This Time

Anthony Barnett, author of the classic *Iron Britannia* and editor of *Power and the Throne* was the founding Director of Charter 88, the influential movement for the constitutional reform of the United Kingdom.

Anthony Barnett

THIS TIME

Our Constitutional Revolution

VINTAGE

Published by Vintage 1997

2 4 6 8 10 9 7 5 4 3 1

Vintage
Random House, 20 Vauxhall Bridge Road,
London SW1V 2SA

Random House Australia (Pty) Limited
20 Alfred Street, Milsons Point, Sydney
New South Wales 2061, Australia

Random House New Zealand Limited
18 Poland Road, Glenfield,
Auckland 10, New Zealand

Random House South Africa (Pty) Limited
Endulini, 5a Jubilee Road, Parktown 2193, South Africa

Random House UK Limited Reg. No. 954009

A CIP catalogue record for this book
is available from the British Library

ISBN 0 09 926858 2

Papers used by Random House UK Ltd are natural, recyclable products made from wood grown in sustainable forests. The manufacturing processes conform to the environmental regulations of the country of origin

Set in 10½/12 Sabon by
Deltatype Limited, Birkenhead, Merseyside

Printed and bound in Great Britain by
Cox & Wyman Ltd, Reading, Berkshire

CONTENTS

Acknowledgments ix
Introduction: Voice, Class and a Nightmare 1

I THE MEANING OF 1997

1. The Defeat of Fear 27
2. A Velvet Revolution Against Corruption 50
3. A Normal Country 77
4. Worcester Woman 101
5. Diana: 'You Was a Rose in a Garden of Weeds' 115

II VOICING THE CONSTITUTION

6. What a Constitution Is 149
   Individual freedom and rights 164
   The distribution of power 172
   Accountability 193
   Voting 199
   Aspirations 203
7. Ours Is Broke, a Story of Nerve Gas and Eton 213
   The culture of government: three examples 218
   Liberty and powers 224
   Arms to Iraq 230
8. Mending It – A Theory of Change 251
   Traditional reform 258
   Free-market populism 261
   Utopian Realism 268
9. The English Question 282
10. This Time 307

Notes 331
Index 351

FOR TOM

ACKNOWLEDGEMENTS AND THANKS

First, and above all, to Judith.

This Time was written swiftly but draws on nearly ten years of work, some of it published in other forms, since Stuart Weir, then editor of the *New Statesman*, asked me to help draft a Charter 88. At the time I was preparing to emigrate. But when the Charter and its call for a written constitution was published in 1988, 10,000 signed and many sent money. This surprised everyone, and meant there was a source of vitality in Britain willing to challenge Thatcherism in a fresh way, when it was at the high of its power. It offered me the rarest opportunity as a political writer, to learn with and influence a movement of opinion. I took it. It has been an intensely enjoyable privilege to become, what should it be called, a 'practical intellectual' perhaps? My thanks to all those first signatories to the call for a peaceful revolution in Britain. If there is one difference between myself and others who write about the constitution, it is that I feel the breath of the public in the argument.

Charter 88 became a professional organisation financed by its signatories, who now number nearly 75,000. It could never have made it without the assistance of the Joseph Rowntree Reform Trust. Its trustees have been fair and radical in their judgement; the Charter being only one aspect of their enormously beneficial influence on Britain. In addition to my personal debt, their Chairman, Trevor Smith, has been a sharp-eyed strategic guide and intellectual colleague who read an early draft. My thanks to him, and them, especially.

As well as the staff who created Charter 88, my thinking and attitudes have been shaped by those who gave their time when I was its Co-ordinator: the Chairs of its Executive and Council; Tim Miller and David Currie; Beverly Anderson and Helena Kennedy; also Leslie Scarman, with his exemplary capacity for clear judgement; George Smith, the most influential political writer of my generation; Richard Wainwright, for his rare combination of experience and encouragement; and Tania Rose and Marna Glyn, who were volunteers at Charter 88 throughout that first period. They read and clipped the newspapers; this book would have been *much* poorer without them. I should stress while all these volunteers and others have influenced these pages, for which many thanks, they have not read them before publication and are not responsible for any of its errors or misjudgements.

These are plentiful. I am acutely aware of the missing references, the partial arguments, and contributions unheeded – especially in the compressed summary of Part II, where I have defied all academic division of labour. Such expertise is essential, and I respect it, but my aim has been to show how the principles of reform, linked and complex though they are, can be debated in an open fashion.

This Time was drafted between May and August 1997 and finalised after the events of September. Caroline Michel, Rowena Skelton-Wallace and their team at Vintage have been creative, extremely fast and exceptionally flexible, Mandy Greenfield has improved the book throughout and Sue Martin has indexed speedily. A big thank you to all. And without Georgina Capel it would not have happened.

The following have read partial drafts, or sometimes just a chapter, and encouraged me to publish: Matthew d'Ancona, Richard Bohane, Neil Belton, Jeremy Hardie, David Hayes, Eleanor Herrin, Judith Herrin, Paul Hirst, Tamara Kate (a big thanks for close criticisms), Tim Miller, Tom Nairn, Ned Pakenham, Andrew Puddephat, Marina Warner, Francis Wheen.

Also thanks to Robin Blackburn for a suggestion; Richard Bohane for help at the start; Will Hutton and Nick Cohen at the *Observer*; Portia Joan for title tracks; and Jonathan de Villiers for two words.

Any change of government which has to be introduced should be one which men, starting from their existing constitution, will be both willing and able to adopt, since there is quite as much trouble in the reformation of an old constitution as in the establishment of a new one: it is just as hard to unlearn as it is to learn.

Aristotle, *The Politics*, Book IV

That's one of the reasons I'm a modernist, why I like Blair, because he is a modernist and I *hate* this old rubbish . . . these old prejudices, these old people who don't want to see anything new, want to cling to the past. The past is like a dead sheep. If you cling to it, you start to stink!
Lord Rothermere, owner of the *Daily Mail*

Introduction

VOICE, CLASS AND A NIGHTMARE

THE YEAR 1997 has altered Britain for good: politically, institutionally and emotionally. Corrupt politicians were exposed. A Tory government was shattered at the election. A Labour government started to reform the constitution. One of the last remnants of Empire, Hong Kong, was handed back and Establishment figures cried. Then Diana – the mother of single mothers – died, and the country's image changed as millions cried. Scotland embraced Home Rule and said it was willing to pay for it. Wales followed if only just – with significantly higher support for a Scottish style parliament than the pup of an assembly on offer. Londoners will confirm that people like radical democracy. Labour and the Liberal-Democrats started to co-operate and consider proportional representation. British citizens, the term is starting to sound genuine, are to have their rights in court. And the government declared that it wanted the European single currency to succeed and Britain to join.

It was a year of positive negatives. Voters rejected Tory sleaze. Popular opinion turned against an old-fashioned monarchy. Racism and hostility to Europe, the twin pillars of what was known as Powellism, were largely repudiated, at least for the time being. And there were plain positives. We – 'we the people', to use a long-coined phrase that may finally become currency in Britain – have changed, especially in our relationship to authority. The election of May 1st expressed the power of the change. The rejection of royal coldness over Diana manifested it. The Scottish vote for a new Parliament began to apply it. The change is about democracy – it is about the freedom to govern ourselves. Many of us have looked forward to this. This time it may happen.

To ensure it does so, we need a democratic written constitution. This does not necessarily imply a republic, in the sense of having a President as Head of State. Something more profound, even if it sounds less radical, has become feasible. Because our political culture is still so deferential we continue to talk about whether 'they' – the royals, the politicians – will change. That, naturally, is how *they* like it. This time, though, the voters have changed. A normalisation has begun that could discard Britain's élitist, unwritten arrangements in favour of a democratic constitution, which decentralises power and is based on human rights. It would be a constitution in which the peoples of the United Kingdom, and not 'The Crown in Parliament', are sovereign. Because voters are ready for it, it could happen. I will argue that it should happen.

What 1997 has made possible is not inevitable. As well as constitutional democracy there are adverse forms of modernisation. Centralised, populist rule from above is one, that rests on the awe-inducing glamour of media and electoral manipulation, rather than the glint of bayonets or coronets. Take the monarchy, for example. The overwhelming public intervention in Diana's funeral upended the Victorian relationship of monarchy and people. Queen Victoria emphasised that 'She *could not* and *would not* be the Queen of a *democratic monarchy*'.[1] And she wasn't. Nor have her successors been. But in the first poll after Diana's funeral the *Daily Telegraph* reported that 71 per cent of the population now favour a 'more democratic' monarchy like Holland's.[2]

Monarchy is a relationship. A modern one like Holland's is not just for them to create, it is also – mainly – up to us to make it happen. Will we-the-people normalise our side of the relationship with a constitution that defines the throne? Once British society belongs formally to us-the-people and not to them-the-Establishment, then, should the majority wish it (which it probably will) the Windsors can breed the country's

Head of State. And do so without the need to endure life as an impossible substitute for the principles of British society. For once sovereignty is inscribed in special words it will no longer be necessary to force a family to personify it as special people. This is the Dutch model.

As the millions of flowers for Diana began to be cleared away, the usual experts were sent in to speak against such an outcome. The monarchy will modernise itself, they assured us; do not upset the young Princes by talking about it; the Queen wears socks so she must be human; and even – a desperate attempt at shock tactics – Roy Hattersley could be President. By one means or another their aim is to recharge a *pre-democratic* monarchy with its old allure.

But special teams of boy scouts had to separate the often mawkish and sometimes eloquent written messages from the myriad bouquets. For the display was a backdrop to a write-in of unprecedented proportions. On the same day this sorting began people in Scotland added their message, when they endorsed proposals for a national Parliament. These had been drawn up swiftly and professionally over the summer by the new government. The referendum on 11th September stamped the authority of the Scottish people on what is indisputably the greatest constitutional change in Scotland since it abandoned its previous parliament in 1707. Even after the dramatic verdict of 1st May, and the unexpected response to the death of Diana, commentators still insisted that everyone was surprised by the large majorities for Scotland's 'Yes, Yes' affirmation of a Parliament with tax varying powers. Much of the London media had hoped that Diana's funeral would induce the Scots to rally to the old Union, or at least abstain from voting. The hope was that collective sentiment would return to its pre-democratic reliability. Instead, Scottish voters confirmed the spirit of Diana as it came to be represented in the days following the accident: defiance of the Establishment, independence of spirit, a reaching out to difference, an insistence on speaking in one's own voice.

The three events – the General Election, the celebration of

Diana and Scotland's whole-hearted embrace of Home Rule – are a potential beginning. *This Time* explores how they came about and where they might lead.

Another development also took place on the day the flowers began to be removed and the Scots voted. It was a reminder that not everything had changed. The IRA announced that it did not support the decommissioning of weapons before a peace settlement and rejected the view that the people of Northern Ireland had the right to decide their own future in a referendum. Instead, the IRA claimed that Ulster's fate could be determined only by a referendum of the whole of Ireland – north and south. While the British State started to discard attitudes of Empire and embrace the decentralising spirit, the IRA declined to relax the prehensile grip of its primitive anti-imperialist nationalism. This illustrated how the Irish process is taking place in a country distinct from Britain. Britain and Ulster are linked, of course, as British actions have rebounded on the mainland police and justice system, to say the least. But all too often, arguments over British policy in Ireland leave little or no time to address the less violent issues of Whitehall rule over the British heartland. This book, if only to rectify the imbalance, focuses exclusively on the United Kingdom of Great Britain, and not Northern Ireland.

What direction is Britain taking? Blair and his advisers have sought, skilfully, to postpone their answer – to put off the denouement – while they assess the strength and nature of the forces at work. Theirs is still an agenda of negatives: they are against statist socialism, free market neo-liberalism, and welfare dependency. They are against strikes as well as windfall profits. They are against the past – and I am with them on that. But what future do they seek?

Part of their answer lies in what are called 'real issues' – as if the constitution is unreal. Labour's programme includes much improved education, a world-class health service and an end to long-term unemployment to prevent the social exclusion of the unskilled and disadvantaged. It can be seen as an attempt to prevent the Americanisation, while reinforcing the modernisation, of Britain. This is most unlikely to be achieved under exclusive Treasury control; there will have to be fiscal and therefore political decentralisation. For a fairer and more efficient society cannot be delivered from the top downwards. If only because command performances are inherently unfair, and centralisation is structurally inefficient, the means will confound the ends.

The issue can be put in terms of society. Margaret Thatcher did not believe in society but only in individuals and families. The new government *does* believe in society. But what, so to speak, does society itself believe in? A society that depends upon the glamorous, or the presidential, or even Downing Street, for confirmation of its existence and purpose, would be a feeble, deferential thing. For a society to believe in itself, though, it has to be able to act in its own ways – ways not dependent on permission from above. For this to happen, two things are needed in the UK: a decentralisation of the old power structures, and the popular energy to animate new structures. British peoples have the latter in abundance. But they also have an over-centralised old State. It requires far-reaching democratic reform.

A written constitution to provide a framework for this development would be good for the peoples of Britain – socially, economically, individually, locally, regionally, nationally, in Europe and in world terms, beneficial for growth and for immediate, personal security. However, the process of achieving it will take time. And written documents do not in themselves solve anything; they can, at best, provide a shared framework for change and for argument over change. All constitutions are lived. The way they are lived gives the meaning to their claims.

Our existing unwritten constitution is also a framework in which we live. But because we-the-people do not hold it in our hands, the meaning of our constitution is defined by those who rule us. Or, as Sir Robin Butler when Cabinet Secretary and head of the Civil Service once said, when asked to define the constitution, 'It is something we make up as we go along'. Just ask yourself whether you could say the same. Of course not. Butler's helpful moment of candour reveals that his 'we' is not the 'we' of 'we-the-people'. It is an exclusive pronoun. *They* make it up as they go along. Perhaps this is why the call for a new constitutional settlement still sounds abstract and strange to English ears. The constitution is a closed, upper-class thing: something that, many people still believe, is not for the likes of us. Well, now it is. Peter Mandelson has claimed, 'It is high time constitutional power was returned to its rightful owners – the British electorate.'[3] The electorate cannot have returned to it something that never belonged to it in the first place. Rather, voters should acquire constitutional power for the first time. The people are, indeed, its rightful owners. And to take possession of it, it needs to be set out in the way of all contemporary countries, so that voters can claim it as their own.

The need for a written constitution is more important now that Britain has a government that is altering the unwritten one so radically. The new Labour reforms, from the forthcoming Scottish Parliament to abolishing hereditary peers, are partial measures. Will they democratise power in an impartial and principled way, or are they designed to gerrymander it, as the opposition claims? Might they prove to be concessions that uphold the existing system, rather than moves towards the 'new constitutional settlement' which Tony Blair called for when he campaigned to become Labour leader?[4] These are fair questions because our existing, unwritten constitution is famously two-faced. Looking backward as well as forwards, it had a brilliant record of preserving itself through partial reform until, under Margaret Thatcher, it was deformed rather than reformed. Then it became clear to everyone that the British State is not a constitutional democracy, it is an elected dictatorship.

In the 1997 General Election the Tories said, in effect, we must keep traditional elected dictatorship. The voters rejected them. Labour did not highlight a call for constitutional democracy, but it could now deliver it. A great possibility lies before us as the Conservatives are scattered. Let us be cool about the odds, but not indifferent or fatalistic about the opportunity.

A great opportunity. Sovereignty has three linked elements: the international, the national and the internal. Under Margaret Thatcher's premiership the three aspects were forged into a specific combination. The nation state was vaunted as the exclusive arbiter of the country's interests. International affairs were seen as a field of combat against foreign competition. Internal differences were crushed and government was centralised, to ensure effective battle against the forces abroad. This set of attitudes was not an imperial ideology, for the Empire was broken as a power. Indeed Thatcher's supporters scorned the post-war approach of 'handling decline' by appealing to post-imperial attachments like the Commonwealth. Yet Thatcher's nationalism, was not a little Englandism as many claimed. Rather, it sought to restore the country's greatness. So I have called the ideology associated with her period 'Great Englishness'. While its Premier was Thatcher, its progenitor was Enoch Powell, who from the 1950s trail-blazed the elixir of monetarism, privatisation and a near mystic obsession with the special nature of parliamentary institutions. Constitutional democracy would drive a stake through the heart of this form of nationalism. The State would decentralise at home, it would willingly share sovereignty with partners internationally, and internal differences would be protected by a framework of rights.

Thus the constitutional moment involves personal and national identity as well as high politics. Throughout *This Time*, therefore, I have tried to combine the immediate with the general to show how we personally experience the historic structures that form and restrict the possibilities of politics. A metaphor much used in legal textbooks is that laws are the skeleton, while conventions are like clothes. This is a suitably emaciated analogy for lawyers. Constitutional law is indeed like the bones of a skeleton. They are lifeless until animated – not by clothes but by flesh and spirit. Yet the body gains its backbone, reach and protection (when it comes to the brain and heart) from the anatomy. Dry as the old bones might seem, we need them in order to live.

The living comes first. A written constitution cannot prevent abuses and corruption if that is what those in power wish – the recent example of the Iran-Contra scandal under President Reagan comes to mind. But it can help to combat such abuses. At the turning point of the Second World War, the American judge Justice Learned Hand said, 'Liberty lives in the hearts and minds of men. When it dies then no constitution, no laws can save it.' This famous caution should be the starting point for every constitution. Such documents are not solutions or panaceas. After all, almost every other country in the world has one and the world is hardly free of problems. The justification for writing down a British constitution is, negatively, to limit if not eliminate the corruption and incompetence of the old system, and, positively, to renew and greatly expand the indigenous spirit of liberty and democracy.

The most frequent objection to such a proposal is that it will 'need a revolution'. So I will meet this point immediately. Obviously, before a democratic transformation can take place the public has to be ready for it. But people in Britain are, and the fact that they do not want a Jacobin-style, year-zero revolution is a sign of intelligence not backwardness. Or, to put it another way, the necessary revolution has already occurred. There are two parts to it, institutional and popular.

After 1945 Britain continued to be ruled by what can be termed an Empire State. It was a complex of interlocking bodies – Church, Army, court, aristocracy, Civil Service and the City – that directed the earthly fate of 800 million souls.[5] Over the last fifty years it has been stripped away. Few insurrections have wrought such a dramatic transformation. Nor was it just a collapse. In 1972 the UK joined what is now the European Union, an act confirmed by referendum in 1975. In constitutional terms this was a truly revolutionary step, yet it was not embraced as such and Britain has been in denial ever since. The result is an oddity. There has been a fifty-year revolution from 1945 to 1995, imposed by world forces and sections of the élite, rather than at the overt insistence of the British public. As a result the outward forms of British sovereignty continue, yet have been largely hollowed out. The stiff upper lip has ceased to express a stalwart inner determination and has become a pretence.

It is as if we have become privately – but not publicly – a modern country. The other side of the fifty-year British revolution has been the transformation in homes across the country. This was manifested at the wake for Diana and in the Scottish referendum. Writing in the London *Evening Standard* about the crowds that filled the Mall and Kensington Gardens, A. N. Wilson regretted Diana's accident but judged that she was a capricious woman unworthy of emulation, let alone the panegyrics that poured forth. Wilson asked, 'Am I alone in thinking that there is a total disparity between the feelings of the mob and the feelings of the well-balanced, intelligent people?' And he went on to damn the newspapers for 'being guided by the mob'.[6]

Wilson's theme was picked up by Bruce Anderson in the *Spectator*. He too regarded the crowds as potentially wild natives involved in a cargo cult, with the potential to turn nasty:

> The mood among the hundreds of thousands of votaries who assembled around St James's last weekend was febrile. It was only because there were no inflammatory speakers that the full potential of crowd psychology was never manifested. It would have been easy for a mob orator to whip up hysteria, or anger; it would not have been impossible to persuade the audience to burst into Buckingham palace or the palace of Westminster, or both.[7]

Along with thousands of others, I was caught in the Mall outside St James's on the Friday evening, as they took the hearse to Kensington Palace in preparation for the funeral the next day. I found myself next to a woman who was breast-feeding a baby while keeping an eye on an older boy who complained quietly in the crush. Her husband was preparing supper for them in Tunbridge Wells. We sheltered under my umbrella during a brief rainstorm. The man in front was from

Guildford. A young woman recognised me from the Voting Reform Group and we all talked about why Diana was different from the other royals and whether the Queen's three-minute speech had been sincere. Were *we* part of a febrile multitude on the edge of hysteria or were we thinking of dinner? Personally I had a date to go to a movie. Had a new Trotsky leapt precariously upon the barrier, whipped off his pince-nez and called on us to storm the Palace, everyone would have been embarrassed. He would have been offered sympathy for being so upset at the death of a Princess, and possibly a cup of tea from the Harrods catering vans or by someone who had brought along a thermos.

Some on the right are obsessed with the caricature of insurrection; possibly because they themselves would like to lead a violent Europhobic counter-revolution. Meanwhile, outside the palaces, it was a crowd of writers: composers of poems, cards and letters. People talked to each other easily; but far from there being a potential for hysteria or mob violence, the mood was quiet and self-contained.

'What is one to make of it all?' Bruce Anderson asked, aware perhaps that his description did not fit what happened. 'The people' are not the trouserless, desperate for revenge. Nor are they walking headlines from the *Sun* or the *Mail*. They are open-minded, against protocol and for authenticity. This is ambiguous, certainly, but its potential was displayed in Scotland. The depth behind the quietness became apparent there on the day of the referendum. The singer Pat Kane told a BBC interviewer that it was 'weirdly placid' as he watched people break off from their shopping in Edinburgh to vote for Home Rule – then carry on shopping. There was no violent, atavistic nationalism on display. Another participant explained, 'The first parliament for 300 years is quite intimidating.' There was an absence of 'buzz' *because* it was important. Reporting on the vote in *The Times*, Magnus Linklater described his profound relief that his fellow countrymen had 'kicked a couple of centuries of retreats into touch, we had demonstrated faith in ourselves'. He quoted a colleague who, significantly, was from Northern Ireland, 'amazed' that in pubs where opinions were deeply divided there was no rancour. 'They never fell out', the Ulsterman said.[8] The calmness meant deep currents not dead water, currents that connected back to the election. This was seen three months before the Scottish vote by Iain MacWhirter, in the *Scotsman*. People were asking, 'Where is the ferment?' he reported. They were wrong to conclude that no one was 'bothered'. On the contrary, 'if there is no debate in Scotland, it is simply because the country has already made up its mind',

> What some have been interpreting as lack of enthusiasm for constitutional change is . . . merely the quiet resolve of a people who have united behind a proposition and are impatient to see it implemented. When you've finally decided where you want to go, the last thing you want to do is keep on talking about it.[9]

Offered a real parliament the Scots knew their minds. Change based on reflection not confrontation is all the more revolutionary in that it is concerned to last.

Voters are acting like grown-ups, changing things when they can without throwing tantrums. The media, however, hates dullness which it mistakes for unimportance. The spectacle craves melodrama not deep currents. The camera zooms in on tears, joy or anger, as it seeks a Delacroix-style sensation of the barricades to symbolise change. It also needs to demonstrate its own importance and uncover the story. But how do you make 'a story' out of an argument without rancour? What the media regard as its strength, its hard-nosed 'cut the crap' search for the angle, is also a weakness; an appetite for sensation over content. This happened during the election, as I will show. It leads the press to over-rate the traditional nature of Britain because it interprets calmness as attachment to the past, whereas, at least in 1997, it turned out to be a settled desire for change and not conservatism.

Britain has a political élite that wants to conserve *its* grip on State power. Its conservatism should never be underrated in this respect. For sure, it will lead a successful resistance to democratic reform if the public wishes to carry on as it has done in the past. The events of 1997 suggest that this is not what the majority want. People like reform when offered the real thing. This changes everything.

I repeat, this changes everything. The argument for a new democratic arrangement of the way Britain is governed is a double argument: about transforming the constitution and about popular readiness for this. In Part II, 'Voicing the Constitution', I outline a case for reform. It opens with what a constitution is, a lengthy chapter which argues also that what is 'constitutional' itself changes through time. I then show that Britain's present constitution is broken (Chapter 7). I do not propose a model replacement. My aim is to help persuade public and politicians alike that the process of writing down the constitution can be embarked upon, not to prejudge an outcome that needs inventive public participation. Instead, I address the fact that Labour lacks a clear strategy for reform, and I discuss the approach it should take (Chapter 8). The government rejects Fabianism, Monetarism, Labourism, Liberalism, but has no method – yet – that it can call its own. It prefers the radical centre to left or right, which is a position, not a route. Perhaps all governments everywhere are caught up in this dilemma. As it wrestles with it, Britain's new one is all too likely to accept the embrace of gravity and default back to a variant of national conservatism, which has always flown the flag of 'necessary change'. Instead, we need a contemporary way of being British – which means in turn that English nationalism must not be abandoned to the right.

The possibilities of reform are governed by popular attitudes. Expert opinion usually insists that the people are a passive not an active part of the argument. In his survey, *On the Constitution*, Lord Hailsham writes in the chapter on 'Fundamentals', 'It is no good beginning with high-sounding generalities about inalienable rights or civil liberties or vain abstractions like "the people" or "society in general".' Having decided not to begin with them he does not end with them either, instead he ignores the people altogether, except for Burkian asides about the 'little platoons'.[10] The complacency is telling. A similar attitude is embedded in the more interesting argument for a reform recently proposed by Lord Alexander. He seems to take a different view, stating it is 'the spirit of the British peoples which may be fairly said to lie at the heart of our constitution', yet he claims:

> Perhaps the most eloquent tributes to the strength of our institutions, and the commitments to the spirit of liberty, are both the historic stability of our society and the virtually complete lack of any strong demand for root-and-branch change.[11]

One can hear the sound of the élite clapping itself on the back for the way the people do not want much reform. Thus Alexander opposes the idea of a written constitution because it 'appears to lack the groundswell of strong popular support'. Implicit in such discussions are three attitudes caricatured by Edmund Burke in his criticism of the French Revolution. Those arguing for radical change are little more than 'a ring of grasshoppers'. No one should imagine, in Burke's view, that just because the insects make all the noise they are the only inhabitants of the field, for 'thousands of great cattle, reposed beneath the shadow of the British oak, chew the cud and are silent'.[12] Should the reliable bovine populace get on the move, however, they swiftly become, in the view of farmer Burke, the 'swinish multitude'. Or, as we have just seen in terms of the people on the Mall in 1997, 'the mob'. The same contrast can be found in Walter Bagehot's nineteenth-century perspective. He warns against the dangers of the great unwashed, then praises the people for being deferential, and insists on the need for a monarchy to keep them this way. For three hundred years British rulers have viewed the lower orders from above and assumed this natural perspective to be the only possible order of government. The populace are praised for their wisdom when silent and denounced as a danger when they speak. Either way they are ignorant.

My assumption rejects this view completely. Contemporary

voters are neither contented cattle nor dangerous swine. A profound transformation is under way. The reasons are familiar: literacy, thanks to the enormous increase in higher education; articulacy, thanks to the penetration of television drama; spare time, thanks to the increases in productivity; understanding, thanks to the feminist revolution. Popular autonomy and self-reflection are gathering pace.[13] They revealed themselves in 1997 and have upended the axioms, the premise, the foundation on which English constitutional debate has rested.

To show that this is so, I have dedicated the first part of *This Time* to the meaning of 1997. I have sought to recapture the moment of 1st May. This means bringing back bad memories as well as good. At some length I sample the press coverage to illustrate how large sections of the Fourth Estate were way off beam in their conviction that voters want the country steered back towards 'Great Englishness'. I describe in some detail the corruption and sleaze voters consciously rejected, even though the full charges were never combined for them to assess as a whole. These two chapters set the scene for the later discussion of the breakdown of the old constitution. Overall, 1997 shows that the British want to be governed by normal rules and not pretentious, old-fashioned ones. This is not a matter of restoring trust in our leaders. Or in asking leaders to trust the people. The British peoples have become different and better, and can trust themselves. Which means that we deserve a different and better sort of constitution.

Achieving it demands political imagination. In contrast to the Tories and the Liberal Democrats, this quality has been lacking in Trade Union and Labour Party thought and culture since 1914; although debates over democracy and reform were central to the peoples' movement before then.[14] A change in attitude and understanding is needed most of all in Labour circles. While I hope this book will be enjoyed by readers of every persuasion, some final introductory remarks may help to free the left, in particular, from its antique mental formulas.

For the constitution is lived in language and attitudes ingrained on the left as well as the right. Whether in opposition or in office, one of the most debilitating aspects of Old Labour's political culture was the way it reproduced the inherited culture of class, or, more accurately, of caste. Deference, defensive resentment, an implicit contempt for working-class expectations . . . the combination is familiar. In a perverse way the labour movement reinforced its own confinement in the name of staying true to itself, while the genuinely popular was disparaged as consumerist.

The main engine of this subordination was, naturally, Conservative guardianship of the ruling culture, which Labour accepted as it was incorporated into the post-war consensus. When the consensus was broken, rougher methods were called for. These were pioneered against Ken Livingston's Greater London Council in the early 1980s. Later they were applied to the nascent Charter 88 when it called for a broad programme of constitutional reform in 1988. Scorn and derision became the order of the day, as those involved were pilloried as luvvy members of the 'chattering classes'. If you expressed criticism of the way the country is governed, protested about the violation of basic rights or just advocated reform, you were derided as a powerless chatterbox. In effect, critics were intimidated from raising the subject.

In America, if you want a good argument you can question the power of the Supreme Court. In Britain, if you raise the role of judges it has to be with a modest cough and an apology for talking about something that 'is not television'. But because it is not drafted on paper, our unwritten constitution *has* to be argued about or it dies. For some three centuries English debates over constitutional matters were one of the glories of civilisation. Pamphlets and books about it sold hundreds of thousands of copies; contributors to them comprise a glittering roll-call of poets, politicians, philosophers, historians and campaigners. From Hobbes and the Levellers, Milton and Locke, through Hume, Blake, Burke, Paine, Macaulay, Shelley, Coleridge, Disraeli, the Chartists, Mill, Bagehot, Dicey and Maitland, the English argument was a high-powered act battling to define a multinational polity, even when the aim was to protect it from democracy. And the debate was reinforced by an exceptional tradition of political novels.[15] By the 1980s the still unwritten constitution had become a silent one. It was almost the silence of the grave.

In November 1988, on the 300th anniversary of the Glorious Revolution of 1688, Charter 88 set out to revive tradition and to do so in style. It launched a public appeal for a new constitutional settlement, endorsed by 350 names. There were distinguished specialists, of whom Lord Scarman was the foremost, and also among the signatories who helped were novelists like Angela Carter, Ian McEwan, Salman Rushdie, who have many more readers than an MP has constituents; scriptwriters such as Harold Pinter, Dennis Potter and Emma Thompson, who express national experience in ways more lasting than some Prime Ministers; and writer-performers like John Cleese, who has raised more laughs than either main party has enjoyed votes. The agora of contemporary culture is a major part of our democracy; those named are some of its many representatives. Within a few weeks thousands signed Charter 88, a degree of public support which suggested that what had been considered impossible could become possible, as the constitution came alive once more. Today, over 70,000 have endorsed the call for constitutional reform.

The original audacity of this call for change was that it rejected both deferential reformism and the melodrama of defiant anger, and so abjured the usual, futile arguments of the British left. Modest as it was, Charter 88's call for a written constitution made – and makes – a claim on the country as a whole. In doing so, it enjoins risk, makes partners of quality and popularity, and maintains a link between excellence and enjoyment. This challenges what might be termed the 'sovereignty of voice' assumed by the established political class.

'They' used to conduct the only conversation about the rules of the game that mattered, and they did so in exclusive tones. The upper-class accent dominated British power. And until now it has been almost impossible to break into the conversation from outside. If you are polite, you are ignored. If you shout, you become easily stigmatised as a disruption. Charter 88 sought to break this taboo and expand what is accepted as 'authoritative argument'. This is why I have called Part Two, 'Voicing the Constitution'. For those who dismiss reformers as 'chatterers', in their stupid way deny the resonance and breadth that arguments about power can draw upon in England. I will give two instances, from the seventeenth century and today.

It has been argued that after the Scots joined the Union in 1707 they 'colonised themselves'.[16] They kept their own education, legal system and church but lost their national-political voice. A similar analysis can be applied to England. The English upper class expresses itself in Westminster. But the people of England lost their voice in the Empire State. Angela Carter once discussed the way that most national stereotypes are folk ones. The typical German, Italian, American, or Irishman, whether urban or rural, is lower or middle class: think of the garlic-eating, Gauloise-smoking Frenchman, or of Marianne on the barricades. But 'the typical Englishman', she observed, 'is represented as a toff'. There are Cockneys and plain Yorkshiremen, but these are regional not national, types. It was not that she thought there should be just one stereotype. She was interested in contesting the definition of popular Englishness, not least its maleness. And she found that its national symbols had been appropriated by the upper class. A surrender had taken place. The voice of regular English people – self-mocking, ironic, disparaging – is also, self-colonising. That is, it is conscious that it should not attempt to rise above its station and that, however idiotic it knows those up there to be, it falters before displacing them.

It was not always so. The clear, contemporary sound of Englishness was heard during the Civil War before the settlement of 1688 closed above it. It can be heard on *both* sides of the Putney debates, for example, held in 1647 to consider 'The Agreement of the People' which had been drawn up by radicals in the Army. The debates were presided over by Oliver Cromwell. The King was held prisoner further down the Thames. The Agreement is quite a limited document, nonetheless its demand for universal franchise is as historic as the Magna Carta, and it has been described as 'the first rough draft of a written constitution in the history of democracy'.[17]

'The Agreement of the People' proposed political equality for free men. At Putney, it seems to have been read out for debate article by article. The first article claimed:

> That the people of England, being at this day very unequally distributed by counties, cities and boroughs, for the election of their deputies in Parliament, ought to be more indifferently proportioned, according to the number of the inhabitants.

Soon after it was read out, General Ireton, Cromwell's son-in-law, defended a property qualification:

> It is said, they are to be distributed according to the number of the inhabitants, 'The people of England' etc. And this doth make me think that the meaning is, that every man that is an inhabitant is to be equally considered, and to have an equal voice in the election of those representers.

Colonel Rainsborough replied in terms that still stir with their immediacy across three centuries and a half:

> For really I think that the poorest he that is in England hath a life to live as the greatest he; and therefore truly, sir, I think it's clear, that every man that is to live under a government ought first by his own consent to put himself under that government; and I do think that the poorest man in England is not at all bound in a strict sense to that government that he hath not had a voice to put himself under . . .[18]

The debate over who should vote was argued over in terms of 'voice'. And the language in which this debate took place was itself free from snobbery. Ireton's view was that those without a fixed property interest should not 'have equal voice'. Influenced by the Levellers, Rainsborough countered that acceptable government needs the voiced consent of all. The Levellers were not full democrats; their free-born Englishman was qualified as free-born to distinguish him from servants and those dependent on alms. My point is not to romanticise either them or Rainsborough. What is striking about the Putney debates is the way that *both* sides argued over the nature of government in a language without royalist affectation and inhibition. The fatalism and conceits that have come to mark what was at first an aristocratic and then an Establishment hegemony over English political culture are absent. In 1647 the outcome was not democratic. Cromwell sided with those who feared anarchy. But – apart from gender – the language of the Putney debates on all sides is freeing itself from monarchist hierarchy.

In 1969 the voting age in Britain was lowered to eighteen and those old enough to fight and die for their country could qualify (a right the Putney gathering concluded soldiers should have, before Cromwell's dispersed them). But well before the long procession of Acts that extended the franchise, Edmund Burke developed the theory that parliamentary representatives owed their opinions to their conscience, and not to the views of those who elected them. Today, MPs are under discipline to subordinate their opinions to their party. Either way the English do not hear their voices spoken through the throats of MPs. A more proportional system of voting could improve this. Britain also needs a more proportional political culture that recognises a wider legitimacy of voice than can be found in Westminster alone.

This is why the freedom of the press is a constitutional issue. An immediate example is conveniently to hand. In 1995, the *Guardian* asked Jonathan Aitken why, when he was a junior Minister of Defence in 1993, he went to Paris to talk to Arab business partners who paid his bill. Aitken lied to cover up his impropriety. The paper decided to make the matter public. A storm of abuse descended upon it and Aitken declared that he would 'fight against falsehood and all who peddle in it'. Leave aside the extent and whereabouts of the peddlers. The way in which the *Guardian* and then

Granada television were attacked was significant. The newspaper was seen as rising above itself. It was told it had no right to 'witch-hunt' Aitken. Withering criticism was aimed at the suggestion that as a responsible paper it had a constitutional duty to raise such an issue. To the widespread approval of fellow MPs, Aitken sued for libel.

English libel laws allow wealthy wrongdoers to intimidate the media into silence. One study 'proves beyond doubt that the libel laws do have a chilling effect in inhibiting the reporting of matters of public concern'.[19] This is another way in which democratic voice is repressed. Under British law the *Guardian* had to *prove* that Aitken was lying, even though *he* had the evidence and knew the truth. This presented the paper with almost impossible obstacles, which it managed to overcome only by happy accident. The system, in which the burden of proof falls on the defendant, apparently goes back to the Tudor laws of the Star Chamber.[20] It is known to have allowed liars to collect fortunes in British courts. More often it prevents papers from publishing what they believe the public should know. Thus, while the innocent can be pilloried and broken by press intrusion, the rich and guilty can silence the media from reporting their wrongdoing.

The law should protect and encourage the speaking of truth and the exchange of opinion. Instead, the 'mess' and 'absurdity' of British libel laws conveniently tangle up

democratic arguments in the toff-speak over-charged, adversarial proceedings, meanwhile allowing thuggish tabloids to masquerade as the voice of the people and intimidate their victims. Some clear overall principles are needed to sort things out. For example: the media must not be above the law; its free expression must be protected; it should feel it has a duty to investigate and report wrongdoing, therefore there must be no prior restraint on it of any kind – no Maxwell style gagging writs that cost many a pensioner part of their livelihood, or State regulation; citizens' rights to personal privacy must be respected; penalties for their breach and for libel should be punitive to deter rich conglomerates and should include the imposition of equivalent space and page position for retraction.

Such a codification would not be exceptional in international terms. However, any such overall approach will *constitutionalise* the law of the press and the public's right to be informed and not to be intruded upon. The debate about these issues, now given a blip by Diana's death, is also reflective in a constitutional fashion, seeking to balance power, interest and accountability. Even the arguments about people buying newspapers with pictures they do not want to have taken are constitutional, for one of the central issues in establishing the rules of government is how to protect ourselves from our own weaknesses.

Why, then, do the political parties and especially their realistic 'hard guys' despise and disparage this kind of debate? Because it challenges their 'official voice'. The clubland moans of 'Who do these people think they are?', when another scandal is exposed by the upstart press, are the expression of a monopoly interest. The left has often believed that *it* should exercise this monopoly. A fool's dream. Instead, it should welcome the multiplicity of voice in a modern democracy. Then the argument can move on to better questions: Are the matey tones of the tabloids just another form of patronising closure? How democratic is the press, especially given its concentration of ownership? How can official debates ensure that others than MPs like Aitken and his friends give throat to British values?

Contemporary democracy needs a practical imagination. Replying to questions at his Charter 88 lecture in 1993, which marked the turning point in Labour's commitment to constitutional reform, John Smith, then leader of the opposition, explained:

> I think I was the last Minister to try to create a new constitution in this country, as the minister responsible for the Scotland Bill and the Wales Bill in the last Labour Government . . . During the process I became very conscious of two things. Firstly, the advocates of change sometimes stand in their own way by looking for the perfect solution, when what they want

> is a start, not an end, to a continuing process. You can sometimes throw out the very good in the search for the perfect. Secondly, it's very hard to make a constitutional change when you're living in the constitution of the moment, when you're actually carrying on the process of government under one set of norms and institutions and trying to change into another.[21]

When 'living in the constitution of the moment', to use Smith's fine phrase, it *is* difficult to look forward to living in a different one. It is harder still if you don't spell out your goals. Smith made his position within his party more strenuous by resisting pressure to rewrite Clause 4 of Labour's constitution, its statement of aims. This was left to Tony Blair. Similarly, members of the public may resist a process when they cannot see where it is leading; it makes them understandably sceptical and more resistant to each step. Smith was right to argue that what is needed is a start, not an end. Yet a sense of the overall destination is also vital. Constitutional culture became more lively and informed in Scotland, for example, because the call for its own Parliament unified the image of reform. The English have no equivalent sense of overall purpose. The menu of partial changes does not provide it. Replacing the House of Lords, proportional representation, a Bill of Rights and regional decentralisation will ensure specific extensions to individual and public 'voice' in England, as citizenship replaces the demeanour of subjects. However, in any constitution the whole is more defining than the sum of its parts. It is here, in the larger context, that voice finds meaning – but how can it be encouraged to speak before this is achieved?

The question began to haunt me. I drafted arduous paragraphs about how, in tangential ways, people already talk about and recognise the importance of the constitution – to show that reform is already, if implicitly, popular. Then I had a nightmare.

It took place twenty or so years in the future. I found myself being interviewed for a research project. A young man was asking me about *This Time*. Why, he asked, had I gone on at *such length* about how constitutional ideas can be popular? Why did I belabour the point when its validity was quite obvious? Could I recall what I was doing and explain?

In the dream both of us knew that the reason for this puzzlement was that the British constitution had already been written down for some years and proved tremendously popular. My young questioner was from the first generation who had learnt it at school. He had grown up without knowing what it was like to be without a written constitution. It was relatively short in length, yet the product of a tremendous nine-month public debate – it had even become a model for the world. It was the first constitution to be drafted after the arrival of information technology and the new possibilities of direct democracy and decentralisation; the first to encompass the new understanding of reciprocal needs and freedoms now that society has replaced the fate of nature with human-created risk; one of the first to be based on the concept of human dignity as social and historically changing, bound up therefore with the dignity of others. It thus entrenched such fundamental requirements of mutual human dignity as access to housing, health and education within reasonable financial limits and in so far as these could be protected by the courts, in terms of universal freedom that allowed for variation rather than uniformity. A National Health Service committed to the well-being of the whole person had become the exemplary institution that gave the constitution symbolic meaning – rather than the monarchy. Liberty was defined in a way that was co-operative, not competitive, while contention was protected. The ethic of fundamental rights was underpinned by the common right to a sustainable environment, which made the British constitution a pioneer of what had come to be known as new democracy... Naturally, the Britain constitution was extremely well written. Parliamentary drafters had co-operated with poets such as Tony Harrison to ensure that its language drew on the cadences of spoken English.

The nightmare was my attempt to explain to my young interviewer of the future why people did not want such a constitution. My justification fell on deaf ears. I became impatient. 'Can't you see,' I found myself saying, 'it is all right for you, but before 1997 it was different. People hankered for magical solutions. They could not see the point of a written constitution. Those who desired a bold overall approach wanted to deal with inequality, balanced growth and a better environment. They thought constitutional reform was a distraction. Others were cautious and desired small changes, which they felt were within their grasp. They did not see the need for a new overall structure. Some thought that proportional representation, others a Bill of Rights or a Freedom of Information Act, or decentralised local government, was the reform that would make all the difference. Most of all, the English people still did not believe they could claim their country for themselves. Democracy starts with a claim on sovereignty, but many were appalled at the way an ex-Premier, Margaret Thatcher, had banged on about it being British and feared they might become as batty as she was if they touched the issue.' And so on.

I hope, and assume, readers will be sceptical. At the same time it is possible to imagine that Britain's constitution can be written down, and written well, so as to join the argument about whether this should happen at all.

PART I

THE MEANING OF 1997

I
The Defeat of Fear

IT WAS A May night to remember – one of relief and delight. I thought poetic justice only came in small portions, when it came at all. On 1st May there was a tidal wave of poetic justice. It had been interminably slow to arrive. The opinion polls hardly varied after October 1992 when Tory support collapsed. The country had long made up its mind that the Conservatives did not deserve to stay in office. But it was nearly five frustrating years before it could deliver the verdict. When the dam broke, the force of long preparation swept Labour into immediate action. For the first time on taking office, a Labour government, as well as introducing new policies, began to change how Britain is governed. A transformation has begun that will not be stopped easily.

At last we will be able to claim our rights in court according to principles, as do citizens in other democracies. The referendums in Scotland and Wales will now lead to a national Parliament and Assembly respectively, as the peoples of the United Kingdom of Great Britain begin to renegotiate a historic union in line with the times. There will be a Mayor for London – an extraordinary initiative that will give the capital a political leader elected directly by a constituency that is more numerous than Scotland. There is the promise of a Freedom of Information Act that will reverse the fundamental principle of Civil Service control over official papers. The Bank of England has been made more independent and accountable as sovereignty over a crucial area of decision-making, the base rate, is openly shared.

None of these changes will lead to anything unusual in world terms. Together, however, they promise the transformation of sovereignty in Britain. In two simple, if multisyllabic words, a constitutional revolution.

New Labour did not advocate this outcome during the election campaign. Instead, it played down its constitutional programme. Tony Blair insisted that people did not want a revolution. When *The Times* put it to him that his forthcoming government would go down in history for its democratic reforms, he denied this, saying he expected that 'The improvements in education will be much more important.'[1] John Major, however, warned the electorate that the consequence of a Blair victory would be the end of Britain as we know it. He called upon voters to 'save the Union' by returning a Tory government, in order to prevent Labour wrecking the constitution. On 23 April he went to Aberdeen and decided to cast aside his set text and to speak from the heart about the possibility of a referendum in Scotland to create a Parliament in Edinburgh:

> I don't just stand here and say to an audience of Scots in their own land that this is something that isn't for Scotland; I do say it is something that would damage every single corner of our country unless we stand up and fight against it and win this election, and then stop it happening in the next Parliament – or the damage will be catastrophic for the people of Scotland and for people right across the United Kingdom. [Applause]
>
> So I speak on this issue from the deepest of instincts. A profound instinct that what is proposed is bad for our nation. What is proposed is damaging for the unity of our United Kingdom. What is proposed is ill-considered and ill-thought out and ought not to be proceeded with because of its economic damage, its constitutional damage and its political damage – all of which will be profound to the United Kingdom. It is a great issue. They don't always arise in general elections, but they have on this occasion. And it is an issue which stretches way beyond Scotland. It's an issue I have raised elsewhere in this election and will do so again in the days that lie between now and May 1st, because of its importance.

> We have to carry this message from the heart to the head of every elector, so they understand what it is that is truly at stake when they cast their vote.

Major repeated his warning in meetings and on television. He had put his magic marker on the issue for over a year. On 26 June 1996 he delivered a special speech on the constitution, then saw that it was followed by a clutch of set-pieces from Stephen Dorrell, Michael Forsyth, William Hague and William Waldegrave. These were delivered in July and published in September, prefaced by a special letter from the Prime Minister himself.[2] He stated that 'Labour's radical package of constitutional change' would make the coming election a 'watershed'. 'The choice could not be more stark . . . our opponents' plans are so dangerous: New Labour would mean no Britain.'

On 14 February 1997, with the election now looming but still undeclared, the Prime Minister accused Labour of being willing to 'throw a bone to the yapping dogs of Welsh and Scottish separatism'. To the ire of the Scots especially, who formally joined the Union less than three centuries ago, in 1707, Major declared, 'A thousand days of Labour government could ditch a thousand years of British history.'

He could not have been more clear in his message. If the way he spoke lacked eloquence, it had the advantage of plainness. But there was even a touch of eloquence. One phrase stands out: 'We have to carry this message from the heart to the head of every elector.' But hearts had changed. The electorate was no longer in love with the supremacy of the Westminster Parliament. And so voters kept their heads. All the stuff about profound damage failed to put the frighteners on us. We were not afraid. This was the first and most important thing about the 1997 election. On May 1st the British rejected fear.

The electors were not afraid of the constitutional reforms against which Major warned them, whatever they might be. They were not afraid of being closer to Europe, either. In no uncertain terms the *Daily Mail* had warned its middle-England readers. In a stark black box imposed on a Union

Jack that filled its entire front page on polling day, it picked up Major's ignorant alarm call:

There is a terrible danger that the British people, drugged by the seductive mantra 'It's time for a change', are stumbling, eyes glazed, into an election that could undo 1,000 years of our nation's history.

The people of middle England were alerted. They did not stumble. Their eyes bright, they strode towards the polling stations. Then most *Daily Mail* readers voted Labour. As did its proprietor.

Election day also brought an end to a rancid fear of ourselves – that we could not change, that *they* would go on and on. The fear stayed alive, despite all the evidence, until the results came in. As they were announced, the sheer relief brought about by the end of this fear created joy even among these with no attachment to New Labour. Most Liberal Democrats shared it, as did those who voted for the SNP and Plaid Cymru. Perhaps the euphoria of Referendum Party voters was tarnished as they watched their leader, Sir James Goldsmith, gloating like a hooligan. Deliberate abstainers also cheered. Non-voters secretly regretted that they did not have a part in it, and promptly altered their memory so that they too could claim the historic moment. Within five weeks 53 per cent of respondents to a Gallup poll said that they had voted Labour, when in fact only around 43.2 per cent had done so.[3] Even many Tories were delighted, at least until the full scale of the catastrophe dawned – Tories who followed the advice of the *Daily Mail*'s leader, which, because it sensed its readers' doubts, concluded its editorial with the words, 'If you believe that this country should retain its independence you must, however reluctantly, vote Conservative.'

Reluctance wasn't the half of it. Similar advice came from Andrew Roberts, the right-wing historian and *Sunday Times* columnist:

> So on Thursday, if you live in a winnable seat, a winnable Tory seat with a candidate who opposes the single currency, with enormous misgivings and doubts, and with a hearty and justified scorn in your heart, hold your nose and vote Conservative.[4]

Anyone who took this advice – and it seems that millions who voted Conservative did have misgivings and were reluctant – had in their hearts, to use Roberts' phrase, not just scorn but also the knowledge that the Conservatives did not deserve to win.

We knew that we lived in an elective dictatorship. Part of the concern was that Britain would become a dictatorship, plain and simple, immune to elective rejection. Whether because they had foreign money, or tabloid support, or could play the race card, or reveal some scandal in Labour's ranks, there was a fear that the Tories would use every trick to pull off another victory, buoyed up by the underlying economic improvement for some sections of society. It was a fear that the Tories could not be ousted. This fear evaporated. To immense relief.

The exemplary campaign fought by the Liberal Democrats helped the public overcome what fear they had. Paddy Ashdown was courageous and good-humoured. He called for modest, dedicated tax rises, which he said were necessary because more had to be spent on education and health – and was believed. The Lib Dems steadied the nerves of voters and emerged with moral authority, as well as more seats. So it is not hindsight that makes the fear hard to fathom, for it seemed unnecessary at the time. Yet it penetrated almost everyone on the left and centre, because its main source was the Labour leaders themselves. *They* feared losing. They were well ahead in the opinion polls. But Labour's campaign directors were not certain that they had earned their lead, or could keep it. They transmitted their fear to their supporters. It restricted their commitments and constrained their voice. The Tories tried to make them afraid. Labour *was* afraid. But most voters weren't. The election result confirmed the gap between the Labour leadership's expectations and those of the public itself.

Labour played down its differences from the government when it need not have done so. It de-radicalised its image. It even, to its shame, refused to make an issue of corruption and the quango state, two factors that had made the government irrevocably unpopular among previous Conservative supporters who had no time for a State plutocracy. As a consequence, the positive vote for Labour remained moderate. Blair did not win the trust he asked for at the outset of the campaign. I am not saying that the Labour leaders were cowards. On the contrary, because they exaggerated the strength of their enemy, they pitted themselves against odds that were greater in their own minds than in reality. They saw cunning in the tangle of Tory policies and feared public support for Major's pathetic exaggerations. Because of the previous election it was also a matter of once burnt, twice shy. As a result they were *genuinely* afraid that the Conservatives could win. Cowards would have flinched; Blair and Brown became all the more determined. But this led them to be over-cautious, to magnify the government's appeal out of all proportion and to diminish the hope of change that they themselves offered, in case it proved provocative.

So the positive vote for Labour was far from stratospheric. Where a Labour vote did not matter in terms of sweeping out a Tory, there was considerable abstention by its supporters. The swing to Labour in its heartland constituencies was relatively poor. In Blair's own seat at Sedgefield, his vote rose by less than 2,000, from 31,391 in 1992, when he was still relatively unknown, to 33,526. The right sought comfort in the national totals that resulted. They perked up contemplating the fact that Labour won less than 44 per cent of the vote. This percentage was hardly more than Major gained in 1992.

Indeed, because of the number of abstentions, half a million fewer people voted for New Labour in 1997 than voted Conservative five years before. It was, frankly, delightful to read arguments based on these figures in the Tory broadsheets, with phrases about how 'this is not a mandate' – phrases identical to ones I first became familiar with in another context: the xeroxed mailings of the Labour Campaign for Electoral Reform. The electoral system of first past the post is indeed unfair and can bestow grossly inflated majorities in Parliament on the winning party.

But any complaint about Labour's power resting on minority support fails to register the determination of a large majority of the electorate to oust the government. Labour pollsters also failed to sense this. They knew from their own returns that they were not picking up the 50 per cent support the rolling Gallup poll had suggested during much of the campaign and NOP predicted in its final survey. They knew they were closer to the 44 per cent they actually obtained. What they did not register was the abiding aversion to voting Tory that possessed many of the government's previous supporters, and the intensity of the will to vote tactically among those who wanted to see the back of Major. Conservative support decomposed, leaving the Tories with their lowest share of the vote since the early nineteenth century. It seems that more than half of the Referendum Party's 800,000 votes comprised ex-Tories; there were two million abstentions; there was an unprecedented switch of perhaps 1.8 million voters straight to Labour; and, thanks to the Grim Reaper, a tithe of older, Tory-inclined voters passed on, to be replaced by first-time voters determined on change.

When Labour won in 1945 bonfires were lit across London's East End, consuming wood used to patch up blitz-damaged windows. The celebration was reported as being like 'another VE day'. It was a victory, they said 'for the common man'. There was massive class identification with the Labour leader Clement Attlee: his party was *their* party. This was not the feeling in 1997, when the high point was the ejection of Tory Defence Minister Michael Portillo. Revenge, not endorsement, was the order of the day on May Day. The Conservatives did not merely 'lose' the election, they were thrashed. They were driven from office. The great amphitheatre of electoral politics gave them the thumbs down. You cannot gainsay this verdict by complaining that Labour got a mere 43.2 per cent.

The Tory right saw it coming and sought to avert defeat by emphasising its nationalism. At the very least, it aimed to emerge as the strongest wing of the Conservative Party in defeat, not just numerically but also morally, with a demonstrable tide of public support. As the election entered its final phase, right-wingers vied to ride what they saw as the anti-Europe wave that could take them to leadership of their party after the election.

The wave crashed short. The election marked the turning of a tide. During the election campaign itself this outcome would have seemed incredible. A presumption was displayed and an 'attitude' taken up which still awaits a convincing explanation. Jonathan Aitken, an early enemy of Europe, was to display it in his brazen denials; Neil Hamilton was to show the same over-confidence when he held a celebration party after the 1689 Bill of Rights was amended to let him take intimidatory legal action against the *Guardian*. The Conservative right had come to regard its own views as public opinion, its own prejudices as those of the people, its own greed as an extension of the economic aspirations of regular voters. Because such Tories wanted to protect their own influence, they called it 'sovereignty' and then regarded it as something 'the country' also wants them to have. To prove it, they seemed to think that all they needed to do was to repeat their claims loudly. Which they did.

As a result two elections took place on 1st May. There was one between the main political parties, the other between the Tory right and the rest – especially their own party. To say that the Conservatives were 'divided', or that they suffered a 'nervous breakdown' (ex-Chancellor Kenneth Clarke's description) fails to register that a distinct force was at work. A cluster of senior and backbench MPs, journalists, newspaper owners, millionaires and certain life-peers, fought their own campaign. Theirs was the 'Great English' Party. Ideologically it stood for the Powellite core of Thatcherism. This was only a stunted and strident version of the politics Thatcher had espoused when Prime Minister. Instead it took on her attitudes of exile, which gave its followers the tone of prophets spurned, even betrayed, by the fainthearted; and filled them even more with convictions of rectitude. The Great English party was more than an item in Thatcher's handbag. Its views included those of Norman (now Lord) Tebbit, of Conrad Black (owner of the Telegraph group including the *Spectator*), of Simon Heffer and a large part of the *Daily Mail*, of MPs such as John Redwood and Michael Howard, and of millionaires who made it in the eighties, like Paul Sykes, who funded every Conservative candidate willing to openly oppose Britain adopting the Euro.

They felt trapped by the Party led by John Major with Michael Heseltine as Deputy Leader and Kenneth Clarke as Chancellor. They were determined to bust it open. The single currency was their obsession but the menace of the Euro meant much more to them than money. It was an omen that stood for loss of sovereignty, identity, independence and other aspects of the national, manly essence they felt was at risk under Major. They decided to fight for it on the pavements in the constituencies, feeling absolutely sure that 'the people' were on their side – for how could they not be?

Both Tory parties – Major's British one and the Great English one – were defeated on 1 May. Their joint defeat was symbolised by the rejection of Michael Portillo, the only senior figure with the necessary credibility (or incredibility) to unite both camps. But in an election marked by restraint and caution, the Great English party and its press fought a well-focused crusade of staggering forcefulness and alarmism. It is essential to place their campaign on the record, even at the cost of making the reader restless for a few moments. For while the replacement of Major's government by Blair's was expected, the electoral annihilation of the Great English party was not. And in terms of the significance of 1997, the defeat of the latter was much more important than that of Major's party, for they were the alternative future for the right. As their call too fell on deaf ears it is important to remind ourselves what it was.

The *Daily Mail* claimed the credit for starting what turned out to be a lesson in the limits of prejudice (and the capacity for misjudgement) of the press. THE BATTLE FOR BRITAIN it announced across its front page on 15 April, two weeks before polling: 'There is a deafening silence at the heart of this election and its name is Europe.' It assaulted the politicians who 'cynically, even contemptuously' refused to debate the 'fundamental decisions' facing Britain. It then welcomed the way the issue of quota-hopping for fish stocks had hit the TV screens and made Brussels bureaucrats an election issue. At the same time the newspaper celebrated Dame Angela Rumbold, the then Tory MP and party Vice-Chairman, standing for re-election in Mitcham and Morden. She had announced that she could not support her party's official line and would always vote against a single currency, whatever the circumstances. She declared that joining the Euro would mean moving our gold to Frankfurt, a ghastly prospect of loss of our vital substance (in fact, part of Britain's gold reserve is already in Washington as a standard IMF arrangement). Little attention was given to the fact that she had been a lobbyist for a company that supported the Channel Tunnel – the very passage through which the gold will pass, if it goes. Instead, what gained attention was her outspoken breach of Tory Party policy, even though she was its Vice-Chairman. If any other cause got as much prime-time television, it would have regarded itself as privileged. Instead, the *Daily Mail* editorial announced that Rumbold and other Tory candidates were shattering a (sorry, *the*) 'conspiracy of silence', when they declared in their election addresses that they would oppose further European integration: 'The *Mail* salutes them. In the coming days, as they make their views known, this newspaper will give them the publicity they merit.'

It began by listing the first seventy-six such candidates, endorsing them by name. It published their photographs in long rows, and declared that these were the candidates who gave voters a real choice. This choice was, 'Can we survive as a free nation or are we to be bulldozed into a federal European state? . . . be warned, nothing less is at stake than the freedom of Britain as a self-governing nation.'

The *Daily Telegraph* reinforced this theme in its editorial on 16 April. 'The issue *is* the single currency,' it declared. Major has described himself a One-Nation Tory, the editorial noted. If so, he should rule us out of ever embracing the Euro. Repeating a phrase of Margaret Thatcher's, the editorial concluded, 'With a single currency we would not be "One Nation" we would be No Nation.'

The next day the *Daily Mail* continued its campaign. It published another two-page spread of Eurosceptic candidates, and declared: EUROPE: THE GREAT REVOLT, as two Junior Ministers broke from the government's line of keeping the options open. Clearly, such ministers and MPs believed that their open hostility to any further European integration would make them more electable.

Major felt forced into action. He made an extraordinary twenty-minute intervention, speaking without notes to the morning press conference. Never have I heard such an unsustainable case argued with such apparent ease (I will return to it in Chapter 7). His plea, that Conservatives should not 'bind my hands', was ignored. MAJOR'S PLEDGE, screamed the *Daily Mail* on 17 April as it highlighted instead the Prime Minister's claim that, 'I will not take Britain into a single currency. Only the British nation can do that. Upon that, you may be certain.' The paper reported:

> John Major bowed to overwhelming party pressure last night and made his most dramatic personal pledge yet in defence of the pound. The Prime Minister's words – in a hastily arranged party political broadcast – were in response to the extraordinary public surge of Euro-scepticism among Tory candidates triggered by the *Daily Mail*'s Battle for Britain campaign.

The *Sun*, alarmed at being outflanked thanks to its support for Blair, also congratulated the Junior Ministers who had spoken out: 'The politicians should be under no illusions – Europe IS still THE issue for many voters.' This just goes to show that even those who write newspapers tend to believe what they read in other papers. The *Sun* had already got Blair to announce in its pages the month before that he is a British patriot and would not allow the single currency to be imposed on the British people. Now Blair wrote for them that he would 'slay the Euro-dragon'. (Andrew Marr, editor of the *Independent*, penned a fine article 'in anger and bemusement', objecting to the way that Blair caved in to asinine nationalist language that betrayed the sentiments of the country's moderate pro-European majority.[5])

The stampede of Tory candidates towards Euroscepticism, however, convinced most members of the political class that they were chasing the popular vote, not heading for the cliff. Politicians of all parties deflected their language against Europe, encouraged by much of the press. The *Sunday Times* demonstrated its wisdom on 20 April: 'The Prime Minister was right last week when he called Europe the defining issue of the election campaign . . . like a fuse slowly smouldering towards the keg of gunpowder it was always going to explode.'

On the same day the *Mail on Sunday* echoed this vision of an electorate about to detonate over the prospect of a shared currency. It declared 'Euroscepticism to be rampant in middle England', based on the evidence of a MORI poll of its own readers. It went further. If Major would come out flatly against a single currency, just 'for the lifetime of the next parliament', then voters 'would flood back. The Tory vote would shoot to 54 per cent and Labour's fall to 33 per cent.'

Tory candidates everywhere rushed to follow this advice. They turned out to be lemmings. Across Britain they found themselves falling to oblivion. Her prominence, and the massive personal publicity for her stalwart, anti-European views, earned Angela Rumbold, the angel of middle England, a 16 per cent swing – against her. Her vote collapsed from nearly 24,000 to just over 14,000.

The right wing was confident that the more right-wing you

were, the closer to the people you would be. Therefore the better your showing would be. Instead, extreme advocates of national prejudice were shot straight off the cliff by voters – if anything, at even greater velocity. David Evans, the Conservative MP for Welwyn Hatfield, described his opponent, Melanie Johnson, as 'a single girl with three bastard children'. The *Daily Telegraph* dismissed expressions of protest from those civilised enough to be appalled. It assured the nation that voters are made of a different pedigree: 'It is not Mr Evans but the prissy ideologues who express deep shock at his words who are out of touch.' Richard Littlejohn, supposed tribune of the people, was even more swingeing in his *Daily Mail* column: 'in the saloon bars and supermarket queues the length and breadth of Britain . . . millions of people think in exactly the same way as Evans'. On 1 May the 'single girl' became Welwyn's MP. 'Prejudice does not have a home here,' Melanie Johnson declared and described the way people crossed the street to shake her hand after learning of Evans' attack. She gained an 11 per cent swing and a 5,500 majority with an exceptionally high turnout of nearly 80 per cent, as bars and supermarkets right across Welwyn came out against a bigot.

In Exeter, Adrian Rogers made an issue of the fact that his Labour opponent, Ben Bradshaw, is openly gay. He called on the electorate not to let 'the pink flag fly over Exeter' and presumed this would help his election. In his final leaflet he asked them, 'Do *you* want an MP who wants to promote homosexuality in schools?' The answer was decisive: up went the pink flag, hoisted by the largest swing in the South-West. Bradshaw crushed Rogers by 29,000 to 17,000 votes (with another 11,000 Liberal Democrats to spare).[6]

What was going through the minds of Tories who paraded such views in the belief that it would win them a popular accolade? One can gain some insight into their thinking by reading the speech of Andrew Hargreaves, Conservative MP for Birmingham Hall Green, delivered to the House of Commons on 20 February in a full-scale debate on the constitution called by the then Conservative government. I went to watch it, nervous about how Labour would perform, and left certain that I had watched power cross the floor of the House. Not least because the debate implicitly assumed that Blair would form the next government. As one can see when Hargreaves argued:

> If the Labour Party does not . . . clarify its tax policy for a Scottish Parliament, we shall accuse it of depending for its majority, undemocratically, on a surfeit of Scottish Members spending predominantly English taxpayers' money, while English members have no say in the expenditure of money in Scotland. That would be mockery, and a travesty of democracy.

These words show that Hargreaves presumed there would be a modest Labour majority, thanks to its Scottish and Welsh votes. He guessed Labour would win. It had not, however, crossed his mind that it would win in England:

> Every time a patient dies unexpectedly or while awaiting treatment in an English hospital – every day, every week; drip, drip, drip – we shall remind the public in England that the Labour Party is holding power because of a surfeit of Scottish Members of Parliament who are spending two and a half times as much English taxpayers' money on someone in Scotland as on a patient in Birmingham. If there was a rail accident or road accident, the case would be more dramatic: we would be able to say, with justification, that, if the money had been spent fairly and proportionately in England, that accident might not have happened.
>
> That form of representation could not survive . . . Should the Labour Party be in a position to implement its policies by undemocratic means, I guarantee that we shall hound it out of England as an undemocratic party of minorities, never standing up for the majority English interests. It would be a party of ethnic ghettos. In local government, it has made such ghettos of our great cities, for purely political advantage. It would be a party of minorities – never the party of an English majority in England. We shall never let the people of England forget the contempt with which the Labour Party treats an English electorate.

This was a chilling tirade. The bully pulpit from which Hargreaves threatened to expose Labour as a 'party of minorities' was removed from under him . . . by the voters of Birmingham. The swing against Hargreaves was 14 per cent. His majority of nearly 4,000 was turned into a Labour plurality of 9,000. People in the middle of England spoke, but not in the language of Hargreaves.

The right sought comfort in the uniformity of the swing against Conservatives everywhere, whatever their views. Hugh Dykes, one of the leading pro-European Tory MPs, went down in Harrow East with an 18 per cent swing, for example. The observation provides small comfort, however. All were swept away on purpose. Never has tactical voting been argued for so clearly, or its consequences so precisely spelt out, constituency by constituency. The liberal broadsheets, the *Guardian*, the *Independent*, the *Observer*, argued for anti-government action and located their hot-spots – it was the *Observer* that identified Portillo's seat as vulnerable. The right-wing press equally told its readers how to vote tactically for its cause. The *Daily Telegraph*, though down-the-line for the Tories, gave prominence to candidates of the right. *The Times* was more selective and endorsed only those who were against European integration. Together, the two sell nearly two million copies, three times the combined circulation of the *Guardian* and *Independent*. The *Daily Mail* sells a further two million. Day after day that paper displayed its mug-shots of Europhobes and -sceptics, in much the same way that the early criminologist Cesare Lombroso displayed pathological types to demonstrate cranial resemblance and other exterior signs of primitivism. There was no such similarity in this case – all types of features can be found among anti-Europeans. The *Daily Mail* even came out for Tony Benn. To no effect. Tactical voting did increase greatly, but in one direction only. There was no discernible swell of support for chauvinists who opposed Europe, whether they did so in sophisticated terms or took the brutal approach of Evans. The more Anglo-nationalist a candidate, the more irrelevant it seemed. There were variations in both directions

– *it did not make any difference*. In an eloquent, pre-election editorial, the *Sunday Telegraph* called on voters to reject 'New Labour's instinctive belief in further European integration'. They did not. England chose instinctive co-operation. It refused to make a stand at Dover.

The greatest symbol was Wolverhampton South-West, where Nicholas Budgen enjoyed a majority of nearly 5,000. Budgen was a pillar among those hostile to co-operation with Europe. He expressed an extreme version of the combination of contempt for abroad with alarm at developments at home. Just before the election he appealed to John Major to make an issue of Labour's alleged policy of relaxing immigration controls. This was regarded as a barely disguised attempt to exploit a difference over the rights of families to be united, in order to play the race card. The then Prime Minister, who, however indecisive, is not racist, rejected the proposal out of hand. He was to prove himself much closer to the feelings of the British public than those who claimed to be its popular tribunes. (He was to suffer a swing against him of only 6.8 per cent.) Budgen's supporters, however, saw Major's dismissal of the attempt to profile the ethnic question as a fatal misreading of public sentiment. In his column in the *Daily Mail*, Simon Heffer claimed that 'Tory MPs winced with shame at Major's failure to see the importance of the issue.' If so, it was the first occasion for a long time that Tory MPs as a group exhibited this virtuous emotion. After all the revelations of corruption, arms to Iraq and BSE, after doubling the income of the wealthy while cutting the low standards of the poor, I thought that (with a few honourable exceptions) Conservative MPs had no shame. Now I know better – they felt shame when the Prime Minister refused to pander to racism.

Heffer's deftly crafted prose can be elegant. This particular column put together references to race, patriotism and homosexuality on behalf of Mr Budgen, whose views Heffer stated (as if it were obvious) are 'popular with the public'.[7] In fact, the public of Wolverhampton threw Budgen out. His support collapsed from nearly 26,000 to 19,539, with no

Referendum Party candidate to take away an iota of support. The swing against him was nearly 10 per cent and the Labour vote rose from 21,000 to a comfortable 25,000.

It was a historic turnabout, for it took place in a constituency once represented by Enoch Powell, whose influence dominated politics in the UK for a quarter of a century. In the campaign's final week the *Mail on Sunday* carried a long article by the Tory pretender John Redwood, in which he said, 'I want the voters to understand that this Election is not just about who will govern Britain for the next five years but whether there will be a Britain left to govern at the end of five years.' Redwood's combination of ambition, high nationalism and intellectualism make him the contemporary closest to Powell, and he might well have written:

> This is the . . . last election at which the British people will be given the opportunity to decide whether their country is to remain a democratic nation, governed by the will of its own electorate expressed in its own Parliament, or whether it will become one province in a new European superstate under institutions which know nothing of the political rights and liberties that we have so long taken for granted.

In fact, these were the words of Enoch Powell himself twenty-three years previously. They come from the warning he gave in the General Election campaign of February 1974.[8] It is worth recounting briefly the history of Powell's influence, in order to see how much the British electorate may now be liberated from its shadow.

Powell swung the 1974 election against his own party and helped bring about Edward Heath's downfall, which in turn put Margaret Thatcher on her path to power. Powell had also helped to clinch the previous 1970 election, this time for the Tories led by Heath. Although banished from the Conservative front bench for his 'rivers of blood' speech in 1968, Powell renewed his warnings about immigration in four well-timed interventions late in the 1970 campaign. He also warned against Labour's efforts under Harold Wilson to smuggle Britain into Europe and thus subvert our historic institutions. Powell may have hoped that his strong call to vote Tory in 1970 would strengthen his claim on the leadership if Heath went down to defeat, as seemed likely. Instead, his advocacy stirred a critical section of the white working class and broke them away from Labour. This was not the only factor that lost Harold Wilson the election, the primary cause being his disastrous economic strategy of defending sterling. Nonetheless, such was Heath's charisma deficit that Wilson would probably have won in 1970 – if narrowly – had Powell not advocated the Tory cause in the way he did.[9]

In 1974, however, Powell found himself completely alienated by Heath's success in negotiating British membership of the European Community. When Heath called the election, Powell announced that he could not stand as a Tory candidate. It would be fraudulent to do so, he declared, given his long-standing criticism of the government's policies. He then waited until the last week of the campaign to announce that Europe was the cardinal issue. With two days to go, he revealed that he supported Labour. 'By skilful playing of the media,' notes Edward Heath's biographer, 'Powell managed to dominate the news for five of the last seven days of the campaign.'[10] An extraordinary achievement for an independent figure. Once more there was a very narrow outcome (indeed, the Tory plurality was slightly larger than Labour's, though Labour won more seats), which makes Powell's grim claim of revenge all the more plausible. Just as Powell swung his supporters behind the Conservatives in 1970, so he swung them to Labour with decisive effect, in February 1974. 'I put him in,' Powell said of Heath, 'and I took him out.'[11]

A significant moment of the next General Election in 1979 was Margaret Thatcher's carefully calibrated aside that she understood why people felt 'swamped'. By then Powell was a Unionist MP in Ulster. From there he saw Thatcher as a leader whom his own influence had helped to forge. In the decisive Commons debate that initiated the Falklands War in 1982, his demand for iron measures had her nodding assent. It is even possible that, just as she had her pronunciation altered by speech training, so her glaring eyes and emphatic conviction were modelled on Powell's example.

Since his 1968 'rivers of blood' speech, every single General Election in Britain has been won by the most Powellite party until 1 May 1997. This time Powell once again intervened. Formally retired from active politics, he had the modest aim of protecting the inheritor of both his views and his own Wolverhampton seat. He sent a public letter of endorsement to Nicholas Budgen. Powell's move was hailed in the *Daily Telegraph* on 19 April as 'ominously prescient'. Powell, it felt sure, would be proved right and 'is now surely entitled to some wry satisfaction'.

The satisfaction that the *Daily Telegraph* anticipated was that the election would be lost but that Budgen would probably win his seat, and certainly do better than most Tories. There would then be the wry satisfaction of claiming that, had the course of Euroscepticism been followed, Britain would have remained Tory. Portillo, Rumbold, Budgen, would – this was the expectation – take their places on the opposition benches emboldened by the wry satisfaction that the people supported *their* views. Labour, according to this expectation, would not be the legitimate representative of Britain, but merely a beneficiary of John Major's irresolute leadership and unpopularity. The inheritors of Powell would then make a man – an Englishman – of the Conservative Party in opposition, as they blasted the Blair government, which was destined to be on its back-foot thanks to its feeble, Euro-diluted patriotism and spineless commitment to devolution.

The confidence of the Europhobes seemed to convince Labour that this might indeed be the outcome. They went chauvinist in the Murdoch press. The *Sun*'s feedback of Blairite Europatriotic clichés further convinced the anti-European Tories that their own drumbeat was the true pulse of the electorate. In 1997 Powellite patriotism turned the heads of English political leaders as never before.

Yet for the first time it lost its hold over the electorate. It drew no extra support. Its call attracted no extra numbers. It gave no added popularity. Electorally, Enoch's army largely dissolved.

Not completely. There is still some support – as well as a sentimental attachment to his finest creation, Margaret Thatcher. But its capacity to topple the allegiance of key sectors of the British electorate seems to be at an end. In part, indeed, Enoch's army may have been dispersed by its most distorted advocate. It would cause more than wry satisfaction, although not to Powell, if the conclusion of all his efforts turned out to be James Goldsmith's Referendum Party.

For while fear of Europe diminished, alarm and disillusion sown by big money increased. The UK remains vulnerable to trends that are at work most blatantly in the United States, where private fortunes have suborned the democratic process in the name of freedom of expression – a right originally conceived to protect private, personal belief, not public advertising.

In the United States, the last election saw cumulative expenditures of well over a billion dollars, as voter turnout slumped despite various efforts to increase the proportion registered. An inverse correlation can be discerned, which first became clear in the 1992 US elections. The more money that is spent, the fewer people go to the polls, so that now, as a cataract of funding pours into American election campaigns, turnout has fallen to below 50 per cent. The inverse correlation has all the makings of a law, rather than an accidental relationship.[12] For there are at least two discernible causes that explain it. First, money begets money. Expenditures compete, especially when candidates must buy television time, making all parties increasingly dependent on similar, and even identical, sources for their funding. As this happens they cease to be able to articulate their differences; indeed, these start to diminish altogether. Are American voters wrong to say that there is little to choose between Republicans and Democrats? Deprived of what they feel to be sufficient choice, and aware that politicians are on the phone fund-raising far more than they are talking to their constituents, voters abstain in order to retain their own integrity.

Capital-intensive politics also reinforces the repulsion-effect, thanks to the negative advertising that is its natural form of communication. Without internal democracy, stripped of the wide interests expressed in traditional party alliances, forced to express its views in short clips and bold advertisements, high-expenditure politics has a built-in tendency to negative campaigning. The cumulative effect is to depoliticise the electorate, as it turns people off politics altogether.

The Referendum Party showed the process at work. Sir James Goldsmith decided to spend £20 million to save the national soul from Brussels. He calculated that this would buy enough support to field candidates right across the country. Their cry was a referendum against Europe; their full-page adverts were unavoidable, their slogans wholly alarmist. A prominent strapline in one piece of their literature stated simply: FRANKLY IT DOESN'T MATTER WHO YOU VOTE FOR. They also told voters: BEWARE of fake referendums.[13]

The Referendum Party made it more difficult to discuss constitutional issues. These were drowned out by claims that the only constitutional question that mattered was saving Britain's democracy from the claws of the European Union. As the EU is undemocratic, this point had some force. Insisting that it overshadowed everything, the Referendum Party encouraged a generalised sense of fear and loss. It presented itself as raising issues that others did not want to be debated, but its own actions *prevented* them from being debated. Like a loud drunk at a dinner party bellowing that no one is talking about 'what really matters', the Referendum Party was both incapable of listening and stopped others from talking. Some at the table simply left.

Money drove out participation, in the name of calling upon the people to save themselves. So great have private fortunes become, that, with a small fraction of their personal wealth, a single person can create an organisation and gain 800,000 votes. This might seem like democracy at work. In fact, it is top-down, subverting the democratic process and repelling electors. The money spent literally buys what should be a public process. Goldsmith privatised politics. Individuals responded privately. Many did so in the only way they can that clearly belongs to them – they withdrew. Turnout fell from 76 to 71.5 per cent, a drop of over two million voters. To this degree there was an increase in fear.

But it was nothing like as great a shift as the positive urge to kick out a government that traded in false patriotism. The Conservatives even acquired a prison ship, adroitly timed to arrive during the election campaign as a warning of the need for toughness within our shores. The voters were not intimidated. They were determined to drop the Tories, and nothing the government did could make them fear doing so. Powell might protest that his is not the politics of fear, but everything he has argued since 1968 can be regarded as a warning: a warning of loss. Loss of institutional uniqueness, of Englishness, of cultural distinctiveness, of a historic legacy that needs protection, of our rights and liberties, of our sovereignty and national character. Powell told us to fear this loss and hold fast to the past. For the first time since he made this call in 1968 it was rejected.

That this rejection was a considered attitude, settled well before the election, was borne out by the response to Diana's death (which I consider in Chapter 5) – for what occurs spontaneously and with great force must have been in existence for some time. Certainly, the younger leaders of the Tory Party were quick to draw the lessons of the election and her wake. Single mothers, gays, ethnic minorities, are now all part of the country. Powellite views are 'prehistoric' and Britain is officially a 'multicultural' nation. William Hague even came out with a snappy phrase to sum it up, saying that he was for 'patriotism without bigotry'. Privately this was Labour's attitude all along, just as – on a personal basis – voters had got there some time ago. It is significant, and rather shameful for Labour, that it took a new Tory to say it with profile. But it confirms that May Day 1997 was a watershed that certainly buried an ugly streak in Great Englishness, and possibly its form of nationalism, completely.

2

A Velvet Revolution Against Corruption

GUARDIAN CORRESPONDENT Matthew Engel called May 1st Britain's velvet revolution – a term coined by the Czechs after they rescued their country peacefully from communism. 'This was our velvet revolution, and yesterday the population went wild,' he reported. The *Daily Telegraph* attacked the description for crass exaggeration. Ian Buruma, writing in *Prospect*, was offended and wondered whether Engel, and others who even compared the events of May Day to the end of the Berlin Wall, 'were blissfully ignorant of what things are like under a dictatorship'.[1] The *Guardian* defended the analogy in an editorial on the Queen's speech:

> It would be wrong to claim that [it] had the same epic, historical resonance as the great transformations which saw Vaclav Havel or Nelson Mandela come from their prison cells to don a presidential mantle. Yet it was, in British terms, our own kind of velvet revolution nonetheless.[2]

Yes and no. The 'no' is more obvious, the 'yes' more interesting. First, the no. The population did *not* go wild. There were no celebrations in the streets across the UK to welcome a Labour government. At the start of the election Tony Blair called on voters to 'trust me'. They did not. Positive enthusiasm for Labour was scarce during the campaign. When Labour won, the crowd that cheered Blair into Downing Street waving Union Jacks was not a spontaneous outbreak of new patriotism; it was a construct of Millbank, the party organisation, which rounded up selected faithful. In a fundamental sense, therefore, 1 May did not represent a velvet revolution in terms of the transition of State sovereignty. It was not an example of the power of the powerless. Rather, it was an exercise by those who wanted to be powerful, wheeling out the already powerful in the shape of businessmen, to show that they were fit to govern. The Labour leaders rode to office projecting the Tories as weak and themselves as strong.

The reason for this was clear. Labour saw the odds stacked against it. It had to fight the election at a time of the government's choosing, on economic terms that the Tories had manipulated. It felt it had to bring in new money to redress the balance of the old and limit severely what it could promise. Its manifesto was a self-denying ordinance. The goal that the leading members promised to attain was that they would win. This they delivered with consummate discipline.

Public gratitude was unstinting. Yet it should not be mistaken for belief in Labour, especially during the campaign. Here, the analogy with Eastern Europe starts to be useful. In those countries too the people tossed aside the past more completely than any opposition leaders considered possible. To make a direct identification of the UK with the communist regimes of Eastern Europe is repugnant and unfair, but, having emphasised this, to make an indirect one and draw out the parallels opens up helpful perspectives. For, while Britain's society and economy had entered the modern world and those of Eastern Europe had not, the ancient British political system had narrowed rather than democratised itself, before – and even after the end of – the Cold War. Our dictatorship has long been only elective. Opposition is free to speak out and organise itself against the government, for which many thanks. Nonetheless, in terms of what Thatcher herself once referred to as 'our regime', comparisons with the Soviet bloc can be made.

Even comparisons with respect to corruption. This was much more important for people than the 'official' record shows, especially for Conservative swing voters. What I mean by the official record is that if you read the papers or follow the television news, you will have learnt of a number of scandals, each one reported as if it were an exception, a matter of individual circumstance. But at the same time that Tory MPs were involved in various illegalities – taking money in brown envelopes, asking cash for questions, staying for free at the Ritz or having their bills paid by Arab dealers – huge windfall gains were being made out of privatisation. In addition, unknown numbers of unnamed Conservatives were getting jobs on quangos. Furthermore, Ministers seemed incapable of resigning when they made bad policy mistakes. Even if some of these errors were not corrupt, it seemed an abuse of office for them to keep their ministerial privileges when in any other job these would have been forfeited. The overall impact of such episodes accumulated in the public mind.

Early on in her premiership, Thatcher implied not only that it was good to be rich but also that public servants paid less than their equivalents in the private sector were probably second-rate. Throughout the ranks of the Tory Party, cashing in by one route or another came to be seen as a measure of worth. Thatcher's call for a return to Victorian values metamorphosed into a renewal of Georgian values of the late eighteenth and early nineteenth century, when public office was a vehicle for private gain – and which came to be known as the Old Corruption. Slowly, as the evidence accumulated, late-twentieth-century Tory government became associated with the lucrative and improper practices of a new corruption.

The picture as a whole remains impressionistic because much of what occurred was underhand, remains under wraps and probably will never be uncovered. The Conservatives have admitted that a perception occurred, that voters *felt* the Tories were heartless in running down vital public services too much; that it *seemed* to the public that many of them, if not most, were over enthusiastic in helping themselves and their mates to the spoils of office. According to this interpretation, the government suffered from the *image* of being a rotten regime. Was it just an image? Normally viewers are taken in by sleight-of-hand when carried out by experienced performers. In this case, we are told, the audience believed it was watching fast ones being pulled when in fact they were not. Was it just a perception? Or did the voters get what they saw?

In 1996, William Rees-Mogg asked a well-placed Conservative election planner if the Tories would win. 'It depends on whether people have got over their anger,' came the reply.[3] Their anger, that is, with the recession and the ERM fiasco of 1992. British voters are notoriously forgiving. Peter Jenkins once referred to 'the British people, who were quick to forgive and forget and to re-elect the Tories'.[4] Why, then, should they change their character and hold on to the 1992 episode? Rees-Mogg suggests that voters' anger might have been assuaged, had there been an apology 'after the exchange rate collapsed'. Such an analysis hardly goes far enough. Failure to apologise became a continuous process; Ministers no longer resigned when they should have done, through affair after affair, from the Scott Report to BSE. The Scott Report, for example, found that William Waldegrave, by then Chief Secretary to the Treasury, had misled Parliament. When the report was published, but before the House of Commons formally debated it, Waldegrave told the *Daily Mail*, 'It will be hairy for ten days. But that will be all.'[5] In the short term he was right, and the government got away with it. At the election he lost his seat with a 12.1 per cent swing and massive Tory defections to Labour. Waldegrave was justly punished for the arrogance and presumption of power that was a general characteristic of the Thatcher and Major years, and to which he notably contributed.

An aura of contempt – and worse – riddled ministerial deportment. In a striking phrase, Anne Widdecome described her Secretary of State at the Home Office, Michael Howard, as having 'something of the night' about him. She was kind enough to reveal her concern only after the General Election, when Howard ran for the Conservative Party leadership. She need not have worried. The people had guessed. Maybe her own colleagues were unaware of it, being used to the dark.

Nonetheless it was by no means only traditional Labour voters who sensed character defects in the Tories holding high offices of State. Many traditional Conservatives also perceived the Cabinet as a black hole. Voters' anger was not caused by a single policy mistake in 1992 (however severe), which the people did not manage to 'get over'. Anger with the Tories was active and continuous, renewed by each episode of incompetence unpunished, windfall untaxed and power presumed.

Even though it probably helped to decide many votes, the new corruption did not become a defining issue of the election for three reasons. First, the Conservative Party and the media denied that there was any systemic problem. There may have been personal cases, often cast as 'tragedies' for the individual concerned, but just as often blind eyes were turned. When the issue was finally forced upon Parliament, it tried to 'handle' it by creating the Nolan Commission. There was talk of the way the Italians are even worse, as if this made things better.

Second and more important, the Conservative government did not need to defend itself from the charge of turning a blind eye to corruption, because this accusation was not made by the official opposition. Labour did not target Tory malpractice during the run-up to the election. The semi-official *Guardian* account of the al-Fayed scandals (in which that paper played a heroic role, and proved the importance of a free and independent press) reports that Labour was 'docile' in its response, even just before the 1996 Tory Party conference:

> A variety of Labour spin doctors and MPs tried their best to explain to the *Guardian* why they were keeping a low profile. The excuses ranged from: 'Some of our chaps may have been up to the same' . . . to 'Well, the truth is MPs just don't have much appetite for investigating each other'. Robin Cook, who had done such a brilliant forensic job on the Scott Report, was not allowed near this one by party managers. Tony Blair's closest aides, Alastair Campbell and Peter Mandelson, blew hot and cold. The cautious Labour Chief Whip, Donald

Dewar, was put in charge of co-ordinating the party's response.[6]

Halfway through the election campaign Conservative Central Office revealed an early version of Labour's *War Book*. This supposedly showed that the then opposition was a scheming, devious, untrustworthy bunch of manipulators, whereas the actual photocopies of the thirty-one-page document showed it to be a well-presented, lucid and professional assessment of the strengths and weaknesses of the two sides. With one exception. New Labour's appraisal of nine 'Conservative Weaknesses' did not include sleaze, corruption or the quango State. Nor was Labour's promise to clean up government and offer a Freedom of Information Act and improved accountability listed among Labour's twelve strengths. This despite well over 70 per cent support for such Labour policies, even among Conservative voters. Labour's *War Book* laid out a professional overview of 'The Battleground', except that it ensured that corruption did not figure in it.

Despite this, it became an issue. Millbank had a vast staff of researchers mapping every Tory move. The Liberal Democrats had two. They puzzled over why John Major had declared a six-week election campaign and prorogued Parliament early, when he need not have, especially as it obliged him to drop legislation to which the government had seemed committed. The two Lib Dem researchers realised that Major's move prevented the publication of the report just completed by Sir Gordon Downey, the new Parliamentary Commissioner for Standards, on the allegations against various MPs made by Mohammed al-Fayed and the *Guardian*. The Liberal Democrats raised the issue in the final moments of Major's government. Major angrily dismissed their request to extend Parliament for the few days needed to publish the report. The *Guardian* then released transcripts of Downey's hearings – which in a grown-up democracy would anyway have been held in public before television cameras. Among other instances, the paper identified two blatant cases of ex-Ministers who were still standing in safe seats in the coming election: Tim Smith and Neil Hamilton. Smith had told Downey that he had received between £18,000 and £25,000 in cash from al-Fayed. He had been retained as a Junior Minister after the Prime Minister had been informed of this – and resigned only when the *Guardian* published the allegations on 20 October 1994. Even then, the government put him on the Public Accounts Committee a year later. Finally, under the blaze of the *Guardian*'s publicity, Smith stood down from the election.

Neil Hamilton did not. He denied taking cash in brown envelopes from al-Fayed. (It is funny how the colour sticks to the allegation.) But he agreed during the Downey investigation that he had taken £10,000 from the lobbyist Ian Greer, had not declared the money to either Parliament or the Tax Revenue and, when asked by the then President of the Board of Trade, Michael Heseltine, whether he had a relationship with Greer, lied and said he did not. Why? 'Politics is a rough trade,' Hamilton explained to Downey.[7] As an example of just how rough, consider the 1987 letter that Hamilton sent al-Fayed, whose hospitality he enjoyed at the Ritz Hotel in Paris:

> Dear Mohammed
>
> . . . I have now been elected secretary of the Conservative finance committee and vice-chairman of the trade and industry committee, all of which gives me a better position from which to act on your behalf . . .
>
> Yours ever, Neil[8]

'To act on your behalf': if voters had been fully aware of the version of representative democracy practised by Government MPs, even more Conservatives might have lost their seats on 1 May. John Major *was* aware of it.

When Hamilton decided to brazen it out, the opposition parties in his Tatton constituency joined forces to support an 'Anti-Sleaze Candidate' against him. They chose Martin Bell, a television journalist well known for his reports from Bosnia. The *Daily Telegraph* was beside itself with rage that:

> a television journalist should oppose Hamilton. It is self-

> evident to the proposers that a television journalist is the natural upholder of goodness, beauty and truth . . . this newspaper can hardly object to fierce scrutiny of politicians and their supposed misdeeds. But we can and do object most fiercely to a media which sets itself up above those who vote.

This is a fine example of the way in which the right wing objects to the intrusion of voices other than its own. The voters were grateful for the opportunity to choose differently. Hamilton's support plummeted from 32,000 to 18,000, while Bell gained nearly 30,000 votes in a 76 per cent turnout. What had been one of the kingdom's safest Tory constituencies fell to a man in a white suit.

The *Daily Telegraph* smelled a plot. 'Powerful interests', it declared, 'have decreed that this election is "about sleaze"; it looks like the best way of getting the Tories out, the best tactic for diverting attention from the main issue of governing Britain.' Both parts of this argument were wrong. Voters feel that corruption *is* about governing Britain – and they are right – it was not a diversion. But the 'powers' to which the *Daily Telegraph* referred, meaning Labour and its friends, did not want to concentrate on the question. Instead, they too felt that the election had become 'mired' in the issue in the first weeks. Public anger at the kleptocratic tendencies of the Conservative regime smouldered rather than exploded, because the official opposition did not make an issue of it.

If the first reason for the failure of corruption to become a defining issue was Tory insistence that it was neither serious nor endemic and the second that Labour declined to draw up the full bill of charges and nail it to the doors of the Commons, the third reason was the confusion inherent in the term that came to sum up the degeneration of political life under the Tories: sleaze.

Lord Nolan defined sleaze as 'a pervasive atmosphere . . . in which sexual, financial and government misconduct were indifferently linked'.[9] The word became a catch-all. Traced back to seventeenth-century houses of disorder, its use suddenly took off in the mid-1990s, and now its application can stretch to all manner of businesses as well as politics – an observation of Trevor Smith, who made a prescient warning in 1985 about the effect of 'hooliganism in high places'.[10]

The problem with the term 'sleaze' is its very elasticity (if that is not too tasteless a metaphor), as it stretches from sexual peccadilloes to the serious abuse of office. The epithet proved especially useful for the tabloids. Unlike 'corruption', the word 'sleaze' is both brief enough to be headline-friendly and vague enough to be almost sue-proof. The charge of corruption invites libel action, but it is much harder to object to being associated with sleaze, for this carries no specific charge of illegal wrong-doing. Rather, it implies unpleasant motivation, shoddy hypocrisy and the odour of cheap sex. Tabloid-speak demonstrably provided a linguistic service, as it repackaged an activity that was hardly new but whose incidence was growing. Yet at the same time as sending out a necessary alarm call, it dulled an essential discrimination. For there is a difference in kind between putting your hand up the skirt of a hostess and putting it in the till. Taking money is not at all like taking a mistress or a gay partner. By taking bribes, politicians are taking something *from* the public, not simply adding a *frisson* to their own lives. The sensationalism of the term 'sleaze' trivialised grave violations of public standards by associating them with personal indulgence. Useful though it seemed, it obstructed perception by making no distinction between the venial and the venal, the private sin and the public wrongdoing, the forgivable and the criminal.

In the second week of the election campaign, the *Sun* exposed a Tory backbencher, Piers Merchant, by setting him up with a teenage hostess, who kissed him in the park while the paper's photographer staked them out. He was asked to resign, but Merchant refused and the voters re-elected him. Meanwhile, Major declined to ensure a similar, public request to Neil Hamilton, despite his blatant involvement in questionable financial practices. British voters proved to be more discriminating. They can tell the difference between personal and public life, between sex and cash. Possibly swing voters of both genders take a lenient view of extra-marital affairs (after all, they swing), but they are stern about honesty in the public purse as they judge which way to vote. From Paddy Ashdown's admission in 1992 and Alan Clark's revelations in his *Diary* to Piers Merchant's re-election and the victory of Ben Bradshaw, the evidence suggests that voters no longer disapprove of politicians behaving differently in their private lives, so long as no one has been deeply hurt. Toleration of lifestyle, supposedly a byword of the cultivated Briton, has migrated to the population as a whole.

The contrast with America helps make the point. In the United States voters are realistically cynical about the financial corruption of politics. Aware that no one can run for office without television adverts and that no one can afford these without massive fund-raising, they see correctly that politics in their country has been irredeemably bought by money. As if in revenge, the American public punishes its politicians in the only way it can, by demanding a ridiculous degree of sexual rectitude. The American media feed these double standards. As major beneficiaries of the same political advertising that corrupts politics, they are perhaps aware of their own bad faith. Having turned a blind eye to the ongoing financial scandal, they magnify the sexual ones as their means of pretending to hold politicians to account.

Thus the American pattern makes what is personal political, and at the same time makes what *is* political invisible. Thanks to its influence, such double standards affect the media in Britain. This leads to two informal and incorrect interpretations about British attitudes to sleaze. It encourages commentators and politicians on the right to assume that British toleration of sexual mores extends to financial matters, whereas the opposite is the case. And it leads Labour politicians to fear that if they campaign against financial irregularity, the sexual behaviour of their colleagues could also become an issue. Labour folk may be less into sado-masochism than their Tory counterparts, but they are at least as strange in their other tastes – as divorced, as womanising and manising, and as gay – as Conservatives.[11] Fear of exposure in this respect may have held Labour back from attacking Tory sleaze. In this way, neither of the two main parties comprehended that the British electorate retains sound judgement. Voters only slowly became aware of the encroachment of big money into politics. This makes their aversion all the more resilient, as, gradually acquired, it will not be easily dispersed.

Three questions: how widespread were the activities perceived as corrupt; how fair is it to allege they characterised the Tory regime; and how unpopular was this? In their analysis of 'the emergence of the sleaze issue' Stuart Weir and Patrick Dunleavy identify seven categories – in addition to unconventional sexual behaviour – of which blatant and shady financial wrongdoing is only the first. Their list includes the dramatic increase in commercial lobbying; the alleged packing of quangos; honours in return for donations; Ministers taking well-paid jobs in the City; secret, large-scale party donations; and windfall bonuses thanks to privatisation. Not all such activities are illegal, but many put public office to less than impersonal benefit.[12]

If we leave aside illegal activity, whose exposure has the largest impact, there are four broad areas of activity that made voters in 1997 feel that the politically powerful were taking advantage of their position and privileges. The first is obviously the massive growth of *lobbying*, especially as MPs themselves became hired lobbyists for causes in which they had no special interest or expertise. The second, generally regarded as a Tory success story, was privatisation. The third was the rise of unaccountable quangos. The fourth (pervasive but harder to pin down) was the rise in privilege as public services were allowed to degenerate, often gratuitously, while Ministers and their friends looked after themselves privately.

Voters gasped at the sums that accompanied *privatisation*, and were unhappy at the way Ministers and civil servants jumped into lucrative positions in companies they helped to create. There was a suspicion of kickbacks as well as windfalls. Meanwhile, hardly a month went by without a story of mystery prizes for which regular people could not buy tickets, thanks to the government's sale of State assets.

Here, for example, are three items that appeared on the same day during the election campaign itself, all in the *Independent* – stories that appeared and then disappeared. On 4 April its reporter Christian Wolmar drew attention to a report by the All-Party Commons Public Accounts Committee that criticised the way in which the Department of Transport sold off railway depots as businesses with a cash balance of £1 million, when they had £17 million in liquid reserves; £13 million was never recovered. He also reported that until 1996 the Department of Transport classified many of its documents as 'Not for NAO' (NAO stands for National Audit Office). The Committee concluded:

> we consider it extraordinary and unacceptable for government departments to use their resources funded from money provided by Parliament to organise and classify papers so that they are kept away from the auditors appointed by Parliament.

Just another story, just another day. No heads rolled. On the same day, but on a business page, Chris Godsmark wrote a story headlined 'Leasing chief shares mystery rail windfall'. This reported that one John Prideaux, 'a former senior board director of British Rail', received an unspecified windfall consideration through a complex deal, in which one of those involved seems to have netted £36 million.

'What a racket!' is how reports like this are generally seen. They clattered through the Tory years – here a windfall, there a windfall – so that one got used to thinking that a few hundred thousand was 'not much' as these things went. They provided unremembered, uncounted reasons for distrust. They linked in the public mind with what seemed like another racket, the rise of the *quango State*. By 1994 there were approximately 70,000 appointed and self-appointed quango positions – more than twice the figure for elected local councillors. Quangocrats spent around £60 billion a year of public money, about one-third of the total central government expenditure, and only £10 billion less than the total local authority spending. Quango jobs could be accompanied by relatively generous salaries from the public purse. Some of this was justified in terms of the work involved, but the method of appointment was pure patronage. *The Economist* reported, 'What power Ministers have taken for themselves, they are giving to their friends.' Not seeing anything wrong in this, Baroness Denton, who as a Minister at the Department of Trade and Industry supervised 2,000 appointments, told the *Independent on Sunday*, 'I can't remember knowingly appointing a Labour supporter.'[13] One Chair of a major quango reported in his organisation's newsletter:

> I became chairman as a consequence of sharing a cab with a stranger. Another Quango chairman was appointed following a pheasant shoot at which the Secretary of State was a fellow gun; the subsequent chairman of a water authority bumped into a Cabinet minister while birding on a Greek island. It is a splendidly capricious way of doing things.[14]

There is method to the madness. It used to be called class privilege. The capricious aspect is splendid only for those who get to shoot pheasant in the first place.

The government refused to publish the lists of those to whom it gave positions. A request made by Shirley Williams in the Lords for a list of those appointed was turned down on the grounds that it would be too expensive to provide.[15] Exposure relied on local circumstances. The rise of the quango was particularly scandalous in Wales, a country of just over two million inhabitants and almost completely Labour, Liberal Democrat and Plaid Cymru in local government, with the Tories in fourth place in the number of its councillors. Nonetheless a Tory Secretary of State made 1,400 appointments to eighty quangos. These spent £1.8 billion and employed 57,000 people. Appointments might be made by a telephone call. The Chairman of the Tourist Board, for example, was not asked a single question about his plans, nor was anyone else interviewed, before he was given the job by phone. A succession of failed Conservative candidates obtained senior appointments. Large-scale financial corruption followed in the Welsh Development Agency.[16]

In the past Wales has been treated as a one-party state by the Labour 'Taffia'. The only defence of quango-ising government was that it would provide better direction and policy. Instead the Conservatives created, in John Stewart's biting phrase, 'a New Magistracy' – a reference to the old, appointed élite who ran the counties before 1888. In Wales there was a new colonialism.

Interestingly, one of the earliest warnings came from the right, before 1979. For it had been Labour that pioneered the use of quangos. The Adam Smith Institute was told:

> Ministers have discovered that the system can be used for shedding personal responsibility, rewarding friends, expanding the corporate state, diminishing the authority of parliament . . . On its present scale, the vast and complex network of Quangos encourages an abuse of patronage and invites corruption.

Thatcher promised to abolish them. Instead the Tories exploited the advantages offered by administrative fiat in a country where local government has no constitutional or democratic security. In its own modest way, the British State created its equivalent to the *nomenklatura*, the privileged functionaries appointed to government positions under Soviet communism by virtue of their party connections.

Any visitor to Soviet-bloc countries was struck by the run-down nature of public services, even while these were fêted as an achievement of the regime. A similar degeneration of the public sector took place in Britain. This was another form of *improper privilege*. The Tories looked after their own, exploited the advantages of their control of the State and then left the population to rot. I am exaggerating the facts – but not the feeling, which was often rooted in personal experience. There can hardly have been a family that has not had an elderly friend or relative who has been stuck on a trolley in a hospital corridor for want of a bed. Everyone whose children go to State schools, as the vast majority do, knows that the Tories installed a national curriculum, but left schools without the money to acquire the relevant textbooks. We all know too that Ministers were untouched by such problems, because they enjoyed private medicine and sent their children to so-called public schools. There was no need for such stark deprivation of the two crucial services that the State was obliged to provide. Its heedless character bred mutual contempt between people and the government and helps to explain why voters did not 'feel good' about economic growth. The regime had become indifferent. This too offers a fair parallel with Eastern Europe.

After the election Kenneth Clarke expressed his surprise about the way in which ordinary voters did not believe that they were better off, despite the economic improvement he had overseen as Chancellor. Yet in his budget only a few months previously, he had cut £700 million of investment in the London Underground. No one familiar with regular life in the capital could have done this. If one could pile Pelion on Ossa underground, he did so – adding the promise of further misery to existing stress. In the election, the Tory vote was shattered across the capital, despite the boom.

Throughout the exceptionally lengthy campaign each of the parties would hold a morning press conference: the Liberal Democrats at 8.30 am, Labour at 9.15 am and the Tories at 10.30 am was the usual schedule. The events were largely contrived, the questions limited, the answers prepared. The conferences allowed the parties to set out their stall for the day and then crowd around the screens to watch their opponents on cable television. The last morning press conference on the last such day was the Tory one. The Prime Minister made the success of the economy his final pitch. 'No one can honestly question that the transformation in Britain has been anything less than an economic miracle. *It is too good to give up*.' He emphasised this sentence, which was underlined in the press release. 'It is not only our economy that has been transformed,' he continued:

> The programme we have set out . . . has created a Britain we can be proud of. The best free health service in the world. The most effective and best funded system of pensions and welfare . . .

And the chance to take forward my belief in a classless society, where more of the have-nots are able to join the haves.
It's too good to give up.

The final question was given to Nick Clark of the much admired BBC Radio's *World at One*. He was chosen to lead the final exchange of the many hundreds of media jousts between the hacks and the politicians. He noted the theme that the Prime Minister had chosen: how well Britain was doing. Many listeners had sent him letters, Clark said, and he asked if the Prime Minister would respond to one that was typical of those he had been getting over the past weeks. It was from a doctor. Why, the doctor asked, if the economy is doing so well, are so many hospital wards closing? If Britain is booming, why are the hospitals so understaffed; why are there so many homeless on the streets; why are there so many schools with outside toilets, poor food, no textbooks and over-sized classes; why, if the British economy is doing so well, are there such widespread shortages in essential services?

As Clark read from the letter, I watched Michael Heseltine, just a few feet in front of me, sitting next to John Major, who kept his impassive, eerie smile throughout, as he had done for most of the campaign. The Deputy Prime Minister, by contrast, had sat through the last press conference grim and red-faced. Suddenly, as the broadcaster read from the doctor's letter, Heseltine laughed silently. His face crinkled, his eyes sparkled with combat.

I was reminded – unfairly, but one has to keep awake at these events – of a joke about the USSR. In the 1930s a Commissar from the Kremlin went out to a Siberian township beyond Tomsk to report on the four-year plan. He told the assembled inhabitants how much steel had been produced, how food production was rising, how the Soviet plan was the envy of the world. When he finished he asked for questions. Slowly a hand went up. 'If things are so good, Comrade Commissar, why are things so bad?' 'A very good question,' said the Commisar, 'I will take it back to our great leader personally. What is your name, Comrade?' 'My name is Sloyankin, I am a worker,' came the reply. Four years later the Commissar returned to the township to report on the further successes of the next plan, the even greater achievements in output, the even higher estimation of the USSR in the eyes of the world. Once again he asked for questions. This time no hand went up. But from the back there came a voice: 'If things are so good, where is Comrade Sloyankin?'

Back in London in 1997, our Prime Minister replied to Clark's question by saying that he was sure that he could find another doctor with a different experience. Quite. That and Heseltine's laugh . . . If they had had five more years, what would have happened to those like the doctor? It would have been retirement, withdrawal, despair and internal exile. It would surely not – you could tell that from Heseltine's laugh and Major's smile – have meant textbooks in the schools or an end to a society with 'have-nots' (a phrase to which I will return).

The perception of a corrupt regime thus went much wider than actual illegality. It extended to a sense of unjustified unfairness, inappropriate differentials, fortunes flaunted in the face of the hard-working poor. This perception was not the expression of a wet paternalism concerned about the 'have-nots'. It was shared by tough-minded middle-class families who had had their chance and wanted the same for their children. If there was a psychological turning point when people started to question what was going on, it did date back to 1992 but was not limited to the ERM débâcle. For, coincidentally with the vertiginous rise in interest rates and mountains of property trapped in negative equity, came the Windsor Castle fire. People were sad to see the Queen actually there, that this was her home and that she was upset at the damage. They were also infuriated by the tones of Peter Brooke who, as Minister for Heritage, announced on the spot that the taxpayer would cover the costs. During the war the royal family had shared the dangers of the Blitz. This had established its late-twentieth-century relationship with the people. What did it mean to be British? It meant that we were all in it together. In 1992 the government had been saying for years that people had to stand on their own feet as tens of thousands were losing their houses as mortgage rates went – almost literally – through the roof. Hospitals were being closed, State hand-outs cut back. But 'they' could enjoy free castle repairs at the taxpayers' expense. There might be one law for the rich and another for the poor, but it should not be so. Nearly 60,000 *Sun* readers phoned in to say that the Queen should pay for her own castle, while fewer than 4,000 phoned who thought she should not.[17] The image of an official plutocracy taking advantage of its position was deeply damaging to the monarchy. It also tainted the government. It may have been legal, but in the larger sense the regine felt corrupt.

Finally, at the core of public discontent was the belief that government indulged in straight impropriety. John Major's image did not help. His claim to be Mr Clean was believed, and thereby implied that his colleagues were dirty. How many were doing it? How much money changed hands, not just as cash for mere questions (for at least these appeared on the public record) but in the form of positions on the Board in return for contracts eased and connections made, or in terms of party donations after business had been rendered, or on commissions for deals struck by one's mother? We don't know. But there was one telling sign.

In 1992 Asil Nadir jumped bail and fled Britain for Cyprus. His firm, Polly Peck, had crashed around him, leaving the usual victims. He had donated £365,000 to the Tory Party via a National Westminster Bank account in Jersey, which the bankrupt company's administrator, Touche Ross, found to have been 'misappropriated' from Polly Peck.[18] The Tory Party refused to return any of this money, saying that it had not been proven that it was actually stolen – as if one could tell which of Nadir's banknotes were gained by kosher means and which by underhand. The *Sunday Telegraph* polled Tory MPs about the issue: 28 per cent of them said that their party should keep the money, *even if it was shown to have been stolen.*[19] A quarter of Tory MPs had no qualms about their party being in receipt of stolen goods. It was when I read this, tucked away at the bottom of the story, that I knew something had gone wrong that would be hard to eradicate. It was not so much that so large a proportion of Tory MPs were indifferent to right and wrong, as that they should not even bother to hide the fact. This suggested a culture of malfeasance in which dishonesty was a way of life and the Whips' office must have known.

Was it really so bad? It would take a small study to establish the facts beyond doubt, and even this would be ignored by those who do not wish to hear the truth. One description can be found in Emma Nicholson's memoir, *Secret Society*. She had been an ambitious and able Conservative MP, and still believes today, so to speak, in the honour of Douglas Hurd and Kenneth Clarke. She finally left the Tory Party to join the Liberal Democrats over Christmas 1995. It is very rare for Tory MPs to leave their party. Nicholson did so after the vote on the Nolan Commission recommendations. The judge had proposed that, in order to limit the corruption of Parliament, MPs should be obliged to publish the extra-parliamentary income they receive for political work. He did not propose that MPs should no longer be hired as official lobbyists for whatever cause pays the most, or that they should tell their constituents how much extra income they were getting from their other jobs, retainers and positions. All MPs had to do, in the opinion of the Nolan Committee, was declare their additional *political* income. 'Honest John' Major's government opposed even this proposal.

It had to allow a 'free vote', in which MPs vote according to individual conscience, undisciplined by the official Whip and its sanctions. Despite frantic attempts by the government to prevent her and others from exercising their best judgement, Emma Nicholson and a few other Conservatives – twenty-one *in all* – voted to support Nolan. Thanks to them, the vote was won. The number of honest Tories is larger than this, but it remains the only unambiguous statistic we have on the number of Tory MPs who believe that honesty is the best policy. Nicholson recalls:

Even after the passage of a very limited measure, the Tories were in turmoil. It was an astounding scene. Their cloak of superiority had been stripped away to reveal the greed beneath. Among those who opposed the vote on limited disclosure, some were already rich who wanted to get richer; greedy above their worth to Parliament, they had no intention of removing their snouts from the trough. Avarice and panic made an unattractive cocktail as they saw the pound signs floating past their eyes. What was to become of the company delegations they took to meet ministers, paid for by the businesses? What was to become of their lucrative contracts? Others began quickly to regroup and address themselves to damage limitation. We will renegotiate our contracts, they were saying. The amendment passed was only about paid work as a result of being a member of Parliament. If we have a contract for a hundred thousand pounds, we can say that only one thousand pounds of that is related to being an MP. As I listened I reached the extraordinary conclusion that I could stay with these people no longer.

The Commons, Nicholson realised, had become a 'grubby, personal, cash-grasping degeneration of the body politic, brazen in its cynicism . . . a procurer's delight, a den of heaving political corruption'. Looking back, she realised that the putrefaction had begun ten years before:

> By the mid-1980s Members saw not the slightest cause for shame in taking complete speeches from a company that sponsored them and pressing the company's case in the Chamber . . . It was no longer possible to distinguish between the tang of commerce and the flavour of genuine debate . . . Money, under the mask of duty, was passing unseen down every corridor of influence as Conservative members of Parliament assiduously feathered their own nests. In the Thatcher days of huge Conservative majorities members were given the green light to earn money in any way they wanted; provided they turned up to vote.[20]

Was this also the voters' perception? Or is it wishful thinking to read into the considerable anti-government swing in 1997 popular abhorrence at what was going on in the House of Commons? There were high, and growing, levels of public disenchantment with politicians in general. The Joseph Rowntree Reform Trust 'State of the Nation' polls, conducted by MORI in 1995, showed massive majorities for banning extra-parliamentary payments of *all* kinds. More generally, in 1973 43 per cent of the electorate thought that the British system and Parliament worked well and only 14 per cent thought it needed a great deal of improvement. By 1995 only 19 per cent thought it worked well, and 41 per cent felt it needed improvement. In addition 35 per cent believed that it required a great deal of improvement.[21] In October 1994 a Gallup survey had found that 64 per cent of the public thought that 'most members of Parliament make a lot of money by using public office improperly'. Only 29 per cent of the public then thought the ethical standards of British political leaders were higher than those in other countries.[22] These perceptions lasted until the General Election, when a pattern of discrimination between the parties became more apparent. On 7 March 1997 a Gallup poll, published in the *Daily Telegraph*, showed that two-thirds of voters thought the government was 'basically dishonest' (even one-third of Tory supporters agreed with this assessment). There is strong evidence to support the voters' view.

I have not yet even raised the BSE disaster (cost £3.5 billion), transport policies (lack of), the scandal of the Pergau Dam . . . Government failures are for later, though mostly in brief. Dreadful errors can be made by good governments. We all make serious mistakes. Large organisations make large ones – indeed, it is a sign of health, because healthy institutions feel the need to take action and undertake risks, some of which, in the nature of things, must go wrong. Making mistakes is not, in itself, the sign of a rotten system. A system is rotten when it does not know how to correct its mistakes, when it denies them, when its own vested interests refuse to correct the errors that others pay for. The key measure of a system's vitality, therefore, is its capacity to assess and correct the errors it is bound to make. The starting point for this is taking responsibility for them. The failure of Ministers to resign, the Waldegrave presumption that one could just tough it out for a few hairy days and then bury the findings of wrongdoing, the 'tough' attitude that all that matters is deploying a parliamentary majority, the culture of permission behind the absolute sovereignty of Parliament – as if this bestows legitimacy – all pointed to the government's determination to persist in its ways, which suggested that it was wickedly incompetent.

Is this fair? Is Emma Nicholson justified in describing her former colleagues as the creators of 'a den of heaving political corruption'? Were those later found guilty merely a few bad apples in an otherwise shining, if not always tasty, harvest? Or is Nicholson right and the system itself actively rotten, heavingly so? *Telegraph* columnist Stephen Glover summed up one widespread response after Hamilton and five others of his colleagues from the Commons were found guilty by Sir Gordon Downey:

> Of course parliament is not riddled with corruption. Of course the Tory party is not rotten from top to toe. My God, even these guilty six were involved with piffling sums by the standards of your average American or Continental crook. They were small-timers, little men on the way to nowhere who wished to make a few thousand pounds on the side without declaring it. Perhaps there are some Tory big-time crooks still out there, waiting to be trapped by Mr Fayed and excoriated by the *Guardian* but we haven't found them yet.[23]

There are four elements to this argument. First, very few people were involved. Second, those who were, were involved with derisory sums – £25,000 here and there – and were themselves equally derisory, in world terms individuals as insignificant as the average brown envelope. Third, their only sin was not to declare their small-time side-shows. Finally, no big-time Tory crooks had copped it.

This was just before Aitken – who was Treasury Secretary and tabbed as a possible Premier – was exposed. But, so the apologists say, he was only caught out lying about whether or not he was the guest of his Arab business partners when he was in Paris while Minister for defence procurement. But he *was* lying. His wife had not paid the bill. The fact that he lied about this to the head of the Civil Service (who believed him), to the Prime Minister and to the High Court, as well as to the assembled media, is unfortunate, but the hotel bill itself was small. The issue was trivial. The problem here is that Britain's libel laws have worked, even in this case when Aitken was finally exposed. Instead of everyone arguing for three years about who paid the bill at the Ritz, the question *should* have been: what was going on between Aitken and his Arab associates in the first place? He had, apparently, 'brokered a £5 billion arms deal from which his associates stood to get more than £750 million in commission'. No one knows how it was shared out, as officially the commission was denied.[24] Try out this sum on the 'average American crook'.

Of course it was more widespread. It was al-Fayed's *failure* to gain citizenship after the campaign against him that led to his disaffection. How will we ever know if other corporations or exceptionally rich individuals have *succeeded* in altering legislation to their satisfaction through bribery? Downey is confined to considering formal complaints made by third parties. There is still no independent anti-corruption team in place. The excuse is that Parliament must police itself, that its precious sovereignty must never be constrained, that the whole point of the UK's informal, unwritten system is that large-scale systemic corruption does not occur, thanks to the public ethic and the culture of British high politics. Gentlemen do not need to be policed.

Simon Jenkins thinks it is not so bad from another point of view. Writing in *The Times*, he argued:

> I recall no outcry, no mind-numbing report, on Richard Branson's substantial accusations against British Airways for its Commons lobbying in the days of Lord King of Wartnaby. In the mid-1980s, many of the MPs who were defending BA's commercial interests were said to be receiving benefits worth thousands of pounds, with precious few declaring them. Lloyd's insurance market escaped regulation as a result of lobbying by MPs with Lloyd's interests – a rare instance of such pressure working.[25]

This description differs from Glover's. It says that there are indeed widespread payments running through the system and those who do not practise it tolerate it, like students who don't smoke cannabis but would not dream of calling the police when they see a joint passing from hand to hand. Furthermore, according to this view, graft is normal and even healthy, rather than harmful. MPs have always had outside interests expressed as other sources of income. Naturally those who are farmers express farming interests, lawyers a special concern for the hardships of the legal profession, businessmen the concerns of trade. All this, in the words of a *Daily Telegraph* editorial, makes Parliament better able to keep a check on the Executive.[26]

This is not how the public sees it. Voters oppose MPs being paid lobbyists for causes they might otherwise regard as harmful or indifferent. Neil Hamilton received a payment that connected him with US Tobacco while that company was seeking to market Skoal Bandits in Britain. This is a viciously carcinogenic chewing tobacco that produces cancerous ulcers in the gum and throat, particularly in young people. When the then Health Minister, Edwina Currie, was seen by a group from what she called 'the smoking lobby', she circulated pictures of the effects of Skoal Bandits. 'Most of those present were shocked but Mr Hamilton indicated that he did not feel the photographs were relevant.' Hamilton insists that he supported Skoal Bandits as a 'cause' (his words) that was 'wholly consistent with my long-held political beliefs'. One hopes he would not have 'lobbied vigorously' (Kenneth Clarke's description) to harm young Britons if he had not benefited financially from US Tobacco's campaign.[27] To put it more generally, the public may accept that MPs represent their personal interests, in addition to those of their constituency, but they strongly condemn MPs being paid *as lobbyists* for causes in which they do not believe. As the main function of Parliament is to hold the Executive 'to account', the electorate's judgement is sound. Of course MPs should be lobbied. But for them to become paid lobbyists themselves undermines the role, as well as the legitimacy, of the House of Commons as the representative of democratic forces that hold government to account.

As MPs put themselves out to hire, a new corruption was born. Its inspiration was Thatcher. Its holy ghost was everywhere, yet nowhere; impossible to pin down, yet pervasive in its influence; its name was permission. It was a child of the 1980s, and it stood on its own legs after the 1987 election. It was then that Tory Whips encouraged MPs to make as much money as they could, provided they were in the House for the vote. Perhaps the traditional venality of previous days was, on balance – like consensus politics itself – moderate, oiling the wheels, aware of the limits. A racket, but nonetheless one that could pass as patriotic and knew how to draw the line at Skoal Bandits. By the late 1980s it had become something else.

In terms of the Glover criteria, we can say that corruption was widespread, at least in what he calls its 'piffling' form of sums below six figures. Nor was the wrongdoing merely that those involved failed to declare their piffles. Nor was such activity limited to men who were 'on the road to nowhere'. Two of the six whom Downey found against had been appointed Ministers. In addition, Aitken was a Cabinet Minister. And, before them was Mark Thatcher.[28] As for the whole thing being small-time, beneath the contempt of 'average' crooks in the rest of Europe or the US, this echoes Gore Vidal's contempt for the 'Lilliput' nature of British politics, as if he were as great a reporter as Gulliver.[29] The British like this kind of put-down, as it serves to reinforce an image of harmlessness.

Oh yes? 'Commission was paid' on the £20 billion Al-Yamamah deal to which Aitken, and not only he, was connected.[30] The Malaysian Pergau Dam deal illegally committed British aid in return for a large arms sale and was signed by Thatcher. The Irish Sea became radioactive. The paid lobbying to which Simon Jenkins refers helped 'the world's favourite airline'. These are not small enchiladas. Nor are they unconnected with the fact that, just down the road from Parliament in the City of London, is the largest single concentration of banks on the planet.

While a clean, non-permissive Labour culture will help to mitigate the corruption, certain measures are also essential. First, because Labour itself is notoriously prone to corruption, especially when it benefits from long periods in office. Glasgow, Paisley, Doncaster are the latest additions to a long roll-call of Labour sleaze, abuse of office, lavender lists, 'bent coppers' and so forth. New men are not immune to old practices. In local government, proportional representation is a glaring need to rid British cities of what must be among the longest-lasting one-party statelets on Earth.

At the level of national government, corruption needs to be seen in a context where multinational interests and international deals and, domestically, the value of permission to develop property, have started to dwarf the budgets of entire departments of State, let alone individuals. In this context it is insane to allow the continued self-regulation of Parliament. Even Downey's presence is still considered by some to be a breach of the fundamental traditions of the absolute sovereignty of Parliament. Such vanity, if continued under Labour, will ensure tears, even if it does not end in them.

Parliament's claim to the privileges of absolute sovereignty brings us back to the constitutional issue and the comparison with Eastern Europe. At the heart of Enoch Powell's view was an incorrigible belief in the Roman rectitude of English institutions – it was the Tiber, not the Thames that he saw foaming with blood. Great Englishness claims that our institutions are not corrupt, like those of other, less fortunate countries; that our public service sets the highest standards; that our way of doing things is in itself a virtue. Today, after the City's 'Big Bang', the turning point of the 1980s, the penetration of the world market into the spirit and practice of British government has destroyed this exceptional character of our institutions in comparative terms. Nor are they regarded as especially honourable by the electorate. This made the Conservative government's attempt to wrap them in the flag all the more pitiful.

Not all the Eastern European countries were puppets of the then USSR. Some, like Romania and Albania, were on the contrary, outlandishly independent of Moscow, making deals with Nixon and Mao instead. All of them proclaimed the eternal verities of their own nation, as they sought to shore up their domestic legitimacy in the eyes of a population that knew their officials had ceased to be motivated by principle and were, instead, on the make. The stench of a corrupt, provincial chauvinism rose from the various members of the Warsaw Pact before it dissolved. They paraded their patriotism and stirred up xenophobia as a smokescreen.[31] The parallel with John Major's rhetoric is almost too painful to pursue. As his government sold off water utilities to French companies, allowed Americans to acquire power stations as cash cows, told us to rejoice at Korean inward investment, to be thankful for the Dutch take-over of Barings and to delight in BMW's acquisition of Rover, to ignore all the cases of sleaze and malfeasance and also to regard him as honest John, we were also told that our government was patriotic, hated Krauts and was alert to Brussels stealing our sovereignty. In the 1997 election, voters made their views about this new corruption quite plain.

3
A Normal Country

THE BEST EXCUSE the British State enjoyed for its centralised form of rule was the Cold War. Unlike the regimes of Eastern Europe it was more an architect than a victim of the international polarisation of Europe, which Churchill first named in his Iron Curtain speech at Fulton, Missouri in 1946. But there were profound internal consequences for the UK. Nuclear deterrence and the so-called 'special relationship' with Washington lent undue significance to British standing. This encouraged the political class to inflate the self-importance of Westminster and to justify the already excessive secrecy of Whitehall.

Thatcher understood that the end of American/Soviet antagonism would diminish Britain's role – not only relative to a much enlarged German Federal Republic but also, crucially, in Washington, where the UK had been a useful nuclear ally against Moscow. However, there was no great national debate in Britain about the consequences of the Cold War ending so abruptly, perhaps because it would have shone an embarrassing spotlight on the dependent status the confrontation had reinforced. Although Brussels figured as a bogyman in the General Election of 1997, the rest of the world was utterly absent from the campaign. There was no sense that either main party had an international strategy, let alone wanted their view of relations with Washington and Moscow to be mentioned – as the government party usually does, in order to show off its greater experience. The absence of international politics was a further sign of how out of step with the world the Conservatives had become. By expelling the Tories so decisively, the electorate recognised that change was also needed in the UK's international attitudes. Gorbachev, and the revolutions that attended *perestroika* in Eastern Europe, ended the Cold War, as communism caved in under the weight of its own incompetence. These were the decisive events. Britain's peaceful transition towards political modernity in 1997 was a delayed acknowledgement of the advent of the new, and much better, era – our 'thank you' for the end of the Cold War.

Thus the UK participated in its continent's velvet revolution. Hostile to their own State's milder corruption and decrepitude, British voters rejected its attempts to cloak itself in patriotism. In so doing, they chose to normalise Britain. It sounds an odd phrase. I heard it first in discussions that preceded the collapse of the Berlin Wall. 'We want to be a normal society,' many from Eastern Europe would say. The free market, an open press, multi-party democracy was what they meant. Notoriously they saw Margaret Thatcher as the leading advocate and representative of normality and freedom. In one way she did normalise the UK as she destroyed the old corporatism. Foreigners were less able to perceive, however, how she also exploited the abnormal powers of an ancient State to centralise, rather than democratise, political power. Today this is more obvious as she rants against co-operation with the EU, in contrast to Labour's greater ease with Brussels. On 1 May Britain began to take its place as a normal country by rejecting Thatcher's successor.

But she and her closest ally, Rupert Murdoch (or perhaps it was Rupert Murdoch and his closest ally Margaret Thatcher) had tagged the winner early and sought to hitch their influence to it. Sociologists have identified what they call 'reflexivity' as one of the factors that distinguishes contemporary society from previous ones. Today humankind not only transforms the world, but knows that it does so. Knowledge is self-reflective. It is not simply that the transaction of information is growing exponentially. There is also a qualitative alteration thanks to self-consciousness, which feeds back upon what is communicated. The effect is most pronounced in the financial markets, but it is also happening in politics. The way the Tories pre-judged the electoral disaster that awaited them in 1991, should they have retained Thatcher as their leader, was a new development born of people who had mastered opinion polls. Now Thatcher in turn sought to intervene ahead of a national vote. She extended her approval to Blair as she sought to head off an electoral victory for more egalitarian and consensual values. She sought, in other words, through association and influence, to ensure the triumph of her kind of normalisation when New Labour took office.

The notion of 'normalisation' is deceptive because it sounds singular, as does the closely associated term of 'modernisation', in the way it was used, for example, by Tony Blair at the TUC in September 1997. 'Modernity', he proclaimed, 'is our spirit as it is the spirit of an age.' The modern is only singular in the way of fashion. When William Hazlitt published his *Spirit of the Age*, in 1825, he wrote of William Godwin, author of *Enquiry Concerning Political Justice*:

> The Spirit of the Age was never more fully shown than in its treatment of this writer – its love of paradox and change, its dastard submission to prejudice and the fashion of the day . . . Is the *Modern Philosophy* (as it has been called) at one moment a youthful bride and the next a withered beldame?[1]

One should not worship the spirit of the age, for the 'modern' has been subject to fashion since modern times began, somewhere around the seventeenth century. Fashion is a dictator. It allows for only one definition or direction. But it is also fickle. It changes its mind and reverses itself in unpredictable ways. The bright, glittering attraction of what is *fashionably* 'modern' is all too likely to be merely novel, condemned as tacky and withered in no time at all.

At an unfashionable, less enjoyable, but more lasting level, there is a phenomenon that we can term modernity. New forces are being unlocked by the economic and scientific revolutions and by fresh forms of social organisation. The delight of fashion is that it puts form before substance and change before commitment. Although apparently willed by human agency, it is a variant of the ideology of the hidden hand of the market. Arbitrary and capricious, it turns luck into fate – either you 'have it' or you don't. But at the deeper level the modern is not a given. It creates, as well as closes, opportunities. The arguments surrounding the fate of the nation state illustrate how undecided its outcome remains. For the global forces at work – economic, scientific and cultural – simultaneously integrate and disaggregate. Politically, they allow unprecedented centralisation of power, yet they also permit *de*centralised democracy for the first time. Labour can end Britain's state of abnormality. And then?

The government is unclear about which direction it should take. It certainly is tempted by the lure of Thatcher-style populist centralism. It is also drawn to constitutional normalisation that would open the way to a pluralistic, decentralised state. The contest could hardly be more fateful. In trying to evaluate the possibilities, one has to assess the balance of forces. If the British governing classes were in the grip of failure, resentful of loss, alarmed at their own weakness, their capacity to embrace reform would be slight. But they are not. Similarly, if the people were in the grip of neo-racist myths, or resentful and nostalgic for the past, the ideals of constitutional reform would remain confined to the liberal middle class. Neither of these descriptions is true any longer of Britain. As I have tried to show, the General Election demonstrated two things. The electorate is no longer attached to what can loosely be termed Powellism and, as we will see, Diana's funeral confirmed this. Middle England – a social category that seems to have been invented to explain the defeat of the old working class – wants to breathe a world atmosphere and has discarded its passion for English exceptionalism and heritage worship, entailed in the belief that we do things differently here.

The active attachment of the population as a whole to the traditional symbols and rituals, to racism and monarchism, has passed away. Whether it has passed away in the sense of dying, or whether it has just swooned before the dreadful hash Major made of it – and can therefore be revived – it is too soon to say. My argument is that the attachment can be *replaced* by new attachments: better values, which renew the best of traditional ones, need a better constitutional settlement that embeds British democracy and culture. If this does not happen, and instead a centralised form of normalisation is attempted, it will prove unstable. Doubtless the new leader will eventually be decapitated. England is the country that put an end to the divine right of Kings. ('Remember Naseby' is a helpful slogan for aspiring Heads of State who are reluctant to decentralise.) In the meantime, a generation will have lost its chance to catch up with modern democracy.

So before we consider what it means to replace the constitution, some cultural considerations are in order. For the inclination to embrace the modern world is also held back by fear of normalisation. I will probe this fear, briefly, then describe the way in which modernisation has already taken place with respect to the Establishment, the monarchy and the political parties – previously three of the greatest impediments to reform of the ruling system. The greatest of these is the monarchy, and I will return to it in Chapter 5.

To be normal sounds healthy. But what if this means participating in a homogeneous modernity, known as globalisation? Surely a loss of essence will accompany the abolition of difference. It *will* end a thousand years of history if we converge into a world society motivated by commodity happiness, regulated by planetary bureaucrats, and sharply divided between rich and poor. 'All happy families resemble one another, but each unhappy family is unhappy in its own way,' Leo Tolstoy told us. Perhaps we should keep our awkward, difficult, strife-riven, divisive, unfair, secretive and unhappy political system, otherwise we will simply resemble other countries in their blandness. Just after the Second World War, the Oxford University Press published a compendium on *The Character of England*, edited by Sir Ernest Barker. It suggested that no Englishman would install central heating. To be able to bear the bone-penetrating cold of an English winter in a damp English house was to *be* English. The unhappiness was *ours*. Without such pains, the national soul would be lost.[2]

Tolstoy was surely wrong. It is unhappy families that are all too predictable, as their quarrels exchange the same clichés of hurt and suffering. But we are discussing countries, not families. Certainly, terminating a now unhappy and predictable British exceptionalism will bring to an end a closed, fatalistic political culture and the institutional narrowness of the UK's constitutional arrangements. What I mean by British exceptionalism is the idea that one can run a modern society on gentlemen's agreements, discriminating in favour of a national Church, giving people funny titles and expecting this to be taken seriously. Putting all this in the museum will release popular energy and encourage creative difference. Being normal will allow us to be ourselves. Normalisation means participating in, competing with and, where necessary, resisting global pressures. It offers possibilities, among which is the renewal of tradition. Sticking with the ancient institutions, on the other hand, turns them into prisons, which eventually will be privatised, bought out cheaply by multinationals, because all inner resistance has been spent.

It was, it should be understood, the success of the past that accounts for its continued appeal. To speak for change is not to belittle what went before. The Empire was not absurd. It colonised one-fifth of the globe. The reach of its financial centre was even greater. The British created, however briefly, a civilisation, which had its own peculiar ethic. This motivated its special élite, and in place of what the French called *cadre* the British succoured gentlemen. They had their own religion, crowned monarch, code and style, and a unique capacity to make lots of money relatively honestly, for the Empire was run by civil servants imbued with a dedication to probity in public service.

It also created a mental universe which clung to those who grew up during and just after the Second World War. Unlike the episodes of Suez, the Falklands and the Gulf, this was not a conflict that took no longer than a school term. This war lasted in effect ten years, from the Munich Agreement in 1938 to 1947, when the Berlin blockade was lifted and the Cold War settled in. People grew up, and were formed, in this period. Margaret Thatcher, born in 1926 (the same year as the Queen) was barely a teenager when war was declared. She was an adult when it ended. As she entered puberty, Winston Churchill declared our 'finest hour'. Economically and socially that proved not to be so, for the lives of the British have been hugely improved since then. But politically, the actually existing British Empire State has experienced pretty much continuous erosion ever since. We will never regain the Britain of imperial greatness. The generation that identified with the intoxicating memory of that period could never introduce democratic political reform. Only those free from its spell can look forward to political sunshine and construction. There is a class aspect to this as well. The old regime was more potent for rulers than for ruled. When the flag came down over Hong Kong, the Governor wept and Prince Charles could be seen wiping away a tear. This was an interesting incident. The stiff upper lip wavered and cracked, while the population at home was healthily indifferent.

For all the constitutional backwardness of the official country, the real country has moved on. The cultural and social legacy of Britain's parliamentary history has encouraged a resilient sense of personal rights, fairness and liberty, conscious of its unbroken character, capable of frankness and satire, with a spirit of freedom that can make America feel uptight. The imperial legacy of Empire may have left the currently existing official State the most closed and centralised political system in Europe, but outside its nineteenth-century buildings, unofficial London has turned the inheritance of Empire into perhaps Europe's most open, multiracial and energetic capital. It is this legacy that contributes to the attractiveness of London as a scene for young people from all over the continent.

In the past, the British élite believed that it knew 'how things are done'. This exceptionalism became a parody and is no longer viable. Normalisation means becoming like the rest of the world in the way we 'do things' – especially in government – as has already happened elsewhere. This does not mean becoming the same, because all the countries of the world are different – but different in the same way that everyone is different: special, but no longer extra-terrestrial.

Britain has always changed, and it can be true to this tradition and change again. This is what normalisation means. A clear way to observe this is constitutional. The UK used to call on Eastern European countries to incorporate the European Convention on Human Rights into their own domestic law, yet did not do so itself. Now it will. As it withdrew from the colonies that gained independence, Whitehall drew up constitutions for them. It was confident that it did not need one itself. Now it does.

Mentioning constitutions brings us to a paradox. When they hear the word 'constitution', most people in Britain think of the United States – and not of Europe, where there are many more successful constitutions. The US is seen as the model for 'the normal' in the supposedly global economy. Constitutionally, however, America's settlement is 200 years old and now stands as a caution, not a model. It was built upon such a distrust of executive power that its checks and balances have led to legislative gridlock. This has had disastrous consequences for its democracy, as lobbyists have moved in on the backstage deals that are essential if Congress is to pass anything. From my point of view, we need a written constitution *to limit, if not prevent* the Americanisation of Britain. This reverses the terms that most people expect. But the speed with which corruption spread under the Conservatives shows how Britain's unwritten constitution exposed the country to almost non-stop Americanisation – after the regime's once commanding ethic of honesty in public service had been eroded. Money is promiscuous. It exploits weakness in any form. At the century's end, it found an ally in the over-rigidity of the US written constitution and also in the flaccid flexibility of Britain's lack of one.

Obviously the reader is not obliged to agree with this view.

But she or he will be baffled if they presume that a growing call for a written constitution in Britain is motivated by the desire to create an American-style, rights-based competitive individualism with a polity dominated by big money. It does not follow that a written constitution cannot have such an outcome. But the *aim* is a better integrated, fairer and more democratic society. Constitutional normalisation will provide no guarantees – only a better opportunity to deal democratically with the dangers of modern change.

Our age is obsessed with ideas of fatality, with beginnings and endings, with the 'new' this and the 'end' of that, exacerbated by the nearing of the millennium. Meanwhile, we spend our lives in the in-between. Endings refuse to be final, beginnings are never clean. In the long term, perhaps, there may be an entire transformation, however, as Maynard Keynes famously observed in the long run we are all dead. Our lives take place in the short term, and at most our span is medium-term. The pace of change now ensures that each generation is condemned and rewarded with its own combination of old and new, its special mixture of the in-between. Each of us is a migrant whose life stretches along a graph of exponential transformation that is our epoch. We are never completely at home, we never arrive.

Nor is the graph two-dimensional. Society, the economy, the environment alter at different speeds. Transformations that are long in coming break quickly, then work themselves out over many years. In Britain we have just entered a period of intensive change in the area of politics and the constitution. Our historical system of sovereignty is changing fundamentally. A settlement that has lasted three centuries will be succeeded by another. The nature of the succession is being contested. One side wishes to retain such traditions as liberty and tolerance, through transforming and decentralising the institutions – through democracy. The other seeks to preserve the centralised institutions, seeing them as 'vital to our national well-being', even if the cost, and I am quoting Michael Portillo, means that 'we must temper our traditional tolerance'.[3] Britain, the oldest-surviving multinational state, will have to make a choice that will test its unity, decide its relationship with its continent and substantially alter the lived constitution either way.

What was the Portillo option (he has generously agreed to change his mind) sounds like a continuation of the politics of Thatcherism: preserving the central institutions, while closing down their consensual character, their tolerance. It does not follow that the alternative is a return to the status quo before Thatcher. What voters decisively rejected at the end of the 1970s they would certainly refuse now. Socially, Britain is now a much less deferential society. Culturally, its voice is no longer resentful and pinched, often thanks to those who opposed Thatcher's policies – for one of the benefits she brought to the UK was the quality of the opposition to her. Economically Britain is richer, it is also poorer – over the course of two decades, the real income of the poorest tenth has fallen by 13 per cent, while that of the top tenth had risen by 65 per cent.[4] This is as modern as the new resistance to it.

The deregulation and tax cuts that aided this regressive redistribution were turbo-charged by the Big Bang that transformed the City and financial sector. In retrospect, the financial revolution may prove to be the most decisive change wrought by Thatcherism. For it swept away a business culture that had penetrated the political elite and government. Describing the modernisation he thought Thatcherism had brought to Britain, Nigel Lawson, Thatcher's formidable, eloquent and over-the-top Chancellor of the Exchequer, argued:

> Optimism was what Britain needed in the 1980s and what it continues to need today. The debilitating pall of defeatism which characterised the Britain we inherited in 1979 had to be swept aside. Not only was it infinitely depressing, but it had become self-fulfilling and made economic success impossible. For too long the British had been learning to live with decline and defeat. The unfamiliarity of optimism and success proved rather too heady an experience in the late 1980s. But it need not and must not do so in the future.[5]

Already when he wrote this in 1991, the justification of

Thatcherism had become defensive. The optimism and success of which Lawson spoke were a phenomenon of the South of England, which is admittedly very populous. The North was far more aware of the price paid when you place your optimism in the hidden hand of market forces. For it can smite you with little warning. When the bubble burst in the so-called Home Counties, they too turned against Thatcherism. But she had nonetheless restored a belief in the possibility of government, for which anyone with progressive hopes should be thankful.

Thus the political normalisation of Britain was well under way in Thatcher's Britain. We can see it in at least three instances: the Establishment, the monarchy and the party system. In the 1960s the political system was gripped by an image of itself as an Establishment. It was a form of hierarchy that was no longer an aristocracy but fulfilled the same functions. Anthony Sampson first mapped it fully in the *Anatomy of Britain*, in 1962. He showed that interconnections stretched across all the high points of society and the economy, from the City and the banks through industry, the key universities, the Civil Service, the judiciary, Church and military to the political parties. A post-war élite, recruited from similar educational backgrounds and often the same secondary schools and shared clubs, interlocked across the whole ruling arc. Its self-confidence and connections were reinforced by the victorious experience of wartime co-operation. It produced in 1966 under Labour's Harold Wilson a heavily Oxbridge dominated Cabinet.

Britain is still governed by a political élite. But its nature has changed. It is narrower and more professional, but also more 'in touch', as it takes its cues from other professionals, especially those in the media, advertising and public relations. The old network of Oxbridge chaps no longer controls politics in the same way it did. Eton still kicks back, as I will show later, but a profound, informal transformation has taken place – in a way this already is a constitutional revolution. The Oxford analyst John Gray, speaking to a Nexus rally in the run-up to the election, observed:

> The Conservatives have launched themselves on a quixotic crusade in defence of the immobility of the British constitution. They pass over the fact that the constitution that the Tories inherited in 1979 exists no longer. It is barely a historical memory. It had been deformed out of recognition by the centralisation of power that is an integral part of new right policies . . . Conservatism is no longer a real historical option in Britain. Its social and cultural foundations have been demolished, partly because of the economic changes that the new right has promoted or reinforced. *The authority of tradition has been largely destroyed.* The social hierarchies and class structures of earlier times have gone. The old order has been torn down; but nothing has been built up to replace it.[6]

We can all recognise some truth in this. The *authority* of tradition has been blown away, even while the forms continue. The most significant proof has been the collapse of the monarchy's standing as (Portillo again) 'the source of the authority and legitimacy of government'. *The* source, he claimed, placing the legitimacy of Britain's government above such mundane things as elections. No one could repeat the claim today. Two weeks into the election campaign, commerce confirmed that royalty no longer symbolised reliability. The Royal Automobile Club announced that it had designed a new logo in futuristic lettering, and the Crown would no longer embellish its vans. The RAC's Chief Executive insisted that the move was 'taken primarily for design reasons'. But the action was also symbolic. Sir Harold Brooks-Baker, who ought to know, as he is the publishing director of *Burke's Peerage*, explained that 'For many people the word "royal" has a controversial meaning, and no business wants a controversial meaning.' The incident, he concluded, was:

> Simply one more indication that the magic has gone out of anything royal. In the past, if something was called royal it gained a lot of support and admiration – but that has all gone now. This shows a loss of interest in the fairy tale aspect of the monarchy – it means the mystique has disappeared forever.[7]

The political truth of this was demonstrated when the

government attempted to ambush Labour just before the election, by announcing that it had found the £60 million needed to build a new royal yacht. John Redwood, the right-wing anti-European leadership contender outside the Cabinet, had proposed the idea. It was nicked by – who else? – Defence Secretary Michael Portillo, the right-wing anti-European leadership contender inside the Cabinet. The announcement was sprung upon the Labour opposition without notice. The assumed popularity of the Crown was used for party advantage. Portillo's wheeze was meant to score a quick victory on two fronts – dishing Redwood, while capsizing the opposition. Perhaps the fact that the government was willing to exploit the monarchy in so blatant and self-serving a fashion was the final proof that the royalism of the traditional constitution had ended. Respect for its shared, cross-party character was central to its post-war role. The monarchy was the commanding long-term asset of the Establishment consensus. Now it was exploited for short-term ends. This alone spelt the end of an era.

The ploy boomeranged. It became another small but significant government disaster for John Major and further weakened allegiance to the throne. Tony Blair's instinct that the proposal would not be popular proved sound. The *Sun* polled its readers, who voted 5 to 1 against their money being spent in this way. Portillo tried to blame the Secretary of the Cabinet and head of the Civil Service, Sir Robin Butler, and leaked his policy advice, exposing Butler in an unprecedented manner.[8] The Tories then tried to forget their own suggestion. But the episode provided a cool campaign line for Blair and Brown. It guaranteed them applause at election rallies and let them display their radicalism in television interviews, when they said that they would rather spend the £60 million on hospital wards. The Defence Secretary himself went on to lose his seat to Stephen Twigg of the Fabian Society.

Previous Conservative Premiers would have stitched up the opposition before making a royal announcement. Previous Labour Prime Ministers were even more steeped in piety towards the monarchy, so profoundly did it define and represent official life for both parties. The royal yacht episode would have been unimaginable twenty years previously. As if to confirm its diminished status, the Palace let out an unprecedented protest within a month of Blair taking office, when Bill Clinton extended a stopover in London at short notice. He gave a joint press conference with Blair in the garden of No. 10, with the flags of the two countries flying in the background as if it were the White House. Senior Buckingham Palace officials revealed the Queen's 'Fury at Blair' to the *Mail on Sunday*. It was a move that the paper described as unusual. One official told the *Mail*, 'The Queen was at home, but Clinton was not wheeled along. They think Tony Blair is getting too grand and that Prime Ministers should play second fiddle to monarchs.' Another courtier expressed the hurt that Her Majesty felt at being left out. He told the paper, 'It was an extraordinary lack of courtesy that no one bothered to pick up the phone and ask whether she would like the President to come to see her privately, even if it was just for a cup of tea.'[9]

The point has been made. To go about it much longer would begin to sound like nostalgia. Even before Diana's death the Queen no longer mattered in the way she once used to.

There is an implicit royalism in the slightly pejorative term that people often use about themselves in Britain when they describe themselves as 'ordinary'. We don't say, 'As a plain citizen, I . . .', or, 'In my view as a regular person . . .' Instead we call ourselves, and are described by BBC commentators as, ordinary. It is an advance on the once familiar description of people as being 'common'. But today's term still implies that there must be extra-ordinary people. Otherwise the phrase would add nothing. Who are the extra-ordinary terrestrials among us, the special people who are not ordinary? Most obviously they are the Queen and other royals.[10] Now, finally, the Queen is also ordinary – that is to say, normal. No one thought to pick up the phone and call us either, when Clinton came to visit. As Michael White observed in the *Guardian* the royal family has become the victim of 'a significant growth in public *indifference* – far more dangerous than niche republicanism'.[11]

Quite right, of course. But, to anticipate my argument, a danger resides in this delightful episode that should be borne in mind. Blair also apparently tried to free himself from the Tuesday afternoon audiences that the Queen has conducted with her First Minister since she came to the throne in 1952. The Prime Minister may feel that to seek her approval is a form of restraint. It may be a small one, but he prefers to be with his children. However, the problem with old-fashioned restraints is not that they are restraints, but that they are old-fashioned. Restraints are a modern as well as an ancient necessity. Newly fashioned ones are now needed. Power has to be accountable on a daily basis between elections to ensure probity and preserve the spirit of the law – if not to the monarch, then to a Freedom of Information Act. Labour has broken free of monarchical hegemony. But 'presidential' power, the normal replacement of monarchy, must be restrained by a secular constitution. Otherwise it *is* dictatorship – another abnormal form, which will not last in modern conditions.

If 1997 saw the first post-Establishment General Election, it follows that something had changed from the previous election of 1992. John Major, with all his weaknesses, is a modern man, having arrived at the top through diligent mastery of the greasy pole. One explanation for his surprise victory in 1992 was that Labour failed to update itself in a similar way. Neil Kinnock tried but could not escape the shadow of the Wilson-Callaghan years of 1974–9 in the way that Thatcher broke from Heath's of 1970–4. As early as 1975, in one of her first speeches as party leader, Thatcher denounced the 'progressive consensus . . . held to varying degrees in all our political parties'.[12] But in 1992 Labour still remained loyal to the past. Not least thanks to the influence of its deputy leader Roy Hattersley, it was unable to discard its role in the 'progressive consensus' that made up Establishment politics and which Thatcher had denounced nearly twenty years before.

Between 1994 and 1997 Tony Blair completed the modernisation of the Labour Party. Neil Kinnock began it and took most of the knocks. John Smith took it further. It was not simply a matter of dropping state socialism, which had anyway been a mere decoration of Labour policy since the 1960s. Blair oversaw something much more radical in British terms – he purged it of Labourism, of the left's version of Establishment paternalism. Blair and Brown made the Labour Party more serious and less indulgent, professional not gentlemanly – in a word, contemporary. And because he and his fellow modernisers were catching up with the example already set by both Tories and Liberal Democrats, they were all the more thorough and dedicated. One key change had been Smith's insistence on one-member-one-vote for appointing the party leader, which destroyed the grip of the unions' bloc-votes. It meant the end of Labour's version of clubland. When Blair was elected by the entire party membership as individuals, Major's claim to be our 'everyman' – the symbolic representative of each one of us, be he ever so lowly – was overshadowed. With Paddy Ashdown already a quintessential modern man, trained by the Army, all three main parties had finally broken from Establishment routines by 1997.

This annoyed Major, who pointed out that he was a mere O-level boy from Brixton, while Blair had been to Oxford. But the fact that Major saw it like this showed that he was, if anything, more attached to the old class system, in a 'chippy' way. Of the three, he became the most outdated. Major championed the status quo in the House of Lords, which hardly fitted the image of an up-to-date person of the people. As Labour embraced the market, the Tories clung to traditional authority. Millions of voters responded by breaking away from tribal loyalties altogether, to enter a more calculating, reflective age.[13]

Events tend to be seen separately. If one looks back on the events of 1997 each development on its own can be dismissed as insignificant. So what, says the person who pretends to have seen it all before, if the voters rejected Powellism: it was all John Major's fault, but they will return to the fold. So what if corruption became excessive: the Tories will clean up their act and the problem will either blow away or despoil Labour. So what if 'the Establishment' has withered: it was a load of tosh anyway, in so far as it wasn't just a journalist's invention. So what if the monarchy is in trouble: George IV had a bigger problem with Princess Caroline and the throne bounced back with Victoria, as it always does eventually. In this way a broad-bottomed person can convince those who wish to listen that nothing has really changed.

But if you bring all the events into view at the same time, 1997 appears as a turning point. For an historic country to become contemporary is a complex process, worked through at various levels: from the economic to the emotional. At a certain point the change becomes irreversible. We can see this if we look back at the start of Thatcherism. Until the Falklands War, Thatcher was unpopular and unsuccessful. But the combination of her second election victory in 1983 thanks to the triumph of the Falklands, the miners' strike and then the Big Bang together spelled the end of the post-war settlement.

In a similar way, the extent of the 1997 election landslide (which removed an incumbent government that was doing well economically), the prompt endorsement of a second British Parliament in Scotland, the introduction of a Bill of Rights and a London Mayor, together indicate the start of political modernisation. The Labour leadership could blow the opportunity it has now created. But the shift has already taken constitutional forms that demand additional action.

If the meaning of the 1997 election comes down to normalisation, is this such a big fish? Here, too, the analogy with Eastern Europe clarifies. The velvet revolutions of 1989 were a liberation from oppressive dictatorships in a way that 1997 was not for Britain. But the outcome for these countries was a slog to catch up with what was already familiar in the West. They were not revolutions of the future, like the French or the American revolutions proved to be (or the socialist ones claimed to be), which created new societies that became a model for emulation elsewhere. They were not revolutions that took 'history' forward. They were revolutions against backwardness, which confirmed, not challenged, global realities: they emulated what was already in practice elsewhere. Equally, while 1997 already seems to be a dramatic break for Britain, in international terms does it have anything special as its destination? What, after all, is all the fuss about? That the Queen is less important and must stop behaving as if she is better than us, that Parliament has more women members, that there should be some decentralisation of a kind that has been familiar in the rest of Europe for decades, that children should be taught to read, write and calculate? Come on! This is no new deal.

Only a narrow breakthrough has taken place. Which brings us back to the differences with the velvet revolutions. Ousting the Tories on May Day was a relief, *not* a liberation. Some might regret it, but British society and economy have already been modernised. In its fundamentals, the UK is already normal. If anything it is even 'ahead', in terms of the unfettered rule of market forces, even if it is lamentably behind in its investment in education. Society is no longer deferential. We do not suffer from the inbred bureaucratic lethargy of the Soviet-bloc workforce, the passivity of the proletariat induced by communism. Many of the difficult aspects of modernisation – good and bad – have already been undertaken. This puts the Blair government in a better position than the governments of Eastern Europe. It also allows us to ask the fundamental question raised but not debated in the election: what kind of normalisation should we choose? For normalisation is a choice not a fate. The key choice is whether there will be democratic reform, from the legal to the local, to open the way to more equality.

It is said that there are broadly two directions for Britain – two roads to modernisation. Either free-market Americanisation with its extreme differentiation, violence and creative energy. Or Europeanisation, with its emphasis on inclusion, high-quality public life and dignified levels of social support. Americanisation seemed to many to be our fate during the election campaign, not least as New Labour fought with techniques widely regarded as imports from the US, while its propaganda stressed the importance of globalisation.

The debate can also be seen as focusing on whether or not globalisation is an unalterable fate. Advocates of the deregulated market are said to assert that it is – that wealth creation and income differentiation go hand in hand; that you cannot have wealth without poverty; that the development of a First World and a Third World cohabiting the same cities is the future for the whole world. The dystopian prospect is familiar. The rich move from air-conditioned apartments to air-conditioned offices in air-conditioned cars, conferring with each other in air-conditioned hotels, and only know what country they are in from the folk decorations in the lobby. Meanwhile, the poor breathe in the pollution from the air-conditioning exhausts and eat processed food from polystyrene cartons manufactured by robots from a branch of galactic chemicals. In between: nothing, apart from school teachers. You are either on the life-support machine that costs a fortune or you are among the myriad paid a pittance to service it.

If this were the only possible future, it could be an argument for clinging on to the House of Lords. At least we would know what country we were in! Inevitability is the first refuge of ideology, however. Market forces will adapt if they must. They are not inherently democratic, but will serve democracy when they are regulated by democracy. The critical issue for any national community is whether it works to include, rather than allow the market to exclude, its own citizens. There is nothing inevitable about the outcome, and in Britain, with its sizeable majority in favour of investing in effective redistribution, normalisation need not mean bowing to American, or Thatcher-style, globalisation.[14]

American commentators believed that New Labour has set its course towards their own experience, and predicted the Clintonisation of the UK. British papers imported American reporters to say similar things. However, the patronising scorn of US correspondents was solipsistic, not investigative, journalism. They presume to see in the Brits a dinky version of America, but their interest in the election was confined solely to the question of how far Britain is becoming like them. They presumed it was. And as the US has emptied its politics of difference, they feigned boredom. I say feigned, because rather than being bored they were obsessed with themselves. As for Britain itself, their own mirror could not reflect back to them that one aim of the New Labour campaign was to halt Americanisation and the creation of an underclass.

On education, employment and health, the watchword of the Labour campaign was the need to prevent a growing two-tier division from becoming permanent: a division between the literate and illiterate, the skilled and the long-term jobless, NHS fundholders and the rest. Perhaps the new Labour government will fail to reverse the chasms that have opened up under Conservative rule. It will be impossible to do so without redistribution. But Labour's leaders, not to speak of their candidates, were largely sincere. They have public housing estates in their constituencies. They have witnessed the vortex of unemployment, crime, drugs and illiteracy that threatens the life of working-class people especially. The pledge to put 250,000 young people into jobs may have seemed a paltry sop to US reporters, but Labour politicians are aware that while the Tories can rule for decades through widening inequality and riots, they cannot. After the election, the decision to ban handguns completely was announced as a legislative priority. This symbolised Labour's commitment to prevent Americanisation if it can.

The party which would have Americanised Britain irreversibly was the same one that sold off British utilities as cash-cows to US companies. The Conservatives embraced globalisation, while turning the State into their compound. When the Labour call to heal the worst aspects of social division became a sub-theme of the election, the government felt it had to respond. John Major repeated a number of times the concern he expressed about the 'have-nots', as at his last press conference. If this lacked credibility, we now know why.

After the election a Tory campaign adviser told the *Sunday Times*, 'I was in a meeting where Major said he was bored to death saying his mission was to help the "have-nots".'[15] Meanwhile, one-fifth of British households had no active wage-earner.

What will the new government do about this? In January 1996 Tony Blair used a tour of the Far East to announce his interest in stakeholding, which was projected for a brief period as the 'Big Idea' of New Labour. The central feature of stakeholder theory is to combine a market approach with an expanded version of participation. There are different variations, but all seek to combat the short-termism of the market, to moderate its baleful extremism and ensure greater security for employees, while enhancing creative investment. In this way stakeholding combats insecurity without creating labour rigidity, overcomes trade-union/employer antagonism with a structure that articulates mutual interests and mutual gains, as value is added by an increasingly well-educated workforce. That is the theory. Above all, it is an inclusive, not exclusive, approach. It takes account of the social consequences of investment. In global terms it seeks to limit the ability of capital to take off into an international circuit that accepts no responsibility for the costs borne by those whom Major so quaintly called the have-nots.

The original theorists of the Welfare State developed a concept of economic citizenship – meaning that there should be full employment and freedom from primary want underwritten by the State. Through its overall management of the economy it would create growth and jobs. Through the organisation of insurance – the safety net – it would secure welfare when things went wrong for individuals. In contrast to the Welfare State, stakeholding places much more emphasis on what can be called welfare capitalism. It views companies and the market, not government, as the providers of wealth, growth and security. The citizen must therefore internalise the norms of the market, aspire, save, own and insure. But capital must also treat employees, suppliers, customers and those working in the surrounding social structures, which provide the infrastructure and environment that secures its markets, as citizens of its enterprise. Its advocates say such an approach will enhance the wealth and welfare of both capital and people.

Blair was not very specific about stakeholder capitalism, his concern being to generalise support for a stakeholder economy. In Singapore on 8 January 1996 he said, 'Successful companies invest, treat their employees fairly, and value them as a resource not just of production but of creative innovation.' But his main emphasis was on 'mutual purpose for which we all work together and in which we all benefit. It is a stakeholder economy, in which opportunity is available to all . . . and from which no group or class is set apart and excluded.'[16]

Within ten days of the Singapore speech, Blair returned to the theme in Derby, where he argued that a stakeholder economy was the key to preparing people, business and country for change. 'It is about giving power to *you* the individual,' and he praised 'business advisers like John Kay and Charles Handy who say that competitiveness and success come from a stakeholder approach'. At the end of the month Blair spoke in Southwark Cathedral on the need for a stakeholders' Britain. He attacked American-style division and inequality as 'the *Blade Runner* scenario' and announced that 'For the new millennium we need a war on exclusion and a determination to extend opportunity to all.'

Within six months of Blair's January speeches, the term 'stakeholding' was dropped from Labour's propaganda. It played no part in the October party conference that prepared for the election. When the history of the period comes to be written, it will be interesting to learn the reason for putting aside the term. Did it fail to go down well in focus groups? Was it seen as too risky for business? Was it felt by some to look like recycling socialism in another guise? Or was it regarded as a great idea that it was too risky to debate further, as it would not win votes and could now be stored away as a guiding approach once in office? All we can do is note that stakeholding has not been renounced, or even denounced, by anyone close to Labour's political leadership.[17] It came and, just as mysteriously, it went. Was New Labour walking softly thereafter, while carrying a big, democratic idea? Or just walking softly?

The episode shows that there is intense discussion among Labour advisers as to the best form of modernisation and what kind of normal, equal-opportunity society they favour. What emphasis should be placed on quality, for example, in the economy and in education, where it will certainly demand more State resources? Labour is convinced that investment and welfare need to be geared to augment the efforts and motivation of the poorest families themselves, whose conditions are threatening to spiral out of control. Even if this approach is right, can it be run exclusively from the centre? On this great question a wager is the best that I can offer. Economic democracy is not going to be delivered by political dictatorship – means and ends contest too sharply. True, the 1945 Welfare State was egalitarian and the creation of a centralised regime, but it came out of the levelling experience of war, when, for once, central direction was also committed to the people. Today, only the people will be committed to the people. Radical decentralisation, constitutional democracy, open accountability entrenched in independent authorities, are the prerequisites for the greater economic democracy that is called fairness.

Since 1979, Britain has become a much more normal country. The monarchy has been secularised, Establishment culture has withered and consensus politics has lost its grip. Yet the UK remains institutionally abnormal. Now Labour's first constitutional reforms have created the possibility of contemporary political institutions. These could give Britain the democratic decentralisation essential to both economic growth and greater equality. Yet growth and equality need not go together. This is why 'modernisation' used in the singular is so dubious. The modern is not a fate, it is a zone of contest. Too often it is taken to mean what commerce and fashion want it to mean. This *must* be contested. At present neo-liberal 'Americanisation' (a term unfairly slanted against US civic traditions) is the current definition of *the* modern. The irony is that it could soon be seen as out-of-date. An alternative, European modernity, is possible. *This Time* argues for such an approach.

So, on the one hand there is a welcome overall transition away from a singular, restrictive past, but on the other, the idea that the future too is singular makes people suckers to the market, as they dismiss history as irrelevant (as Henry Ford famously desired). *In fact, respect for history is completely modern.* Without a historical culture differences cannot flourish and dissent will die. Knowledge of history, indeed, suggests that a simple notion of 'the modern' belongs to a previous age of mechanical politics. Today we have entered a time of ecological politics. This seeks to conserve as well as to transform. Constitutional reform can be seen as an aspect of this overall approach – an attempt to create a balanced system of democratic government capable of sharing and distributing power in contrast to the winner-takes-all machinery of old British sovereignty.

That it is possible to have this discussion over the direction Britain should now take, is entirely due to the Labour victory on May 1st. And in government Labour has promptly delivered historic reforms to the constitution and begun a politics of co-operation. At the same time it continues to retain the high-command approach laced with caution and concessions to the Thatcher-Murdoch version of modernity, that won it the election. As a consequence of its self-denial prior to May 1st, New Labour is still at variance with itself.

4
WORCESTER WOMAN

THE LEADERS caught electoral frigidity. Their only outburst was John Major's unscheduled appeal to his own candidates to keep to the party line on Europe. When leaders speak to their followers there is often a degree of edge and frankness, as the nature of reality is argued over and a real attempt at persuasion made. This was true of Labour's efforts to face up to the modern world throughout the 1980s. However, when politicians speak to the public they are less candid. Questions are parried, accusations are met by evasions, images and speeches are designed to reassure. The exercise becomes an impediment to comprehension. Major ordered a six-week campaign – double the usual length – both to delay the Downey Report on corruption and with the idea that the more voters looked, the more they would 'see through' New Labour. But the public had been looking at his own government for long enough and had no desire to observe it any longer. When the main BBC News at 9 pm extended its half-hour format, its audience plunged, as 'forty per cent of viewers actively turned over whenever election news came on'.[1]

A world-historic but now sclerotic and crippled constitution was under challenge. Would the dictatorial powers that its feebleness granted the Executive be used to divide British society into an island playground for the super-rich and a cheap workforce from which they could recruit servants? Or would this threat be resisted by the only credible alternative, a Labour government? There *was* a fundamental choice. But who would have known it? The two main parties presented themselves with a smile and then told us sternly not to trust the other side.

The Labour campaign was imprisoned in the straitjacket of its own fear. For six weeks not a memorable phrase, not a striking metaphor, no frank and vivid sentiment left the lips of its spokesmen and -women. The only phrase that has lasted from their campaign is the need to be 'on-message'. What that message was few now recall. When reports from his focus groups told Blair that he lacked conviction and this was damaging his image, he made a speech saying, 'I am a man of conviction.' He opened the campaign with a magnificent speech in which he called upon the people of Britain to have faith in him. But who trusts a salesman whose opening pitch is to ask you to believe in him? It takes two to trust, and Labour provided little evidence that it would risk placing its trust in the people.

Why was the gap between its election language and its purpose so great? Everyone can see, now that they are in office, how serious the Labour leaders' intentions were. It was also clear beforehand to those who knew them. Their impatience to get on and 'do' something made Blair's staff ratty in the months after the final, pre-election party conference in October 1996. John Rentoul's semi-official biography of Blair foretells swift actions from him and Brown on winning office, and identifies 'semi-independence for the Bank of England' as one such move. Yet it came like a thunderbolt for the media when Gordon Brown took prompt action four days after he became Chancellor.[2] Labour did not communicate during its campaign its determination to govern differently. Why were such brilliant communicators so hamstrung and choked? The moment that stays in my mind as the most visible expression of Labour's self-denying ordinance came after a joint Church document on poverty and unemployment was published. It called for more taxes and public expenditure to combat raging inequality. Brown was asked at the morning press conference if there would be any redistribution of wealth when he got into power, so that inequality would be less under Labour. In a pained attack on the Labour election campaign Martin Jacques and Stuart Hall, writing in the *Observer* commented:

> Gordon Brown refused to say whether, after five years of Labour government, the gap between rich and poor, which has widened to make Britain one of the most unequal Western societies, would have narrowed. So, pray, what's the point? Blair embodies the ultimate pessimism that there is only one version of modernity, the one elaborated by the Conservatives over the last eighteen years.[3]

This assessment was unfair. Only two months beforehand Brown had delivered the Crosland Lecture on the need to ensure that 'everyone should have the chance to bridge the gap between what they are and what they have it in themselves to become'.[4] More than most he had thought hard about how to diminish inequality.

When Brown ducked the question at the press conference it seemed obvious that he wanted to say that the gap *would* narrow. Normally the discipline of Labour spokesmen was so well rehearsed that you couldn't notice their self-restraint. In this case one could, for a moment, sense the processes flashing through Brown's mind. If he said, 'Yes, the gap will narrow', he would be *off-message*. He might then be asked, 'By how much might it narrow?' or even 'How would this be paid for?' The headline was just waiting to be written: NEW LABOUR: NEW DANGER: NEW TAXES!

But who would be so afraid of this? Upstairs at Labour's Millbank centre, above the press conference, were the computers of Labour's Key Seats Unit, which held the names and phone numbers of the one hundred thousand or so swing voters in the ninety target marginals. Throughout the campaign they were being telephoned. Theirs were the only votes that absolutely mattered – or so it was thought after the experience of 1992. Labour was talking to them, but the restriction this imposed upon its policy and thought processes was crushing: *76 per cent* of the population want 'to extend health, education and welfare services even if it means some tax increases'. This has risen from 64 per cent in 1991. As well as representing a very large majority, those who favour redistributive taxation are growing in number.[5] But most of the swing voters Millbank phoned are upwardly mobile, financially stretched and insecure. They don't want more tax. And in the past they have not trusted Labour. Down the Millbank computerised phone lines they held the country to ransom.

Hindsight shows us that in 1997 they need not have done so. On 28 April, four days before voting, the Millbank Unit projected only a moderate overall Labour majority, of forty to fifty seats.[6] Obsessed with those swinging to Labour, it could not measure the anti-Tory tide, a classic case of psephological myopia. Yet, as Paddy Ashdown saw at the time, the movement of opinion to Labour would be strengthened, not reversed, by a pledge to raise limited and measured amounts of extra finance for better health and education.

One of the few respectable arguments against reform of the British voting system is Tony Blair's. He accepts that our first-past-the-post system is unjust, but feels that any alternative may also end up being disproportionate. For proportional representation (PR) often gives small parties an over-large share of power. The British electoral system is unfair, this argument runs, but so is life. You always have to balance one unfairness against another. A party with 20 per cent support at present gets an unjustly small share of seats in the UK, but were it to win 20 per cent of Parliament it might exercise an *unfairly large* share of power. Which in turn could harm the influence of the parties for which the vast majority have voted.

However, the British voting system is becoming increasingly imperfect. Because elections are decided in the marginals, these constituencies have an overwhelming influence on the outcome. Today's combination of information technology and sophisticated marketing techniques has moved in to identify the actual individuals who swing in the swing marginals. The result is that 0.03 per cent of voters hold the fate of the country in their hands. The possibly unfair margin of advantage gained by a small party under a more proportionate voting system could not possibly be as grossly unfair – and indeed topsy-turvy – as the UK's current electoral system. It is as if we are voting in an upside-down pyramid, in which one small move at the tip can send the whole edifice crashing.

We should not place all the blame on the swing voters themselves. The monopoly of influence corrupts the responses of those seeking to woo them. Labour was not merely piloted by the objective analysis of the Key Seats Unit as to what would win and hold the votes on the margins of the marginals; it took some of its initial guidance from Tory thinking. Andrew Lansley, who directed Conservative Party Research (notably during the 1992 election), published a valedictory article in the *Observer* in 1995 when he resigned to run for Parliament. He advised his own party to 'mount a successful negative campaign', describing how 'immigration was an issue which we raised successfully in 1992'. These cynical observations aroused the most public comment. But perhaps his assessment of Labour's vulnerability on tax was more influential. 'For Labour,' Lansley claimed, 'the only way to defuse the tax issue is not to promise any extra spending', and he rubbed his hands because he thought Labour could not credibly pledge itself to implement Tory cuts.[7] Within a week of its appearance, an influential Labour leader said privately that Lansley's article was 'seminal'. The swing voters were hardly in a position to call it into question when, in January 1997, Labour – in order to ensure that its pledge on taxes remained credible – made its breathtaking promise to stick to Conservative spending targets, which everyone knew had been contrived to help the government win the election.

The consequence in 1997 was that Labour leaders lost their tongues. Afraid of the fear-factor, they did not harness hope, nor lash the Tories for their corruption and incompetence, in case this might put off swingers who had previously voted for Major or Thatcher. In the end, even right-wing papers were better at taking a firm measure of the Conservative Prime Minister than Labour representatives – at least in public. It is worth reminding ourselves of what most voters rejected by quoting from previously pro-Tory newspapers. This will help recall what all the relief was about on election night. More important, this was the hard talk that New Labour abandoned. The contrast allows us to perceive an absence more clearly, in detective terms it shows that Labour's campaign was a bulldog that did not bark.

The eve-of-election editorial in the *Evening Standard*:

> The chief executive of a reasonably stable and successful company is usually selected . . . on his record of competent management, of appointing and promoting the right people and of reacting to unexpected opportunities and threats . . . These have buffeted Mr Major. The Danish referendum, White Wednesday, the Maastricht paving debate, the Mellor scandal, the sacking of Norman Lamont, the 'back to basics' fiasco, the election of Jacques Santerre, the mad cow crisis, the 'whip-less' Tory rebellion, the bungled cabinet reshuffles, the Scott Report, the scandals over the child support agency and the management of prisons, the endless aborted re-launches and impotent assertions of authority, right down to the latest fiascos over Neil Hamilton and free votes on monetary union – the catalogue of tactical errors, misjudgements, confusion and pathetically ineffectual leadership just goes on and on. None of these farces and fiascos on its own could explain the public contempt for John Major's government, but putting them all together shows a pattern of unrelieved incompetence the like of which has rarely been seen before.[8]

The economics editor of *The Times*, Anatole Kaletsky:

> Since his last election victory in 1992, Mr Major has been pulled and pushed, bumped and tossed across the political stage by his own party and above all by its vociferous right-wing minority . . . The collapse of his cherished European Exchange Rate policy dealt a blow to his credibility from which it has never recovered. It was Mr Major whose jape it was to appoint Norman Lamont to the Chancellorship as a reward for managing his leadership campaign. Mr Major protected, then belatedly ditched, Mr Lamont, who in turn delivered the viper's curse on his mentor's government 'in office but not in power'. Last year Mr Major plumbed to his

> lowest point when he launched 'the war of Hogg's career' . . . he has presided over as many sordid little political transactions as any of his predecessors, yet he seeks to promote himself as 'honest John' . . . the Tories make much of Labour's 'threat to the constitution'. Yet one of the gravest charges against this Government is that it has created a pernicious centralisation of power at Whitehall . . . The Conservatives have forfeited this election by their accumulated record of incompetence, division, petty corruption, inadequate leadership and failed foreign policy. Hatred of Europe is the nearest this tired and ragged gang can approach to a ruling passion.[9]

In these passages one can feel the anger that underlay the electorate's decision to oust Major.

Labour abstained from such appraisals of its opponent's legacy. The electorate drew a line, New Labour didn't. It broke from its own Labourist past, but it did not, in public, break from the Tory past in its campaign. Instead, two weeks before the vote, it unveiled a new mascot, a bulldog, which it used in its party political broadcasts to project an image of itself as patriotic. The dog selected, a pedigree, seemed peculiarly white in colour and turned out to be castrated. There were understandable protests from minority groups at the deployment of this most exclusive and least sympathetic image of Britishness – one which even the *Daily Mail* pointed out was 'thick-skinned, impervious to pain and not terribly bright'.[10] In the 1987 general election the Tories used a poster that boasted Britain was overtaking other European countries. It showed a pathetic French poodle, a ridiculous German Alsatian and a great big British bulldog, as visual proof of its claim. When it was unveiled, Norman Tebbit posed personally with the bulldog in front of the poster. Ten years later Peter Mandelson did the honours as Labour's Campaign Manager. He also wanted to draw the attention of voters to the confusion in the ranks of the enemy, and said at one point, 'The issue is not the single currency, it is the divided state of the Conservative Party.' This was not a claim that Labour had a better policy than the Tories; it simply emphasised that the Conservatives were unfit to govern.

Indeed, they were. But it did not follow that Britain needed a Conservative Party that *was* fit to govern. Labour's campaign managers drew up the wagons and even then refused to fire a sharp phrase that might upset swing voters in the marginals.

Roy Jenkins, now an elder statesman and leader of the Liberal Democrats in the House of Lords, spoke at his party's penultimate press conference. The Conservative campaign seemed to him, he said, like Moby the whale, a sad creature that had recently been marooned in the Firth of Forth. Struck by a disorienting illness, it died after every effort to get it back out to sea had failed, and its decomposing body was exposed at low tide. All of us attending the Lib Dem press conference laughed in recognition at the comparison. It was not an image for posterity but it had a vivid edge – it was politically strong and it damaged the Tories more than the ya-boo, 'You're divided, we're not.' No one dared to say anything so colourful at Labour's press conference, where every answer was 'on-message'. Robert Harris witnessed Labour's preparations behind the scenes: 'Nothing comes up which they haven't just rehearsed or answered before.'[11] It was Moby versus a machine.

The worst place to be was on board the machine. The journalists who travelled on Blair's battle-bus were driven out of their minds with boredom. Iain Jack accompanied them on the last phase of the campaign for the *Independent on Sunday*:

> On Tuesday evening, at a briefing in a hotel outside Luton, Alastair Campbell, Tony Blair's press officer, acknowledged the problem to the journalists who travelled with the leader. 'I know', he said, 'you're bored shitless with it.' A reporter mentioned that there are a lot of other issues Blair could take on, some of them even mentioned in the manifesto: the minimum wage, the environment, public transport, or (a big thing surely?) constitutional reform – Scotland, the House of Lords. 'Constitutional reform?' Campbell was incredulous. 'You think Mrs Woman-in-Worcester is interested in Constitutional Reform?'

For readers who are puzzled at the reference, Worcester

Woman is not a strange Ice Age mummy. She is a construct who has become a modern myth. She is the powerful goddess of swinging opinion who emerged, fully clothed, from the forehead of market research. She is the female-in-the-middle, on whose decisions the election of 1997 allegedly depended. An upwardly mobile, lower middle-class mother of two children in a suburban marginal constituency, with a mortgage and a husband who feels the need to wash his car, Worcester Woman is a contemporary allegory. In earlier days female allegories were cast in stone and metal across our capital cities to represent all the male virtues, hopes and fears – Justice, blindfold, holds out her golden arms to the barristers and shysters of the City; on Admiralty Arch, as one astute female critic observed, the allegory of navigation sits with her sextant like a dildo in her lap.[12] Today, our guiding allegories are virtual. No one would sculpt Worcester Woman except in irony. But her every inner statistic is measured by narrow-eyed, serious suits as she weighs power in her balance. Men of influence wake at night for fear that she has left them for another.

Labour asked for her trust but never extended their trust to her – the muse, mistress and even mother of their election campaign. Instead they selected a bulldog – a Thatcherite symbol of grasping, violent, white supremacy, except that this one had no balls – to reassure her that Britain would be great under New Labour. And by extension, that her lawn would be safe from intruders.

Like all allegories, Worcester Woman does not think for herself. She is the creation of experts who project onto her their fears and desires. But what if she *does* think? What if she stirs of her own accord? Worcester Woman does not say, 'I want to be a citizen not a subject.' Nor does she tell the canvasser at her door, or the pollster on her phone, 'My number-one priority is constitutional reform.' Yet in all sorts of ways she cares about the constitution. She wants to know if her family has the right to a health service. She will have a view as to whether Britain should be more like America or Europe. She is concerned about the fate of the monarchy and how the Queen should behave – evidently a constitutional question. On 4 September Pamela Methley, standing in the queue at St James's Palace after the death of Diana, told *The Times*, 'We knew how to behave. Why didn't the Queen and the rest of the royal family?' – a clear, constitutional sentiment. She came from Ilford in Essex, where both of the town's seats swung to Labour in 1997. She could just as well have come from Worcester.

Those who disparage the idea that Worcester Woman has an overview sleep more comfortably believing that she does not. After the election, Alastair Campbell was reported to be 'less than enamoured by the prospect of a statutory right to know'.[13] When he briefed journalists about the promised White Paper on Freedom of Information, he taunted them by saying that it did not mean there would definitely be legislation. But a Freedom of Information Act is a constitutional reform that most certainly interests Worcester Woman. It means she will be better informed about the quality of the food she and her family eat, the safety of the medicine they take, the extent and history of radiation accidents in Worcester and elsewhere. At present MAFF, the old Ministry of Agriculture, has a Committee on Toxicity. This ominous-sounding body classifies safety levels in foods and drugs, such as dosages in vitamin pills. The committee 'meets in secret and is not obliged to give any reasons for its conclusions'.[14] Has Worcester Woman been taking, or giving her children, too much vitamin B_6 (a newly understood danger)? She would like *the right* to know.

The contempt and scorn for Worcester Woman's limited horizon presents itself as realism. But its purpose is to keep her in ignorance. Worcester Woman needs to be extricated from the condescension of politicians, spin doctors and the media. She is much more interested in constitutional reform than they want her to be. Perhaps not in the details of its administration, for few people are. It is the meaning and implications of reform that touch her directly. 'Too many people are put off by the word "constitution", and make the mistake of thinking it a technical subject that only the experts can understand,' John Major argued when he was still Prime Minister in June 1996. His speech writers had clearly been reading the publications of Charter 88. 'Well, I don't claim to be a constitutional expert,' Major continued:

> But I am a politician and a citizen, and it is from that practical experience that I want to address the issues. Because the constitution is not, to me, simply a matter of institutions – Parliament, the Crown, our legal system. At its heart I believe it's about individuals and individual freedom. How we influence and control the kind of nation we live in. The Constitution is shorthand for our rights and our democracy.[15]

This reads strangely, does it not? A Conservative Prime Minister tells us that he is a citizen and that our constitution is about our rights and democracy . . . 'What constitution is that, then?' would not be a stupid response. For over seventy years the Conservatives of Britain *have* been telling us that the constitution is a technical matter, that it is *not* something sensible people are interested in, or one that practical, 'ordinary' people need to bother their heads about. This made the country much easier to govern. Alastair Campbell's scoffing is merely the latest echo of a thousand Pall Mall clubland jeers deriding and patronising the Worcester Women of their day.

At the last quarter of an hour, historically speaking, Major saw the constitutional writing emerging on the wall. It was being written by the hands of the people, not the spirit of God. He sought to appeal to the people – who else? – to stop it. He did so in the language of constitutional democracy itself, using such terms as citizen, freedom, democracy and rights. This language still has little purchase on the popular imagination, nor could it with respect to the old regime. For the whole point about the existing British constitution – and it does indeed have a wholeness – is that it is not owned, let alone controlled, by the people. It does not belong to us as citizens and we do not have democratic rights. We may enjoy exceptional freedoms compared to some other countries, but we do not possess them, as recent Conservative legislation has made abundantly clear. Major used the language of reform to defend the unreformed constitution *from* reform. Little wonder it sounded strange.

Stranger still, Major was right to say that the constitution is shorthand for our democracy – such as it is, at once considerable and lamentable; it does concern individual freedom, national power, public accountability and common identity. Today, it seems, British people want their government to be held to account in an open fashion that cuts through mystique and jargon. They do not want to be represented by people who behave as if they were different from, or better than, us. Indeed, just as any sporting club or local association has a written constitution to empower and regulate its officers, most Britons would be pleased to have one for their country. This view, until recently regarded as the irrelevant fancy of marginal radicals, is now held by a massive majority of the electorate, including Worcester Woman.

The Joseph Rowntree Reform Trust *State of the Nation* opinion survey commissioned from MORI in 1995 showed that an overwhelming majority of all social classes, in all regions, across all age groups, support the idea of a written constitution. A representative sample was asked to consider the statement 'Britain needs a written constitution providing clear legal rules within which Government ministers and civil servants are forced to operate' and 79 per cent agreed. Only 7 per cent disagreed. Of those who agreed, nearly half agreed strongly.

The question presented a written constitution as something that is normal and that might help prevent corruption, by making the powerful accountable. It did not ask, 'Do you want to surrender a thousand years of history by letting know-nothing intellectuals concoct a new-fangled written constitution that will hamstring officials and ministers who are doing their best?' Well, they could always ask the question if they want. Meanwhile, the results of the Rowntree poll tell their own story – and, incidentally, a written constitution *is* normal and would provide clear legal rules, unlike our own.

Support for a constitution of this kind is not a middle-class, metropolitan phenomenon. It is higher among so-called C2s (74 per cent) than among ABs (70 per cent), and higher among those who read popular papers (79 per cent) than among those who read the quality press (69 per cent). It is higher everywhere else in Britain (69–81 per cent) than in the capital (62 per cent).

A closer look shows that the main reason for the variations is that a significantly larger proportion of those who *oppose* a written constitution are ABs who live in London and read the quality press (10 per cent of ABs oppose a written constitution compared to 5 per cent of C2s; 8 per cent of those who read broadsheets compared to 4 per cent of those who read popular papers; 9 per cent of Londoners compared to 6 per cent in the North of England).

A *Spectator*-reading intellectual would have told you the opposite: that we live in a 'sensible' country, which holds the present unwritten constitution to be 'a good thing'. And that only a few middle-class, progressive types want it written down. The Rowntree/MORI survey shows that it is the other way round. It is the proponents of the status quo who are a small, but significant upper middle-class, broadsheet-reading, London-based minority, with far too much influence for the country's good. Across the land, almost everyone else, from 65 per cent of Conservative voters to 75 per cent of skilled workers, would be happy to have a written constitution.

A large majority of Tory supporters like the idea. Their party leaders are so against it, however, that they have never yet considered making it policy. An even larger majority of Labour supporters (78 per cent) want a written constitution. While Gordon Brown has called for 'a new constitution for a new century' (and this *has* appeared in Labour documents), this phrase did not appear in Labour's manifesto. And even this phrase carefully avoids the term 'written'. Such is the yawning distance that passes for government being in touch with the people. To put it in language that may seem strange to outsiders, Worcester Woman is not averse to having a constitution that belongs to 'us' and not to 'them'. We – 79 per cent of us – would not object to an honest, modern constitution that we can call our own. It is not the people of Britain who are not yet normal, it is the political élite.

5

DIANA: 'YOU WAS A ROSE IN A GARDEN OF WEEDS'

ALL REVOLUTIONS INVOLVE the rapid movement of large masses of people who 'surprise themselves', as the regime gives way. It was fitting that the British equivalent should be the complete opposite of an insurrection as millions of people seized the device that the old constitution itself deployed to confirm and renew its apparently lasting superiority – the ceremony of State. Since Queen Victoria was made Empress of India, 'they' have decided the route while 'we' cheered and bowed our heads. This time, the people altered the route and doubled its length, after the Palace stated that it could not be changed. This time, it was the Queen who bowed her head. She was even obliged to fly the Union Jack at half-mast from the Palace, something that 'is never done'.[1]

The Diana event was a stumbling upon ourselves as we are now. As Suzanne Moore suggested in the *Independent*, 'What we have witnessed is, in Raymond Williams's phrase, a new "structure of feeling" that was already present but surfaced as a result of Diana's death.'[2] Because something is new does not mean it is faultless. The new structure of feeling is sentimental and credulous, as well as respectful and determined. There was a demystification of the monarchy but at the cost of a sanctification of Diana. Both expressed a form of the contemporary that connects to the landslide of 1 May. The main novelty was that it confirms the British are normal. I have argued that the election was a vote for normalisation and a rejection of Great Englishness with its myths of exceptionalism, obsession with sovereignty and allegiance to arrogant, Westminster-style narcissism. The monarchy is part of this self-important system although its influence, especially thanks to the honours system, penetrates much further. The celebration of Diana confirmed the rejection of this system as representative of ourselves.

In her few speeches and her *Panorama* interview, Diana broke a key taboo when she exposed the royals for their coldness and inhumanity towards her. In a country that was still deferential, Diana reinforced the relaxation of inhibitions and endorsed private doubts about the monarchy; she punctured the reverence in which the Queen was held. It was a strange route for social equality to take, through the privileged opinions of an extraordinarily rich and glamorous daughter of a hereditary Earl, keen for her son to be King.

For official Britain it was to herald a dramatic turn. Even after the divorce, the shift had yet to be recognised. In its editorial on the Queen's seventieth birthday, on 20 April 1996, for example, *The Times* hailed Elizabeth II's 'virtue', 'wisdom' and 'restraint'. Through her long reign, it proclaimed, she had been 'more sure-footed than her ministers' and had become 'an emotionally satisfying focus for national loyalty'. It wished her a long life and endorsed the view of a typical constitutional expert: 'The Queen, in the words of Vernon Bogdanor, "interprets the nation to itself".' No longer. In 1997, more people than ever before at a single moment in Britain's history interpreted the meaning of the nation through its relationship to the royals. And the Queen was very definitely not the one who was doing the interpreting. On the contrary, the nation was saying that she was no longer the mirror in which we see our country reflected. We are no longer stiff and buttoned-up; we grieve openly, hug each other and believe in talking through our troubles.

But good grief! The French and the Italians have mourned openly, hugged and talked through emotions for decades – was there ever a time when they didn't? – *and* they have a higher standard of living than the UK; stiff lips did not even pay popular dividends. The September days echoed, if more theatrically, the shift made evident by the election earlier in the year. The astounding numbers who were swept up by Diana's death confirmed the internal revolution – an entire society embraced publicly a redefinition it had already achieved privately – its Britishness was no longer that of bigotry and bulldogs.

If 1997 brought the Victorian monarchy to an end, the sound of its coming demise was already familiar, as we have seen. The monarchy's psychic hold and quasi-religious sanctity had already been broken and increasingly people now live without them. This means that the throne has to a large extent been republicanised. Since the fatal wedding of Charles and Diana in 1981, its royal sanctity has been eroded. First by the demotic gaze of Murdoch's *Sun*, then by the Thatcher period's assault upon Establishment consensus (which above all else the Queen represented). The upper decks of her great liner still sail onwards, with her impervious features on the bridge. It is strangely impressive – even if her trusties polishing the brass railings to glorify her reflection are ridiculous. Especially so because most of the ship has sunk below its water-line. Diana's death pulled the vessel even further towards the bottom by bringing it 'closer to us'.

It does not follow that the public is, or will be, rudely republican. Both sides of the formal monarchist/republican debate were weakened in September. Because both argue over something that the Diana days made less relevant. For in a strange way Britain's first secular Head of State was installed on 6 September: a President of Hearts. The public clearly proposed Diana as their ideal national representative, in the decorative sense. This preference was communicated symbolically – in an amphitheatre of flowers – but this too was apt. Over the course of a week, in front of the palaces of London, the massed subjects of the Crown acted out the two measures needed for the inauguration of a President: a *non-royal* was selected and then *endorsed by the people*. To make it even more symbolic, the people selected Diana after she was dead. This showed good judgement, however, for Diana-dead was a very different figure from Diana-alive. Dead or alive, Diana was a figure of power and privilege. She was a right-wing 'President'; but then the most influential republican in Britain is the right-wing Rupert Murdoch.

Tony Blair responded adroitly, recognising the loss that many would feel. By calling her the People's Princess, a phrase that came from Julie Burchill via Alastair Campbell, the Prime Minister gave permission for the public to claim Diana – and through her the 'official' country – as its own.[3] This permission will not easily be withdrawn. In the process Blair emerged as a patriotic, rather than a merely partisan figure and made the critical transition to national leader; a move that had always proved beyond John Major's reach. In so doing, he left Major's successor as leader of the Conservatives, William Hague, stigmatised as a party hack.

Yet the ease with which Blair achieved this meant there was something almost discordant about the emphasis he then began to place on the need for Britain to *become* modern. As he pressed the theme on the Trades Union Congress in September with increased urgency, it was like insisting that everyone must pull really hard to open a door that is already unlocked and needs merely to be pushed. Where was the resistance coming from, which made the Labour leader so insistent on the need to modernise? It came from within, as he tested the alternative forms of modernisation, each with its own uncertain outcomes. Diana's death floodlights the options.

Blair and his colleagues have a choice. It is not a simple either/or. Nonetheless, I will put it crudely. Now that New Labour has made Diana the People's Princess, the spin doctors have let it be known that there will be a modernised People's Monarchy advised, if not run, by the People's Prime Minister. This option is possible because the Prime Minister, with popularity ratings around the 80 per cent mark, is far more popular than the Queen. For the first time since 1945, Downing Street stands in higher public esteem than the Palace.[4] Never before in Elizabeth's reign has she needed her Prime Minister's support more than the Prime Minister has needed hers. Blair would not be human if he were not tempted to fold the aura of the Crown into his own influence, so as to reinforce his role above party politics. To do so would be modern in the way Diana was modern, a representative of the global spectacle – glamorous, digital and defining. The Prime Minister would absorb the symbolic role of the occupant of the throne and become the representative of the whole nation. If they go down this route, Blair and his colleagues will choose populism rather than democracy.

Writing in *The Times* the day before the funeral, John Lloyd spotted the danger:

> It had been one of the received wisdoms of anti-communism that whenever one met the People capitalised, one knew something undemocratic was afoot. A People's Princess is not a People's Democracy to be sure; but in recasting the people as the People we move into dangerous territory.[5]

Lloyd goes on to imply that popular feeling about Diana was largely constituted by the media and that the nation was being subjected to an 'awful mobilisation', drummed up by the need for an icon on 'the left'. This description is a sophisticated version of the mob theory. The people who gathered did so of their own accord, not as obedient subjects, or as manipulated fools, or as angry Jacobins – but not yet as citizens. Perhaps we can call them lower-case people. In doing so they created an opening, not a closure, an overture to a new period.

But Lloyd's point is salutary, as a warning of what an alliance of government and glamour-hungry media could make of the legacy of the Dianorama: a People's Government run by the People's Premier, who heads the People's Party to create the People's Britain, using the glamour of a People's Monarchy, itself built on the memory of the People's Princess, as one of the devices to ensure its supremacy. The last check and impediment to the dictatorship of the Executive, the royal warning, would have fallen.

An alternative was proposed by Shirley Williams at the 1993 Monarchy Conference. She criticised the then Conservative government for the way in which it abused the powers of the Royal Prerogative. Williams thought that the monarchy could help to mitigate this development, but:

> The Royal family has made an attempt to change but I believe that it has gone in the wrong direction ... The royals themselves have paid a terrible price for becoming stars on a stage which was not made for this purpose . . . the transformation of the Royal family into a soap opera has also exacted a terrible price from the rest of us because it has reaffirmed what we were rather than what we are, and distracted us from what we might be.

Williams then called for a Citizens' Monarchy. In the absence of an unwritten constitution, this could become a guardian of liberty and a defence against the abuse of the Royal Prerogative by the Executive, she suggested. It would be 'less magical', 'more real' and would concentrate our minds on, 'That troubling aspect of our historic legacy: a powerful executive that is checked neither by a constitution, nor by a bill of rights, nor by a truly independent parliament'.[6]

The suggestion that the monarch should personify not just the constitution as a whole, which is bad enough, but especially its residual ability to defend liberty against the abuse of power is wholly unrealistic. Only a democratic constitution can do this; there is no substitute for it. But the point that Shirley Williams makes which can be retained is that we need citizenship reflected at the very top of our constitutional structures, and not the centralising force of the media-spectacle – royal or not – that ventriloquises the People and subverts democracy.

The importance of the September days for Britain lies with the lower-case people. If we look at Diana's death from this perspective, it is easier to see both the possibilities that the crowds signalled and the danger of their trust being misused. Individuals themselves harboured quite different feelings. Contrary reactions drew those who mingled in the vast crowds, making it possible to project onto the popular reaction almost as many different interpretations as are being thrust on Diana herself, she who bestrode the spectacle with her long legs – taunting the camera to find a spot of cellulite upon them – during her last weeks of showing-off at St Tropez. So first a few remarks are necessary about her.

The car crash fused widely differing stories into one sudden, catastrophic moment. The breadth of identification was possible because Diana was into transgression. She turned herself into a medium whereby the public could dream of being both themselves and something else. Medieval scholars recognised the two bodies of the King – one holy, the other mortal. Diana had four bodies: earthly sex symbol, regular loving mother, charismatic royal healer, and glamorous yet manipulative star. Critics say she was less deserving of her fame than those who are singers, actors, politicians or racing drivers. But she raced through life. Much of the attraction she generated and renewed came from the way that, from the safety of their own lives, people lived out vicariously their desire to be different through her. The rationalist sneer that she was contradictory misses the point that we all harbour contradictions. She wanted royalty *and* normality, fame *and* privacy. She wanted to be commanding but also vulnerable. As she strode the minefields of Angola in her khakis and protective clothing she *was* all those things. She had achieved the impossible. But – and this really was impossible – she wanted it to stay that way, a desire that condemned her to ever more extraordinary escalations. After meeting her for lunch in New York two months before she died, Tina Brown, the editor of the *New Yorker*, perceptively noted that Diana wanted to go to China to 'straighten out' their heads! And observed that a 'frantic Diana lurked beneath the shining surface'.[7]

Brown relates this to Diana's reckless tryst with Dodi Fayed. The suggestion is that she called in yet further hypercharged lightning strikes of the media-spectacle as she swallow-dived off Fayed's yacht in order to upstage Camilla Parker-Bowles. For Charles was about to host her rival's lavish fiftieth birthday party in what was once supposed to be Diana's home. He had sustained the relationship across a quarter of a century in which Diana was just an episode. She could not abide the prospect of life as the reject, stuck in Kensington Palace, her official residence, which turns out to be a block of flats for fading royals, a Margaret here, a Gloucester there – poking their heads into the corridors to see who is sleeping with whom, a 'ghetto' Diana called it, understandably. Who could she turn to but the one true love of her life, the lens? It was not her only relationship but it was the one that sustained her.

Such celebrity is international. But this then intensifies national attachment, as the recipient comes to symbolise the larger world of fortune and opportunity for those at home. Diana lived dangerously. She took risks, shared the pain and succeeded at a time when her countrymen and -women craved success. Hence the mass grieving when her life was cut short. An immediate comparison is with the gigantic outpourings of grief in Brazil in 1994, after the death of their world-champion racing driver Ayrton Senna, whose foundation for helping children in need has since raised $100 million.[8] Evita was a more frequent comparison. But the film of the musical, which many had seen, skimped on Evita's politics. She came from a poor background and sought to transform the economic lives of exploited workers, the kind of people Diana never hugged. So Evita's support mixed glamour with class – real class – and it lasted as an expression of the Argentinian labour movement. This was not Diana's role. Instead she has entered the morbid twilight zone preserved for stars who die young, ruled over by Monroe and Kennedy, where the two-dimensional obsessions of those sadly granted only a half-life here on Earth find compensation in the paranoid inter-net of their common projections. Such obsession leads into the pathological. Diana-after-Diana will live on as a stereotype of the beautiful woman who died for love. 'Christ was also persecuted' was one of the ominous messages, thankfully infrequent, attached to the flowers. A cult will grow.

It will eventually die out, say around the year 2020. In the immediate future an effort will be made, by the Palace and its Trusties to persuade us that Diana's sudden death, and by implication the royal relationship with her, was an accident that merely happened to accelerate reforms already under active consideration. The monarchy's official presentation of itself is to insist that it is not influenced by the judgements of anyone other than its courtiers, and certainly not by the lower-case people. The Queen has said there are lessons to be learnt. She will learn them, thank you very much. Further public dialogue will not be amusing. When the arguments over Diana's death became public, the Palace denied them. It let it be known that the Queen herself had decided to make her live television address and have the flag on Buck House lowered for Diana and that she had done this on Wednesday, *before* the press amplified the volume of protest that had been gathering on the Mall. It was only because the Palace is stately in its ways that the news was rushed out on Thursday – I mean, delayed until then. So you see it was good royal judgement, and not a caving-in to pressure, that saved the day.

The monarchy must remain untouched by the hands of citizens. Advice it receives needs to be hidden from view to preserve its sanctity in the eyes of its subjects. After Tory leader William Hague protested about the way in which Downing Street had claimed credit for its role in advising the Palace, his Shadow Cabinet colleague, the constitutional expert Stephen Dorrell, went on the radio to defend his boss. Nothing, Dorrell argued – not the smallest detail of transactions with the Palace – should *ever* be revealed. A similar attempt at contamination prevention can be heard in most interventions by those constitutional experts who see their role as protecting the Crown. Norman St John Stevas, for example, used the *Today* programme to praise the wisdom of the Queen in paying some taxes, as evidence of her 'openness' to change. The real purpose of such praise is to argue that there is no need to argue for any change whatsoever. There will be adaptation, of course, but we are already in safe hands. This is the first tenet of the British State. You remorselessly oppose the slightest reform, and then, when it is forced upon you after massive resistance, you blithely turn round and, without the tiniest speck of conscience or self-reflection, take credit for it. Indeed, you proclaim that the system always was progressive and anticipated the way ahead. This is the instinctive response of top-down authority everywhere: whatever *you* have is by *our* grace. It is amazing that such judgements can still be uttered without everyone else choking with laughter.

The difficulty such experts now face is that it *was* people who forced the Queen into her belated acts of wisdom. While Diana's death was an accident, the millions upon millions who laid the flowers and wrote their notes and poems did so on purpose. What changed was not the monarchy – it showed itself quite unchanged. Nor was it underlying public attitudes – for these had already been expressed on 1 May. What changed was that through their enormous congregations and the oceans of flowers, cards, letters, poems and contributions to condolence books, including those in every Tesco and tabloid paper, millions *manifested* a desire to be represented differently. They did so with more deliberation than was allowed on May Day in one respect. In the election they merely had to mark their X, the sign of the illiterate. When Diana died they wrote, the first signal of citizenry. How they wrote! Nearly 300,000 inscribed their messages on the official books alone, while when George VI died only five books were opened.[9]

Was it all a put-up job, a mere acting out of the media's call to adulate a star and increase circulation? Clearly, the experience of Diana's death was mediated by press and television, through which she had lived and which allowed millions to identify with her. Of particular importance were the continuous television documentaries that presented a full-colour cameo of her life in the hours after she died. Many said they were surprised at their own reaction to her death. In part that reaction came from turning on the news and watching her come back to life before your eyes: holding children, getting married, being a mother, shaking hands with an AIDS victim, touching a leper, being interviewed in close-up about how there were 'three of us in the marriage', then talking about bulimia, having fun on a water slide with her boys, protesting about landmines. Each image was sharpened by the knowledge of imminent termination and the grim glamour of the smashed Mercedes. It was hardly surprising that people sought to assimilate this heady amalgam by doing something. They took to their feet and, especially when they saw that others were marking the event, decided they should too.

So, clearly, the firestorm of sentiment was fanned by the high winds of non-stop television and massive newspaper coverage. But the media was also swept up in the firestorm fed by its oxygen. It did not create the response. On the contrary, as I have tried to show in examining the coverage of the election, while the media is all too prone to believe its own sensationalism, the population is quite capable of remaining unmoved by it. 'The public is corrigible', to use a phrase of Jean Seaton's,[10] meaning that it learns from its mistakes, and reflects on the way it is presented with stories. The public is more media-wise than the media gives it credit for.

Further evidence that people were moving in large numbers of their own accord was provided by the funeral and its immediate aftermath. More than one million, though fewer than the predicted two million (because of police warnings about the crush and instructions not to bring children), lined the streets for the actual funeral on Saturday, 6 September. To the astonishment of the authorities, Sunday brought another three million to the royal parks. There had been no suggestion of this, or encouragement in the press. No one had called on 'the people' to pay their respects the next day with their families. When the hearse carrying Diana's coffin drove off from Westminster Abbey to her family estate for her burial it looked strange, for there was no cortège behind or wreaths upon the car. People started to throw flowers at the vehicle and covered much of the roof, forcing the driver to turn on the windscreen wipers and then stop to deposit a small, jumbled wreath at the beginning of the motorway. No one had thrown flowers at an official car before. Or cast them in front of the gun-carriage that bore Diana's body to the Abbey, as many did. Nor did these spontaneous responses show evidence of mass hysteria or pathological obsession.

On the contrary, people clapped the coffin as it went past. This was another innovation. The flowers were like a physical manifestation of the applause. They were thrown at the coffin like confetti, a sign of wanting to keep faith, rather than an acceptance of loss. More people clapped than cried. They wept as well. But mostly, as a careful account by Grace Bradberry in *The Times* emphasised, the occasion was marked by 'emotional restraint', although not the stiff-upper-lip variety. The flowers and the clapping suggested gain alongside the loss. Just as one claps a brilliant innings, which destroyed the other side's bowling but failed to win the game thanks to a stupid run-out. Of course you are sad that the player is out. You curse the character defect that led to the risk that ensured the run-out. You also forgive it, as you acknowledge that the same exceptional willingness to take risks had created the innings in the first place. The other side is obliged to stand and ruefully applaud the lonely withdrawal of the genius, an innings cut short. *Well played, Diana!* The game is suddenly much duller. In some ways it was not like a funeral at all.

When Winston Churchill died in 1965 he was a commoner – as was Diana, now stripped of her titles. Churchill too was an international figure who had palpably entered the experience of millions of lives, if for quite different reasons. His funeral *was* a farewell. He had lived life to the full (he was also a great one for crying). Yet he represented a done past, of Empire and heroic stubbornness, which had fallen as all things must. When his body was taken on the Thames to sail towards his chosen burial ground near Blenheim, the gaunt cranes of the London docks that lined the river bowed before the catafalque as it passed. It was an extraordinarily moving, officially organised farewell. The docks that had withstood the Blitz, those who had died in them, the vital seaborne supplies that had sustained Britain at war, and the common organisation which the country managed and Churchill inspired – all these living memories were caught up in the silent adieu of the cranes. When their black frames dipped towards the coffin as it slowly sailed past, it was as if the war effort itself had returned to salute its historic leader. And, of course, we now know that the same magnificent determination to resist and preserve a way of life led the dockside crane operators to defy containerisation. Within a few years, undercut by Felixstowe, the cranes themselves were dismantled. Churchill's funeral was a domestic, as well as a historic, farewell. It marked the end of an era, an ending to be proud of, a true valedictory.

Diana's funeral was not like this at all. Rather, it was the site of a contest over the future. One that began from the morning of the Sunday she died, when individuals started to leave flowers and messages, and to gather outside the palaces, while the royal family went to church without a public signal of regret or a mention of Diana's name during the service (apparently at the Queen's instruction). Within four days the monarchy capitulated. The Queen was forced to do a live television broadcast. Grudgingly short, it was subjected to immediate, blunt assessment in the crowds outside the Palace itself. Did people think it had worked? That the Queen could be questioned in this way, as if she were a normal Head of State, confirmed the end of the covenant that sustained the Crown through the twentieth century. Then the Queen's words were upstaged the following day by Earl Spencer's funeral address. There was no question that *his* words worked. The applause that swept through the holy doors of the Abbey from the public outside and engulfed the congregation inside, stopping only at the Queen's own party, endorsed Spencer's declaration that his sister's 'natural nobility . . . needed no royal title'.

The point is not whether this was true, or whether Diana deserved it. The point is to register the applause of a nation that shouted 'Yes' at its television screens at that moment. For it confirmed a beginning, not an end. This is not undermined by the fact that Diana herself was a royalist. Her views are now beside the point. For when literally millions join in to support one side or another meaning changes. The post-war era was initiated in 1945 by celebrations led by the King from the Buckingham Palace balcony after his family had shared the Blitz. The 1953 Coronation marked the pinnacle. The 1969 television film about the royal family was seen by over 60 per cent of the population. The wedding of Diana and Charles inaugurated the 1980s. The Queen Mother's funeral was supposed to be the next such occasion. The nature of the country is unlikely to be defined so confidently from above to grateful subjects on great occasions again. These will still occur, but they will never be as great as Diana's. It was their instant foreboding of this that made Palace officials do everything possible to diminish the obsequies for the Princess. This merely inflamed the response.

Did the people 'love' Diana more than the Queen? Many did. But not nearly as many as joined in the occasion of September. Odd as it may seem, it is a mistake to over-personalise what happened. This was precisely the mistake that the Palace itself made. By seeing how this happened, it may be possible for us to avoid it. A 'senior member of the Royal Household' told the *Sunday Express* in 1996 that Diana and Sarah Ferguson were held responsible for the way royalty had lost its popular standing:

> There is no doubt that those two women have done more than anyone else to bring the Monarchy to this sorry state . . . Charles has not helped but . . . before they came along, the Monarchy was in a healthy condition and looked to have a long and stable future. Now look how things have changed.[11]

Anyone can see that this attempt to scapegoat Diana for the decline of the monarchy's esteem, and exculpate the Queen, has all the forward motion of completely stalled judgement. Now, with hindsight, we can observe that Diana *increased* the standing of the monarchy as its living critic. In the Hegelian sense that nothing really exists until it is divided, she gave a decrepit institution the kiss of life, when she became its adversary. It was as if, in this more democratic age, the public needed a monarchy which included Her Majesty's Opposition.

To take the side of Charles, for example, or feel that his mistress Camilla Parker-Bowles could be accepted publicly, was a view that took into account the strength and security of Diana: if you thought the Princess had recovered from being a victim, then Charles could be punished less. Thus popular identification with – or just low-level background interest in – the royals, assumed Diana to be intrinsic to them. The monarchy, meanwhile, acknowledged her as mother of an heir to the throne, but otherwise regarded her as an increasingly irrelevant nuisance – a fatal misunderstanding. The resounding silence from Balmoral, with no one flying down to London to pay Diana their respects, excited disapproval and stimulated more flowers. This in turn drew attention to the monarch's desire to be rid of her. It became clear that the royal glacier intended to push aside her life as so much moraine, and proceed on its frosty way as if she were no more than a mistake. This was unacceptable. Diana-now-dead had come to represent hope, change and modernity. The Queen and her subjects started moving apart. Then, thanks to the government, the message got past the shut windows of Balmoral and Her Majesty flew down just in time.

I will argue in the next chapter that all societies have aspirations and that the monarchy personified Britain's. Reminded by the films of her life, the public suddenly saw Diana-now-dead as an alluring symbol of unity reaching out to everyone – whereas Diana-when-she-was-alive had been an exhibitionist divorcee in a family fight. To lose the 'healing and appealing' openness represented by Diana-now-dead would mean to default back to the past, to the rigmarole of status and to believing that those born to privilege are better than us.

At the same time there was a loyal opportunity for the public to object – and to overrule the Queen. Another way of describing what happened in terms of symbol-systems is that Charles and the Queen stand for the rural values of those who own and enjoy acres. For them the city is a pity. Diana represented the city as hope – the flashy lights of opportunity rather than rural fatalism. Most of us live in cities. A monarchy that *included* both sides of the argument between town and country was bearable, even when it favoured the latter – for most would like a place in the country. But a royalty that institutionalised pastoral privilege over terraced regimentation was an unacceptable emblem of inequality and closure. This was rejected by the cowards.

One reader of the *Independent* wrote a letter that compared the response to the time the Berlin Wall came down, which she had witnessed. She went on at length about how the situations were quite different. Nothing had happened in Britain, she felt, that compared to the end of communism:

> I couldn't find any rational explanation for my feeling; in fact I was ashamed at comparing this profoundly sad occasion with the excitement of the East German revolution . . . I am not in any way drawing a comparison between the oppressive Communist regimes of Eastern Europe and the British monarchy. But a new ethos was vindicated on Saturday – one which allows the heart parity with the head.[12]

An internal wall, a division that had run through British society was being demolished. There would still be rich and poor – Diana certainly did not stand for economic egalitarianism; indeed, her wealth was part of her attraction – but there would no longer be 'them' and 'us'. People felt freer as a result. When the comparison with the Eastern European revolutions was made after May 1st, some observers were scathing, and I have quoted Ian Buruma from among them. This time he confirmed the watershed, adding his own apposite comparison:

> There was an atmosphere of protest in the silent crowds queuing up for seven hours to pay their respects to Diana. I was reminded of Chinese crowds paying homage to Zhou Enlai in Tianenmen Square, after his death in 1976. Defying official orders, they came *en masse* to lay flowers and wreaths. They were not revolutionaries, but their gesture was a silent rebuke to the Gang of Four who still ruled China. The mood among the mourners for Diana was summed up for me by a

semi-literate letter on a bunch of flowers laid on the Mall: 'You was a rose in a garden of weeds'.[13]

The events of 1997: the destruction of Tory corruption, the shrugging aside of Europhobia, the election massacre of May, the Diana days, the Scottish vote *together* were comparable to a change of regime: to a European normalisation. A polity moved from being trapped in a self-regarding, archaic order to becoming part of the – lower-case – free world. It was a defeat for socialism. September saw the celebration of a very rich woman. But it was to her, and not her antecedents – her life, not her inheritance – that her mourners spoke in their letters and notes. This was a defeat for the social order of the old regime represented by the Crown. The year as a whole was a declaration by the British people that they wanted a contemporary, inclusive, relaxed, European-style country, living in peace and mixing history with the future.

It was typical of the old mental royalism of the still actually existing British polity that the penny did not drop. Much of the discussion in the weeks after the funeral was obsessed with the royals and how they would change, as if the public had not moved. 'Will the weeds modernise?' became the topic of the hour. Heavyweight experts were wheeled out and asked, in effect, 'How can the weeds grow petals, just like New Labour?' They recommended a cut-back on the number of palaces or abolition of curtsying, a proposal of such moment that I will return to it in Chapter 6 because, like most debates over royalty, it is a detour – in Britain the debate over constitutional representation still takes place in a cul-de-sac. The fundamental question is: have the people changed? Are *we* contemporary?

It was widely and immediately argued that Diana's death marked the end of Thatcherism. Millions were being more than simply individuals and families. As Anthony Holden, a republican, put it, 'It finally gave the lie to Mrs Thatcher's cold, hollow dictum that there was no such thing as society. Never have I, and millions of others, felt such a sense of community.'[14] September 1997 saw a celebration of caring and concern, a validation of the message that none should be cast out, that we have a responsibility towards the weak and the maimed. Diana's wedding gave a glamorous start to the Thatcher period, as a symbol of the idea that anyone can make it. The reactions to her death endorsed the way she changed her role and reached out to the disinherited. The *Zeitgeist* had gone into reverse and Diana's life symbolised the U-turn. Normally I would be adding plentiful supplies of salt to any such analysis. But there was one striking fact about the week of manifestations that validates it. Blacks, Muslims and gays played a full part in the mourning. It was the first official, mass event since large-scale immigration into Britain began that was open to being experienced equally by every section of the population. Multi-culturalism defeated Norman Tebbit.

Diana's affair with Dodi broke the last taboo. Racism and bigotry are fiercest at the top of British society, and snobbish remarks about Arabs still reflect the judgement of what passes for civilisation among the upper class in Britain these days. But below the upper classes, the country has become more civilised. Even if theirs was a jet-set liaison, this distinctly unveiled woman had held out her arms to a Muslim and the people did not object. When he was serving as one of Thatcher's Cabinet Ministers, Norman Tebbit defended himself from the charge of racism, but added that he did apply the cricket test. It was okay to be black, provided you supported England. Everyone understood this to be a narrow criterion – blacks could not begin to be one of us unless they were willing to be *just like us*. Tebbit's version of Englishness may not have been racist, but it did not welcome difference into our midst. The Diana test is far more generous. The multiracial crowds that mourned for her also shared their reflections with each other. It was a naturally integrated, multiracial national mourning. I am not saying that every black person identified with Diana or that all Muslims felt she was their girl. That would be ridiculous. In each section of the population, people felt differently about her, many indifferently. The point is that each section of British society had an equal claim on the experience. It was in effect the first Anglo-British state occasion from which no one felt excluded because of their background.

A comparison can be made with the previous full-blown parade in London. This too was not formally a State occasion but was nonetheless an official, national one. It was the Falklands victory parade. This is how Enoch Powell described it:

> There was this huge crowd spreading out into all the streets radiating from Mansion House, and one big band came down and started to play Rule Britannia, and the entire crowd, right as far as one could see or hear, took it up. That was what it was about. And England had known itself, it had recognised itself. The England which tolerated the British Nationality Act of 1948 . . . was an England which had not recognised itself.[15]

Like that parade, the *use* to which Thatcher put the Falklands victory sent a shiver of alarm down the spines of many minorities in the UK. Even though much of the support for the Falklands War stemmed from public sympathy towards the poor islanders, it was not concern for the underdog that the Prime Minister emphasised when her victorious fleet returned. Instead, she rejoiced in the rediscovery of imperial virtue:

> There were those who . . . had their secret fears that it was true: that Britain was no longer the nation that had built an Empire and ruled a quarter of the world. Well they were wrong. The lesson of the Falklands is that Britain has not changed and that this nation still has those sterling qualities which shine through our history. This generation can match their fathers and grandfathers in ability, in courage, and in resolution. We have not changed . . . Britain found herself again in the South Atlantic.[16]

We have not changed: this claim frightened many of those whose grandfathers were not English. With good reason. Powell had spoken against them a few years previously: 'The nation has been, and still is being, eroded and hollowed out from within by implantation of unassimilated and unassimilable populations – alien wedges in the heartland of the state.'[17]

Powell never accepted that such sentiments are racist. As an Urdu speaker, he would praise Indian civilisation, saying that it was greater than England's. He did not regard immigrants as inferior, but as different. For 'the unbroken life of the English nation over a thousand years' has produced 'the deepest instinct of the Englishman – how the word instinct keeps forcing itself in again and again!' This cultural gap, he claimed, would produce 'a fight for power. People fight for domination.'[18] Indeed, 'It is . . . truly when he looks into the eyes of Asia that the Englishman comes face to face with those who would dispute with him the possession of his native land.'[19]

Most of these quotations are taken from Paul Gilroy's *There Ain't No Black in the Union Jack*. He takes issue with a fine analysis of the nature of nationalism in Benedict Anderson's *Imagined Communities*. Anderson says that nationalism is different from racism and can incorporate different colours and religions within its structure of allegiance. Gilroy disagrees with respect to English nationalism, saying it is not capable of such openness, and that ethnic exclusion is essential to it. The case he makes against what he terms Powellism/Thatcherism was irrefutable. But clearly something has changed. Egyptians will excuse me, but from an English point of view, Diana, the English Rose, 'looked into the eyes of Asia' and liked what she saw. It was impossible to mingle with the crowds on the Mall and around Kensington Palace and regard blacks as 'alien wedges', because in these defining circumstances none of the millions of white citizens of England regarded them in this way. The England of Powell has evaporated. It could no longer be recognised in the crowds outside the Palace. Britain *has* changed. A former member of John Major's Cabinet told Matthew d'Ancona, 'I walked through the crowds in St James's and realised this was no longer a country I truly understand.'[20] In this way 1997 was indeed a velvet revolution.

Does New Labour understand the country? Those who questioned its concessions to chauvinism during the election, and argued that there is a pro-European majority in the making and that people will support paying tax for dedicated purposes, such as education and health, can feel vindicated. Tony Blair led the mourning for Diana and stated that the celebration of her showed that the country believes in 'compassion'. Too right. There had been no need for the bulldog. Labour had dragged out of the cupboard the emblem most removed from compassion that it is possible to find. The point needs to be emphasised. Not because it is enjoyable to say 'told you so', for Labour leaders were fearful that racist symbolism might be used against them and wanted to secure their flank. They can be forgiven for the mistake, not least because the tabloids reinforced it. What would be unforgivable is to continue to believe it is necessary. For what the shift in attitude shows is not just that there has been a gap between the real country of the people and the legal country of Parliament, but also that there is a gap between the country of the people and the country of the press.

Why did it happen? If the episode was so significant, can it have been merely a matter of chance? Rumbling above it, it seemed to me, were two sounds. The first and loudest was the sudden crush, ricochet and scream of metal – the ghastly impact that made most of us fear that our lives too might crash in an instant. Much of Diana's projection of herself as being normal was contrived. Nonetheless, the carapace of fame, wealth and importance that surrounded her caved in. She died, just as we might, as a casualty. The sound of this reverberated forwards into the everyday fear that the life of a loved one might suddenly flicker out in the inhuman surroundings of metal and road. Her death was a moment of modern time, when simultaneously a quarter of the world was shocked to hear the news.

A second noise, replayed frequently on television in Britain, echoed backwards into the past and into the strangeness of the monarchy. It was the throttled half-laugh that Charles emitted after he became not only the first heir to the throne to be asked if he loved his future wife, but also – which was to prove even more inauspicious – the first person in the world to be asked in public whether he loved Diana. He qualified his answer, 'Yes. Whatever love means, hoa, hoa.'

In one sense it was to his credit that he added this philosophical supplement and did not just lie. But millions winced in anticipation as the familiar clip was repeated after Diana's death. The monarchy had hitched itself to the anachronism of an arranged marriage. The alliance itself was flawed from the start, and this could have been foreseen. If one asks why the sixteen-year crash that was Diana happened to the British monarchy, one can say that while the end was an accident, the beginning was not.

For a start, it was protocol that the heir to the throne had to marry a virgin. Given the history of the royals since the 1950s, not to have lowered the flag on this stipulation seems extraordinary. No one has reliably explained just who insisted on it – whether it was the monarch, the heir or his father. At any rate it was insisted upon. Apparently Diana agreed to gynaecological confirmation. The way she put it was, 'I knew somehow that I had to keep myself very tidy for whatever was coming my way.'[21] The protocol went back to the days when Christian women did not have full sex before they were married, if only because contraception was so unreliable. But it seems to have been insisted upon for another reason. The normal – that is to say, non-ordinary – source of a future King's consort is other royalty. But the British royal family proved too parochial, and the supply of royal blood-lines elsewhere too few, for this option to materialise. Had there been a genuine continental Princess able and willing to tryst with Charles, and to whom he had been attracted, then the tidiness test might have been waived. But if Charles had to marry a commoner (such as the daughter of an Earl), then the passageway through which the future monarch would emerge into the vale of tears had to be pristine. The consequence, in these times, was that the lucky girl would have to be very young in order to be inexperienced, thus making an emotional mismatch likely. In this way the historical decline of monarchy as a world force and the rise of modernity in sexual behaviour twisted Charles and Diana into their fateful union.

For where could the royal family find someone suitable who would meet their criteria? The answer had to be from among their own circle. The foreshortened gaze should not be blamed on the limited nature of the Windsors, but rather on the imploding world they inhabit. The process began in the 1950s when Princess Margaret fell in love with an equerry and was separated from him because he was divorced. She later married her photographer. Likeways, when Princess Anne remarried, she chose a royal equerry. Once, the circles that royalty moved in represented a social and political order that spanned the world. Elizabeth's grandfather arrived in India and declared that the entire subcontinent would have a new capital built for it in Delhi. That was global reach! But even his eldest son, the future but never-to-be-crowned Edward VIII, could not find a satisfactory wife within its ambit, and looked across the wrong ocean to an American divorcee and had to abdicate.

Nowhere is the compression that British royalty has undergone clearer than in the choice of Diana as the attempt to avoid another such débâcle. The story is enough to make Oedipus shudder. For the Windsor and the Spencer families had been intertwined in a double helix of subordination and dependency for half a century. Diana was born on the royal estate of Sandringham; her eldest sister had a nine-month affair with Charles, during which Diana, a young teenager, met him for the first time; her other sister is married to the Queen's private secretary (who was also born on the Sandringham estate). It was the two sisters who talked Diana through her traumatic pre-wedding fears, telling her that it was too late to cancel as the commemorative tea-towels were already on sale. Her younger brother (who gave the savage memorial address in the Abbey) had the Queen as a godmother and had served as her page.

The Spencer family had already provided close support to the royals for two generations. Diana's father was equerry to both George VI and his daughter, the present Queen. And *his* father had been Lord Chamberlain to George V. *Both* Diana's grandmothers were members of the court of Queen Elizabeth, the present Queen Mother, the most important being her mother's mother, Lady Fermoy, who was Woman of the Bedchamber. When Diana's parents divorced in the 1960s, their separation was regarded as a scandal. Lady Fermoy gave evidence in court against her own daughter, no less, in order to ensure that Earl Spencer retained custody of the children, a highly unusual outcome. According to Andrew Morton's account, Diana and her brother blamed the Queen Mother, who they thought forced Lady Fermoy to give evidence, thus driving their own mother away from them. Nor does the granny's role end there. According to Charles Nevin's obituary of Diana in the *Guardian*, it was Lady Fermoy's 'close interest', as well as the connections of the elder sisters, that 'combined to bring Diana to the attention of the Prince and the Palace in the summer of 1980'. A grateful Palace must have presumed that she 'knew the score'. Instead, the helix became a vortex for the nineteen-year-old.

She refused to be crushed. But the energy Diana released as she forced herself free was uncontainable. Not least because 'the Firm's' constant efforts to stigmatise her as paranoid and unstable provoked her into dramatic efforts to prove her health and vitality. The decisive moment came when she decided to speak directly to the people – over the heads of the monarchy – in her famous *Panorama* interview and was denounced by Nicholas Soames, a junior Defence Minister and friend of Prince Charles, as being in 'advanced stages of paranoia'. To the public this confirmed Diana's allegations of their ruthlessness. Nor, it seems, did they relax in their desire to destroy her. A year later there were still reports of members of the Royal Household collecting details of Diana's 'impulsive and tempestuous behaviour' to generate a psychiatrist's report that she suffered from a 'personality disorder'.[22]

She sought to preserve her *popularity* against the Palace's attempt to undercut it. But she was not a democrat and certainly not a republican. In the *Panorama* interview she opposed a European-style monarchy and advocated the regeneration of a magical one, which she described in what now seems a tragically prescient way: 'I would like a monarchy that has more contact with its people – and I don't mean by riding round on bicycles and things like that . . . I think the British people need someone in public life to give affection, to make them feel important, to support them, to give them light at the end of their dark tunnels.'

Many viewers, taken in by the modern, urban manner of Diana's presentation, failed to appreciate that her attachment to the divinity of kingship was even more archaic than that of Charles. She argued for a return to the scrofula-curing, royal healing touch of old. Whereas Charles called for a better nineteenth century, Diana spoke out for a return to the sixteenth century. Writing before her death, I was dismissive of her project, though admiring of her audacity:

> Her vision for the monarchy is ludicrous. But the way that she has insisted that she be heard is a victory for equality . . . Diana's refusal to be marginalised as 'a failure' is emancipating for everyone. Her defiant unwillingness to be parked in a spare palace as the inadequate wife punctured a centuries-old male ruling culture. The fact that it was already withered and weak enough to give way does not lessen the courage it took to burst it from the inside.[24]

Her vision was not so ludicrous after all. More people wanted the 'love' she claimed to offer them than I gave credence for. ('I know that I can give love for a minute, for half an hour, for a day, for a month, but I can give,' was how she put it.) The popular desire, and even need, for figures like her is something she experienced. The need for a glamorous alternative to everyday life, the transformation of intimacy, the sporting excitement of fame, these are all part of modern political representation – which can be assessed more clearly in the aftermath of Diana's death.

For the way Diana argued her case and restlessly developed her role was quite unroyal, despite her royalism. The fundamental character of royalty is to be – well, part of the fundament. Its role is to be permanent. As the Queen is said to have told John Major about Prime Ministers, 'I count them in and I count them out.' This posture is much easier to adopt if you are at the top. Elizabeth was fortunate to arrive there when she was twenty-six. And there she stays.

Or does she? Her September crisis was prefigured in February 1997. In an extraordinary television show broadcast by Carlton TV from a giant studio that is used to stage *Gladiators*, the monarchy was turned over to the public. It was hardly a debate in the sense of an exchange of views. It was a mass row. While it was on air, the programme ran a phone-in for viewers' opinions on the once venerated institution. It generated two and a half million calls. Many were made thanks to the redial buttons. Yet both sides seemed to have redialled equally, for, when the results were announced, the proportions were broadly accurate: 66 per cent wanted to keep the monarchy, a substantial majority.

The show generated a furious response and had vigorous defenders. Most of the argument concerned the spectacle, as mediacrats exchanged views about the power, responsibility and limits of the media itself, rather than those of the throne. Meanwhile, a more orthodox survey of opinion carried out before the programme went ignored. This showed that 69 per cent of the public support the idea of a referendum on whether or not to keep the monarchy. Thus around half of those who support the monarchy also want to choose it.

Another way of putting this is that while a clear majority of the British public want to retain the royal family, another equally large majority made up of a different mix of people want the decision to be taken in a non-royal way. Traditionally the point of a monarchy, in contrast to a republic, is that the Head of State is chosen by God through the vehicle of biological fate. Only Poland seems to have elected its King, and in the end this did not do it much good. As far as Britain goes, some experts argue that a referendum on the monarchy is a category mistake – an impossibility, because the monarch embodies divine, not earthly, will.

The public understands the reality better than such experts. As Britain becomes a modern democracy, sovereignty will increasingly rest with the people. They can still retain a monarchy. But this has to be *the decision of the citizens*. After the death of Franco, for example, Spain held a referendum that brought back its monarchy to guard its new written constitution.

The most influential description of the monarchy still remains that of Walter Bagehot in *The English Constitution*. He proclaimed that the Britain of 1867 was already a country where 'the appendages of a monarchy have been converted into the essence of a republic'.[24] In Bagehot's view, the throne provides merely the 'dignified' aspect of government, inspiring deference to it. Meanwhile, the reality of Cabinet government was, in his view, republican. It was 'an *un*royal form of Cabinet government' (his italics) and a 'modern' one – 'Its essence is strong with the strength of modern simplicity.'[25]

There are three things to say about this theory. First, Bagehot correctly grasped that a republic can have a hereditary Head of State as decoration. Second, he was completely wrong about the republican aspect of Britain. What people saw in the Empire then and afterwards, up until our own day, was what they got – this point has now been well argued by various authorities.[26] Third, Bagehot was right to see the monarchy as crucial to the organisation of consent. Consent, controlled from above, kept full-blooded democracy at bay while ensuring the loyalty of the populace.

Today, the Diana events show an increasingly self-confident public keeping the monarchy in line. The change in attitude was confirmed, not created, by September 1997. The Royal Yacht episode had demonstrated people's underlying republican attitude to the monarchy, like that of ex-soldier Simon Phipps, who phoned in his view to the *Sun*. He told the paper, 'If the Queen wants a new yacht, she should pay for it.' His and other reactions like this suggest the development of a new force in British politics, Murdoch Man. The Conservatives have always depended on the support of a working-class vote – their 'Angels in marble'. Often ex-soldiers loyal to flag and country, they were patriotic, tough-minded but also subordinate, deferential subjects of the Crown. We are witnessing the emergence of a male, working-class republican, who was once pro-Thatcher and is currently for Blair. Republican, that is, with a lower-case 'r'. The ex-soldier probably does not want a President. But nor does he want a King or Queen to think that they are any better than he is. This is what I mean by having a republican attitude towards the royal remainders.

It is as if the servants are intent on taking over the Victorian house for themselves. They will install central heating and other modern conveniences that release them from drudgery. But they will keep the grand fireplace (if not all the small ones). By doing so, the fireplace will come to symbolise not their subordination but their ownership. This is the new decorative role of the British monarchy. It is quite different from the one Bagehot conceived.

The problem we face in the present circumstances is that the fireplace has not yet been fixed, there being no written plans to guide the reconstruction. Like the great Victorian gothic structure that is St Pancras Station (which was designed for the Foreign Office and, when rejected, was turned into a railway terminus), the magnificent Victorian monarchy that Britain has inherited is no longer attached to the real constitution and we are looking for a place to position it. Should it be the front door? Does it still have the function of expressing what we are, or a vision of who we will be? Or is it a sentimental convenience – or inconvenience, according to taste – best put in the spare room?

The answer has to be provided by the inhabitants now heavily engaged in home improvement (and not by the fireplace itself). One does not ask the fireplace to install modern heating. Similarly, it is not up to the monarchy to modernise itself. To ask it to do so is to make an impossible demand. But just like Diana, the monarchy is full of illusions and believes that it exercises the deciding role. It set up its 'Way Ahead' group to discuss how the Crown should adapt to modern times in order to re-establish the trust of the people.[27] But the royal family views the people with the same distaste with which it viewed Diana. And now the public knows it. This is why discussions about what 'the monarchy' should do next are so painfully unpolitical. The real question is what the citizens should do with it.

And here we come to the question of what 'it' actually is. That thing called monarchy. Is it a position that people must bodily inhabit? Or is it a person, the Queen, who – and it is not incidental – has no intention of abdicating? Actuarial probability suggests that she will outlive her mother. We can expect her, therefore, to remain on the throne until 2026, when she will send herself a telegram. So even if Tony Blair is Prime Minister for a record-breaking fifteen years, Elizabeth assumes that she will still 'count him out'.

The historical answer was that monarchy is both person and position, a representative of the divinity of Kings sent to us in the body of a mortal. The answer today, in a democracy, is that the only viable monarchy is secular. It has no heavenly existence but is entirely down here, both in person and in the attitudes of lower-case people. This is where modernisation has already taken place and where leadership is needed to consolidate the change.

The monarchy is a relationship. The point bears repeating but is hard to retain. So imagine a Britain without titles and handles before people's names (except for just the monarch). Immediately the relationship between the Crown and the country, between the people and the Queen, would be more modern, and a massive weight of snobbery would be lifted from public life. The Prime Minister told the Cabinet, 'Call me Tony', as he felt the spirit of the times course through his veins. But then the government declared that it would make achieving headmasters Knights of the Realm – 'Sirs for sirs' – as if this sets an example of modernisation for the country's school children. Instead of such reinforcement of the old mentality, all the 'Right Honourables', the Lord this and the Baroness that, the Sirs and Ladies and other obscure ranks and prefixes – by which the British regress their brains and 'monarchise' attitudes towards each other – should go. Titles are one way in which official society reproduces its belief that some people are 'better' than others. All prefixes, except for that of the monarch and Dr for a medical doctor, could be abolished from official discourse. Republicans say we must get rid of royalty to rid the country of snobbery and backwardness. I say, why wait? Let us get rid of the systems of snobbery straight away – off with their garters!

The second step, which will take longer because it is a much more important process, is, as argued in my introduction, to replace special people with special words: the aspirations of a written constitution. Then – and only then – can Britain be represented by human beings who are 'like us', in that they pledge allegiance to the same constitution. After which royals can inherit the position as 'a kind of hereditary presidency', to quote a Swedish MP about his Head of State, if this is what the citizens want.[28] For the British would then *be* citizens. Already the British people are no longer a single great mass – the view seen from the gilded carriage and the media-spectacle that threatens to replace it. The time for democracy has come.

This, then, is the alternative route for Blair and his colleagues. The choice of democracy rather than populism. Democracy can be popular and authoritative, and depends on the endorsement of freedom. Populism is directive and authoritarian, even while it draws glamour from the licence of the market. Both are modern, both are republican in the sense of secular, and both can retain the Crown to endorse their methods; such is the variety of government.

This is one reason why the September days left people puzzled and curious. The people were unified, yet the meaning of what they did remains unclear, because, while people knew what they wanted to leave behind, none knew where we are heading. September confirmed the potential of

May. But different routes are possible into the modern world. And commentators found themselves in difficulty, because the terms in which we think and expect, when faced with large crowds, are still embedded in old stereotypes. The received categories for describing lower-case people taking to the streets are out of date. They were neither republican hordes itching to boo the Queen, nor gullible, infatuated dupes reproducing traditional royalism. Yet both caricatures hovered behind much of the thinking, as the starting point for an assessment. The common assumption behind such stock images is that, whether oppositional or conventional, the masses are mindless.

The millions who responded to Diana's death were mindful. A thinking multitude, the great washed – with flowers – rather than the great unwashed; well dressed not *sans culottes*; a vast movement of people who by their very existence demonstrated that the premise of the 300-year-old British constitution had been swept away. The people are now independent-minded and capable. Their letters, messages, and applause, which carried official UK before it, demonstrated that the country is ready for full democracy, British-style: informal, good-humoured, inventive and measured. The question now is whether the political élite will allow the constitutional transformation to proceed.

PART II

VOICING THE CONSTITUTION

6
What a Constitution Is

A CONSTITUTION IS the set of relationships that proposes how a country is run. A society is defined by its constitutional aspirations as well as its grim realities. All constitutions combine the written and unwritten: in the shape of basic laws, institutions and the way these are lived. While the balance of these elements can differ widely, the constitutions of all societies are inscribed, institutionalised, lived. And the living is the most important in all cases, because it interprets the written and reproduces the institutions.

Every society has basic rules – whether written or not – that determine how laws are made, what rights people have, who holds power and how they can be removed from power. These rules have a special importance because they decide how we are ruled. Normally, a democracy has a written constitution, which stipulates the special measures needed to change these rules, such as weighted majorities, or a second vote in the assembly or Parliament, or a referendum. Britain is exceptional in that, while it has fundamental laws, these can be changed as if they were no more significant than any other law. As we will see, the Bill of Rights of 1689 was amended by John Major's government using procedural sleight of hand.

The reason why this could happen in 1990s' Britain is that the lived tradition that once ensured a restraint upon the abuse of power has withered. Its lungs no longer speak out against impropriety. Mostly they only just manage to wheeze clichés about wonderful chaps, parliamentary sovereignty and the best system of government in the world. The impertinent might ask: If it is so good, why not write it down? In a way this simple question hits the spot. Just as the first purpose of the law is to ensure that people do not need to go to court, so the main purpose of a written constitution is to provide a framework for living with rules. In short, what matters most about constitutions is *how* they are lived; writing them down can help to facilitate this; and the first concern of a constitution is with what should and should not be easily changed about a country's laws and arrangements.

It follows that an important question to ask about any country is: Who can change these rules and how? Countries like Britain, where those in power can make up these rules 'as they go along', are ones where there is only convention, and not the rule of law, at the level of the constitution.

It does not follow that countries like Britain do not *have* a constitution.[1] We do; but those in power can alter it with little, if any, constraint. An example may make this clear. In 1984, Clive Ponting, then a high-flying civil servant, when asked by his new Minister of Defence, Michael Heseltine, to correlate the evidence concerning what happened when the British sunk the *Belgrano* at the start of the Falklands War, as a matter of conscience, gave copies of the material to an MP, Tam Dalyell. When he was identified as the source, Ponting resigned. But the government also took legal action against him under the Official Secrets Act, to have him jailed. Ponting pleaded the national interest: Parliament, the forum of the nation, was not, in his opinion, being told the whole truth and so he informed it – this was the core of his defence. However, the judge told the jury that the interests of the State were the interests of the government. In effect, he instructed the jurors to find the defendant guilty. But the jury refused to convict and found Ponting innocent of treason.[2] The government was furious. Later it passed a new Official Secrets Act making it illegal for a civil servant to plead the national interest, as Ponting did. Today he would have to be sent to jail. Not only are juries no longer to be relied upon to weigh up the national interest, no civil servant will be given the chance to explain himself or herself before one. At the same time there is no statutory code that binds the government to be truthful in its dealing with Parliament. On the contrary, as we will see, the government was to use its prerogative to weaken ministerial responsibility to be honest with Parliament, by ruling that henceforth Ministers must not 'knowingly' mislead the House.

Clearly, the new Official Secrets Act changed the constitution, in that it altered the rules of government affecting relations between the top of the Civil Service and the nation. It also strengthened the government in relation to Members of Parliament. Two different kinds of issues are raised. First, the rights and wrongs of the change. Second, the way it was carried out. The latter shows that the rules governing the rules of government in Britain have become the possession of the Executive (and not, note well, 'Parliament'). The Prime Minister, Margaret Thatcher, was embarrassed by a jury and decided never to let this happen again. And Thatcher usually decided matters outside full Cabinet. She once opened a Cabinet saying, 'I haven't much time today, only enough time to explode and have my way.'[3] In this case the right of a public servant to plead the public interest before a jury made up of members of the public was withdrawn in just the same way as legislation on dog licences can be altered.

Britain has became so used to arbitrary alterations of its constitution that *the way* in which they are carried out is hardly remarked upon. Take, for example, the abolition of municipal government that Thatcher also instituted. A written constitution would enable municipal authorities to be abolished – provided this is what the people want. It would stipulate a more considered process than simply the Prime Minister's insistence and a Whipped majority of MPs and the Queen's signature – for example, referendums in the effected municipalities. So we can say three things about the British constitution. Within the limits of the electoral system, British governments are chosen democratically. Nonetheless, they can alter the constitution undemocratically. At the same time, however, there *is* a constitution. Governments can alter it but they still have to abide by it: the Conservatives were not able to slap Ponting in jail after the jury's verdict.

Britain can no longer entrust its constitution to the sole will of the Executive. Instead, it should become a constitutional democracy – two terms that have equal emphasis and qualify each other fundamentally. I don't argue that we should write down the constitution that we have at present. I do not call for democracy in the sense of the unchecked power of the majority to do as it wishes. Either of these outcomes would lead to a closed system of unchallengeable power. What I am arguing for is open democracy, governed by laws and rules, in which differences are protected and people have different kinds of input in how they are governed.

For Britain to take such a step civic society must be prepared for it – in its common spirit, self-confidence and sense of responsibility. I showed that it is prepared in Part I. Second, it will only happen if the existing constitution has broken down and has ceased to enjoy historic legitimacy. I attempt to summarise why this is indeed so in the next chapter. Together the two developments mean that change from a closed to an open system of government in Britain can be achieved: from the Empire State to a democratic State. Members of the political class, and its tame experts and hangers-on, argue that the present unwritten constitution *is* open or, to use their word, flexible. And so it is for them. For the rest of us, however, its concepts, language and ownership shut us out.

To make the case it is necessary to trace the basic elements of any constitution, written or not, to establish what it is that needs renewal in Britain. I hoped this would be straightforward. Instead, this chapter is a lengthy and difficult part of the argument as it raises concepts rather than puts them in their place. For example, the classic division of State authority into three branches – legislative, Executive and judicial power – is inadequate. Another branch of the State is now growing, namely, accountability. Those engaged in it do not make the law, execute policy or judge conflicts; instead, they exercise an official power which, while of long standing, is becoming a fourth branch of the State. The more that official authority is decentralised and shared, the more clearly accountability becomes essential to legitimate rule. This, at least, is the conclusion I come to. And it points to something even more important: the nature of constitutions is altering. Advocating constitutional reform often seems to have a vintage quality in Britain. It is somehow assumed that one is trying to go back to the eighteenth century. But in fact it is sharply innovative, not just so far as the UK is concerned but more widely. For the nature of constitutions is itself being transformed by modernity.

I am painting in broad, crude strokes. The picture needs a further preliminary remark to frame it. Since the three great horse-riders, industrialisation, capitalism and science, began to revolutionise the world after the European Renaissance, the rule of religion and monarchy has been replaced by nationalism and democracy. This essay is in the main about democracy. But democracy is inconceivable without nationalism. It is *nationalism* that draws the boundaries that define who 'the people' are, who then exercise democracy. Almost everywhere these borders were drawn in blood. The very definition of democracy itself, 'government of the people, by the people, for the people' was made on the battlefield of Gettysburg at the turning point of the American civil war. A war that pioneered the application of mechanical reproduction to military affairs and pre-figured the killing fields of the twentieth century. Furthermore, Lincoln's compelling words were directly descended from the debate over previous decades as to whether Blacks and slaves were fully American.[4] The forging of a modern 'people' was not a civilised experience anywhere. And while far-reaching democratic reform can be introduced consensually, the drawing of the boundaries that define 'the people' still remains explosive.

Progress has a dark side. It reaches deep into our feelings and plucks without mercy at relationships that we desire and rely on. Democracy is neither simple nor always benign. Its progress has seen at least three levels of intensification, which overlap in world terms and are still far from complete. The first was the development of secular, legal government by a capitalist élite. More or less gentlemanly, it was republican in the way Walter Bagehot described nineteenth-century England as a 'disguised republic', as well as Lincoln's.[5] It oversaw the introduction of representative or administered democracy. It was driven as much by war, imperial mobilisation and defence as by national development – and it created the modern party organisation. David Held calls it 'competitive élitist democracy' and has listed its features.[6]

A second stage began after 1945 with the defeat of fascism and the containment of communism, both of which were products of a popular mobilisation of democracy that went wrong. With fascism vanquished and the need to secure the West from the initial lure of communism, the inclusion of citizens through welfare and economic rights became part of the expectation of democracy. Equality of opportunity (both human and legal) was its governing ideal, in sharp contrast to the earlier period. Contemporary notions of fundamental or human rights are a development of this time. The polities involved were still largely administered from above, but for the first time the entire population, not least women, were expected to be literate and to live like voting humans. This is our period: the golden age of consumer capitalism.

Now, a third democratic transformation looms, that of planetary liberalism. As global influences interlace national economies, countries are less independent, individuals more autonomous, warfare more professional, nationalism concentrates downwards rather than expands imperialistically, opportunities increase dramatically, as do drastic inequalities that deprive large numbers of the capacity to pursue their liberty. We are witnessing the beginning of a more reflexive democracy with its emphasis on higher education, open connections and complex consequences.

Britain adapted better than other empires to representative democracy. It helped to pioneer the second stage of welfare rights, bending its unwritten constitution to do so, while preserving its inherited élite. It will need an explicit constitutional framework to respond to the third intensification of democracy, however. This will entail a simultaneous catching up with the twentieth century in terms of constitutional measures *and* a going forward. In catching up we will have to do something new.

It follows that constitutional reform in Britain has a dual character. There is an acute need to deal with the legacy of exception, as well as to move forward to a more participatory citizens' regime. The past has delayed modernisation but not, as the 1 May election showed, dimmed the potential energy of a society that has, despite its conservative reputation, always also been committed to change. The twofold nature of reform is not fully understood. Those impatient to embrace the new in the economy and society tend to disregard the need for constitutional measures, which they feel force them to look backward at the clinging tentacles of ancient institutions. They see the past as a distraction. 'Let us use the trusty sword of the absolute sovereignty of Parliament to cut our way into the future,' they shout, not realising that its blade faces the wrong way. Constitutional trainspotters, on the other hand, who are fascinated with how to manage reform in their sector, often do not want to know about novel techniques of participatory democracy, or anything else that might make their reforms seem even more radical, difficult and dangerous than they already are. For them, it is the future that is the distraction, as they try to unpick the mortmain of yesteryear.

The introduction of a written constitution requires both historical insight into traditional forces and an eye for the new global realities that have penetrated British society with great rapidity. The outcome will certainly not create the alleged checks and balances of the Enlightenment. On the contrary, the background of reform is the future. Catching up will also be an opening up to what has been termed the 'democratisation of democracy', which has only just begun.

In other words, what a constitution 'is' has changed successively, since the first secular definitions of national sovereignty began in the seventeenth century. Redefining Britain's constitution can mean reconnecting with that intense, pioneering English debate that, as I noted in the introduction, has been pressed into silence. But it does not mean returning to that time (before women had the vote!) and its presumptions. I will therefore look at a crucial reform that shows the way in which constitutional reform is itself a moving target.

The argument over a Freedom of Information Act illustrates vividly the way that what is regarded as constitutional is itself changing, as reformers try to change the constitution. Britain became an official secret society in the First World War. Until then it was a confidential one. But when, for the first time, Cabinet minutes began to be kept, official papers were formally closed to the public. The first result of this was that information on what happened during the First World War was censored and even destroyed. A cover-up began to protect the Generals that remains a lodestone for British government. Its justification is that what it shields is too important to be known, and that the quiet wisdom of the impartial Civil Service would be shattered by the threat of publicity. (Some say that if government really was as efficient, far-sighted and exemplary as it claims to be, officials would be tempted – even eager – to open their papers to scrutiny.)

When it was first introduced, official secrecy was accepted as a necessity for competitive élitist democracy. But as the second stage of rights-based democracy developed after the Second World War, information came to be seen as, precisely, a public right, and it began to hover as a policy issue for the UK itself. The issue was addressed by Lord Franks in 1976. Franks was *the* representative of the British political-administrative élite. When he died in 1992, he was aptly described as 'the undisputed doyen of post-war British fixers'. Among the positions he *turned down* were 'Governor General of the Bank of England, Secretary General of NATO, Director General of the BBC and editor of *The Times*'. His obituary in *The Times* stated, 'He was not just a member of the First XI of the Great and the Good. He was its captain, wicket-keeper and last man in . . . we shall not look upon his like again.'[7] 'Knowledge is power,' Franks stated:

> It is important to recognise that the issue of open government is about power, political power, a shift in power, its redistribution. The government of the United Kingdom has in its possession a vast store of information, and the ability to withhold information and to judge the timing of its publication is a part of political power. Open government entails increasing publication of official information to the press and the public who, with the power given by greater knowledge of the activities of government, are better able to assess, criticise and bring pressure to bear on the government's performance.[8]

In this view, crisply expressed and to the point, the government is seen to be in control. Its power is singular. To loosen this control would be to give voice to the media and public. Such was the decision to be taken, in Franks' view, and at the time few on either side of the argument for and against a Freedom of Information Act would have disputed his description. But today such an Act has begun to take on a further meaning. The failure of Labour to legislate will make the government look weak, even warped, as if living in the past. Whereas twenty years ago a refusal to legislate on the right to know about official information could be respected, along Frank's lines, as a tough-minded determination to hold on to power and control, now it is seen differently. In modern societies, openness increases motivation and leads to better decision-taking (BSE, for instance, might have been avoided). Legislating the right to know is likely to *increase* the legitimacy, authority and hence the power of government to lead and be followed. As Gordon Brown put it after he became Chancellor, 'Information is power and by devolving information, we can help to devolve power and in doing so, make for better government.'[9] Furthermore, when Franks issued his warning, there were no personal computers – there might have been a rat in the store, but no hackers. The Lord Franks model of a vast but passive store of information with one gatekeeper is outdated. A new information environment exists, with which freedom of information will interact.

So, first, catching up. What Franks said in 1976 remains true. Freedom of information reverses the ownership of State information. Officials will no longer be able to decide for themselves what it is best for the public to know. In a country like Britain, where the Crown and not the people are sovereign, a Freedom of Information Act with a statutory right to know subverts the old, top-down presumptions. It *is* about power. But catching up will not return us to a better yesterday. That opportunity was lost. Today, the revolution in terms of power that Franks feared will be less, because Britain is already more decentralised and more open and the need for a different approach to government is much clearer. Freedom of information is also moving ahead in what is now an information-based society. It hooks up to the future at least as much as it clears up unfinished business from the past.

Central to both representation and voice is *effective* voice: the ability to speak and decide with authority and influence. In Britain there is plenty of free speech. Yet, as the Conservative MP, Richard Shepherd, has pointed out, while 'we have freedom of opinion in Britain, we are not free to base our opinions on facts'. The capacity to advocate knowledgeably, to argue with information, to base judgements on the evidence, is the starting point for constitutional democracy and an open society. Equal access to information underwrites political equality and equality of opportunity. This ethical principle is also a practical one. It will lead to better decisions, more effectively carried out.

The point is painfully obvious. Why, then, is resistance so tenacious? The simple answer, in the words of Franks, is that the élite do not want to surrender power. But if power is better exercised and legitimacy greater when secrecy is not the commanding culture, this answer becomes less convincing. Another answer suggests itself. The attachment to official secrecy is a pathological symptom of the dishonesty of the British system as a whole. When the Emperor has no clothes, the discussions of his courtiers must be hidden from view in case the record reveals that they are aware that all the waffle about Royal Prerogatives just comes down to naked power.

For example, everyone knows that the Prime Minister's Press Secretary holds regular briefing sessions with political correspondents. These are formal sessions. But they must appear as indirectly attributed, sourced as 'the Prime Minister's Office'. Under Thatcher they were slightly more obscurely referred to as 'Whitehall sources'. It cannot be said that these sessions are secret, yet they cannot be acknowledged for what they are. In America, the equivalent sessions are televised. Recently the *Guardian*'s political correspondent, Ewen MacAskill has argued they should be on the record here too. The reason they are not, according to convention, is because all policy announcements must first be made to Parliament, because 'Parliament is sovereign'. If the Executive revealed its thinking directly to the press, this would manifestly undermine Parliament's claim to priority. But Parliament's claim is a falsehood. Actually, in Britain today, the Executive is sovereign and Parliament is largely decorative. The media, interested in real power rather than in the pretence, concentrates on the Executive briefings when it can. So of course these should be open – everyone knows this. Yet they seem to remain off the record so as to preserve the pretence of Parliamentary sovereignty. The pretence of the constitution creates further dissimulation that makes openness supposedly impossible. In this way the secrecy of British government does not just cover up falsehood – it is also what can be termed a structure of hypocrisy.

A simple modernisation – televising the routine press conferences attended by all the journalists and broadcasters – cannot be carried out because it would create a constitutional crisis. And this is not the only way that the past holds back the present. As Clausewitz observed, politics and war are part of the same continuum. Discipline matters in short general elections that are the culmination of long campaigns. British politics in particular is a matter of winner takes all. Yet just as a country cannot be run successfully on a war footing, so you cannot lead a country in the same way that you would run a political party preparing for an election. The British political tradition, however, has become imbued with the victory/vanquishing mentality. This has a number of sources.

It is rooted in the Empire that forged the dominant institutions in the nineteenth century. It has been reinforced by the role of war in restoring the regime through the twentieth century (the Boer War, the First World War, the Second World War, the Cold War and the Falklands War). It is kept intact by the knife-edge nature of the electoral system, as we saw in Chapter 4. It is encouraged by the adversarial culture of the House of Commons. It is embodied in the almost military-style concentration of State power in the hands of the Executive. In 1971 the canteen in the Cabinet Office was still called The Mess.[10]

This inheritance is deflating as its traditions ebb into history. It has left us bereft of a public culture that values open political co-operation and can handle the concepts of separate powers and shared sovereignty. It is as if the salt deposits of the retreating flood still sterilise domestic political life. Yet renewal is taking place, unnoticed by the public and within the system. Here I want to recount a story of how I witnessed a moment of renewal that enhanced the ability of MPs to hold Ministers to account. The episode reflects on the relationship of all three classic branches of power, while its animator was the fourth, the spirit of accountability. It also demonstrates an absence – always a hard thing to do – in this case of constitutional intelligence in the media.

It was 1993. I had phoned Anthony Lester, QC, only for him to say that he was too busy to talk. He explained, 'I am about to go to court on the most important constitutional case I have ever worked on. Its concerns whether judges can read Hansard. It is being heard in the House of Lords now – why not come along?'

I thought it was ridiculous that reading Hansard could be important. But Pam Giddy, the editor of *Violations of Rights in Britain*, explained that judges had been forbidden to read Hansard in the mid-eighteenth century, in a ruling that went back to the Bill of Rights of 1689, which protected the freedom of MPs. Perhaps judges really were about to take power from the politicians!

Three of us jumped into a taxi. When we got to Parliament

there was a long line of people waiting to get into the Strangers' Gallery of the House of Commons. We told the policeman that we wanted to see the Law Lords. We were immediately let in and sent down a corridor to a large committee room. There were the Law Lords, sitting in a semi-circular arrangement. Another surprise: none was wearing a wig or gown. At the back there were a large number of empty, uncomfortable chairs. There seemed to be no journalists present and just one or two members of the public.

Anthony Lester and the Attorney-General (both of whom were wearing wigs) were arguing over the meaning of the 1689 Bill of Rights. While its larger purpose was to ensure a Protestant succession on the throne, it also spelt out a deal between Crown and Parliament. One part reads:

> the freedom of speech and debates or proceedings in Parliament ought not to be impeached or questioned in any court or place out of Parliament.

This had led to the historic ruling that the courts could not read Hansard, which publishes the proceedings of Parliament. But it seems that one of the Law Lords had peeked at it. On a matter of taxation, a Minister, in response to a parliamentary question, had told the House of Commons unequivocally that a particular clause meant a modest tax cost. But the language was unclear and when it became law the courts decided that, as written, the law had to be interpreted in a way that was contrary to the Minister's clear assertion.

The government wanted to keep things this way. The Attorney-General argued in favour of preserving a situation in which a Minister could tell MPs that the legislation meant X, when in fact it meant not-X. Think about why the government should want to do this. After due consideration the Law Lords decided against the government. They ruled that, henceforth, when there is an ambiguity in the law, and provided the responsible Minister had specifically referred to that ambiguous passage in Parliament in a way that clarified it, then those words can be read by the courts to assist their interpretation of the law.

There was an entertaining aspect to the case, known as *Pepper v. Hart*. The Attorney-General suggested that an MP's right to freedom of speech would be restricted. A judge asked him if thinking before you spoke was really a threat to freedom of speech. Outsiders to legal philosophy, like myself, need to be careful before we cheer or boo a decision that seems like common sense. For there is a long-standing argument as to whether laws should be interpreted as meaning what they were 'intended' to mean when passed, or whether they mean what they say. This is an especially important debate for constitutional questions. Be that as it may, the British constitutional court – for such it was when it made this ruling – shifted the balance of power in Britain and undid a 200-year-old precedent.

Judges already exercise constitutional power. This is point one. It puts much of the verbiage about the 'absolute sovereignty of Parliament' into perspective. In this case also the court ruled against the government. Yet by so doing it *increased the power of Parliament*. Until now, drafted legislation could say something unclearly and Ministers could say that it meant something different. Whether or not you think such a thing could happen deliberately, the Law Lords' decision means that it can happen no longer. Today, if a backbencher demands clarification of a piece of legislation, then the Minister's clarification carries weight in law. You might have thought it always did. Because it did not, the Executive was shielded from being held accountable by Parliament for the legislation it drafted. The judiciary in this case empowered the MPs, at the expense of Ministers, and increased the ability of Parliament to hold government to account.

The story shows how ill served we are by our media. In the United States or Germany such a case would have been a major news story in the quality papers and in anchor television news programmes. In Britain, few knew it was going on. As we left the Houses of Parliament, we bumped into one of the most intelligent, hard-working MPs concerned with constitutional reform. He was unaware that the case was taking place. Parliament was ignorant, while its powers were being reviewed and changed. The public never had a look-in.[11]

My concern is with the constitution as a whole. *Pepper v. Hart* shows how the details count, and how they go back 300 years. But we cannot look to the past to make sense of the present unity. To do so would be absurd, thanks to the unofficial modernisation that has taken place as the constitution is on the move. The kind of backward-looking, constitutional nit-picking that would rightly make Alastair Campbell shut the book of reform at the first page can be found in the learned attempt of the esteemed constitutional expert Vernon Bogdanor to defend the claims of Prince Charles in *The Monarchy and the Constitution*. The sovereign, Bogdanor points out, should not be referred to as the Head of the Church of England. The monarch is *only* Supreme Governor of the Church, and not 'its Head, which is Christ'.[12] It would be all too easy to be drawn into bizarre disputes with an Oxford don as to who is the governor and who the head of the Church of England; why he uses such funny grammar; and how, *empirically of course*, we might establish the real facts with those concerned.

Discussion of the constitution as a whole can go in two directions. It can examine the joints and gristle beloved of experts, 'which is skeleton', as they might put it. Or, as I will try to do, it can consider the forces that animate the body, always bearing in mind that without its bony substructure, life would fall apart. On to the constitution as a whole then, with the purpose of identifying its distinct components and the issues they raise.

Once the rule of law has been established, there are five discrete areas of a constitution, which can be summed up as: rights, powers, accountability, votes and aspirations. Just as with Freedom of Information, in all five areas the UK confronts a double-act of catching up on the past and preparing for future prospects. We need to assess them in this way. I should emphasise once again that my purpose is to identify the issues, not issue edicts about what is best for Britain.

INDIVIDUAL FREEDOM AND RIGHTS

If voice is the starting point of sovereignty, then it has two sides. It speaks to power, demanding influence – to vote, to call to account and to assess. But it also asserts *a right*: a claim to be heard and to count, however different you may be. Rights matter especially if you are weak, isolated or opposed to the dominant views of the day. They therefore also matter because you might find yourself in this position. One of the glorious moments of Britain 1997 was the desperation of those who favoured fox-hunting as majority opinion swung against *them*. All the notions that the gentry had scorned as ludicrous suddenly walked with green gumboots: it was a workers' movement, country folk had the right to their special way of life, diversity had to be protected from uniformity imposed by the centre. It was a sweet victory for the sixties. 'Let it be' now rode with the hounds!

More seriously, to have a right means to enjoy it as a possession, not a permission: such as the right to speak out or be silent, the right to believe, to privacy, to know, to gather in public, to be innocent unless found guilty. Such fundamental political rights are a claim on the political community, especially by those who are out of sorts with it. The dominant majority has no need for its rights to be protected, for it will exercise them anyway. When written into a fundamental law, rights are a commitment by society as a whole to protect the *equal opportunity* of those who stand outside the majority.

Rights were first proclaimed before there was universal franchise, when 'the rights of man' were claimed against arbitrary, despotic and monarchical power. This sense of rights asserts the rights of the 'whole people'. It was not a minority claim except for conscience. The amendments to the American constitution that are today known as that country's Bill of Rights, and which people in Britain tend to associate with the modern claim of equal rights, were in fact made by men concerned about the possibility of too great a State power arising among them. Their aim was liberty, not equality. The American *constitution* and Bill of Rights makes no mention of individual equality. The word appears only once, and then with respect to States having equal votes in the Senate. The Declaration of Independence famously declared all men to be born equal – and it inspires today. But it had little influence on the laws of America until our own time. One historian states 'only in the mid-twentieth century did the courts decisively expand the definition and protection of equality'. Equality, as we know it, as the claim of equality of opportunity and treatment for all:

> long important in American political rhetoric, has become a core constitutional value only in the last half century . . . Substantive equality, the notion that there is only one community of rights holders, that everyone is entitled to equal treatment in all aspects of life, came to maturity in constitutional jurisprudence in 1954.[13]

The concept of equal rights protected by law is a *contemporary* development everywhere, even in the USA.

The modern concept of rights is based on the need to limit the raw force of 'the People' deployed as a unity in the name of the nation. Today's ideal of inclusive citizenship takes account of diverse interests that must be protected from the dangers inherent in the unchecked machinery of party representation that dominates the nation state. The international conventions on human rights that have been drawn up since 1945 are a response to the holocaust and not, as many in the UK still tend to believe, to the French absolute monarchy.[14] In the US, pluralist democrats reworked the protocols of the American Bill of Rights to eliminate segregation, with its obvious parallels to Nazi supremacist propaganda and policy.

So to argue against entrenching our own fundamental rights, as many still do in Britain, as if what was proposed was an eighteenth-century device, or taking sides in the clash of Burke and Paine, is to petrify the terms of the debate. Thus the Bill of Rights in the South African constitution, adopted in 1996, came out of a movement originally rooted in the Leninist tradition yet it also expresses a democratic reflection on the *dangers* of mass-based revolution. One of those who fought to free South Africa from Apartheid and helped draft the constitution is Albie Sachs. He witnessed other popular struggles in Africa:

> The party would act in the name of the people, and then the leadership would act in the name of the party, and the people got more and more remote. We came to see that the people also had a diversity of interests. There are male people and female people, who didn't always see things in the same way. There are urban people and rural people, not least amongst the oppressed. There were employed people and unemployed people. So one needed factors, criteria, mechanisms and principles to reconcile divergent interests . . .[15]

In Britain advocacy for a contemporary Bill of Rights began with Anthony Lester's Fabian pamphlet published in 1968.[16] Roy Jenkins was Home Secretary and had overseen a liberalisation of Britain's oppressive domestic legislation, but his approach did not extend to codifying a coherent framework of liberty in society. Ten years later, Margaret Thatcher (who, coincidentally, made her first call to limit the powers of the State in 1968) began the liberalisation of the economy. Had they been rigorous in the application of their favourite thinkers, such as Frederick Hayek, the Thatcherites would have embraced their own version of a Bill of Rights, entrenching property rights especially. Once again – as from the other side – an opportunity was missed. But the consequences of arbitrary legislation were more widely perceived as the Thatcher years rolled on. A classic statement of the modern case was made by Leslie Scarman, by now a retired Law Lord, when he responded to an attack by Lord Beloff on Charter 88's Constitutional Convention in Manchester in 1991:

> Max Beloff asks a question, which he wisely refrains from answering: 'Will a single Bangladeshi family in Tower Hamlets feel more secure if Britain has its own Bill of Rights?' I will

> give him an answer. A Bill of Rights would secure to the members of that family protection enforceable in the courts against harassment: their private and family life, and their home, would have the protection of an enforceable law, itself protected by the constitution. Their colour, language, religion and minority status would not expose them to discrimination to their disadvantage in the countless ways in which they currently suffer. Their constitutional rights could be enforced by injunction and, where proved, could earn the remedy of damages by way of compensation . . . They would have the support of a public opinion educated in the fundamental social importance of the basic human rights of everyone present within the jurisdiction of the British state . . . Constitutions are not designed as automatic purveyors of jobs, homes and prosperity. Their purpose is to establish and protect a framework within which government and people can attack these problems on the basis of equality and justice for all.[17]

It cannot be put better.

The question of rights has now become an area of exploding philosophical debate. New forms of rights are being advocated and tested. Against this, the advocacy of fundamental rights so well articulated by Lord Scarman is under assault from communitarians. They denounce the selfish 'rights culture' as an encouragement of egotistical and divisive individualism. Obviously a society without social obligation and reciprocity and leached of any sense of duty would disintegrate. It is sensible to be reminded that rights are not consumer goods, and that a society that wishes to see them flourish must itself be respected and replenished by those who claim 'their' rights. The legal and political culture of rights is new, as we have seen. We are just beginning to learn how to live with and look after them. The communitarian critique of excessive rights-selfishness is salutary, but as it gets into its stride, political communitarianism puts duty to society above people rather than alongside them.

When pushed, communitarians assert that they are not opposed to rights, and even that they support the existence of a formal constitution – if they are American, this almost goes without saying. They are opposed to 'duty-less rights'. Except that when leading British communitarians argue this, they don't take rights as their starting point, and qualify them with duty, but rather defend a version of social sovereignty. Thus David Selbourne, perhaps their leading exponent, draws on Hobbes to authenticate his claim that 'there cannot be two sovereign powers in one society: either the civic order, or its instrument the State, must be supreme'. This is a staggeringly archaic premise. It is like Lord Tebbit's claim that no one 'can serve two masters' in his attack on multi-culturalism. But anyone with a job and a family knows that modern life is about negotiating the co-existence of different sources of authority. *Not*, it seems, for communitarians like Selbourne. He insists that 'the principle of duty' will restore sovereign power to the civic order, as against the State. Any hope that this might relieve us of a repressive, if occasionally beneficial, power is soon dispelled. Civil society courts will be needed to protect 'civic social-ism', as Selbourne calls it. They will ensure that citizens undertake their 'self-regarding duty' to avail themselves of the education and training that their capacities make possible. Courts will decide whether citizens are up to duty and whether 'special penalties, controls and deprivations' are needed if they are not. This sounds very much like the State, to me, only now it appears that it will have the power to decide what is best for me personally. As Selbourne concludes, he is not seeking to *balance* the rights that, say, the Bangladeshi family might claim, with an assertion of their duty to support the civic order. Instead, Selbourne claims that *duty* is, in his emphasis, the *sovereign principle* among all ethical principles on which the civic order is to be built.[18] In this way, while British communitarians present their arguments as a critique of personal rights, they turn out on examination to be apologists for an all too familiar leviathan.

By contrast, advocates of rights support an open society with shared sovereignty. Many would agree with the communitarian rejection of neo-liberalism, which puts the free market above everything, but the answer is not a new form of State control, this time dressed up as the authoritarian voice of civil society. Instead, the listing of fundamental rights is seen as essential in order to protect individuals against the power vested in the State with its wealth, administrative reach and monopoly over coercion. Rights are listed in a Bill of Rights because they conflict. Were this not the case, we could simply say, 'People have the right to be free' and leave it at that. But in all sorts of ways – complex and simple – fundamental rights collide.

If you own a newspaper, does your right to freedom of expression allow you to exclude adverts from a cause with which you disagree, or does this interfere with other people's right to freedom of expression? Do cigarette companies have the right to advertise, as part of their freedom of expression, provided that they make the life-threatening character of their product clear, or does this harm the right to life of the weak and gullible? There is an ancient right to silence, implying that no one shall be forced to give evidence against herself or himself, which goes back to medieval times, to protect individuals from forced confession. This right has recently been removed in the UK. People's refusal to speak may now be held against them, and this clearly alters the balance of power between suspect and police at the point of arrest. The weight of experience tells us that this is wrong and that miscarriages of justice will result. But what if the head of a large pension company, holding assets in trust, is asked to explain various improper transactions? Should he be allowed to plead the right to silence? Does not the fact that he is holding other people's savings place an obligation on him to explain how he discharged the trust? Do the pensioners not have the right to know? Whose right should prevail?

Justice is particular. A constitution will lay out only those rights a society regards as fundamental. Courts then balance the outcome in each case. But there are different kinds of conflict. There are those where the rights of one individual clash with the rights of another. More common and serious is the clash between the individual or family and a branch of executive power, whether local or national. Finally, and most controversial, there is the clash between legislation and basic rights – if Parliament itself passes a law, that may breach a Bill of Rights. Suppose Parliament, to popular acclaim, makes cigarette advertising illegal, yet the courts rule that this violates the companies' right to freedom of expression – who then decides? Mainstream thinking in the judiciary today (unlike yesterday) says that judges should arbitrate the validity of the law. In a sustained account of the application of human rights law in English courts, Murray Hunt argues that it has already become the 'special responsibility' of judges to ensure 'the effective protection of the rights enshrined in the international instruments' and to recognise the 'transformation which has taken place in English legal culture . . . and embrace the constitutionalism which embodies the spirit of the times'.[19]

The danger is that judges will take it upon themselves to become constitutional overlords. Clearly many enjoy the prospect of becoming a hegemonic authority. We are seeing the emergence of judges with attitude. A distinguished academic Jeffrey Jowell has shown how the British judiciary took it upon itself to become the instrument of the administrative State after the First World War and how this was a historically specific, not a traditional, role – one that he also shows is demonstrably coming to an end.[20] Alongside the example of their international colleagues, British judges have begun to make amends for past subservience and regard an increasing part of their role as keeping government in check.

Are all rights so well established then, that they can be placed in the hands of the courts, beyond the reach of Parliament? Surely not, because two processes are taking place. At the legal level the notion of rights is expanding. At the same time, human ingenuity increases power over life and ability to communicate speech and images at will. Conflicts over the use of such powers are bound to arise, and they will be cast in fundamental terms. The South African constitution even states, 'Everyone has the right to an environment that is not harmful to their health or well-being.' The process seems positive, but casting it in terms of rights can be driven by weakness. One party demands that the right to a sustainable environment should be part of the constitution. Who will say 'No'? Who wants to appear to be saying that people should *not* have a right to a sustainable environment? Certainly not politicians, if it will lose them votes. So an unbelievable criterion gets logged in. The case against this process can be summed up in that one word: voice. If judges, whose appointment is opaque, whose tenure is for life, and whose representative character is questionable, rule over an ever-expanding field of rights, they will increasingly adjudicate not just political questions but the most novel and important political issues concerning new powers over life, death and reproduction. Just as the public's capacity to participate in decision-making has increased, thanks to modern technology and education, so the élite threatens to whisk away its say into the hands of a small legal clique. Even if the decisions then handed out are progressive, the method cannot be democratic; it will further alienate people from politics, and give the rhetoric of democracy to reaction.[21]

What began after 1945 as a protective philosophy to ensure the access of all to equal treatment, now runs the danger of becoming a device that deprives people of their democratic say. Nonetheless, fundamental political rights are essential to ensure the claim of free and equal citizenship. And without the prior security of basic rights, demands for responsibility and duty move implacably towards ideological fundamentalism. Only those who are already free can act with responsibility. The securing of freedom based on political equality is the threshold of democracy. It is a sign of its coming constitutional revolution that the British State will step across it, and that a code of rights will finally become part of our law.

The White Paper on the Incorporation of the European Convention on Human Rights will prove as historic a document for Britain as any to be published in the extraordinary year of 1997. The government has sought to protect the powers of the legislature from being directly overruled by the courts. Is it protecting a democratic legislature or a rampant executive? Either way it will claim that the sovereignty of

Parliament has not been disturbed. This then leads on to the distribution of powers.

THE DISTRIBUTION OF POWERS

For the individual, the most important aspect of a constitution concerns personal rights and freedom. For society, the backbone of a constitution deals with the distribution of State power. As the argument on how far the courts should judge legislation shows, rights and power connect – to codify rights means giving judges the authority to say whether the State or its agents are in breach of them. This means that a clash is possible between the judiciary and the Executive, and even the legislature. The issue of rights then turns into one about sovereignty. In Britain this debate tends to take on apocalyptic tones. If 'the power to decide' – here the voice tends to fall to a grave tone – is given to the courts, then we will be 'ruled by judges'. Implicit in this view is the theory that there *can be only* one sovereign source of all authority. Power over the State, by this definition, is a singular endowment. Either Parliament has it, or the judges do. Debate about who is the 'final arbiter' is sometimes presented as a technical matter. Yet it soon takes on that tell-tale language of 'loss' that has accompanied post-war British politics and is shared by right-wing and left-wing conservatives alike. If power is gained by one party, then it must be lost by another. It is the traditional, Hobbesian, view.

But power is *not* a zero-sum substance. It is not a question of: 'it is mine'; 'no, it's mine'. In contemporary society, power has grown beyond such childish arguments. Its character in a post-Hobbesian society is different from the notion of power still lodged in the heads of British politicians and civil servants. The more power is shared, the more it can grow. This does not mean it is conflict-free. It means that power struggles are complex and many of them can take the form of mutual agreement and even co-operation rather than smashing the other side. Britain too is leaving the age of zero-sum absolutism. Parliament's claim to *absolute* sovereignty – the assumption that it is and must be 'supreme' – has withered away in fact and will soon be seen as a denial of democracy. For the term is a fig-leaf for the supremacy of the *Executive*, and already that fig-leaf is so badly weathered that it only achieves the desired cover-up for those who do not wish to look.

We are witnessing the end of the most distinctive feature of the UK's system, one that a legal expert described as 'an omnicompetent and elective legislature'. The legal expert in this case was Lord Hailsham, Lord High Chancellor from 1970 to 1974 and then again from 1979 to 1987.[22] In between, when his party was in opposition, he described government omnicompetence more famously as 'elective dictatorship'.

The new Labour government says that it wishes to distribute power but retain parliamentary sovereignty. It is trying to share out the competence while keeping the 'omni'. Nothing is impossible, but Ministers will find the exercise painful. At present they refer to devolution or decentralisation as if these concepts were interchangeable. They will find that they imply contrasting principles that will have to be sorted. In dealing with rights and legislation, the government can get away with verbal face-saving, while European courts will retain their power to overrule Parliament. We all need cosmetics to help keep the show on the road.

When it comes to decentralising institutional and territorial power, however, it will take more than vanishing cream to overcome the problems that are bound to arise over the coming decade. A democratic second chamber will need to be created after hereditary peers are abolished. The new Scottish Parliament will have a political hue different from that of Westminster. The Mayor of London may come from a different political party from the Prime Minister. This is a healthy state of affairs. It will put pressure on the unhealthy claim that Westminster is supreme.

Power can be distributed between institutions at the same level, like the Commons and the Lords. It can be distributed vertically between local, regional and central authorities. It can be distributed along a vector that strikes between these two directions, to national Parliaments within the polity. The new Labour government is redistributing power partially, but simultaneously, in all three directions. It will reform the second chamber; dynamise a section of local government, with a directly elected Mayor for London; empower the regions with appointed chambers; and create a national Parliament in Scotland as well as a less important Welsh Assembly

The programme's obvious caution is laced with radicalism. A directly elected London Mayor is a constitutionally unprecedented move that is completely at odds with inherited tradition. Ironically, it is the one reform that the Conservative opposition has already supported in advance – clear evidence that the old order has lost its orientation. Abolishing hereditary peers has been attacked as a limited reform. But because it is largely symbolic, it will focus attention on the overall history and nature of the constitution. It is an improvement. Yet it is unsustainable because it further exposes the dictatorial powers of the Prime Minister, which the ermine legions once cloaked with the respectability of the ages.

There are only two ways in which power can be distributed. Either sovereignty is not distributed at all and one central authority continues to exercise unquestionable dominion, which it may lend to others on terms that it decides, while retaining the ability to call it back. Or power is shared. Shared power does not mean equally shared – there can still be a hierarchy of authority. What it does mean is that the higher authority does not have the power to alter the sovereignty of the lower one at will. At present Britain has the worst of both worlds. A central power that claims to exercise authority over every corner of the land – a mantra of the sovereignty of Parliament which is also a pretence that denies the actual reality of permanently shared power with the European Union. The anachronism of parliamentary sovereignty also weakens the legitimacy of the Commons, undermining its ability to hold government to account. Sooner or later an overall agreement will be needed to explain how power is going to be shared, which binds all parties to procedures for the resolution of conflicts between them. Such a contract would be a constitution. At present, as the first great reforms of 1997 unfold, tension rather than resolution has developed in the three main sectors where Labour intends to decentralise – or is it devolve? – power.

1. Lords

What happens to the UK's extra-ordinary Upper House poses the question of whether or not Britain should have a normal form of government, and whether, in so doing, it must be a dull one. Labour's intentions are to do away with the voting rights of hereditary peers, probably in the next session of Parliament (Stage One), and establish a cross-parliamentary group to consider how to create a democratic chamber (Stage Two). In 1995, when a Blair victory first seemed likely, a group of peers, headed by the well-connected Lord Carnarvon, gathered together to discuss how to resist Blair's commitment to rid the country of hereditary aristocratic power. A discussion paper to rally the forces and rehearse the arguments was their Lordships' first step. Until then, they felt, it had been best to ensure that the sleeper did not awake: 'Constitutional debate is not endemic in our national life. For long periods our central institutions are taken for granted. This is a sign of their underlying strength.'

In this self-satisfied way they justified a narcoleptic polity, in which their own mausoleum of self-interest went unquestioned. As they proceeded with their investigation, however, they were unable to discover any contemporary justification for their status – no authoritative confirmation from expert outsiders that they should continue, no sociological evidence that they are wanted by the public, no young men and women to endorse their red leather benches, and no international examples that showed them in a good light. Yet one should never underestimate the guile, stubbornness and audacity of inherited privilege in need of a line of argument. They wrote:

> Hereditary members of the present House of Lords – who are well aware of its shortcomings – would vote themselves into history with barely a backward glance in favour of a reformed House which was more effective, and whose composition commanded wider acceptance, than the present one.[23]

There will be lots of backward glancing; it is happening already. Hypocrisy and bluff have served them well for centuries, so well that they are almost natural characteristics. Their instincts for survival still intact, their Lordships decided that their best form of defence was attack – with the best weapon around, namely democracy itself. Their line of attack is to expose the logic of constitutional reform and dare Labour to implement it, betting that it will back off. By removing the power of the hereditaries, Labour will create a completely appointed Upper House. This is undemocratic and the peers reckon that it will not be accepted by the public. The Carnarvon 'groupescule' – typically, it denied that it had any formal existence, even though it published its conclusions – calculated that it might be able to roll this lack of acceptance backward into the here and now. Labour had promised to proceed to a second stage of a properly democratic chamber. But it has not as yet thought about how to do this. Things constitutional can take generations to change – as their Lordships know full well, since an earlier promise to reform the Upper House was made in 1911! So the great procrastinators, hoping that the electorate are still idiots, express their alarm that Labour's quango chamber could last for generations. How undemocratic – and they should know! Surely Labour *must* tell the people what its real intentions are: how and when they will complete their reforms. Until they do so, 'fully aware of their shortcomings' as they are – indeed, chock-a-block with their renowned modesty – the hereditary peers will have a duty, in the name of democracy itself, to reject Labour's proposition. In December 1996, Lord Cranborne, the Tory leader in the Lords and a Salisbury by lineage, made a barely disguised threat to bog down Labour's programme, while kindly suggesting:

> Were the Labour Party to win the next election they really would be better advised to abandon their plans to stage one and concentrate on developing plans for a second chamber that demonstrate a little more coherent thought on their part.

Thus the line of resistance concedes: 'Of course we are undemocratic and have to step down.' Then it adds, 'provided that we are replaced by something that is genuinely democratic. Until then, we must try to protect the public from the arrogance of power.' However hypocritical it may be coming from their Lordships, it is a good argument.

Surely Labour should first decide how it will replace the Lords with a democratic chamber? Otherwise it will create an Upper House that is so pliant and illegitimate that it will expose the government to the charge of dictatorship. However, replacing the Lords raises thorny problems. In effect, it starts to put the entire system of government on the line. Briefly, if it is directly elected, the second chamber will become an alternative focus of authority to the Commons, and Britain may end up with American-style deadlock over legislation. To avoid this, and to limit its role to scrutiny and approval, the Upper House could be elected indirectly, on a regional basis as in Germany. But Germany is a federal republic with regions and Britain is not. The Labour approach to the regions is that they are likely to be offered the possibility of some self-government only if they choose it by a referendum. This decision cannot be pre-empted via a new Upper House. To have a new Upper House also poses the question of what to do about the Law Lords. At present they sit as a constitutional court as well as a court of last appeal, and contribute to the legislation via the upper chamber. How could this set of fused roles survive in a new Upper House?

Designing a democratic second House is not a traditional sort of partial reform that the old constitution permitted. It will mean drawing up a blueprint for a new centre of power. This will affect other parts of the constitution. Logically, it would be more sensible to draw up a new overall settlement first, which defines the role and character of an upper chamber, planning the whole before building the parts. As no one except the Liberal Democrats is proposing this, Carnarvon and his chums are rubbing their hands in anticipation. Unable to change everything – which would be most un-British, even unpatriotic, think about the Queen! – the government ought to change nothing; at least as far as they themselves are concerned.

Fortunately, Labour seems oblivious to the impeccable logic of their Lordships. Perhaps because they know that if they go into the next election, at the start of the twenty-first century, saying, in effect, 'New Labour has changed its mind and decided that hereditary peers are wise and, anyway, we want our children to be legislators without people having to vote for them', they would be laughed at.

Fear of being laughed at is an occupational hazard for politicians. As a non-politician I can float a suggestion for reform of the Upper House that most politicians would fear. It is well off the radar screen of current British politics. Nonetheless, I make it in order to show that thinking about constitutional reform can be enjoyable. Also, I want to focus on the most important question about a second chamber. What should its powers be? Because the question of how to elect a second chamber should follow from a principled definition of what we want it to do.

There is an argument for not having one at all. From Tom Paine to Tony Benn, there is a populist approach that states that the people should elect one assembly, which is the representative of 'the people'. Nothing, then, should stand in its way. Experience suggests, however, that the people most prone to fits of panic, mob reactions and foolishness, aside from journalists, are politicians themselves – a second House empowered to check such excesses is essential.

My premise is that the dominance of the House of Commons is an accepted part of British government and that it will remain the prime site for legislation. A number of functions then remain for a second chamber, such as:

• *Scrutiny and constructive revision*

Legislation needs to be scrutinised to ensure that citizens can understand what it means. And, to test through debate and listening to evidence, whether it is likely to achieve its stated purpose.

- *Full and free debate*

There is an occasional need for set-piece debates to act as a focus on areas of public concern where there may not be legislation and where the adversarial structure of the Commons is unhelpful.

- *Limited capacity to delay and exceptional power to refuse legislation*

The Lords at present has the power to delay legislation, which it hardly uses, although it does symbolically send legislation back, which the government usually just forces through. This general power of delay has become otiose. A new second chamber should be able to return legislation with a specific request for the government to think again, which obliges the government to do so by reformulating its arguments to meet the objections (or accept amendment) But the general power to impose a two-year delay should be abandoned. On the other hand, any new upper chamber should have the power to reject outright legislation, or parts of legislation, that would undermine fundamental constitutional principles, such as the right to equal exercise of political choice – it must be able to pass what can be called 'the Poll-Tax test'. A second chamber that was simply unable to stop a such disaster is too powerless to be justified.

The Poll Tax was not simply a staggeringly costly political blunder. It also drove hundreds of thousands from the electoral register. When it was under discussion, the Home Office produced a Cabinet paper expressing its concern that it would be seen as 'a tax on voting'.[24] When the Conservatives' narrow victory became clear on election night in 1992, Margaret Thatcher was quoted by the *Sunday Telegraph* as saying, 'The Poll Tax worked after all.'[25] Even in the United States, which has notoriously unfair electoral laws, the Poll Tax would have been ruled unconstitutional.[26] It was a flagrant abuse of power, quite apart from its other inadequacies. A reformed system of government needs to be able to prevent such abuses on principle. So while a renewed second chamber should not have the power to reject or block the policies of the government, it should have the democratic authority to protect basic constitutional principles, if the government goes off the rails.

One way to create such a chamber, that would not compete with the Commons but would be able to exercise legitimate scrutiny on the above lines, would be to select one by lot. This can be termed the Athenian Solution. In classical Athens there was a 201-strong governing jury drawn by lot on an equal basis from each of the city state's twelve tribes, so that as well as being a random selection of the citizens it was also a *representative* body, drawn in proportional fashion from the free men of the city state. In the 1990s, experiments have begun with deliberative assemblies, representative bodies of citizens asked to come to a view, or take decisions, after a concentrated presentation of evidence.[27] A British House of Peers could draw members by lot on a regional basis in proportion to each area's population and with gender equality. Recently, different proposals on these lines have appeared independently, perhaps because the proposal is the democratic version of the one positive virtue of the existing House of Lords – that it is not made up of professional politicians.[28] The point is not that random selection is better than election, but that elections already take place to the House of Commons. If a second chamber is to be a constructive addition, and not a destructive alternative to the electoral primacy of the Commons, it may benefit from being less party political. When watching the House of Lords debating its own future in 1996, I was amused to see Lord Cranborne, who was leading for the government, coyly suggested that hereditary peers are such 'normal people' these days that they could be compared to the Athenian jury! This was a further example of the audacity of privilege. Even he knew that he was pushing his luck. If it is randomness that is to be recommended, there is no doubt that we can do better than the present occupants.[29]

The government is right: the sheer number of hereditary

peers, their reactionary and Tory bias, their self-seeking role, their pious proclamations of disinterest – none of this should have a place in a modern democracy. So out with them! But neither is the absolute sovereignty of the Executive a modern form of democratic rule. By removing the hereditary peers, Labour removes the cover from its own inheritance of royal power. It will need a new second chamber that does not simply put the cover back on. I have floated one suggestion, and there need to be others, so that instead of clinging to the wreckage, a free and stimulating debate about the future of Parliament can take place.

2. *Regions*

As Jim Bulpitt demonstrated in his now classic account, *Territory and Power in the United Kingdom*, English local government was developed as an applied form of the 'indirect' rule developed in the colonies. This allowed the natives to administer themselves under the control of the imperial authority. Bulpitt shows how the same pattern was re-created at home. Many good measures were taken and aldermanic chains distributed. But they were confined to what he calls 'low politics'. The 'high politics' of strategy and co-ordination was strictly and jealously guarded by Whitehall.

There seems to have been only one moment when decentralisation became a reality. When war broke out in 1939, regional authorities were created to wield executive power in case of invasion. They became the co-ordinating agencies of the war effort and organised the response to emergencies brought on by heavy bombing. A. J. P. Taylor believed that the organisation of the war 'would not have worked without this system':

> Administratively it was a vast improvement on the historic arrangement, where nothing was interposed between the central departments in Whitehall and the elected local authorities of the counties and country boroughs. But . . . the regional commissioners were abolished at the end of the war

> . . . and the chance was lost to give England the blessings of regional government.[30]

Without it, the term 'local government' reeks of administrative contempt. No one identifies with their local government, which is a planner's phrase. 'The local' means the pub, if it means anything at all. Political decisions that are within one's own reach, whose impact one can see, are a starting point for involvement. Most such popular influence has withered to a shadow. The big cities especially, where most of the population lives, have been evacuated of practical democracy. Few understand how, and by whom, decisions are taken. Levels of participation and voting are accordingly derisory compared to other European countries – not because people are not interested in local politics, but because there is little in local politics for them to be interested in. The Commission for Local Democracy made the point. The ratio of elected officials to the population in the UK is 1:1,800. 'The average in other European countries between 1:250 and 1:450.' Voter turnout in local elections is around 40 per cent in Britain. In no other EU country does it fall below 54 per cent (Holland) while in most it is close to 70 per cent (France, Germany).[31] Why is this? Because other countries have a genuine politics of place. British politicians talk about community, but in local terms they might as well be worshipping pharaonic tombs – looted both of the dead and of all inanimate valuables as well. The first deeds of community action, such as knowing a local representative, remain alien experiences in Britain.

I am fed up with hearing MPs, whom most people regard as somewhat extra-territorial as it is, say, 'My constituents have never asked me for more regional government.' Only the rude tell someone that a different sort of person should be doing their job. The abstention rates *are* saying something. They are saying that community politics as it is organised at present is meaningless. Perhaps the only way to communicate the point is by putting it in market terms. Local politics is a wonderful site for effective voice. Yet what people have to say is made irrelevant in our over-centralised country. As Stephen

Dorrell, then Tory Secretary of State for Health, put it in a special speech in defence of the constitution:

> The Westminster Parliament is currently the decisive voice in every part of Britain not just in economic and foreign policy, but also in health, housing, education, law enforcement, social services, and a wide range of other fields of domestic policy.[32]

This being the case, why bother with local elections for administrations stripped of 'decisive voice'. It is not Parliament that should have the decisive voice, in all local matters it is local electors. Deprived of it, electors can either buy (vote in) local elections or 'exit' from the market of local politics, to use the language of economics.[33] By choosing to exit, they reject the product called local politics. It is not the buyers who are disinterested and apathetic, but the manufacturers of local government, who are 'bankrupt'. In any market situation, the enterprise concerned would change the product, not blame the consumers.

Deputy Prime Minister John Prescott is now overseeing the regions. He is a keen advocate of regional economic development but less so, at the moment, of political decentralisation. Typecast as a traditional shop-steward Labour bloke, Prescott was transformed by the opportunity of further education at Ruskin College and became an appointed member of the European Parliament before it became an elected body. For many upwardly mobile Tories, a career in politics represents a narrowing of their options, compared to the choice of finance or industry. This is one reason they are so keen to defend Westminster's mythical power to do what it likes. But for Prescott, politics has been a broadening of experience and he can understand the need for new arrangements that empower people 'on the ground'.

But for local and regional government to sustain a revival in the UK, it will have to become constitutional. For the idea of community to have political meaning, there has to be a transfer of real power and initiative. This must mean the ability to raise and spend money. As accountability has improved, so has the ability to track and report on specific revenue sources. The popularity of hypothecated taxes – of paying a tax specifically targeted for the NHS or education – is evidence of an English interest in 'doing something' about a problem and believing that concerted public action can then achieve this. As one expert on citizenship put it, 'hypothecated taxes are the fiscal equivalent of referendums'.[34] The more local they are, the more interesting local government will become.

Trust the people! When this was uttered as a Tory catchword at the end of the nineteenth century it contained a note of irony. It meant trust them to trust 'us', and trust them not to rock the boat. Now the same words need another meaning. Trust must be vested in people locally to renew government outside Whitehall. The question at issue can be put simply – decentralisation or devolution? In a consultation document *A Choice for England*, Labour floated its ideas for the encouragement of regional government. Well-meaning and, in part, creative, it considered the prospect of Spanish-style decentralisation, in which the regions choose for themselves what level of self-government, if any, they want. But the weakness of Labour's constitutional understanding was illustrated by the way it included an example of 'Conservative support for regional government', as if this would make the case more acceptable. It cited ex-Premier Edward Heath, who once stated, 'Devolution gives communities the right to exercise greater influence over the way in which they are governed.'

This nicely sums up the *old* Labour and Conservative attitude. The right to a bit more 'influence' is, of course, no right at all. It is merely a concession that your opinion will not be dismissed out of hand. 'Communities', in Heath's traditional view, 'are governed' – and they had better know it. They are the recipients, and not the initiators, of their own government. It is done to them – not by them. The phrase of Heath's old enemy, Enoch Powell, summed it up: 'power devolved is power retained'. In this respect the two Tories were at one: when it comes to the exercise of power at home, sovereignty is not to be shared.

On the other hand, when power is decentralised, it finds its own roots if the soil is responsive. Decentralised power is different in kind from the indirect form of power-sharing that the British State has utilised since the nineteenth century.[35] The familiar forms of indirect rule and devolved power developed then are accountable upwards, to the central State, which retains the monopoly of high politics. Decentralised power, by contrast, is accountable downwards, to the citizens. Obviously, there can be devolved power where positions are filled through local elections, and decentralised power that is regulated by a central framework of defined functions. The critical factor is that decentralised sovereignty is sovereignty shared, however unequally, between the centre and the locality. For the centre loses its absolute control: to rewrite the rules, to abolish, to pay what it wishes.

The larger the decentralised local authority, the more challenging the relationship between it and the centre. Hence the explosive potential of a Mayor for London directly elected by five million people. Technically, traditionalists will hold that Parliament retains its absolute power. But in fact the scale of the democratic mandate will shift the real relationship of legitimacy. Deprived of a powerful administrative executive, the Mayor will seek to hold the capital's quangos to account, to encourage bold strategic renewal, co-ordinate democratic initiatives, handle issues of tension and inequality within the city, and link up with the mayors of other, similar European cities. This brief is the politics of voice, rather than the humdrum, low-level practical problems that have, until now, been the domain of local government. It is high politics hence its radicalism.

Even if the government denies it, the hitherto ruling principle of British domestic administration will have been reversed by this reform. Primaries, whether official or unofficial, may select the main party candidates. Voting will have to be preferential in some form or another, as Londoners vest their choice in a representative with a far greater constituency than any MP. Could the government then abolish the position of Mayor if he or she became troublesome but remained popular? This did happen with the abolition of the GLC. A decade later, it was that astoundingly undemocratic move that led to the even more radical innovation in Labour policy and to the new government's Green Paper. Any attempt to repeat such an abolition ten years on from now is likely to precipitate an unstoppable, popular call for a more permanent settlement. This time, we are offered city-based democratic sovereignty, quite unlike the precept-funded GLC. As the natives throw aside indirect rule, the constitution will never be the same again.

3. *Nations*

Scotland has led the way to constitutional reform in Britain. The Union was formed when Scotland joined with England in 1707. Tom Nairn has argued that the Union is now likely to break up as a consequence of the new Parliament in Edinburgh. He makes a supple, historical case rooted in his familiarity with the national forces at work across the UK and Europe. It is a view that rests on a growing body of international scholarship, which has shown how nationalism, while it has regressive examples, is not the anachronism that élites in large, historically early nations tend to view it as. The nation is a motor of development, of 'being modern', to use a New Labour phrase. In Scotland's case we need merely note that it was Old Labour that was a determined opponent of Home Rule. A larger comparative overview suggests that it is the *hostility* to national determination of domestic affairs that is backward, regressive and old-fashioned. The same social, cultural and economic forces that have propelled New Labour towards a more relaxed, pro-European, non-monarchical culture in England are also propelling Scotland towards its own Parliament, and – if necessary – statehood.

So the first thing to say about Nairn's case is that irritated dismissal is misconceived. He does not foresee the short-term electoral success of the SNP. On the contrary, he argues that 'Home Rule is far too serious a matter to be distracted by Independence'. His thesis is that Scottish Home Rule is likely to lead to the break-up of Britain because *Westminster* will prove incapable of altering its own character so as to make a success of decentralisation. Instead, it is likely to continue to regard Edinburgh as a subordinate, even engorged 'local' body until it is too late. Unable to accept Scotland's voice as a suitable interlocutor with its own, the Westminster élite, Nairn predicts, will continue to regard the Union as a singularity and not as an evolving partnership. This will then drive the Scots out.

I have suggested that his argument is overly pessimistic.[36] It is also one that is difficult for the English to understand. Constitutional brain cells have been so stunted south of the border that many English flip from 'What is the problem?' to 'If that is how they feel, kick 'em out', and a vapour-ridden lament that the English are now the victims exploited by greedy Scots. In her novel *Orlando*, Virginia Woolf imagines her hero being given perpetual life at the end of the reign of Elizabeth I. Soon afterwards James VI of Scotland came to the English throne as James I. If we imagine that a couple had been granted a similar immortality, and that, after a century-long engagement they married in 1707, we can reflect on their relationship as a new millennium hoves into view. The weaker partner had no property rights, let alone the right to divorce, at first. Of course, she played an important role in the reproduction and success of the family, and benefited from it. But she was not her husband's legal equal. In the nineteenth century, when women around her began to claim equality, she spurned such new-fangled ideas. Then, after the middle of the twentieth century, with the family estates in decline, she thought, 'Why not?' After a false start followed by twenty years of wrangling, her husband finally concedes her a public, legal voice. She remains weaker and smaller, while he still earns more. But she has changed since 1707 and wants the equality of a late twentieth-century marriage. She wants to stay married, naturally, after all the centuries of psychological investment and family picnics around the world. The real question is whether her husband Mr England Britain wants to renew his marriage to Mrs Scotland Britain in the same way that she does. Does he any longer regard it as a Union, or has he, over the years, forgotten the courtship and come to regard 'the wife' as nothing more than a subordinate? Now she has joined the conversation as an equal voice, and her appearances in the front room are no longer limited to performances at which she wears funny skirts, what will happen when there is a disagreement, for example over whether he takes his trips to Brussels on his own? Must she still plead with him as she did before, or, when there is a disagreement, will both sides now see that it must be solved by *mutual* agreement, as in a modern marriage? If not, then her legal voice will lead her towards full independence ('If you *won't* let me come with you to Brussels, then I will go on my own!'). Especially if he responds by saying, 'I earn more money than you, you benefit unfairly, therefore, if you want more independence, I will cut your allowance.' At present he is displaying the pathology typical of such a husband, veering from aggressive threats to show her the door to lachrymose complaints that he is the injured party. If this attitude continues, any guidance counsellor will predict that the relationship is soon likely to end. For it implies that he regarded her as a kept woman of convenience all along . . .

Another English criticism is that it is all exaggerated. The Scottish Parliament will not be very powerful. Unable to do much, it *will* settle down as 'another tier of local government'. Here, Nairn's response is convincing. Because the Parliament will not have much direct administrative work, it will be all the more concerned to become the voice of Scotland. To prove itself, it is bound to seek a defining role, just like London's Mayor. The dynamic behind the creation of the Scottish Parliament lies in the feelings of the Scottish people. It is not being created in order to overcome administrative difficulties, or to ease problems at the centre, as has usually been the case with Westminster-style 'devolution'. It will be a real Parliament, either within or – if necessary, then without – the UK.

The government's White Paper, *Scotland's Parliament*, and

the substantial endorsements in the referendum on 11 September of both a Parliament and its proposed financial power suggests that it will be a real Parliament. Bold in its presentation, clear in its proposals, a pleasure to read, the White Paper radiates self-confidence. The lessons of the abortive attempt at devolution in the 1970s have been learnt, not least by Donald Dewar, Labour's Scottish Secretary of State. A veteran of the earlier battles, he drew on the cross-party efforts of the Scottish Constitutional Convention established with the Liberal Democrats, a precursor of the Cabinet's constitutional committee now meeting in Downing Street, which has brought the Liberal Democrats into planning future constitutional reform. Their influence and experience will be unfairly under-recognised, as Blair's mastery of the media sweeps all before it. (It will also be under-discussed in these pages, which are not a history.)

In contrast to the Welsh proposal – which was a half-loaf – the Scottish White Paper has helped to provide high-quality momentum that will feed back into England. It has also been an object lesson in the influence of political culture. For in addition to the exceptionally creative, patient and determined national pressure for the peaceful construction of a Scottish Parliament, their call for reform and decentralisation *has* been recognised and acted on in England. This is the first reason to think Nairn may be overly pessimistic. James Cornford's work as Director of the policy think-tank IPPR, and then in overseeing the creation of the Constitution Unit, is one unsung contribution. At the unit, established specifically to consider the difficulties that a Labour government will confront, Robert Hazell oversaw the publication of a series of authoritative reports which transformed practical understanding of constitutional legislation. The Scottish White Paper benefited directly from the unit's recommendation that the Act should list only the powers Westminster will decide to retain; that there had to be a procedure for disputes established in advance; and that a short, powerful Bill is more likely to overcome English objections.[37] The actual White Paper states, 'All matters that are not specifically reserved will be devolved.' English preparation has already contributed to the reform of the Union – a welcome sign that there is recognition of the need for a new relationship in the South, as well as in the North.

The White Paper not only assigns legislative power over devolved matters, it also agrees that the Scottish Parliament will be able to 'debate a wide range of issues of interest and concern in Scotland, whether devolved or reserved'. This gives the Parliament voice, even in areas where it does not exercise power. It will, for example, be able to debate the advantages of even greater tax-raising powers than it has or, more obviously, the issue of Scottish independence. It does not have the authority to decide such issues – foreign and constitutional sovereignty reside with Westminster. But if the White Paper had limited Edinburgh's freedom of speech to those issues within the proposed legislative remit, it would not have been a Parliament at all. As it is, those who drafted the White Paper took the necessary risk for Scotland to identify with its coming national assembly.

One significant limit has been placed on the Scottish Parliament's ability to legislate on domestic matters. Although health is obviously domestic, 'abortion, human fertilisation and embryology, genetics, xenotransplantation and vivisection will be reserved' – in other words, they will still be decided by Westminster, because, the White Paper adds, 'of the need for a common approach'. But surely this is an area where uncommon approaches might be called for. That bio-ethics should become an area of dispute in the Cabinet committee drafting the White Paper vindicates the arguments developed by Ulrich Beck in *The Risk Society*. Across the world, he shows, the politicisation of the previously non-political is under way, in the environment and with respect to the human body especially. Biological and medical ethics are today areas of important differences and unpredictable outcomes, no longer issues that the public is willing to abandon to experts. It is a hot zone for 'voice'.

From Hume through Ferguson to Adam Smith, Scotland can claim to be the home of the moral economy. If there is anywhere on the planet where politicians can draw on a politico-cultural tradition capable of a sustained discussion of bio-ethics, it is in Edinburgh. And in its vicinity, large mammals have just been cloned for the first time. A Parliament with close on 50 per cent women, non-adversarial in its style, perhaps with a practice of insisting that those who speak must then attend the rest of the debate, with a crowded chamber of those who are well educated (this being Scotland) yet dour in repartee, could conduct the equivalent of an intense teach-in on the issues posed by medical ethics in today's world. As witnesses, they will be able to call on the world's most experienced genetic engineers on their doorstep. The proceedings could become a reference point in a debate unfolding everywhere. To forbid such a chamber from then acting on its conclusions, but instead to insist that it must bow to the empty benches and vacuous barking of the House of Commons, would make the world shake its head in disbelief. The English should want Scotland to debate and legislate in this area. We can all benefit, whether the new Parliament establishes exemplary rules or instead demonstrates the stupidity of Presbyterian fundamentalism.

But whether the English want this or not is beside the point, should the people of Scotland themselves want it to happen. This is the key question. If they do, it will. For if they do, and the English government persists in saying that they cannot, the Scots might choose to decide from outside the British Union.

Scotland alone is sufficient to conclude that Labour's reforms will not be assimilated in the manner of previous reforms of the British constitution. Partial reforms have hitherto renewed the old order. They have quietened, not encouraged, the demand for further change. A Scottish Parliament will sit apart. Its impact will generate new problems. It will inflame the English to call for some kind of parity, despite their own dominance. It will inspire those English regions avid for their own development and voice. England will have to alter the internal character of its own constitutional arrangements or the Union will break up in some fashion: either the Union State will become pluralist, or it will lose its multinational character. This is the choice facing the UK over the coming decade. It is a welcome one – a crisis that has the possibility of a positive outcome inscribed in it from birth, unlike the Irish crucible.

The second national reform is in Wales. Here, Labour conceded in advance to the opposition to Welsh home rule and watered down its proposals. If a low turnout can resound, then the abstention in Wales on 18 September was thunderous and led to the slenderest possible majority for the Yes campaign, scored by a mere quarter of the electorate. There were special reasons for the opposition to a Welsh Assembly. The principality is linguistically divided, historically and institutionally more integrated with the UK than Scotland, geographically split, economically settled by the English, and so on. There are three Wales, according to John Osmond of the Institute for Welsh Affairs: 'Welsh Wales' of the Valleys, 'Welsh-speaking Wales' and 'British Wales'.[38] The first two voted Yes, the third No, to the Assembly. At the same time, right across Wales, when they voted people divided generationally, with youth on the side of the Assembly.

The London media took the outcome as a signal of regional opposition to decentralisation and a reason for the government to slow down its programme of reform. The resounding Scottish vote, and the current 80 per cent support for a London Mayor, are exceptions, according to this received wisdom. Wales is the rule. There is indeed one sense in which this perverse analysis accords with reality. The Welsh turnout was comparable to the pathetically low arousal ratings of British local government. For the biggest vote of all in Wales was abstention – representing a good half of the population. Here was a truly historic opportunity to initiate a representative body for the country – and most people stayed in bed. This was not opposition. If there had been strong opposition, the proposal would have been crushed easily. It was indifference.

Before those opposed to decentralisation welcome the

Welsh outcome as proof that people do not wish to be citizens, and prefer deference to the wisdom of Whitehall and its appointees, they might reflect on the evidence. When offered the real thing, response rates rose towards Scottish levels. An NOP poll taken across Wales in the week before the vote prefigured the very close result. It found only 37 per cent in support of a Welsh assembly, with 29 per cent opposed and 24 per cent don't knows. But it also found a much larger 57 per cent support for an assembly 'with law-making powers'. The lesson seems to be that the less people are offered, the less interested they are. Further evidence of the intelligence, not the apathy, of the electorate.

The new Welsh Assembly was ratified only by the skin of its teeth, but the grain of opinion is with it. In the 1970s, Wales voted by four to one against an assembly. A much larger turn-round of opinion took place than in Scotland. Young people are on the side of an assembly, and there is already, the poll suggests, a clear majority favouring an increase in its power. The energy points towards success. There is a good chance that the Welsh will make a mess of the Assembly thanks to the depth of their divisions and lack of an overall national culture. But there is a better chance that they will make it work. This will then rebound back, to secure the kind of changes needed in Westminster to enable a plural constitution to emerge that will also ensure constructive relations with Scotland. If Wales had voted No; if there had been no proposals to give London its voice; if the government was not committed to a Bill of Rights and was seeking to keep the House of Lords as it is – then Nairn would be right to argue that an unchanging Westminster is unlikely to adapt to the rise of Scotland. Instead, reformers are able to thank the thousand voters in Wales who made sure that the constitutional revolution was not aborted before it began.

ACCOUNTABILITY

In one of the earliest attempts to describe a secular constitution, Montesquieu praised Britain in his *The Spirit of the Laws* published in 1748. He defined three activities – law-making, governing and judging – being carried out by the legislature, the executive and the judiciary. In London, he said, instead of these activities being fused in the authority of a single monarch and his Court, they are carried out by different bodies. He described this as the separation of powers. The concept greatly enhanced constitutional understanding. It provided a theoretical structure, which in turn justified the independence of the rule of law – and Montesquieu's analysis helped inspire the American constitution. But Montesquieu got Britain wrong. He failed to perceive how the Glorious Revolution had preserved some of the old fusion of powers, especially between legislature and executive. A hundred and twenty years after Montesquieu, Bagehot trumpeted the real nature of his country's constitution, in contrast to America's:

> The efficient secret of the English Constitution may be described as the close union, the nearly complete fusion of the executive and legislative powers. No doubt by the traditional theory, as it exists in all the books, the goodness of our constitution consists in the entire separation of the legislature and executive authorities, but in truth its merit consists in their singular approximation.[39]

Both Montesquieu and Bagehot wrote prior to the advent of democracy (which the latter despised), but at least they understood the term. The creation of modern, large-scale government would have been beyond even Bagehot's comprehension. Its regulations and responsibilities go well beyond the apparatus of authority of the old State. It now reaches into every corner of society, with total expenditure of between a quarter and a half of the national economy. It guards infants and pays pensions. When the local-authority nurse comes round to observe your new-born child, you know that government is expected to check on, if not protect, every vulnerable life when it can. It may be costly, but it is money well spent.

But is it well spent? Those who endorse the essential role played by government in protecting a fair standard of living wish to ensure that expenditure is not wasted or corrupted, just as much (if not more) than those who are hostile to State expenditure of all kinds. The information revolution has heightened our ability to set and monitor standards. There is a growing awareness of how public expenditure can be suborned. Voters are more conscious than ever before of the consequences of good and poor regulation, in health and safety matters especially. The public wants to know about the impact of welfare on motivation and long-term outcomes, it wants accountability for the consequences.

Accountability has become a new branch of government. It can be added to the three outlined in *The Spirit of the Laws*. Elections have provided the ultimate, after-the-fact weapon for holding government to account. But elections are crude devices, and the civil servants and bureaucrats who take the administrative decisions can still remain shielded from responsibility. As society becomes increasingly knowledge-based and reflective, demand grows for a better kind of responsiveness from officials and for more transparent assessment of their work. A battery of measures is being created to monitor and improve administration, from the development of administrative law since the 1960s, 'the most rapidly developing area of public law in this country',[40] to the so-called reinvention of government. The call for freedom of information is linked to the same demand to hold power to account. An independent statistical service and the National Audit Office are parallel mechanisms. Citizen's Charters, although pioneered to provide 'remedies not rights', are also devices of accountability for everyday users. Now experiments with Citizen's Juries are taking place to explore democratic methods of assessment.

Accountability in this sense has three characteristics. It is ongoing, rather than occasional. It is about getting the right results, rather than punishing errors. It provides a direct bridge between citizens and the State or local administration, unmediated by politicians. We are familiar with the State sending out its inspectors. Now accountability inspects the State.

From earliest times politics has included a strong element of this, as leaders have been obliged to give an account of themselves. But previously such accounting took place in two constrained arenas, at least in Britain: at elections, when governments asked to be returned to office; and in Parliament, where Ministers answer questions. Public accountability has now left the political arena to become a permanent, ongoing aspect of democratic government. In doing so, one issue has begun to be posed above all others. Will the new techniques of communication and feedback take the politics out of power, or will they put democracy into administration? This is a fundamental question about the character and authority of the reformed or reinvented State. The authors of *Reinventing Government* extol the methods of business: 'Democratic governments exist to serve their citizens. Businesses exist to make profits. And yet it is business that searches obsessively for new ways to please the American people.' Their explanation for this paradox is money: 'Why is it this way? Simple. Most public agencies don't get their funds from their customers.'[41]

Their solution is to reorganise State services so that these simulate market conditions – for example, by building in continuous accounting of results, including consumer satisfaction, such as response times, waiting lists and other league tables. In this way, government provision will build accountability to the public into its motivation.

Without doubt the methods they propose are an advance on the oppressive treatment that monopoly services once doled out to the public. But there is a clear danger in turning the citizen into a customer, especially in a country like Britain where people are not even full citizens yet. Approaches that present themselves as being neutral have a built-in tendency to be reactionary. The reinvention of government is no exception. In a cautionary overview, Peter Miller has pointed out that there are no accounting 'solutions'. Even trying to attribute true costs remains controversial, and 'we should ask whether the technologies of distrust that pervade the new public sector are appropriate to services as diverse as sewage disposal and medical care, refuse collection and school teaching.'[42]

This is a welcome warning from a professional in public accounting, against the notion that there are impartial answers to social and political issues. But the apparent promise of American techniques were leapt upon by upper-class Conservative politicians, who saw in them a new way to reproduce their traditional approach to government, that of monopolising power while ensuring consent. When he was responsible for the Citizen's Charters, William Waldegrave argued that:

> Services are not necessarily made to respond to the public by giving our citizens a democratic voice, and a distant and diffuse one at that. They can be made responsive by giving the public choices, or by instituting mechanisms which build in publicly-approved standards and redress when they are not attained.[43]

In this way a Minister depreciates democratic voice in contrast to monitored services, as if these are alternatives. In effect, Waldegrave advocates the latter in preference to democracy. Some of his predecessors used to praise Mussolini for making the trains run on time, even though he abolished elections. Their tone of approval prefigured the more refined appreciation of the reinvention of government that can be heard today. It can be seen as modernisation without politics.

In two ways such modernisers have a case. There was, and remains, a danger that services will be taken over by producer interests, which then run them for themselves rather than for the public. Prison officers should not run prisons, nor doctors and nurses hospitals. These institutions need to be directed on behalf of the public with publicly accountable controls. (The same argument applies to the Permanent Secretaries at the top of the Civil Service.) Second, there is anyway a secular decline in party politics, now reinforced by the demand for responsive services and open and accountable administration. The new methods of accountability cut across tribal allegiances and whether organised from above, or giving new form to voice from below, they undermine traditional adversarial politics.

The gleam in the eye of those in power is not so sociological. They can spot the possibility of controlling the polity through mechanisms of market responsiveness. Through the use of focus groups and opinion research, they will register their voice privately and observe the trends of opinion on the graphs projected onto the screens at their policy assessments, before those opinions have had time to express themselves publicly. In the short term this will tend to silence public resentments. Eventually, as with environmental issues, citizens will start to organise their views through their own modern pressure groups and other forms of highly geared and well-focused response, not least in direct action aimed at the television screen.

Television is altering the way that power accounts for itself to the people. (The press has a different impact because it is not live.) The *image* of accountability has become part of policy and as a consequence the television interviewer has become a professional who holds power to account, or fails to. Clearly, the media has a growing constitutional role as the mediator between power and the people. No constitution specifies what this role might be, except to safeguard its special freedom. But if holding the government to account is becoming a constitutional role of the media, what does this signal about its responsibilities?

Finally, the national focus of public accountability remains Parliament. The Commons has been extraordinarily weak in holding governments to account as the State grew. Part of the frustration with its adversarial rituals is that they fail to bite on real decisions. Since 1979, Select Committees have begun to ask officials (and experts) to answer for and explain policy. The power of such committees is still weak, the growth of their role further evidence that this area has an autonomy and impetus of its own. The accountability of those in the highest offices goes to the heart of government and I am going to consider the most extraordinary study there has been of it in Britain, the Scott Report, in the next chapter. Increasingly, politicians and civil servants will find the demand for independent scrutiny of *their* affairs too strong to resist.

When the call was first made for a new settlement in which the people, not the Crown, were sovereign, it seemed rhetorical rather than plausible. Accountability is fast developing a variety of forms that have started to make democracy more plausible, helping it to become informed as well as direct. By undermining representative, party-driven politics, this process is dissolving the old system of centralised rule in favour of new forms of sovereignty.

VOTING

Casting a vote is becoming more frequent and variable. During the next four years a Londoner will be able to vote in a referendum on having a Mayor. If the proposal is endorsed, Londoners will then be able to vote in elections for the Mayor using a form of alternative vote. The elector will also have a vote in European Parliament elections in 1999 using a proportional system, probably a regional list. There may well be a referendum on the national voting system, so that the elector votes on how he or she will vote in future general elections. It is even possible that the next General Election itself will be held under a new system. There might also be a referendum on joining Europe's single currency. In addition there will be elections to the new London-wide authority, and the usual local borough elections.

Different *kinds* of votes, different *systems* of voting, different *sorts* of representatives. This admirable confusion reflects the democratisation of democracy. Two issues are posed in the question of voting. How can regular citizens intervene directly in the questions that affect their lives and the destiny of their society? And what sort of representation do people wish to have, given their growing awareness of the complexity of life and the multiple influences at work upon them?

The first great democratic exchange at Putney in 1647 was over who should have the vote. It continues to this day, with arguments over how votes can have an equal value and ways of ensuring that the franchise is proportional.[44] This debate, to which a few have dedicated the best portion of their waking lives, is coming to a head with the creation of a commission to report on the best possible alternative to the UK's ridiculously unfair system of first-past-the-post. The outcome will have a profound effect on national politics. Roy Hattersley, who supports the existing voting system, sees two rival views: 'Should the people, by a first-past-the-post system, directly choose the Prime Minister and the party of government or should they, through proportional representation, create an electoral college, which makes that choice for them?'[45] This argument defends the existing system by turning elections into a form of referendum on, as Hattersley puts it, competing party manifestos. (This, of course, undermines the historic justification of electing representatives in the first place, whose role was to be independent.) The core of the argument is that proportional representation will create a Parliament that will have no single-party overall majority. The Commons therefore, not the electorate, will become the arena for choosing the government. Hattersley defends the status quo as providing a *more* direct voice to the voter than proportionality, which will end up in 'backstage deals' (they are no longer in smoke-filled rooms).

Given the alienation that people feel from politics, their disbelief in manifestos and their growing ability to judge front-of-stage deals, Hattersley's view is over-traditional. The best way to ensure that voters have a direct say in the choice of competing views is to have referendums on major policies, and voters know and like this. The underlying public culture within which the argument about electoral systems is taking place is itself changing enormously. Three issues stand out: the new role of referendums (two having made a significant contribution to the changes of 1997); the disenchantment of the electorate, especially with the kind of manifesto politics that Hattersley recommends; and the future reform of the voting system now about to be considered for the first time by an official, independent commission.

Politics is being transformed by referendums. They remain potential plebiscitary devices of the kind that reinforced fascism. But, in a fully constitutional context, the danger of their becoming undemocratic is diminished. Britain's referendums are part of a global phenomenon and signal the normalisation of the UK's politics. Across the countries of the world, in the five decades from 1920 to 1969, there was an average of fifty-seven national referendums per decade. In the two full decades since the 1960s, the average rose to 165. This is precise evidence to date the onset of the democratisation of democracy.[46]

It links up to a revolution in the way in which citizens' views are registered. This too, like the development of continuous accountability, weakens party politics and the exclusive claims of representative democracy. But the values of more participatory decision-making remain confused. Fairness is one principle. All should be able to vote with equal effect. Participation is another. Do we all need to take part to reach a fair decision? Citizen's Juries and deliberative assemblies are techniques that could allow a representative sample of the electorate to decide an issue after hearing all the evidence over a number of days. They offer the prospect of fully informed decisions taken by regular people, a much more sophisticated process than single-question referendums.

To ensure fairness, rules are needed, and financial controls over expenditure are essential so that outcomes cannot be bought. Once referendums become constitutionally regulated – and in a number of countries referendums are needed to alter the constitution – the sovereignty question follows. Who should have the right to call them? In Italy and Switzerland referendums can be triggered by citizens' initiatives. Should the right to referendums belong to the people, or remain in the pocket of politicians? And while they sound like a shared way of resolving differences that cut across party lines, referendums also contain the seeds of antagonism and divergence and their use in California shows that they can be exploited to secure privilege.

Behind all these questions looms the issue of turnout – of who votes. Increasingly younger people are abstaining from politics altogether, as the vote is being presented to them as a symbol of commitment to the system. They do not want to make the pledge. Increasingly, too, the marginal, the dispossessed, the homeless are not able to vote. The underclass is growing, but it is not on the march. Instead, many who are on the edge, say, 'Fuck the system, I'm not going to register.' They believe that they have found their own voice. In fact, they are reading lines from a script written by the status quo. Behind the mock outrage at such behaviour, the wealthy laugh up their sleeves, drink a toast to the stupidity of the poor and enjoy a sound, warm sleep. The last thing they want is for those living outside on the pavements to register their opinions in elections.

Disenchantment, marginalisation and abstention, intensified (as we saw in Chapter 2) by the expenditure of vast sums on negative advertising, create a vicious cycle in which the 'irrelevance' of elections is proven by the numbers who abstain. Divisions will harden around the lines of exclusion. Harsh divisions will regiment a society into sameness on the separate sides of the divide, as within each social bloc demands are made for a common front towards the other. Liberty and relaxation cannot be acquired behind the razor wires of American-style housing compounds. Freedom requires that all of us not only have an equal right to a vote that counts but that everyone does vote. Returning officers should be obliged to ensure this if they can.

The best way to do so is through compulsory voting. In Denmark, Greece and Australia there is a legal obligation, although voters are free to spoil their ballot papers and thus say 'none of the above'. The liability for fines on those who fail to turn out is light, the policing minimal. But the obligation is there. A similar measure should be introduced in the UK. The British system has functioned to deprive voters of their sense of relevance, and alienation is understandable. The demand that the young 'should' register has a touch of presumption. Instead, the obligation of the electorate to make their choice should be codified.

What system should be used? In a massive study of 8,000 voters taken as they left the polling booths on 1 May, the Democratic Audit re-ran the 1997 election on a range of different voting systems. The results showed that the Additional Member System is the only alternative that would have produced a fairer outcome. Leaving the outcome aside, there is one advantage to this system from the voter's point of view. A citizen voting in an election is doing two things at once. First, electing his or her own representative for the constituency and, second, making a choice about the government of the country. The AMS system allows this double-choice to be clarified by giving the voter two votes: one for the local representative on a straight, first-past-the-post system, as we have at present; the other for the outcome that the elector wishes to see in Parliament. Another system, called the Single Transferable Vote, gives electors a sophisticated choice over a number of candidates. The Democratic Audit paper, *Making Votes Count*, describes the various methods, and the outcomes they would have led to in the 1992 and 1997 elections. Any form of proportional representation (PR) means the composition of Parliament will better reflect the views of voters, the electorate will also have a richer and more interesting vote. Certainly, the outcome can produce a stalemate or a coalition. But the *voters* can learn from this and re-think accordingly. And meanwhile the existing system also produces weak governments. John Major attacked the idea of PR in the House of Commons on 20 February 1997 and claimed it would lead to governments depending on small parties. A few shouts reminded him that he himself led a minority government that depended on the votes of Ulster Unionists. He scurried on. The British system confines voters' choice to the crudest, most patronising form possible. This is why PR is not only essential for a fairer, if never perfect, House of Commons, it will also be an important step towards transforming subject-natives into citizen-rulers.

ASPIRATIONS

Along with Britain's, the next major constitution about to be written down is Europe's. Because the Brussels élite has no democratic mandate and distrusts popular sentiment, it is likely to go about writing the European Union's constitution in the wrong way. But because it is familiar with institution-building, it will also proceed with its task in a more forthright intellectual fashion than Britain's Establishment would do for the UK. The two are opposites. Britain has a lively tradition of thrashing out arguments in public and of puncturing pompous grandiloquence – it may not have a democratic constitution but it has a democratic culture. The EU, on the other hand, has almost no democratic culture but it does not suffer from the constitutional illiteracy, institutional nostalgia and regressive symbolism to which the English Establishment clings, in the hope that it can keep things as they are. At any rate, it is an Englishman, Frank Vibert, who has produced an early, book-length, formal account, *Europe: a Constitution for the Millennium*, that examines the way forward for the continent's government. 'A key purpose of a constitution,' he writes, 'is to express the fundamental values of the political order. They provide a basis on which all can agree that the endeavour of political association is a good endeavour. They help legitimise the political order.'[47] This aspect of a constitution – its expression of purpose and values – is what I term its aspirations.

A society's constitutional aspirations need not be included within the written document when it has one. But all constitutions explicitly or implicitly provide an ideal, a vision of the political order to which the country aspires, however far it may fail in practice. Vibert compares different sets of values and plumps for prudential, precautionary ones, rather than high ethical principles. He takes the approach that James Madison argued for, after he had helped draft the American constitution in 1787:

> In framing a government which is to be administered by men over men, the great difficulty lies in this: you must first enable the government to control the governed; and in the next place

> oblige it to control itself. A dependence on the people is, no doubt, the primary control on the government; but experience has taught mankind the necessity of auxiliary precautions.[48]

These precautions – the US's famous checks and balances – would make for a dull country if America had only its constitution as its governing document, with its calibration of the slave as worth three-fifths of a free person; dull and even oppressive. But the US also has the Declaration of Independence, drafted ten years before:

> We hold these Truths to be self-evident, that all Men are created equal, that they are endowed by their Creator with certain unalienable Rights, that among these are Life, Liberty, and the Pursuit of Happiness – That to secure these Rights, Governments are instituted among Men, deriving their just Powers from the Consent of the Governed . . .

These words are not precautionary or prudent at all. The declaration remains a model expression of a spare yet exhilarating set of aspirations. The constitutional values of America are, therefore, not contained within its formal constitution alone. To take a different, modern example of the expression of constitutional aspiration outside the formal constitution, it is striking that the South African constitution has a brief sentence on the inside cover page of the edition that went out in millions of copies to every household: 'One *law* for One *nation*'. This phrase, with its italics, is not contained in the legal constitution itself, although its preamble includes a more wordy version of the same intention. The curt phrase sums up the aspirations of the entire country seeking to recover from Apartheid.

A society may aspire to be obedient to God or to Allah, and to live out His values on earth, or to a classless society organised by the party. It might simply aspire to survive, or, if it is imperialist, to conquer. Britain, without a written constitution, has no accepted set of words. Instead, 'Rule Britannia, Britannia rules the waves' jostles with 'God save the Queen'. The latter wins, as the official national anthem. The aspirations of the British constitution are embodied in the monarchy and its surrounding rituals: she or he, who 'interprets the nation to itself'. But such expressions are now becoming collector's items. Here is a recent one from William Waldegrave, made when he was still a Cabinet Minister and MP, after Charles and Diana officially separated. He accepted that, like the rest of us, Charles is made of human clay, but:

> it is not to the fellow human being that we bow our heads, or in whose name our laws are made; it is to the mighty symbols we have asked them to embody for us that we pay allegiance . . . the British royal family is . . . an institution we are going to need more, not less, in the future. Far more will change in the next fifty years than will stay the same . . . The things we will need to know and understand; these things will change with ever more terrifying pace. It will not be possible or right to seek to resist many of the changes. But if we are to keep our sanity and our sense of community then we must preserve our ability to demonstrate practical allegiance to the age-old aspirations to unity, to service, and to those values higher than self-interest. The British way of doing this has been, and remains, above all by offering our allegiance to the Crown . . . By carrying the symbols of our highest traditions, its representatives help us to have a vision of what we should be.[49]

This description of the monarchy as embodying 'our age-old aspirations' is full of pathos – as well as being ridiculous. The hyper-importance that Waldegrave gives the monarchy is not traditional at all. He sees the universe changing and the Crown as the last bulwark standing against the tide of change, like a pillar for us to tether ourselves to, in order to prevent our sanity being swept away in a community-less future. Our aspirations to unity, service and values higher than self-interest (such as doffing our cap to old Etonians like himself) are embodied in the mighty symbols animated by the royals.

In its heyday, the monarchy was *never* seen like this. On the contrary, it was at the symbolic apex of a fully working order, of Church, Army, aristocracy, City and Empire that represented the future as it expanded and enforced its domination. Today, in the Waldegrave version, instead of being a symbol, the monarchy has become a substitute, an isolated last stand. In this role, the human character of those who wear the crown matters all too much. The pressure this puts on them is insupportable. How can they represent 'a vision of what we should be'? The aspirations embodied in a constitution set out a way of life and social organisation within which, whether citizens or subjects, a clear majority aspire to find themselves. Britain's old regime provided this because, while hierarchical and class-bound, it also worked. The monarchy symbolised a promise: to know one's place but also to belong; to behave properly but also to be part of a country that ruled the waves, or at least beat Hitler. It was a lucrative social order in which it was a privilege to be included. When it issued titles, people were proud of it. Now, most people with titles are embarrassed by them. 'Don't call me "Sir" ', they will say, or 'Lady', in conversational situations. If they insist on it, they would probably be regarded as peculiar, as having airs and thinking themselves better – meaning socially and intrinsically better – than the rest of us. Knowing this, intelligent, forward-looking people with titles do not wish to be regarded with abhorrence and so avoid the use of the handles before their names. How can the monarchy represent this modern feeling when it stands for the its opposite?

This is why much of the discussion about how the monarchy 'can modernise itself' is so teeth gritting it is humiliating even to read it. Take a two-page survey in the *Daily Telegraph* of the views of 'Establishment figures' about the royal family after Diana's death, and 'what changes might be made to bring them closer to a nation that still values its monarchy'.[50] One authority says there should be fewer royals to whom one has to bow. Another 'would go even further and abolish curtseying altogether'. This is revolutionary stuff. All insist that 'style and attitude will be crucial'. Sir Anthony Jay, 'an ardent Monarchist', is convinced that Charles should dress 'much more informally when appropriate'. Others feel that this is not enough to do the trick. Some 'Former courtiers who have known both Prince Charles and Diana well, insist that the change must go much deeper', so the *Telegraph*'s correspondent informs us. And just what is the deep change they must undergo to modernise themselves for the democratic age? 'They have got to learn to look interested in what they are doing.'

What planet are these people on, craving glory for licking the golden plates? The conservative advisers whom the Queen prefers are probably wiser. At least they can see that selling off a palace or giving the Gloucesters the chop is not going to make any difference. Another form of 'modernisation' is also proposed, of a kind that, as we will see in the conclusion, is being floated independently by other figures in order to manage the constitutional crisis. This is the classic Establishment move: create a private committee of . . . well, people who can be trusted like themselves. Former Cabinet Secretary Lord Armstrong told the *Telegraph*:

> I'd like to see the Queen appoint a much wider group of outside advisers. There could be perhaps 10 of them, certainly limited to the number who could comfortably sit round a dinner table with five or six people from the Palace. They'd be people she could grow to like and trust [Me! Me!] they could meet every six months and they'd give her additional eyes and ears to tap into national life. The only proviso would be that they were prepared to be totally discreet.

This is desperate stuff. Fifteen people, at least ten of whom are tapped into national life, discussing whether one should have to curtsey. Can this be the vehicle of Britain's aspirations? Such is the fate of our mighty symbols.

I return to the question asked in the Mall, after Diana's death and quoted in *The Times*, which expressed the view of millions of reflective men and Worcester Women: 'We knew how to behave. Why didn't the Queen and the rest of the royal family?' It is not a revolutionary query, or a Jacobin interrogation. It is not the kind of pre-revolutionary sentiment expressed by Russian peasants who thought their ruler was being a 'bad Czar'. Failing to understand the implications of this guileless disappointment, the rulers of Russia went to their doom. British rulers have not made this mistake since 1688 – having learnt the lessons of the Civil War that preceded it. Pathetically, they seem to think that this is what they are faced with today: that the top royals need to be better at being royal in modern conditions. But the spirit and message of the notes and letters, pithily summed up by that question are not deferential in style. 'We knew how to behave' is a different kind of message. It means that people have moved on from believing that the monarchy is better than them. It means that a change has occurred. Most of the British public still like their royals but they no longer defer to the political values of royalty in the same way – they need formal, democratic aspirations.

Britain is now a relatively open society, while the monarchy represents a relatively closed system. Britain is now a relatively egalitarian society, while the monarchy stands for a hierarchical one. This incompatibility is not going to be resolved by Charles wearing more informal clothes, or by the Queen, who is seventy-one, spending the next twenty years 'learning to look interested' in poor people.

What *are* Britain's aspirations and how will they be expressed constitutionally? The royal family – the traditional, non-political, pre-verbal resolution of this question – has ceased to provide the answer. Because Britain's culture is still so pre-constitutional in the modern sense, thanks to residual but still massive royalism, the best way to illustrate the importance of the answer resides elsewhere: the European Union. At present the Treaty of Rome states that participating members will strive for 'ever closer union'. Britain signed this treaty and its meaning is clearly federalist. More than this, it is liquidationist so far as nation states are concerned, for it implies a never-ending process of dismantling differences. Today, European courts use the injunction to help them interpret decisions. Like all active aspirations, it is a surprisingly influential force. As a proper constitution is drafted for the EU, it may deepen this aspiration. There seem to be two possibilities: either EU members can aspire to a Europe that integrates its peoples as one people and strives to create an even closer union that aims to supplant national differences;

or it can aspire to be an association that aims to encourage the development of its member nations within the shared structures of the union. It is clear, therefore, that what the EU aspires to matters. Well then, what does Britain aspire to? The answer to this question is constitutional.

I now realise why books on the constitution tend to be lengthy. There is so much more that needs to be said: about the police and security services, international finance and the constitutional role of the banking system, local government, the role for quangos in modern government, the ways in which welfare can encourage or demobilise recipients. The Army is especially important and remains undiscussed. As does the BBC as a constitutional institution of central influence, transmitting voice and authority – but is it that of the Establishment or that of independence?

My purpose has not been to provide a systematic account of modern government that would survey all this and more. I have simply tried to show how a constitution is a complex unity that provides a changing framework for the relationships of citizen, locality and State in terms of voice and representation. The extent and nature of a constitution are not adequately described by the three branches of government: the legislature, the Executive and the judiciary. In Britain the legislature has almost ceased to have an independent existence. The Executive is a huge body of administration, while the judiciary is threatening to become a law unto itself as it connects to the international circuit of legal standards. Within this trio, it is the Executive that demands the most attention. One of the commanding *aspirations* of the old constitution was that Britain would be governed by a clean and competent Civil Service recruited and promoted by merit. In the next chapter I will look at why we need a new constitutional framework, by showing how the present one is irreparably fractured especially in this respect. Britain can no longer rely on the old public-service ethos to guide its politicians and administrators. The machinery of State has lost its constitutional gyroscope; issues of responsibility and accountability are confused; buck-passing is standard, secrecy essential to hide the mess. There are still considerable assets to draw on, nonetheless there is a fundamental disorientation at the heart of British government.

There is one final issue, however, that has to be dealt with in clarifying the nature of a constitution. This is the notion that it is impossible for Britain to have a written constitution. It is the kind of point that experts love to make to puncture idealists. Even if a written constitution is a good idea, they say, feigning sadness, it could not be done. Bogdanor again:

> The British Constitution can be defined in eight words: 'What the Queen in Parliament enacts is law'. It is largely for this reason that we have no codified constitution; for there would be no point in having such a constitution if its provisions could be amended through the same procedures as ordinary, non-constitutional legislation.[51]

We should beware of such seemingly casual, yet devastating asides. Niels Bohr, the Danish physicist, once said that 'an expert is a man who has made all the mistakes which can be made in a very narrow field'. The technical phrase for the argument that Bogdanor endorses is that no Parliament can bind its successors. It alleges that if Parliament were to declare a constitution, this could still be ignored by the next Parliament because nothing could be done now to limit its absolute sovereignty.

This is obviously untrue. Parliament could call for a constitutional convention that would promulgate a supreme written code which, once endorsed by referendum and passed into law, would bind the institutions under its jurisdiction, including Parliament. Indeed, the famous flexibility of the old order makes this possible rather than ruling it out. Anyway the expert claim that no existing Parliament can bind its successors is not so expert after all. De Smith and Brazier's standard account notes that the issue is 'difficult' and that 'an orthodox opinion does not become unassailable merely because it is widely held by distinguished authorities'. They point out that 'a fundamental change of a political nature may bring about a fundamental change in legal doctrine'. What they mean is that the sovereignty of Parliament is based on legal decisions and that the law can change. For example, the courts might decide that an earlier parliamentary decision *does* overrule a later one, and if the courts so decide, then this will be the case.[52] This view is supported by another authority who accepts there is force to the argument that, 'if an Act were to be passed requiring, say . . . a referendum before the law on a given subject could be amended, a future parliament would be bound by such a requirement.'[53] Indeed, this may have already happened. The 1973 Northern Ireland Constitution Act states, 'it is hereby affirmed that in no event will Northern Ireland . . . cease to be part of the United Kingdom without the consent of the majority of the people of Northern Ireland voting in a poll held for the purpose'. The wording has been described as a fundamental pledge in official papers. It clearly implies that it is binding – 'in no event' can Parliament relinquish Ulster without prior consent. Whatever Bogdanor thinks.[54]

In addition there is the fact of being in the European Union. The British Parliament has agreed that EU law is superior to its own. If its Acts conflict with the rulings of the European Court, British courts have already ruled that what the Queen in Parliament enacts is *not* law. And so the power of the current British constitution is not summed up by Bogdanor's eight words. The argument that Parliament can always leave the EU, and thus see its powers remain intact even if they have been suspended for the moment, is quite beside the point. For there is no intention of leaving the EU. On the contrary, the fact of near-irreversible membership, on current probability, and the growing pressure inside the EU for it to draft its own constitution, provide two of the strongest reasons for writing a British constitution as soon as possible. And if I have done anything in this chapter, I hope I have shown that the exercise can be as stimulating as it is important.

7
Ours is Broke, a Story of Nerve Gas and Eton

> If I might say so, the gassing of the Kurds acted against the country and then one says, is it really a very, very different guideline in substance?
>
> Margaret Thatcher, giving evidence to Sir Richard Scott

'PARLIAMENTARY SOVEREIGNTY IS a busted flush.' This is the brutal conclusion of the magazine that Walter Bagehot used to edit, *The Economist*.[1] It won't be too long before everyone recognises the truth contained in its stentorian verdict. The Commons is fast losing its legitimacy, its standing and authority, as its power to make and check the law evaporates. Bagehot celebrated the 'close union, the nearly complete fusion of the executive and legislative powers' but it was a fusion of equals. Now we are looking at the subordination of the elected chamber, as legislation is reduced to a chore that places only a marginal drag on the Executive.

Bust within and bust without. For Parliament now shares its sovereignty with the European Union, as it agreed to the superiority of European law over its deliberations. As Enoch Powell put it:

> In 1972 Parliament, including the House of Commons specifically, in the most comprehensive manner by statute destroyed the parliamentary sovereignty of the United Kingdom by vesting the overriding power of legislation, the overriding power of jurisdiction and the overriding power of taxation in an external body.[2]

In a pungent essay that has the qualities of an adieu, he adds, 'This was not something which I personally believed the House of Commons would or could ever do.' He intimates for the first time that there may be no reversion, no promised land lying ahead, even after his lifetime. One does not need to share his regret to recognise the truth of what he describes.

Yet Labour's Lord Chancellor, Derry Irvine, says that incorporation of European Human Rights into British law 'must not disturb parliament's supremacy'. As if that historic supremacy is as fine and dandy as ever it was. The supremacy to which Irvine refers is formulaic. Already the Commons is the site of the submission of the legislature to the Executive. The claim of the 'supremacy' of Parliament raises rather than resolves the issue of democracy, therefore. A strong party system has knee-capped the power of MPs to hold Ministers to account. With the Lords otiose, the supremacy of the Commons means the supremacy of party. In modern conditions, the supremacy of party means the supremacy of the leader. And if basic rights do not disturb the supremacy of the leader, then this is not England.

But it is England, which leads on to another fracture, for the distance between official talk and real talk will be constantly exposed, as politicians dissemble. Peregrine Worsthorne, at least, was frank about it:

> Telling the truth about the reasons for Britain's fishing policy, for example, would almost certainly involve telling Parliament a murky story which any self-respecting minister would rather not tell; and, if told, would cause one hell of a stink . . . in short, the myth of parliamentary sovereignty would not long survive if ministers always told the truth. So perhaps it is a mercy that even the best of them do not do so.[3]

The proud language of the front benches has become a joke. The English enjoy frankness. Worsthorne's language reflects this, as does the laughter offstage at the truth of his remarks. The trouble is that even those who snigger will put on official language, like official robes, when they have to talk from the front bench themselves.

Especially in relation to Europe, British leaders feel obliged to stick with pseudo-patriotic formulas about sovereignty and their version of 'no surrender'. Even Labour reformers have found themselves drawn into claiming they will 'preserve' the sovereignty of Parliament in the context of the EU. The need for consistency obliges them to repeat that same formula in relation to Scotland, or the Lords, or London government, or Freedom of Information and fundamental rights. The issue of sovereignty and Europe came to a head in the General Election campaign when John Major delivered his extraordinary twenty-minute address to the morning press conference on 16 April. Usually all the parties began with a senior spokesman reading a brief statement. Major's intervention was exceptional and was presented as spontaneous. (Apparently he had rehearsed it some time before in the Cabinet Room, with advisers pulling their hair out.) But he spoke without notes, steadily, with no 'ers' or 'ums'. He has a first-class back-of-the-envelope mentality. It was weirdly impressive. On the one hand, he listed the advantages and, on the other, the disadvantages of the single currency.

The *Daily Mail* had just launched its Battle for Britain, Tory candidates were declaring their undying opposition to joining the European currency, and pressure was mounting on Major to do the same. He was obliged to hold his line of 'negotiate and decide'. This is indeed a sensible, traditionally Conservative, pragmatic attitude. It drew from Major a forceful expression of a fundamental principle that I had never heard a politician advance: the uncertainty principle, although Major did not put it in philosophical terms. He claimed that with great ventures one cannot know the outcome. The Euro might turn out to be a great success. What, then, if Britain remained outside: 'Can anybody honestly put their hand on the heart and say that they know for certain what the outcome would be?'

Did he *want* the Euro to succeed, though? This was the central question a true national leader would have to answer after he put down the pros and cons on his envelope. Major passed over the question in silence. Instead, having insisted that we must keep our options open in case things went right for the Euro, he turned to the drawbacks if it went wrong. One was that it might fail. Another that it might suceed, yet in doing so claim further powers, such as a uniform fiscal policy and tax system, thus transferring direct control of public expenditure to the EU:

> Would that inevitably be entailed to a decision to go into the single currency? I have to say to you that these are practical questions that genuinely do touch upon a word often abused but right to use. They genuinely do touch upon the sovereignty of the British nation and upon the sovereignty of the British House of Commons. I can tell you upon those issues, upon those practical issues which beyond doubt touch upon the sovereignty of our Parliament and our nation, the question of the transfer of fiscal policy, the question of tax and spending, there is no question whatsoever that I would advise my Cabinet, and my Cabinet would agree without a single shred or word of dissent, that such a transfer would not be acceptable to the British nation.

Now Britain is not fiscally untouched by the EU, which already has some control over VAT. This is not a minor detail, as it explodes the actuality of Major's distinction, but it is a mere fact. Major was addressing an obsession. That poor, abused word, sovereignty. Our food, health, agriculture, working week and international trade policies are decided in a legally binding partnership with Europe, and now even our currency could be, but still our sovereignty would not, according to Major, be 'genuinely' touched. Whereupon suddenly a line appears. No, more than that, he promises that it will be a trench, a Hadrian's Wall, a Dover cliff, a never-in-a-thousand-years, they shall not pass, here we stand, at this point the beer is warm – and nothing else would be acceptable to the British nation. A border-line.

This simply is not credible. The term sovereignty has become a conceptual cul-de-sac for British politicians. If you take the Austinian or Powellite view of sovereignty's absolute nature, Britain's participation in the EU *already* represents a 'comprehensive destruction' of it. The Conservatives lay claim to this spirit of absolutism in words. But they did not in deeds. Their claim that sovereignty has been preserved is bogus. For some it survives up to and including a single currency (if that is a success) but no further, as Major claimed during the election. For others it survives up to but *not* including the Euro, as some of his more 'sceptical' colleagues would believe. In reality, British national sovereignty *is already shared*. The traditional conception of supremacy is dead.

Long live the new one! The transition – far from being all loss – is a multiple gain in power and influence as well as civilisation, though *not* yet in democracy, where the critique of the EU is well founded. Instead of making a fist of this, and giving the old principles a decent burial, British political leaders continue to leave old claims undisturbed, frightened to expose any rigor mortis. Don't disturb Uncle Sovereignty in his high-backed chair, they tell us, for he has sat there for as long as we can remember.

The funniest form of this argument is the old saw, 'If it ain't broke, don't fix it'. The linguistic appeal to cowboy utilitarianism bears the hallmark of patrician striving for the common touch. When Brian Mawhinney was still Chairman of the Tory Party, he told a television interviewer that proportional representation should not be introduced for the elections to the European Parliament. Searching for a reason he declared, 'If it's not broke,' and then paused, as if he realised that more conviction were needed. He raised his voice an octave, '*why*' – then another, tiny pause, to make it seem that he was thinking the words for the very first time – 'mend it?' It was like a screen test, in which an amateur actor is asked to make a cliché seem spontaneous.

Well, the old British constitution is definitely broke and conceptually bust. Renewal – and replacement where necessary – is called for. The means are at hand, and reconstruction is already beginning. Nonetheless, it is essential to drive home the argument that the constitution *is* broke because of the humungous scale of self-deception and wishful thinking concerning it. To show that its central concept of sovereignty is unable to withstand scrutiny is not sufficient. In this chapter I will try to illustrate the way in which its all-important culture of government is now risible; how general surveys show systemic failure and comparative backwardness in human rights and the distribution of power; finally, I will use the massive evidence of the Scott Report, whose implications remain undigested, to look into the heart of British government and show how the aspiration for a clean, efficient and honest administration has been betrayed.

The culture of government – three examples

Once, when the word 'sterling' stood for quality rather than 'crisis', the British could argue that their country was among the best governed in the world. We did not have democracy in the formal sense. We were privileged to enjoy something that made it unnecessary: a law-abiding society with a government that was honourable and even capable. Other countries have constitutions that include fine words like freedom, equality and the right to free speech, which exist on paper but not on the pavement. In Britain we were privileged to have it the other way around.

How was it done? It was done because we knew how to do it – or, rather, 'they' knew how to do it. There is a succinct, contemporary justification of the unwritten order. It was made by Lord Mackay, John Major's Lord Chancellor. He was opening a two-day debate on the Constitution in the House of Lords on behalf of the government in July 1996. He described the way Britain is ruled and placed singular emphasis (the italics are mine) on the people who run things and their reliability:

> In the absence of a written constitution in the conventional sense, we place considerable weight on practice and convention. The judgement, discretion and good faith of those operating our constitutional arrangements is of the greatest importance. It is a strength rather than a weakness. It inculcates mutual recognition and understanding of the respective roles, and permits flexibility and adaptation to developing circumstances. As long as we have *people* in public life with the *necessary qualities* – and I believe that we are very

> fortunate in this respect – I think our arrangements work at least as well as, perhaps better than, many others.

Mackay had a reputation for exceptional integrity as Lord Chancellor. Discretion, good faith and fair judgement are in his character. Yet his Scottish upbringing was far from the fleshpots of today's English public schools. So in questioning his description of the way we can rely on government by People with the Necessary Qualities – for short, PNQs – I am not saying there cannot be such chaps, Mackay is proof to the contrary. I am suggesting that the very fact that his character is described as rare should alert us to the likelihood that others are not like him.

What is the normal PNQ like? In the absence of a written constitution we place a special trust in them, as Mackay describes. Yet the very 'flexibility and adaptation' of the species means that they are difficult to observe in action. Meeting one on a sunny day is likely to be a pleasing experience, naturally. But the test of their constitutional reliability comes when the pressure is on them in a tight corner. Modern societies would normally regard it as a nonsense to base their government on the 'judgement, discretion and good faith' of State employees. They have written rules and professional investigators. Proposals that similar measures are needed in the UK are dismissed with remarks to the effect that critics 'do not know how things really work'. But how do they work? Do PNQs pass the test? Can they demonstrate that their discretion and good faith are up to the job of ensuring clean and effective government? One example of failure would not be sufficient, as it would be dismissed as an exception. Perhaps three will suffice.

Case 1: Tim Smith

The first test of government by PNQs is to see how they react when dealing with someone who has done wrong. The Downey Commission into parliamentary conduct seemed a good place to look. It found Neil Hamilton guilty and was widely praised. No one, to my knowledge, has criticised the men involved: the Commissioner himself, Sir Gordon

Downey, and his Counsel, Mr Pleming, QC. They are outstanding PNQs.

They had to look into what Mackay calls 'our arrangements' and consider the action of the ex-Minister Tim Smith MP. He had admitted that he took at least £18–25,000 of undeclared cash in envelopes. The machinery of investigation turns out to be the Commissioner, and a small team of his legal council and a secretary. For them to do their work there has to be an 'complainant'. MPs did not give the Commissioner the power to investigate wrongdoing in Parliament for himself. Instead, a member of the public has to prepare a case before anything can be investigated. This is a daunting if not prohibitive task (undertaken in this case, 'reluctantly', by the *Guardian*). A cynic might suspect that this alone was sufficient to undermine belief in the 'good faith' of Parliament. Ask yourself: who else, apart from criminals, would want policemen not to have the power to investigate a crime until someone else has laid charges?

Anyway, the *Guardian* laid its charges and Downey investigated. Those concerned were interviewed in secret, to ensure that the public could not see the process for itself. Eventually, the proceedings were published. After much preliminary detail and minor questioning, Mr Pleming finally raised the key issue with Mr Smith:

> *Mr Pleming*: What I wanted to ask you is your reaction to cash. This is not the usual way, I trust, that members of Parliament get paid for consultancy work. They would have an agreement or arrangement. Cheques would be paid in the normal way. Cash would be very unusual. Again, I hope that is right.
> *Mr Smith*: Yes.

That was the beginning of it. And the end of it.[4] A regular citizen who had been caught taking up to £25,000 in undeclared notes would be asked: Do you do this often? Did you accept cash from other people? If you thought it was okay at the time, and leaving names aside, *how many of your colleagues were doing the same?* The reason why any professional investigator would press such questions is that Smith had admitted taking cash, he was clearing his conscience, he was feeling bad about what he did – he was turning into a witness. Discretion alert, to use Mackay's terms, good-faith emergency!

No alarm bells are needed – that would have been (er-hem) improper. Pleming, like Downey, is an instinctive PNQ. The exchange is a vivid example of the judgement, discretion and good faith of those trusted and acclaimed for operating our constitutional arrangements. No hard questions asked, no probing of the extent of the rot, sympathy for the poor chap whose weakness is exposed. The whole thing could hardly be a more pathetic investigation of wrongdoing. If such arrangements are 'better than many others', as Mackay coyly puts it, trying not to let his patriotism become boastful, then they should not be good enough for us.

Also, of course, they do it better in other places. In the words of Geoffrey Robertson, QC, the *Guardian*'s Counsel in the Greer-Hamilton case and before the Parliamentary Commissioner:

> Parliament cannot be trusted to regulate itself, the only satisfactory method of combating corruption in public life is the machinery [that] advanced Commonwealth legislatures have already put in place. This takes the form of a permanent independent commission against corruption, headed by a judge and staffed by full-time investigators, whose work is not subject to the vagaries of parliamentary prerogative or to the in-built Government majorities on the Standards and Privileges Committee.[5]

Case 2: the quiet voice of truth

When Tony Blair and Gordon Brown took office they brought with them their teams of political advisers, a reasonable and professional thing to do. The Conservatives complained that they were 'politicising the Civil Service'. Jonathan Hill, who was John Major's Political Secretary from 1992 to 1994, admitted that he too wished at times to 'silence that nagging Whitehall conscience'. But, he argued in the

Daily Telegraph, in an article that is a perfect statement of the British constitution's political culture: 'all politicians need to have that decent, quiet voice drawing them back'. This is the voice of the Civil Service, the tenured guardians of our way of doing things:

> Who in No. 10 is now going to say to Mr. Blair, 'I'm not sure it would be quite right to do it like that, Prime Minister'? Who is going to say, 'Convention suggests that we ought to consult on that, Prime Minister'? Mr Blair will become cut off from the reality of day to day life . . . When that moment comes, the Prime Minister will need that dispassionate Whitehall voice to tell him the truth.[6]

This passage is a fine summary of the vanity of the permanent Civil Service, with an even stronger fragrance than Mackay's puff. We are supposed to believe that PNQs in the Civil Service will act like poets and speak truth to power.

Within days of the *Daily Telegraph* publishing Hill's article, the actual character of Civil Service instinct for the truth was confirmed. When the Secretary to the Treasury, old Etonian Jonathan Aitken, MP (whose deceptions over Middle East investment in his television company were a matter of record), met old Harrovian, Sir Robin Butler, head of the Civil Service and Cabinet Secretary, did Sir Robin say, 'I'm sure you would not lie or embarrass us, old chap, I hope that is right?' or words to such effect, and Aitken reply, 'Yes', or words to that effect, while he crossed his fingers? At any rate the dispassionate Whitehall voice reported to the Prime Minister that all was well. This is a clear example of the way that Lord Mackay's *practice and conventions* are cut off from the reality of day-to-day life.

Case 3: altering what Bill of Rights we have

Our constitution has some written elements. One of these is the Bill of Rights of 1689, which protected the role of Parliament as a partner with the Crown. As we saw in the last chapter, to protect MPs in the seventeenth century the Bill of Rights stated that no law court can judge what MPs say in

Parliament. Now fast forward to 1996. The *Guardian* accused Neil Hamilton, MP of corrupt practices. He sued. The paper stuck to its allegations and wanted, naturally, to plead as evidence Hamilton's interventions in the Commons – the questions he asked that the newspaper said were paid for. The judge hearing the case ruled that this would breach the Bill of Rights of 1689 and that Hamilton could not proceed with his libel action. To force the *Guardian* to back down, Hamilton hit upon the wheeze of amending the 1689 Bill of Rights. This, he thought, would really crush the upstarts. To achieve this he needed to use the Conservative Party's narrow majority. Yet he had to argue the case in terms of natural justice. A plot was hatched in Downing Street, its broader aim being to intimidate the media. The Prime Minister, the same John Major who paraded himself as protector of the constitution, agreed, in a Downing Street meeting with Hamilton, actively to support his wheeze. It was also agreed that everyone would pretend that the reform was non-partisan. Lord Hoffman was tricked into putting an amendment forward to allow MPs to waive the immunity granted to them by the 1689 Bill of Rights. When it came to the vote in the Lords, an extensive underground whipping operation ensured a lopsided turnout of Hamilton's supporters, led by the greatest of them, Lady Thatcher. Hoffman was so appalled at the sight of the obviously whipped support that he abstained from his own amendment. Having passed the Lords, it went through the Commons, with Hamilton voting in his own cause. He was convinced that the *Guardian* would, as he put it, 'back off – end of case'.

The amendment became law. It means that MPs may now defame, say, a woman from Worcester, when speaking in the House of Commons, and be safe from her seeking legal redress. Should she, however, criticise the way her MP behaves in the Commons, the MP can waive immunity and sue her for libel. In the words of Lord Simon, a former Appeal judge, an MP can now 'pick and choose to stand on his privilege when it suits him'. Thus the constitutional amendment cooked up at a private meeting in Downing

Street ended equality before the law. The Conservative Party stated officially, 'Neither the Prime Minister nor his office has ever been involved,' but according to subsequently published reports it was later admitted that Major had 'steered it through'.[7] This is how our constitution has recently been made up 'as we go along'.[7]

It is bad enough that there should be an outrageous constitutional amendment to the 1689 Bill of Rights to alter the balance of power between MPs and the public, that gives MPs the privilege to claim or waive immunity at will. But how could such a constitutional alteration be made by sleight of hand in a deceitful atmosphere with no checks? The answer is that Mackay's 'practice and convention' have broken under the weight of modern times. The 'judgement, discretion and good faith of those operating our constitutional arrangements' is no longer reliable. This is not because public life is bereft of *People* with the Necessary Qualities. It was never a personal matter, so much as a special culture reinforced by a politics of loyalty and belief, in the Church, in the Old School, in the Queen, in the Club. It is facile to mock these ties, and I am not doing so. They worked. They were a big success. They built the world's greatest Empire. Now they are broken. They no longer hold in any way that can be relied upon. The public cannot be expected to defer to them. The unwritten constitution is *spiritually* bust. As it depended on spirit more than the letter, it *is* broken.

Liberty and powers

The three examples remain impressionistic. Part of the beauty of the unwritten constitution is that it can be praised in awesomely vague terms. Critics who respond to the general claims are then accused of suffering from vagueness. Perhaps the *culture* of the constitution is threadbare, but does not Britain continue to set an example for the world in its actual practice? Recently, protection of rights and the centralisation of powers have been surveyed explicitly to test this proposition.

The Democratic Audit was founded at Essex University to

assess the state of British democracy in a systematic, comparative and objective fashion. Its first volume, *The Three Pillars of Liberty*, is a 376-page survey of political rights and freedoms in the United Kingdom. It confirms the trend suggested by the Criminal Justice and Public Order Act of 1994 (which abolished the right to silence), the new Police Act and the asylum legislation. The survey audited such legislation and compared it to the standards set out in the international agreements that the UK has signed.

The Audit built its conclusions on case-by-case assessment. For example, it shows that there has been no right to freedom of assembly in the UK since 1976. In 1994 the Criminal Justice and Public Order Act added a new power to limit peaceful gatherings, that of 'trespassory assemblies'. The way the legislation, which gave police and government some draconian powers, became law is briefly summarised. The Audit tabulates the parliamentary time taken in the Act's various stages and the paucity of references to international conventions. When the Bill was first introduced, it consisted of 117 sections and 112 pages. By the time it received royal assent, it had almost doubled in size to 172 sections and 214 pages. There were 480 government amendments, often introduced late. Members of the House of Lords complained about the piecemeal treatment of basic rules of the country's liberty and order, and of having to debate them 'after midnight in an inquorate House'.[8] Once again means and ends, rotten law and bad procedures, reinforced each other without constitutional resistance.

And so to 1996. Because more than twenty people gathered on a grass verge near Stonehenge they were breaking the law. Two of them were prosecuted under the 1994 Act, even though they caused no obstruction or disturbance of the peace. They were found guilty. The director of the pressure group Liberty described as 'bizarre' the fact that 'a peaceful, non-obstructive gathering on the public highway . . . is trespass'.[9]

After trawling through the defining cases, the Audit's balanced conclusions are worth quoting at length:

As may be expected, we found no examples of widespread or gross violations of human rights, other than disturbing responses to terrorism in Northern Ireland. Government in this country does not kidnap, or torture, or kill its opponents. Citizens in this country are free openly to criticise the government and can combine at free and regular election to turn it out of office, if they are so minded. Citizens generally have ready access to their elected representatives and civil liberties groups may raise matters of concern with politicians, public servants and the public with no fear of reprisals. In other words, British citizens live in a democracy.

But our audit found that the United Kingdom offers far less formal legal protection of fundamental political rights and freedoms than international standards require and ordinary citizens are entitled to expect. Our findings disclose a series of breaches of those standards, across the spectrum of such rights. They raise a number of very serious issues for UK citizens and their governments. For what emerges from our audit are not fairly random pockets of non-compliance – the odd statute too narrowly drawn, this or that protection ineffective in practice – but a pattern of systemic weakness. It is a weakness at the very heart of Britain's political and constitutional system and calls into question the adequacy of the UK's arrangements for protecting its citizens' democratic rights on the verge of the twenty-first century.[10]

Three hundred and fifty years ago General Ireton, who today would be considered 'right-wing' for linking the right to vote with property, stated:

We talk of birthright. Truly by birthright there is this much claim. Men may justly have by birthright, by their very being born in England, that we should not seclude them out of England, that we should not refuse to give them air and place and ground, and the freedom of the highways and other things to live amongst us . . . that I think is due to a man by birth.[11]

'Due to a man by birth', 'freedom of the highways' – to speak such words now is to risk being regarded as a subversive. In terms of the protection of basic rights, the British constitution has become a relative failure internationally.

Rights and liberty are one part of a constitution: power is

the backbone. We are fortunate to have a clear portrait of the logic of power under the Conservatives, supplied by Simon Jenkins. *Accountable to None, the Tory Nationalisation of Britain* is a vivid, pioneering and now, it seems, definitive account. Rarely can essential reading be such a pleasure. I say it is definitive. What I mean by this is not that I agree with it, for one part of his argument, that the Treasury made Thatcher its victim, is unconvincing. What I mean is that the description Jenkins gives of what happened (as opposed to why) has gone unchallenged. Accounts such as *The End of Whitehall* by Colin Campbell and Graham Wilson, or *The State under Stress* by Christopher Foster and Francis Plowden, paint sober pictures of an administrative machine now disabled by over-centralisation and in need of comprehensive reform or replacement. However convincing and authoritative these studies may be, they are not written in a public voice. British political argument can, and does, ignore such studies. But Jenkins is an ex-editor of *The Times*, an influential columnist, and as his book was widely acclaimed its indictment was heard.

The failure to rebut it can be compared with Will Hutton's *The State We're In*. Hutton's fine polemic is a coruscating account of the institutionalised short-termism of a finance-dominated economy and society that condemns the UK to boom and bust. Hutton calls for a radical version of stakeholding. Like Jenkins, or, on the centre-left, David Marquand, Hutton developed a thesis that criticised the system and not just the scandals of the British polity. Because he advocated radical economic measures, Hutton's prescriptions have been combated. The right and the centre have more than enough mental capacity and alertness, as well as the contemporary interest and concern, to try and rebut a strong case that they do not like. They cannot have liked Jenkins' book, either. But *Accountable to None* drew no equivalent response. A silence descended. No one leapt to the defence of Thatcherism by rebutting Jenkins' charges item by item or by providing an interpretation to justify them. No one dissented from his thesis that Britain has become way too over-centralised. His description stands unchallenged. In this sense it is definitive.

Most books about the Thatcher–Major years focus on the personalities and policies at the apex. Jenkins provides a sweeping survey of the impact of Conservative policy outside Westminster from 1979 onwards and a brilliantly sceptical review of the Treasury. He diagnoses a vicious pendulum. A process in which central government intensifies its control in order to prevent waste, cut costs and improve standards, which then leads to pressure on government to increase expenditure to stave off ministerial embarrassment. He argues that power must be decentralised, and that money needs to accompany power to ensure diversity and experiment and to release Whitehall from responsibility over details that it cannot adequately assess. Jenkins traces a centralisation *à tout azimuth* – in every direction: local government (nearly 150 pieces of local government legislation since 1979), the police, health, education, the universities, housing, the law. In short, almost everything. He is incisive on the creation of a uniform business rate, which took the totality of commercial building revenues into the Treasury, cutting them from local control and their relationship to place – 'the biggest single act of nationalisation undertaken by any government since the war'. The British once regarded *other* European countries as monstrously centralised: 'Since 1980 Britain has moved in the opposite direction to the rest of the world . . . determined programmes of constitutional devolution have been in countries as widely scattered as Sweden, Norway, Denmark, France, Spain and Portugal.'

In a sombre conclusion Jenkins states, 'As long as Britain has no written constitution and concentrates all governmental power in the hands of the leadership of a Commons majority, that leadership will always seek more.'[12] Together, *The Three Pillars of Liberty* and *Accountable to None* would shake the complacency of any legislator capable of reading. You could not put them down and repeat after Lord Mackay, 'I think our arrangements work at least as well as, perhaps better than, many others.'

But there is one aspect of our rights and powers that neither account touches: the point where the practice and conventions put the law into effect, in the legislative process of the House of Commons. One assessment that does is Andrew Marr's *Ruling Britannia, the Failure and Future of British Democracy*. Written without malice or rancour – and with an appreciation of the moderate temper of British government, and the moderate public interest in it – Marr's book contains among its other attributes ten pages that are enough to make you weep. Concerned to show how 'real people really suffer' through bad government, he looks at the way Parliament handled pension reform in February 1986. Tens of thousands of people are now suffering from the loss, sometimes a considerable loss, of their savings, through being mis-sold pensions after the government 'bribed' people to leave SERPS, the State earnings-related pension scheme:

> The disturbing thing about re-reading the committee minutes afterwards is the accuracy with which MPs pointed to the key flaws in the legisation – the lack of proper protections against high-pressure salesmen, the opacity of the all-important information about how much of the pension holder's money would be swallowed up by commissions and administrative costs, pocketed by the companies; the danger of innocent people (in both senses of the word) being bilked. All were preventable. What was predicted, then happened. In some cases the very proposals which were laughed at by ministers were later adopted by the government to limit the damage that followed.[13]

One of the Ministers doing the laughing was John Major.

In the first part of this book I recognised that all organisations, big or small, make mistakes, because to grow they must take risks. Their quality as an organisation should not be judged on whether they commit misjudgements but on whether they are able to correct them. Does the organisation know how to listen, assess evidence of possible errors and respond to such evidence so as to prevent a reoccurence? The British government fails this test. The pensions tragedy was a compressed version of the Poll Tax. The government was warned that it was in breach of trust with voters' savings. Those warnings were entirely justified. They could make no impact, nor arrest the disasters forewarned. This is evidence of a system that has become structurally flawed – because it cannot correct itself; with no decentralisation of power, no legitimate second chamber of scrutiny, no effective brakes to stop mis-government. It is not just concepts like sovereignty that are bust. No government can escape the consequences.

Arms to Iraq

In 1988, when Charter 88 drew up its list of constitutional reforms, the machinery of administration was not identified as a major issue. It was Westminster, rather than Whitehall, that was seen as the constitutional problem. Freedom of Information would open up the latter; apart from this, the traditional routines of a neutral Civil Service were not widely regarded as an impediment to democracy. The failure to address how government takes place still remains a weakness in the arguments for reform. Defenders of the status quo quote Pope: 'For forms of government let fools contest, whate'er is best administered is best.' As a justification for contempt towards all constitutional discussion, it is easy enough to counter. It is harder to answer the challenge of how administration should be bettered, when secrecy makes it impossible to see what goes on.

Finally, it is possible to look into the heart of the constitution, thanks to the Scott Report. *The Inquiry into the Export of Defence Related Equipment to Iraq and the Related Prosecutions* by Sir Richard Scott was a strange affair. It saw – for the first time before a public tribunal – the entire senior range of Ministers and civil servants straining to justify how they worked. The Prime Minister, John Major, his predecessor, Margaret Thatcher, his deputy, Michael Heseltine, and the head of the Civil Service and Secretary to the Cabinet, Sir Robin Butler, led a small army of lesser politicians, officials, arms-salesmen and intelligence officers (referred to by mysterious letters, such as Mr P and Mr Q), who submitted answers to questionnaires and responded to lengthy oral questioning; 278 witnesses gave written evidence, 81 of whom also gave oral evidence, 20 in private. Over 160,000 pages of official documentation were obtained by the inquiry team, 20,000 of which are reproduced on its CD-ROM. The public hearings alone took more than eighty days as the processes of government were laid bare.

The inquiry was established in November 1992. As it proceeded, it aroused intense opposition from officialdom. Its report was expected to have a devastating impact. In the course of its three and a half years numerous attempts were made to undermine it. Mysterious sources rubbished Sir Richard Scott's credentials. The end result, published in February 1996, was five volumes of unprecedented length and detail – but without a coherent summary of judgements. On publication there was a classic House of Commons battle. The government lost the argument but won the division, by a single vote. Then pop went the weasel. Rarely can something that was for so long predicted to be about to change the future have been so swiftly consigned to the past. The system defaulted back to normal. For the time being, at least. What was it all about?

On Wednesday, 16 March 1988, Halabjeh, a town of 50,000 mainly Kurdish inhabitants, situated in eastern Iraq and at the time occupied by Iran, was bombed. The bombs contained a mixture of the nerve gas Sarin, cyanide and mustard gas. An estimated 5,000 inhabitants were paralysed and died. Technically, the decimation made it an act of genocide. It is the largest recorded incident of indiscriminate, airborne chemical warfare against civilians.

Western journalists got there on 22 March, via Iran. Nicholas Beeston in *The Times*:

> Like figures unearthed in Pompeii, the victims of Halabjeh were killed so quickly that their corpses remained in suspended animation.
>
> There was the plump baby whose face, frozen in a scream, stuck out from under the protective arm of a man, away from the open door of a house they never reached.

> Near by a family who had been sitting in their garden eating lunch were cut down – the killer gas not even sparing the family cat or the birds in the tree, which littered the well-kept lawn.
>
> Their neighbours had had the foresight to hide in an underground shelter. It became their mass grave . . .

The British government, which had recently extended Iraq a £200 million export credit, protested at the lowest possible diplomatic level, even though it accepted that chemical weapons had been used 'contrary to international obligations'.[14] The previous month British government Ministers had approved the sale of 'non-lethal' machine tools to Iraq, which some officials knew were likely to be put to military use. No attempt was made to reverse that decision.

At the beginning of August, Iraq and Iran agreed to a ceasefire of their long war. There had been a Western policy to ensure that Iraq was not overwhelmed by Iran. That policy was now redundant. But instead of clamping down on arms sales, the British government moved swiftly to sell Baghdad as much as it could. It felt unable to sell overtly lethal kit. Instead, it set about encouraging and guaranteeing credit for everything that would not threaten its ability to deny in public that it was relaxing restrictions on Iraq.

The materials attached to the Scott Report in CD-ROM allow one to read many of the documents for oneself. Within ten days of the ceasefire, Foreign Secretary Geoffrey Howe sent a memorandum to the Prime Minister called 'The Economic Consequences of Peace in the Gulf'. To produce it, his officials had consulted with the Treasury, the DTI, the Ministry of Defence, the Departments of Transport and Energy and the Bank of England. At the same time as sending the paper to the Prime Minister, Howe circulated it to the Overseas and Defence Committee of the Cabinet, where it would have been read by all his senior colleagues. The concentrated assessment of the opportunities offered by peace, in other words, was a collective exercise by the government as a whole. It was conducted as a priority, less than five months after Halabjeh. The aim was to identify the factors for 'reformulating our policies'. The memorandum noted that Britain had a 'fully functioning commerical section in our Embassy in Baghdad which is eager to exploit every opportunity'. On defence equipment, the document predicted a considerable potential for sales and concluded, 'We should aim to get the non-lethal business and build on that.' As it was drafted, circulated and considered by the government, further gas attacks were mounted against the Kurds. Within a week of the 'Economic Consequences' being drawn up, David Hirst of the *Guardian* reported, 'There are, it seems, only two words – gas and extermination – on the lips of the thousands of Kurdish refugees who had flooded across Iraq's northern border into Turkey in the last few days.'

In his summary for the Prime Minister which Thatcher's Private Secretary, Charles Powell, attached to her copy, he noted:

> there is likely to be a great deal of defence sales business. We shall need to consider fairly soon whether any amendment to our existing guidelines is required to enable British firms to compete for this. But there would be great difficulty in the case of Iran, particularly while the hostages remain in captivity.

A few paragraphs later he referred to 'the price of following a consistent and honourable policy' *over Iran*. There was, it seems, no difficulty in extending 'non-lethal' credit for weapon-making and communication equipment to a genocidal maniac in Iraq. Powell also noted, 'both countries are likely to require substantial credit cover'. The Prime Minister endorsed the paper's strategy and asked to be 'kept very closely in touch at every stage and consulted on all relevant decisions'. Six weeks later, on 14 October, she approved a further export credit to Iraq of £340 million.

The government was fully aware of what was happening to the Kurds. Later, Howe justified his memorandum, telling Scott, 'The Kurdish issue was an important part of the general awareness at the time', while his paper 'only dealt specifically with the economic consequences of the end of the Iran/Iraq conflict, not with the wider questions of international politics or human rights issues'. The judge rejected this, stating, 'since Lord Howe's paper was addressing the "factors" to be taken into account "when reformulating our policies to the region" the absence of any reference to the "Kurdish issue" or to the hostages does seem surprising.'

After Howe's circular, the Foreign Office generated a draft internal paper that argued, 'we need a policy that tenables [*sic*] us to justify re-entering the defence equipment market . . .' But Howe would not allow the document to go forward. His Private Secretary noted on 22 September that the Foreign Secretary was 'reluctant . . . to initiative [*sic*] a process whereby it will become known that our line on arms sales to Iraq has relaxed, while the Kurds/CW question is still hanging over us.'

It is worth noting in parenthesis the collapse in language that accompanies the collapse in ethics, much as in the US military during the Vietnam War. To refer to CW (that is, chemical warfare) as 'hanging over us', not the Kurds, is bad enough. Worse, linguistically, the Foreign Office sought to 'initiative' a process so as to 'tenable' an outcome.

In his report, Scott highlights the words that state that Howe did not want it to *become known* that policy was being reformulated. The judge observes, 'He was prepared for the new approach to be adopted but not for it to become known. In his oral evidence to the Inquiry Lord Howe confirmed that this was so.' Under questioning Howe agreed that there was a divergence between policy and its presentation. In his view, relaxing the restriction towards Iraq could not be made public because of 'the extremely emotional way in which such debates are debated in public'. 'A sort of "Government know best" approach, is it not?' Scott asked him at the oral hearings. To which Howe answered, 'Yes'.

Scott notes that Howe's defence was not based on grounds of national security. The judge concludes that a prime 'reason why no public announcement was made' was fear that:

> public knowledge of an intended relaxation of the restrictions on the supply of defence equipment to Iraq would provoke such indignation in the media and among vociferous sections

> of the British public as to be politically damaging. Public pressure might . . . have . . . even brought about the reversal, of a new relaxed policy.

So, within weeks of the ceasefire, the government had agreed to encourage defence-related sales to Iraq, had extended Saddam Hussein substantial new credits and had decided not to inform the public – because of the protests that would follow, due to Iraqi nerve-gas attacks on Kurdish civilians. As Howe's Private Secretary put it on 28 October 1988, the Foreign Secretary still did not want the paper, which suggested a need to justify the shift in policy, circulated, 'particularly when Iraqi use of CW is still so sensitive an issue here . . .'

This was the starting point for the scandal that led to the Scott Report. The government chose to ignore the genocide and shift its policy. But when it was asked questions about this in Parliament or in letters, it was evasive and, as Scott was to find, misleading. It did its best to ensure that the 'emotional' public was unaware of the new direction policy was taking. At this point the old constitution hits ground zero. It was built on the assumption that the people are a danger to order and good judgement. They are likely to be a 'mob', at best swayed by weakness and foolishness. But as we have seen, the British public is reflective and self-possessed. It knows how to behave. The government did not know. Howe was completely wrong, while the public that he regarded with undisguised distaste as 'emotional' was quite right. All the technical arguments – which Howe himself did a great deal to generate – about whether the Scott Report was necessary, or proceeded in the proper way, distract from this central point. Knowing that the British public would not accept that restrictions on arms sales to a regime that had just gassed the Kurds should be relaxed, the government should not have relaxed them. Then the scandal would not have occurred. Instead it defied public opinion and tried to hide the fact. But it was wrong and the public was right.

Richard Scott was not concerned with this larger question. He wanted to know how the process went wrong that allowed the government to hide its policy shift and to mask it from Parliament. He kept on asking officials this. And was repeatedly assured that nothing went wrong and that the procedures that had been followed were quite normal. This, he was told, *is* how the British government works. It was usual to give 'accurate but incomplete answers' to Parliament, he was told by Sir Robin Butler (yes, the one who makes up the constitution as he goes along). Witness after witness agreed:

> The truth is a very difficult concept.
> Half a picture can be accurate.
> Whitehall cosmetics.
> The avoidance of controversy was not an uncommon concern in the presentation of policy – or, in this case, the non-presentation of policy.
> 'Unquantifiable' [damage] can mean unquantifiably large or unquantifiably small.
> The way in which questions are answered in Parliament tends to be something of an art form rather than a means of communication.
> Screwdrivers are also required to make H-bombs.
> I quite simply misled myself.
> The damage to the public interest . . . would be the exposure of the decision-making process.
> I am using 'accountability' to leave out, as it were, the blame element of it.
> The inner workings of the Government machine . . . should not be exposed to the gaze of those ready to criticise . . .

And so on. The last statement comes from the government's written response to the Scott Report. In effect, it says that the inner workings of government should be exposed only to the gaze of those willing to praise it. Mirror, mirror on the wall.

And remember, all these things were said by People with the Necessary Qualities to run our constitution. From the government point of view, nothing went wrong. The 'inner workings' worked, as they usually do. They never allowed moral questions, issues of fairness, public opinion, or the principles of democracy to prevent them carrying out the necessary policies. On the contrary, the system as a whole believed that 'it knew best'. Not a single member of the Cabinet *or* senior Civil Service, it seems, suggested that there should be a limit to British defence business in this particular case, because the regime was using weapons of mass extermination against civilians. Complicity at all levels, not least at No. 10, is established by the test of the dog that does not bark. Within months of the mass gassing of the Kurds, a memo was duplicated to most corners of the government about how best to maximise sales without saying so: the note on Howe's desire that it should not be known that 'our line on arms sales to Iraq has relaxed' went to *nine* departments. The only significant debate was over how much could be got away with, without going public. The attitude of the inner machinery of government was thus fundamentally undemocratic.

One consequence was, and is, that the House of Commons is regarded as a problem to be handled, not a forum to which the Executive is genuinely answerable. It led to the art-form of the half-truth, which in the judge's view in turn led to answers to parliamentary questions in which Ministers failed to discharge their constitutional obligation 'not to deceive or mislead Parliament and the public'. But all this was usual, normal, regular, nine-department, inner-working-of-government stuff until something went wrong. A senior Whitehall official told Richard Norton-Taylor of the *Guardian*, 'The cover-up is greater than the original sin; the greatest sin of all is to be found out.'[15] They were found out because Iraq invaded Kuwait.

The Iraqi invasion upset the calculation because it led to Customs and Excise prosecuting businessmen who were breaking the public policy of an arms embargo, but who were doing so with the encouragement and connivance of Ministers and the security services. The narrative can be briefly summarised. In April 1990, four months before the invasion of Kuwait, Customs and Excise had seized a set of highly engineered steel barrels. They had been prepared for a 'Supergun' – designed to be one of the biggest lethal weapons on earth. So big that it escaped the guidelines, for the pipes were destined for Iraq. Soon afterwards a company called Matrix-Churchill received its first visit from Customs. At the end of July 1990 the full Cabinet decided formally to approve a liberal export policy towards Iraq. This would have had the effect of retrospectively validating previous policy and arms sales, and any prosecutions could be stopped. The fix was in.

A few days later Saddam invaded Kuwait. All exports were banned. The fix collapsed. In the heightened atmosphere, as Western forces invested the Middle East in preparation for their counter-strike, Customs and Excise mounted a full raid on Matrix-Churchill and discovered false export documentation. But then they were obliged to drop the prosecution over the Supergun. It turned out that the manufacturers had warned the government well in advance of the order's military potential. Furthermore, they had done so through a Conservative MP, who informed the House of Commons of his role and committed himself to appearing in court to testify that the businessmen were honourable.[16]

Customs and Excise officials were angered that, as Britain prepared for war with Saddam, they had been stopped from prosecuting one of his illegal arms suppliers. As a matter of pride and patriotism, (the sort of value the utilitarians in the Treasury regard, as we will see in the next chapter, as 'inefficient') they therefore insisted on taking the directors of Matrix-Churchill to court, and in November 1991 they were committed to trial at the Old Bailey. Ministers then signed so-called Public Interest Immunity Certificates, to prevent the public from learning of government involvement. This would have deprived the defendants of their ability to show they had co-operated with government officials. Geoffrey Robertson, QC, who repesented one of the defendants, let it be known that his client would confirm in open court that he worked for M16. The trial judge ordered the documents to be released. The case collapsed. It seemed that innocent men were being wrongly prosecuted to cover up for the government and that the House of Commons had been misled. The government was forced to set up the Scott Inquiry.

Three years later, Richard Scott published his panoramic survey and exercise in open government. Concluding the lengthy section on 'the divergence between actual policy on exports to Iraq and Government statements on policy', Scott concludes:

> the failure of the Government to be forthcoming . . . precluded a public debate on this important issue taking place on an informed basis. Parliament and the public were designedly led to believe that a stricter policy towards non-lethal defence exports and dual-use exports to Iraq was being applied than was in fact the case.

Some poor sod had to undertake the misleading. It was William Waldegrave. Sir Richard Scott states in his report:

> Mr Waldegrave knew, first hand, the facts that, in my opinion, rendered the 'no change in policy' statement untrue. I accept that, when he signed these letters, he did not regard the agreement that he had reached with his fellow Ministers as having constituted a change in policy towards Iraq. In his evidence to the Inquiry, he strenuously and consistently asserted his belief, in the face of a volume of, to my mind, overwhelming evidence to the contrary, that the policy on defence sales to Iraq had, indeed, remained unchanged. I did not receive the impression of any insincerity on his part in giving me the evidence he did. But it is clear, in my opinion, that policy on defence sales to Iraq did not remain unchanged.

And a few paragraphs later the judge concluded that there was a 'deliberate' failure to inform Parliament. Nonetheless, he made a critical concession by accepting Waldegrave's sincerity, to which I will return.

Waldegrave felt the need not only to insist on his own sincerity, but also to defend the policy. He wrote to Scott:

> It is worth remembering the limited extent to law-based, democratic Government, with a respect for human rights in the world. Amongst the regions I was responsible for – the

> Soviet Union and its satellites; Africa and the Middle East – there was scarcely one country which would have passed the test – Botswana perhaps – at that time. Iraq's vicious regime was very far from being unique . . .

But it *was* unique. Viciousness may be rife, but not genocide. The inability of the Foreign Office to retain even the most elementary degree of judgement over the difference between viciousness and nerve gassing civilians was staggering. It is less a matter of individual stupidity, callousness and public-school arrogance than a consequence of having no rules, and relying instead on the flexibility of believing one knows best.

The government, as we have seen and as Howe admitted, could never have won an argument in public for exporting more to Iraq. Illiberal regimes, yes: those involved in the aerial gassing of civilians, no. This is the heart of the argument for democracy – for the sovereignty of the people being the ruling force in the country – articulated through constitutional rules that are publicly assessed. The public knew better, was more street-wise and more principled than the People with the Necessary Qualities. Voters understand that you do not trust regimes that gas whole sections of their population. There is, after all, some history about this, with which the public is familiar. A price can be put on the value of the public's good judgement. Approximately £1 billion of export credits to Iraq were lost, which the government had to pay, after the war broke out.

Worse still, the government knew that it could not proceed in the full light of day. It therefore decided to proceed by stealth. The entire British administration, we can now see, is familiar with the ways of the dark. This was known long before. Paul Johnson, in his populist battle cry *Wake Up Britain!*, argues the point passionately:

> in the art of government, there is a particular problem in translating popular wishes into foreign policy. The instinct of the rulers is to regard such wishes as highly dangerous. Foreign policy, they think, is a matter for the informed few, the experienced and wise elect, who see all, know all and

> decide all . . . Let no one argue that central decisions of foreign and defence policy cannot be taken through the democratic process, directly or in spirit . . . Foreign policy and democracy can be reconciled. That has not, alas, been the working assumption of successive British governments . . . most of our leaders have taken the view 'Not in front of the children'.[17]

The government was roasted for its failure by Robin Cook, who led for Labour on the Scott Report and delivered a peach of a parliamentary performance:

> The Government are fond of lecturing the rest of the nation on the need to accept responsibility . . . yet when it comes to themselves, suddenly, not a single Minister can be found to accept responsibility for what went wrong . . . Sir Richard returns a verdict of guilty. You can tell, Madam Speaker, the importance that he attaches to the conclusion because, like all his key findings, it is expressed as a double negative, 'It is clear that policy on defence sales to Iraq did not remain unchanged.' Three years ago the Prime Minister told the House: 'The suggestion that Ministers misled the House is a serious and scurrilous charge and has no basis whatsoever in fact.' The suggestion does have a firm basis, in the five volumes beside me. I agree with the Prime Minister that it was a serious charge. Will he now accept that, far from being scurrilous, it was entirely accurate?

Cook stabbed his finger at the Tory leadership. All attempts to subdue him by interruptions had been stilled. He looked at them with contempt. No one moved. 'Suddenly we have a row of limpets stuck to the Treasury bench.' Cook proclaimed.

It was a tremendous moment to witness. A moment of collective guilt, rather than collective responsibility. It made the then government's determination to win the Commons vote utterly naked and professional. They *knew* they were guilty. Of course they misled Parliament. But they were determined to stay in power. They regarded themselves as realists and the arms to Iraq business as small change. What had happened, after all, was what you did when you governed. In taking this attitude they were strongly supported by senior civil servants. Complicit in the guidelines, they feared that once Ministers started to resign, their methods would be exposed. It was crudely done. The government insisted on having a week in which to analyse and respond to the report it had commissioned, and allowed Robin Cook a mere three hours to scan 1,800 pages before the first parliamentary exchange, and MPs just a few minutes. Scott said lamely that he regretted this and would have preferred equal time. He failed to insist on anything like it. As a result of his failure, when copies of the Report arrived in the hands of journalists, who had almost no time to summarise its findings, the Report was accompanied by a Treasury press briefing. This claimed, falsely, that Ministers had been cleared. A Cabinet Office paper was also issued, which summarised the Report. This summary stated that Scott had found that, 'Answers given to Parliamentary Questions gave an accurate description of the Government's policy on exports to Iran and Iraq.'

Later, Tony Wright, MP read this to Justice Scott in a Select Committee consideration of his findings and asked him, 'Could any reader of your Report believe this to be true?' To which Scott replied, 'I do not think so, no.' But when Sir Robin Butler was asked, also by Tony Wright, if it was not 'troubling' that our civil servants assisted in an untruthful exercise, Butler replied, 'No . . . Ministers disagreed with Sir Richard on his findings and the press notice to which you are referring represented the Government's view of the matter. That is perfectly proper.'[18]

A shameless answer. Just how shameless, the reader may not immediately realise. When the Matrix-Churchill trial collapsed, it seemed that the government had misled Parliament in its answers to questions. As Parliament, not the Executive, is supposed to be supreme, for a Minister to mislead Parliament is one of the gravest constitutional sins there is. So a judge was called upon to mount an inquiry. After exhaustive assessment, he concluded that Parliament was indeed misled. The government then issues a press release, which the civil servants then print and distribute to the media and MPs, as the Report is released to them. It states that the judge's Report has found that the parliamentary answers were 'accurate'. We have now gone through the looking-glass. When asked by a parliamentary committee if any reader of his Report could come to this conclusion, the judge says they could not. The head of the Civil Service is then asked to justify how, in their official capacity, his neutral colleagues are allowed to distribute such a false summary. He answers that the government is entitled to its own view – which its civil servants, will then distribute. In other words, the government is not only entitled to disagree with the judge, it is also entitled to its own conclusions about what the judge's conclusion in his report *is*. And civil servants will then print and distribute the government's version in flat contradiction to what he actually says. In the previous chapter I observed that although the government was angered by the jury's decision to find Clive Ponting innocent, it accepted the verdict even if it afterwards changed the law. That was in the 1980s. In the 1990s, the government decided it could rewrite verdicts after all.

The government was helped to get away with it because Richard Scott's report was so long, his double negatives so obscure, his decision not to write a summary of his judgements hopelessly misguided. Pathetically, he relied on the good faith, integrity and probity of such PNQs as Sir Robin Butler, if not John Major. Despite all the evidence that he uncovered, he presumed that the scruples necessary to make an unwritten constitution work, in the way it is supposed to, were alive and well.

The debate that followed was a brief and crushing warning to those who retain such good faith. On the night Cook's words were mightier but the votes counted more. Ten Conservative backbenchers spoke in support of the government's refusal to allow any resignations or accept any wrongdoing. They were almost all ex-Ministers (such as Hurd, King, Channon, Mellor and Sainsbury) or arms traders (Sir Michael Marshall, 'lifelong exporter and adviser to

British Aerospace'). As significant was their social background. Overwhelmingly Oxbridge, one went to school at Harrow (as did Sir Robin Butler), one was from Rugby, while six went to the same high school – Eton. Only one, David Mellor (the Minister who defended sales to Iraq immediately after the gassings) went to a state school. None went to a regular British university. Three went to Ivy League colleges, one (Richard Needham, MP, the 6th Earl of Kilmorey) went to Eton but did not bother to go to university at all – all the rest were products of Oxford or Cambridge. It was a mobilisation of SPNQs – *Special* People with the Necessary Qualities.

The issue was raised during the debate by Labour MP Barry Sheerman, as a point of order, 'This debate is about parliamentary democracy and tonight we have heard from nine former Ministers, six of whom are ex-Etonians . . . all of whom have close connection to the Chief Secretary to the Treasury (Waldegrave).'

This was a very pertinent observation. But Michael Morris, the Deputy Speaker, who was then chairing the debate, told Sheerman to resume his seat and also told him to 'think before he speaks on another occasion'. But Michael Morris is co-author of *Helping the Exporter*. Surely he knows that such connections can help.

Eton is too rich to be a mere conspiracy. Alan Clark and William Waldegrave are both old Etonians but argued over arms sales. The mutual antipathy of a family quarrel does not prevent loyalty under fire from a common enemy, however. In a diary entry about an early parliamentary trial that he had to undergo as a Junior Minister, Alan Clark described how he had been wine-tasting and was incoherent. A Labour member rose to ask him what his last paragraph 'meant'. 'How the hell did I know what it meant? (People) started bobbing up and down . . . this had the makings of a disaster. Never mind. "Heads down, bully and shove".' When he published the diary, Clark provided a helpful footnote for his readers. 'Heads down, bully and shove' is a slogan from the winter-term Field Game played at Eton.[19] Clark survived the onslaught.

With the help of fellow old-Etonians, Waldegrave too survived the Scott debate with 'Heads down, bully and shove'. In the late twentieth century, the British constitution is made up on the playing fields of Eton. 'Heads down, bully and shove' is the blunt reality of Lord Mackay's 'judgement, discretion and good faith'.

One more shove was needed, to change the constitutional culture Britain once enjoyed. Scott granted that Waldegrave, the most senior of those directly implicated, was sincere, even though he was wrong. Because he was wrong, he should resign. But his sincerity was conveniently exploited to get him off the hook.

How should Ministers conduct themselves? In August 1945, as a Labour government looked forward to a full term in office for the first time, chaps were no longer in control of things in the same way. Guided discretion was needed. The first Questions of Procedure for Ministers (QPM) was drafted for Attlee to issue to his Cabinet. It was secret code on how Ministers had to behave. Over the years it was further developed. Finally, in May 1992, it was published. Peter Hennessy, the contemporary historian with a close knowledge of constitutional development, asked his students if QPM was not, by definition, a document of constitutional force. He encouraged them to write to the Cabinet Secretary to confirm this. Sir Robin Butler replied, 'I don't regard it as having a constitutional force at all . . . It would be perfectly possible for an incoming Prime Minister to scrap the whole thing and to devise entirely new rules.' A year later Hennessy asked for permission to quote this view. Butler wrote back to say that in fact only 90 per cent of QPM was at the complete discretion of the Prime Minister: 'It deals with some things which are not at the discretion of a Prime Minister to change, for example, the description of accountability to Parliament in paragraph 27.'[20]

The key passage in paragraph 27 read, at the time, 'Ministers must not mislead Parliament and the public and should correct any inadvertent errors at the earliest possible opportunity. They must be as open as possible with Parliament and the public.' It was precisely this paragraph on ministerial accountability to Parliament – the one that, supposedly, it was not within his discretion to alter – that the Prime Minister *did* alter. In 1994, as Scott was conducting his inquiry, the Prime Minister, presumably on advice, inserted the word 'knowingly' before 'mislead'. When Lord Nolan published his first report on *Standards in Public Life* in May 1995, he recommended that QPM state: 'Ministers must not mislead Parliament. They must be as open as possible with Parliament and with the public.' Instead the post-Nolan version of QPM added a key word. It reads, 'Ministers must not knowingly mislead Parliament and the public.'[21]

The law does not say that people must not 'knowingly' commit a crime. If it did, ignorance of the law would be a defence. It may be a mitigating circumstance, but it does not relieve the individual of guilt for breaking the law. Apparently, ignorance does now relieve British Ministers of part of their duty to be truthful to Parliament. The ludicrous principle of *ministerial sincerity* has become a constitutional one. It offers a further escape route, in addition to the confusion between accountability and responsibility that I will come to in a moment. The Labour government has retained the escape clause of ministerial sincerity, even though it claims to have accepted Lord Nolan's recommendations.

In Chapter 6 I argued that accountability has become an increasingly important part of official power and democratic government. Historically, it has always been a key element in the role of the House of Commons, even if the way MPs hold Ministers to account is negative. The culture of integrity – of being answerable – was central to the legitimacy of Britain's informal constitution. But, as the demand for accountability grew, so the need to evade it became more intense and the weakness of adversarial theatre allowed a new form of accountability avoidance to be developed, the so-called 'Butler Doctrine'. This states that while Ministers are accountable for their departments, in that they must give an account of them to Parliament, they are not responsible for what they do. Accountability does not carry blame. Civil servants, at the same time – although they carry out the duties of the department – are the creatures of their Ministers and may not be singled out for blame, either. The first are blame-free; the second blame-less.

Tony Wright, MP drew the reality out of the Doctrine's author, Sir Robin Butler, in their exchanges over the implications of the Scott Report:

> Are we not . . . back to the jelly then; because what on earth is the point of having a doctrine, which we enunciate, a doctrine of responsibility, if, when tested, we do not know what it means and it seems not to be able to be applied? Is it not a kind of fiction that we trot out on State occasions but in terms of daily reality it does not add up to a row of beans?

Sir Robin Butler disagreed:

> the doctrine that Ministers should resign if they are at fault is one which people would generally accept, but then there is a question of whether they are at fault. Now how is that question to be decided: it is to be decided precisely by Parliamentary accountability, by Ministers being accountable to their peers in Parliament; that is what happened in this case and Parliament reached its conclusion.[22]

Traditionally, it is not the case that wrongdoing was resolved by a majority in the Commons (unless a full impeachment procedure was involved, with Parliament acting as a medieval high court). Ministers are employed not by Parliament but by the Crown – in the form of the Prime Minister – who decides the standards of their behaviour. When illegality was alleged the Prime Minister brought in a judge to establish the facts of the case. The judge found that Parliament had been misled. For the government simply to disagree, to say that no one should resign, to put it to the House and win by a single vote means, according to Butler, that Ministers were *not* at fault. But this is a doctrine of *might is right*. While it holds sway

Britain has no constitutional values worthy of the name. Despite 1 May, the doctrine still holds sway.

In a blistering memorandum to the Public Service Committee, the Conservative MEP Graham Mather noted:

> The result of the Butler Doctrine is that ministerial responsibility for departmental acts has been defined away almost to nothing. Ministerial accountability can be discharged by statements that turn out to have been knowingly misleading, whilst officials have no responsibility other than to Ministers and cannot give an account independently of them. This is clearly a very unsatisfactory position indeed for constitutional government.[23]

He argued instead for a clear statement of ministerial *responsibility*. This in turn could be clearly distinguished by degrees of responsibility, while civil servants would get defined codes of conduct and contracts.

Recent attempts to put things right help to illuminate what went wrong. On 2 May 1997 Robin Cook became Foreign Secretary. He had observed the Scott hearings, queuing up to get in along with members of the public. It is said that Labour was inexperienced. Cook, however, had seen more of the inside of government than most Ministers have after years in office. He was aware that the Civil Service was in free fall, so far as its values are concerned – not so much disoriented as without orientation, unable to tell right from wrong or genocide from 'viciousness'. As soon as he entered the Foreign Office he instigated a new approach. From now on, British foreign policy will pay regard to ethical values and will seek to ensure that citizens of other countries enjoy the democracy and human rights that we would like for ourselves.

There are able members of the Foreign Office and there are lads from the old school. The latter despise Cook's new policy. One of them wrote a memo calling it 'bollocks', and Andrew Marr reported that it found its way to Cook's desk. The author was, apparently, from Eton. He and his allies *have learnt nothing* from the arms to Iraq affair. They are still unable to see that a moral foreign policy would have helped to prevent the Foreign Office from treating genocide as the equivalent of 'viciousness', saved them a scandal and the taxpayer £1 billion. They are blind to the fact that codified values will assist, not hinder, effective international relations; and that such values need to be internalised. Cook saw that change was vital. He has opened up the Foreign Office, shown the public round and instructed that recruitment policy must ensure fair employment for qualified women and minorities on the basis of values.

Some radicals have attacked Cook's declaration of an ethical policy as being mere window-dressing. Doubtless it will be imperfect, and arms will be sold to a regime that misuses them. Nonetheless, the new policy is a qualitative and democratic improvement, thanks to its constitutionalism. It sets out criteria for identifying wrongdoing. These will start to act as markers for public, as well as internal, argument. They thereby open up the judgements of the Foreign Office to scrutiny. This in turn will help British diplomats conduct affairs on a better footing than the cynical calculations that entail stealth and subterfuge. The 'bollocks' memo is a memorial to the old culture of 'heads down, bully and shove'. Labour inherited a Bollocks Constitution, and by bollocks it's broke.

In this chapter I have shown that the damage sustained by the old constitution as it sails into modern times is extensive and goes deep. Its fundamental concept of sovereignty is a farce. Its culture of discretion (vital for unwritten arrangements) has broken down. Its legacy of fundamental rights is in disarray. The distribution of power is woefully over-concentrated, especially in comparison with other countries. The system has little capacity to learn from mistakes, or to accept critical scrutiny in Parliament. Finally the Rolls-Royce machine of the inner administration turns out to be stuffed with lead and refuses to consider as a possibility what is now a fact: that the public may know what is best.

Far from being stretched for examples of the way the British system is broke, I could have gone on for hundreds of pages, telling the stories of needless woe. The BSE disaster was not Europe's fault, it was a national disease that came about thanks to the toxic cocktail of deregulation, secrecy and short-sighted cuts. The Pergau Dam scandal has evaporated. THORP, the nuclear reprocessing plant, opposed by Greenpeace and controlled by BNFL (now headed by John Guinness, who moved there from the Department of Trade and Industry and who opposes Freedom of Information), is going to turn into another Poll Tax/SERPS billion-pound disaster, in which warnings of the sensible will prove true. In addition there are more hidden aspects of the constitution that cannot sustain the light of day. The Royal Prerogative is the holiest of the holies in the very centre of British power, allowing the Executive to override all parliamentary processes, should it wish to. What is the Royal Prerogative? David Gladstone, now retired from the Foreign Office and a descendant of the Great Man, set out to find out, and it has proved nearly as elusive as the Holy Grail, or at least the peculiar snark. At one point in his entertaining account of his so far frustrated expedition, he asks, 'But here is a puzzle. If Ministers *embody* the Crown, as masters of the Civil Service, how can they simultaneously *serve* the Crown?'[24]

Enough! From its concepts to its culture and its administration, the constitution has comprehensively failed its 300-year test.

8
MENDING IT – A THEORY OF CHANGE

FAILED. BUT IS it just a temporary breakdown? The sound of mending and construction is everywhere. Since the seventeenth century the British constitution has never changed faster. It is being changed in new ways, with new forms of consultation, from referendums to focus groups. It is being altered fundamentally in a wholly novel context of shared international sovereignty, along with fourteen other countries in a European Union that is itself undergoing rapid transformation of extent, powers and institutions. The relationship between the nations of the UK has been put to referendums that have voted for change. The capital will be offered an unprecedented form of voice. Fundamental rights are soon to become part of the constitution for the first time. Both Houses of Parliament, but especially the Lords, are being modernised. The main electoral system will undergo scrutiny and a referendum, while other elections are already being shifted to new systems of proportionality. The base-rate decision is being taken openly by an independent, public committee, as the Bank of England is put on an accountable footing. Foreign policy has begun to be constitutionalised with ethical rules. The monarchy is being re-thought, as never before this century. And, overarching all these changes, the entire constitutional environment has been utterly altered, as voters have made it clear that they want to put an end to the deferential mentality of 'them' and 'us'.

But when he heard that his leader, the 36-year-old William Hague, may not oppose Labour's abolition of the political power of hereditary peers, Lord Hailsham said, 'He should leave things as they are. The system has worked well since time immemorial.'[1] If so, time immemorial ended in 1997. Neither government nor the people of Britain are any longer humbled by the past, their backs bent under the weight of tradition, moving at a snail's pace so as not to disturb the ermine and bauble shell above them. Instead, the spirit and reality of reform are abundant.

But what will Britain be like when the reconstruction comes to a halt? The question is of special importance, because the building site's chief foreman (in so far as there is one, an important point) claims that the question does not need to be answered. Derry Irvine, the Lord Chancellor, 'in effect Labour's Minister for the Constitution', the main author of the constitution section of its election Manifesto, who accepts his 'pivotal role' in reform, says that he is motivated by 'cautious empiricism'. 'People,' he has stated firmly, 'will have to live with our manifesto . . . Our traditions are of gradual, empirical, step-by-step change.'[2] In *The Times* he stated that 'the Labour Manifesto gave a complete picture of our policies and the thinking which binds them together'.[3] However, the only passage in the constitution section of the Manifesto that describes Labour's thinking states, 'There is unquestionably a crisis of confidence in our political system, to which Labour will respond in a measured and sensible way.'

As a calming tactic in the election campaign, these words may have been adroit. Now that Labour's programme is becoming a reality, their approach cannot be summarised with a gruff 'it's measured and sensible'. It is not that more needs to be done immediately. The amount of legislation is impressive. And the description of each of Labour's specific commitments in the Manifesto is clear and compelling. What alarms those who *are* sensible is that a government so concerned with presentation, projects an image of its aims that is so fuzzy. Will British voters become full citizens? If government is to be more open, will it be an open society? The values of Labour's constitutional programme go unstated as questions like these are left unanswered. But then Irvine's deeds belie his words. The White Paper on Scotland is an *overall* package that combines extensive devolution of powers, a legal framework for resolving disputes between Edinburgh and London, and a reduction in the number of Scottish MPs at Westminster, to make a fair settlement for the English. He is rightly proud of it for this reason. Furthermore, when challenged, Irvine makes much bolder claims. A fortnight before telling the *Observer* that the government was gradual and empirical, he wrote in *The Times* to assure its political editor Peter Riddell that the Manifesto commitment meant that he need 'have no fear that the programme is piecemeal, or that its interconnections are not being thought through'.[4] In a lecture on how he will incorporate the European Convention on Human Rights into British law, the Lord Chancellor declared, 'We are making a new history – not for a year or two, but hopefully for the great long term', which is not the sentiment of those who live in the gradual, step-by-step policy universe. They never speak about making change for 'the great long term'.[5] It is not a *sensible* activity. 'Ambitious' would be a better term for it. Ambitions that are planned often go wrong, but hopes that are not imagined will never be realised. The government seems to be in need of a new language to describe how it wants things to change.

The tension is patent. Irvine states, 'the British Constitution is firmly based on the separation of powers. It is essential that incorporation (of the European Convention on Human Rights) is achieved in a way that does nothing to disturb that balance.' And also, 'What is critical is that the form of incorporation sits comfortably with our United Kingdom institutions. It must not disturb the supremacy of Parliament.' Firm separation of powers, undisturbed supremacy, comfortable institutions – these terms do not describe the present British constitution, let alone its unparalleled modifications. If they did, the constitution would not need what Irvine himself calls 'the most ambitious and extensive programme of constitutional reform and modernisation this century . . .'

Anyway, as we have seen, it is well known and authoritatively described, since Bagehot and Dicey, that in Britain the powers of government are not clearly separated; the Executive is unchecked; nor, since joining Europe, is Parliament supreme; and internationally established rights cannot possibly sit *comfortably* (a term redolent of the old complacency) with the UK's institutions. There are counter-quotations to be sure, as seen in Blair's preface to the Manifesto, where he calls for decentralisation and democratic renewal. There is change strongly advocated – but also continuity emphasised as if change is feared. There are striking reforms – some made already, others coming soon – but there is also a desire to preserve. Or to have it both ways.

Caution is understandable. After being burnt in four elections, Labour is eight times shy of lefty blueprints (or what we might call pinkprints) that sound radical, yet are remote from people's lives. It is not keen to adopt another ideology that might bog it down. It is feeling its way. If the old institutions are pretty irrelevant anyway, their alteration may matter much less than would once have been the case. On 20 February 1997, the then Conservative government called a debate on the constitution in order to attack Labour's plans. Their critique was feeble and made Blair impatient. When Sir Cranley Onslow interrupted him with a stupid point of order, Blair waved his hand and declared, 'If anything demonstrates why our institutions need reform, he does.' It was not a parliamentary answer (the Hansard record of it fails to capture its flavour).[6] Instead, it had a contemporary temper. Blair feels that Onslow's chamber is irrelevant to British life. To get too deeply concerned about reforming a constitution incarnated by 'the supremacy of Parliament' risks becoming irrelevant oneself and losing touch with the British people. Best to leave MPs barking behind the portcullis.

This is not so much an argument as an attitude. The institutions do not touch the souls of New Labour men and women, so why should changing them? But, then, perhaps rather than being of little consequence, reform might indeed prove dangerous. This too could be a reason for Labour to play down the significance of its actions, in the hope that this will make them less inflammatory. William Rees-Mogg put the danger eloquently just before the election:

> Once a nation starts to change its constitution in fundamental ways, change is bound to continue . . . Each of the constitutional reforms proposed by the Labour Party would be the beginning not the end of a process of change . . . Since women were given the vote, Britain has not seen rioting in the streets over constitutional issues. New Labour may live to regret setting out to sea in this particular sieve.[7]

A safe response is to claim, as Irvine does with emphasis, that each reform is undertaken strictly on its own merits and need have no further consequences than the ones he has taken into account – that they are not starting a process, but stopping the rot. This justification draws on a conventional notion of nineteenth- and twentieth-century reform – that change *should* be piecemeal, its aims being to leave the fundamentals unchallenged. When people say, 'Of course the House of Lords is indefensible, but look how awkward it would be to replace it', it is *the spirit of the whole* that is fortified by an apparently pragmatic defence. What New Labour has done is turn this language on its head. 'Oh no, we *are* defending the spirit of the system,' they say, as they set about altering its fundamental parts. However, its unwritten nature makes a unity of our constitution. Written ones have sections with headings such as: Basic Rights, Parliament, Administration of Justice, which can be isolated from each other. To touch one part of British sovereignty, however, is to touch it all.[8] To agree that the Scots should have a Parliament if they so wish, or that we should all enjoy possession of a Bill of Rights, *is* to change the nature of Britain as a country, not only in the general sense, but in the knock-on effects. Scotland raises the West Lothian question – that is, the English question – about severe anomalies in the distribution of parliamentary authority. A Bill of Rights must affect the sovereignty of Parliament, even if this is supposed to be impossible. There is no need to foresee rioting to accept that Rees-Mogg has made a valid point. As John Smith put it in his 1993 lecture, constitutional reform 'is a start, not an end, to a continuing process'.[9] It can authoritatively be asserted that what Labour has begun with its constitutional reforms will continue, and not stop. So it is essential to ask in what direction these changes will take Britain.

In his Cardiff speech on the constitution in 1994, Blair declared that Britain needs 'a new constitutional settlement to express the new relationship between individual and society, citizen and state, for the world today'. Reform could hardly have been put in a more ambitious framework, as a part of a larger effort to define the place of government. This is surely right. If one sums up the programme of constitutional reform in a word, then that word is 'democracy'. It raises modern relationships of power, risk, responsibility and demands for freedom. This view of constitutional change has the future stamped all over it. But again, the brakes were applied, just as they were to the idea of stakeholding. To start to explain Labour policy in terms of a new settlement connects to the slippery slope of modern times.

There is no way off this slope. In Britain's case it is worse because our constitution, being seamless, makes the slope more slippery. *Glissez!* Powers that others formally separate are closely fused in the United Kingdom. Important reforms will connect to others. Anomalies will survive only if everyone regards them as fair. After the destruction of consensus politics, unfairness has become an issue. The principles of government that Irvine at the moment wishes to leave unstated will be raised and go on being raised. The system as a whole is in play. How to change the constitution links to a much larger question: the nature of political change in modern society.

In his early, fertile masterpiece, *Thought and Change*, Ernest Gellner took a measure of Marxism. In one remarkable paragraph, after noting that the French Revolution of 1789 littered the world with constitutions that are 'often a dead letter' and predicting the Soviet-style five-year plans will suffer the same fate, he writes, 'Revolutions do not occur in developed societies, now that capitalism has gone through its counter-reformation: this gives us something to be grateful for, namely affluent societies with strong liberal traditions.' He then emphasises that there can be no complacency about shocking poverty or concentrations of power. The total population must be enriched, he argues, while preserving liberty. And he concludes, neatly reversing one of Marx's most famous aphorisms, 'As for the thinker – his job is plainly to try and help by understanding the world, not to change it. It is now changing much faster than he can write'.[10] This was in 1964, before global change accelerated to its present pace. Gellner observed in a single sweep two apparently contradictory, but actually related, phenomena: the end of revolutions and the accleration of change. Revolutions as violent insurrections do not occur in developed societies, because their 'unity of rupture' takes place only when societies *fail* to change. When the State seeks to prevent the transition to modern life, modern attitudes force themselves upon it catastrophically. Liberal democracy, being built upon the conscious idea of change, has adaptation built into it.

The British version of this, however, built adaption to change into the old institutions and never had a clearing-out style revolution. Could Gellner be wrong in the British case? Might the new government today be stimulating, not preventing, an explosion with its wholesale reforms? Sovereignty, far from sitting comfortably and undisturbed, is now bound to be transferred from the Crown to the people. Classic revolutions entailed just this secular humbling – so are we not building up to a revolution of this kind? Will Hutton suggests the possibility in his seminal argument:

> No state in the twentieth century has ever been able to recast its economy, political structures and society to the extent that Britain must do, without suffering defeat in war, economic collapse or revolution. Only traumatic events on that scale delegitimise the existing order to such an extent that a country conceded the case for dramatic change. In this respect Britain's

> prospects must be viewed with great caution. The royal state is deeply embedded. The networks of City institutions, public schools, regiments, landed estates and boardrooms that form the conservative base is no less entrenched.[11]

To prove the point he kindly refers the reader to an essay of mine on 'The Empire State', in which I describe the interconnected buttresses that kept aloft the historic cathedral of British rule.[12]

But I don't think there need be such a trauma to recast the political structures now, after the fifty-year revolution has dissolved so much of the imperial culture and institutions forged in nineteenth-century Britain. The economic structures may go deeper, because of the way that finance capital predated and dominated manufacturing interests from the start. But the contention I asserted in my introduction rests on some coherent analysis, and not just wishful thinking. While civil society has renewed itself, the old constitutional, order is suffering its own necrosis. It can therefore be replaced without an insurrection, or defeat in war, because, sociologically, as Gellner argues, liberal traditions have change built into their genetic code. At the level of the State, the way Britain is governed can be refashioned over the next twenty years, or even ten. The reforms that Labour is introducing have begun this process.

There are three different kinds of change in play. First, there is what can be called *traditional reform*. Second, there is *free-market populism*. Third, there is *utopian realism*. The last two are both forms of modernisation, and the future of Britain is now in contention between them. But the first still matters because its language of change is so influential that both competing forms of modernisation tend to express their ambitions in its familiar tones.

Traditional reform

Traditional reform remains a cause of present frustration. It has monopolised the language of authority and 'practical experience'. Reassurance that reform will be limited to adjustments that will sit 'comfortably' with the supremacy of

Parliament is an example. The British system has had a unique capacity to change *in order to remain the same*. It has a brilliant record of preserving itself by means of partial alterations. Without this, it could not have lasted so long. Despite the blast of Thatcher, there is a longing in the political class to curl up and carry on as before. Complacent this may be, but attraction of the past comes from the fact that success was implanted within it for centuries. So it is not merely slothful conservatism that leads those in authority to hanker for the good old days. Indeed past success was founded on an adaptability whose wellspring was the glorious compromise of the Glorious Revolution – the settlement of 1688 that bestowed a patrician system of class alliances and the capacity to alter government peacefully, within a continuing structure of the rule of law. It was a 'preserving revolution', to use the description of Lord Macaulay, whose account of it in *History of England from the Accession of James the Second* towered over Victorian attitudes to their past. And their politics. When Lord Grey introduced the Great Reform Act of 1832 to rid the country of rotten boroughs, he stated, 'The principle of my reform is to prevent the necessity for revolution.' Macaulay, supporting the Bill in Pariament, explained that it would prevent the danger of democracy – this being 'fatal to the purposes for which government exists'. Writing about 1688 itself, Macaulay argued:

> The highest eulogy which can be pronounced on the revolution of 1688 is this, that it was our last revolution. Several generations have now passed away since any wise and patriotic Englishman has meditated resistance to the established government. In all honest and reflecting minds there is a conviction, daily strengthened by experience, that the means of effecting every improvement which the constitution requires may be found within the constitution itself.[13]

Macaulay expressed the Victorian perspective on the constitution. It is the assumption implicit in the thinking of nineteenth-century reformers. They saw their constitutional arrangements as an inclusive *machinery for improvement*. The forward motion was an essential part: it did not merely adapt to change that was thrust upon it. It had not just spared Britain from bloody upheaval, though that was seen to be a considerable benefit. It was a positive mechanism for better government and administration, always within the framework of the élite compromise of 1688. Only in the 1960s did the dynamism of the settlement finally putter out. A still adroit ruling class promptly negotiated accession to the European Union, if on the third attempt. This, however, while a comprehensive improvement in the situation (or so the public judged it in the referendum), was not a change that could be 'found within the constitution itself'. Looking back, we can see that the settlement of 1688 ended in 1975.

The British polity's near 300-year record of improvement under the banner of the Glorious Revolution was much more than administrative. It was able to grow because it managed to widen the base of its inclusion, so that at its peak, after the Second World War, the entire labour movement was incorporated within its socio-political consensus, as well as the upper and middle classes. At each point it tackled reform piecemeal, so as to 'retain traditional centralism in a modern setting'.[14] Nonetheless, it embraced the male franchise, extended it to women and created the Welfare State. Hence the paradoxes of a country at once conservative yet evidently always modernising, and a strong, unified and self-conscious working class that yet accepted its place.

Perhaps inevitably the historic progress of adaptation became riddled with maladaptation. Today, a fundamental question faces those concerned with constitutional reform. Is it plausible to see the new reforms as an extension of the traditional method of incremental change, whose aim is to secure and reinforce the old order in a new world? Are these too improvements of the kind Macaulay venerated? As we have seen, some of Derry Irvine's phrases suggest that they are, although the fact that he is incorporating the *European* Convention into British law suggests otherwise.

Free-market populism

Whatever some government ministers might hope, the incremental adaptation that was the secret of the old regime has already been undermined – by Thatcherism. A year after she first took office Nigel Lawson wrote:

> To describe what we are engaged in as a peaceful counter-revolution would be somewhat fanciful. Whatever else they may be, Conservatives are not revolutionaries. But there is no doubt that our chosen course does represent a distinct and self-conscious break from the predominantly social-democratic assumptions that have hitherto underlain policy in post-war Britain.[15]

If we look at Thatcher's impact from the point of view of the constitution, we can see that what Lawson calls the 'self-conscious break' also shattered the unwritten settlement. For what he terms 'social-democratic assumptions' cannot be separated from it. The socialist and social-democratic element in post-war British government had been rather weak, not least because most of the time the Conservative Party was in power. But what there had been – the development of welfare and Keynesian full-employment policies – had been fused into the base amalgam of the seventeenth-century settlement. What the government after 1979 attacked as 'socialism' was, in character if not in name, the inherited tradition of rule by chaps who knew best: that is to say, the old regime itself. The breaking of this made Thatcher the least conservative and most radical of Prime Ministers.

Economically, the Thatcherite advocates of the free market can make a case for saying that they returned Britain to the status quo, meaning to the previous state of affairs at the end of the nineteenth century, before the rise of Labour. But you cannot turn back time in such a fashion, as the dynamics of the forces involved do not revert to their past. To take the most obvious point, the majority of the population were then starting to make their entry into the process of government through the vote. Men through the trade unions, followed by the women's suffrage movement pioneering direct action, represented efforts to secure a democratic franchise. They looked to the regime to make progress within it. After 1979, for the first time a large, already enfranchised section of the population was driven out: not from the vote – although the imposition of the Poll Tax achieved that also, as we have seen – but from being part of the incorporated interests that defined the nation. Thatcher reversed the orientation of the State away from its historic pattern of inclusion. She did initiate a revolution – there is no other word for it. 'Do you know,' she told a British Ambassador in 1978, while leader of the opposition, 'there are still people in my party who believe in consensus politics.' 'I think most people in the country, including me, believe in consensus politics,' he replied. 'I regard them as quislings, as traitors . . . I mean it,' said the future Premier.[16]

It was not only her own party colleagues whom Thatcher anathematised. Everyone who believed in consensus was a traitor. It is a mistake to regard this as just a matter of temperament. Nothing could be further from the truth. It expressed an assault upon the fundamental values of the constitutional settlement as it had been improved from within, to use Macaulay's terms, during and after the Second World War. The monarch as the inclusive symbol of all our aspirations; the Commons as a club with shared values beneath its adversarial theatre; the Civil Service as above politics and 'managing decline'; the BBC as neutral broadcaster seeing all points of view; the trade unions as the legitimate representatives of working people – *all traitors*. Yet this consensual order *was* the unwritten constitution. She ploughed it up. Nor was her approach empirical or gradualist. Cautious when she had to be, opportunist when she could be, Thatcher was ideological. And she continued to be ideological when the patricians in her party thought such intellectual forcefulness would 'blow over'. Once ideas and arguments had been a living part of the improvement in government that Great Britain pioneered, helping it to become one of the foremost countries of the world. As preservation became the order of the day, however, theory became foreign. Anything that offered an alternative *overview* could find no space within a constitutional settlement that was no longer self-improving, but seeking simply to survive.

Thatcher blasted all this apart. Just after she became Conservative leader in 1975, she intervened in a policy seminar. She interrupted the talk 'by reaching into her handbag and hauling out a copy of Hayek's *The Constitution of Liberty*. Disregarding the speaker, she banged the book on the table and announced, "This is what we believe." '[17] Really? Hayek's study is a lengthy, historical claim that liberty needs constitutional rules: 'A free society certainly needs permanent means of restricting the powers of government, no matter what the particular objective of the moment may be.'[18] She did not go that far. When her free-market ideas hit the Powellite bedrock of 'belief' in British institutions, the ideas crumpled. Nonetheless, her ideological approach remade a regime that was stifled by inertia and, until then, mentally paralysed by its own decline. Thatcher brought in outside thinking to re-orient the old polity.

Thatcher's revolution has made possible the constitutional one that has now begun. It also makes it necessary. The two-sided nature of Thatcher, the reactionary-revolutionary, sets the poser that New Labour seeks (we hope) to resolve. Democrats who delighted in the Thatcher government's assault on vested interests and restrictions, who celebrated council-house sales and privatisation, found themselves wondering why she centralised power too much, instead of extending democracy further. Ferdinand Mount, who wrote the 1983 Conservative Manifesto as a Downing Street policy adviser, became the most eloquent spokesman of this disappointment. In his book *The British Constitution Now*, he fruitlessly proposed that democratic reform be sutured onto traditional virtues and institutions. Macaulay would have been proud of Mount's book. Rarely can so eloquent a case, by an influential figure, have been so utterly ignored. A despairing Mount voted Liberal Democrat on 1 May. Traditionalists meanwhile, who had welcomed Thatcher's emphasis on strong institutions and patriotic exceptionalism, suddenly found globalisation crashing around their heads.

Those who recognised her novelty earliest were also clear about the dual nature of her project. Stuart Hall was the first to use the term 'Thatcherism' when he wrote about her approach prior to the 1979 election, as Labour wilted. He identified her 'authoritarian populism' and the way that her break with consensus politics allowed her to position Labour as representing,

> the power bloc, enmeshed in the state apparatus, riddled with bureaucracy, in short 'with' the state; and Mrs Thatcher, grasping the torch of Freedom with one hand, who is undividedly out there 'with the people'. It is the Labour Party which is committed to things as they are – and Mrs Thatcher who means to tear society up by the roots and radically reconstruct it! This is the process by which – as they say – the radical right has 'become popular'.[19]

The widespread admiration for Thatcher's radicalism was the first sign that the people of Britain are not nearly as conservative as their traditional masters. Obviously as far as the Labour movement was concerned, Thatcher assaulted their position. Less blatantly, but more subversively, she also unravelled the culture of the dominant institutions. At least the unions survived, battered and bowed, as themselves. She even democratised them, insisting on regular leadership ballots and proper internal procedures. She did not democratise and thus renew the inner workings of the various branches of the State. Instead, her governments reinforced the facade while demolishing its procedures from within.[20] Alongside Stuart Hall, Martin Jacques identified the mix as 'reactionary modernisation'. Their orginality was to emphasise the modernity of Thatcherism, the forward-looking, market-driven direction that she sustained through 'conviction politics' – her answer to consensus. At the same time their analysis recognised the regressive narrowing of controls that regarded all resistance as treason. Geoffrey Howe, reviewing Thatcher's memoirs, observed:

> For Margaret Thatcher in her final years, there was no distinction to be drawn between person, government, party, and nation. They merged in her mind as one seamless whole. Her interests were axiomatically those of Britain. Any criticism of her was an unpatriotic act.[21]

This is a precise attack on Thatcher's absolutism. Given that Howe was so firm in his own view that he himself knew best (for example, about how to relax the sale of arms to a pioneer in the mass gassing of civilians), and that this entitled him to hide matters from the British people, one is tempted to say, 'It takes one to know one.' The arrogance of power became so complete within the inner core of Thatcher's government that most of its members criticised each other for being arbitrary and dictatorial. Behind this indulgence was a shared assumption that voters would remain the compliant putty into which they had been turned by consensus politics.

But the personalised form of rule of Thatcher's period, in which individual fates of Cabinet members moved from high drama to sordid farce as you blinked, should not divert us from the fact that it had a specific and novel character in British history. I want to establish, or at least assert, one aspect of the Tory period from 1979, to distinguish it from what went before and what needs to happen now. It is helpful to see the British government and its constitution as they emerged after 1688 as a special form of organised change. The form of change adopted by Thatcherism was different in kind from it – from the complex machinery of improvement by adaptation and incorporation that prevented revolution. Historically, one of the exceptional characteristics of the British State, in European terms, was that it consciously foresaw the possibility of an insurrectionary opposition to it and, thanks to the freedom and toleration it offered and to the concessions it made, prevented this challenge: it was a prophylactic regime. This is one reason why, in the end, it became so stifling. But for all its thorough, preventative construction, it was not prepared for an attack from one direction, and perhaps one direction only. Ideologically motivated radicals had stormed it fruitlessly from every possible angle, except the leadership of the Tory Party. Margaret Thatcher ran an insurrection from above. She had her cadre, inspired by her own courageous example. She had the inevitable force of history, the world market. She had her cry: riches, freedom, enterprise! Above all, she controlled the State, the traitorous machine itself was in her hands, unprotected by a written constitution. This is why she kept the State as it is, so as to be able to use its untrammelled powers to transform everything else.

As the successor to Thatcher, Blair inherits her example. He cannot revert back to the old machinery of the 1688 State. Should he, therefore, follow her and impose change from above, retaining the initiative by forcing the deregulation of the economy onto a reluctant and divided population, by means of an unchecked supremacy of the Executive, which will be renewed thanks to an unfair electoral system and the unfettered endorsement of the tabloid press? If the number-one aim is to win a second election, this must be a temptation.

Furthermore, Thatcher has also profoundly altered the State machine itself, compared to the one that she inherited which resisted her modernisation. The mandarins were always traditional improvers. She turned many of them into something else, cutting their bonds of allegiance to consensus values. The new mandarins who rose throughout the Tory's eighteen years are not constitutional traditionalists or stick-in-the-mud fuddy-duddies. Well connected to the board-rooms, they are avid for a modern, economically vibrant country and are keen to do away with any resistance to the global market that stands in its way. They would even abolish the House of Commons if they could – just as they helped to dismantle local government. Since the age of absolutism, able men with such attitudes have always risen in the service of the State. They seek to exercise traditional supremacy in a new way, using all the methods of contemporary science. Civil servants working for New Labour will encourage a Thatcher-ite approach, presuming it to be a natural, even technical, non-political method. A Treasury strategic review, leaked in

1996, sets out the vision of one such group of modernisers. In its 'Key Assumptions' it states that 'Treasury officials have a high level of commitment to the efficiency of the market . . . and utilitarian ethics,' no less, and it went on:

> In general the limits of the utilitarian-market approach come when people believe that virtues other than efficiency and self-interest should dominate, e.g. responsibility, justice or patriotism . . . The Treasury acccepts the analysis that everything is tradeable and ultimately has a price and that all that is needed is a sensible allocation of property rights.[22]

If these Treasury high-flyers were to draft a constitution, their Declaration of Independence would read:

> WE HOLD THESE TRUTHS TO BE SELF-EVIDENT, THAT EVERYTHING IS TRADEABLE AND THAT ALL MEN HAVE THEIR PRICE – AND THAT TO SECURE THESE TRUTHS WE HAVE THE DUTY TO THROW OFF RESPONSIBILITY, JUSTICE AND PATRIOTISM AND ALLOCATE PROPERTY RIGHTS.

It is not funny. They mean it. Furthermore, they know that they can make no such declaration in public, but still they mean it. The signatories of the American Declaration of Independence felt that 'A decent Respect to the Opinions of Mankind' required them to 'declare the causes which impel them to the Separation . . . and let the Facts be submitted to a candid World'. This is the model for all constitutional proposals. They should explain themselves to the public: outline the grievances they hope to remedy and summarise the values they wish to guide them to 'a candid world'. By contrast, the Treasury's strategic assessement, with its total commitment to the open market and a constitutional perspective that liquidates patriotism, is candid only when it hides behind the Official Secrets Act. It has no respect for the opinions of mankind, for it would not survive in the open market of ideas.[23]

In the open market of ideas, a straight pitch has been made to the leader of New Labour to continue the approach of Margaret Thatcher. Reporting before the election, on her disgust for Major and admiration for Blair, Paul Johnson recommended the Labour leader to the readers of the *Daily Telegraph* by comparing the two:

> The most important respects in which he [Blair] is Margaret Thatcher's successor do not concern policy so much as style. They have five vital things in common. They are both conviction politicians. They both talk, think and act in moral terms. They are both radicals. They both place the highest possible value on will-power and its handmaiden, courage. And they both inherited parties which were hidebound and therefore inefficient in securing political objectives.[24]

And then he continued with his attempt to entice support for Blair by suggesting how it could be that 'Blair's historic destiny is to lead Britain out of a proto-Federal Europe . . . If that happens, no one will be more delighted than the Iron Lady who handed onto him, albeit furtively, her sacred mantle.'

Utopian realism

Blair needs to spurn this ghastly offer. For the 'sacred mantle' of the Iron Lady is embossed with steel lettering, which reads: 'Britain has not changed', even if the way it has changed may prove the best legacy of the Thatcher years. For there were two responses to her 'revolution from above'. Through the long and apparently stagnant years that followed the bust of the Lawson boom, the Poll Tax débâcle and drawn-out misery of John Major's premiership, the Labour Party proceeded to modernise itself. To do so it drew on Thatcher's example. What other example of success was there? It created its own strong leadership, clear image, ruthless appeal to self-interested middle England, and it assumed that voters hate all taxes, respect business and think compassion is for wimps. But underneath, mourning the Health Service, angered by the new plutocracy, caring about social disintegration, desiring education (hence the stampede into universities when offered) and embracing the end of snobbery and deference, a progressive, cellular modernisation was taking place. Family by family, across the country, pet bulldogs in their various forms – from Scargillism to Powellism – were put to sleep. A revolution from below caught up with the revolution from above that Thatcher had inaugurated. It has the potential to reverse its terms.

The need now is for an approach to change that gives formal and institutional expression to the transformation. The political theorist Chantal Mouffe, drawing on the work of Quentin Skinner, has called for articulate citizenship. In a parallel argument, Paul Hirst argues for what he terms associative democracy.[25] In both cases citizenship is seen as open. They reject a crude opposition of rights and duties. Instead they seek to sustain a creative tension between individual freedom and civic participation. But theories about what kind of citizens it is possible for people to become do not resolve the more important question of what approach a government and its supporters should take to achieve such change.

The main form of *change* associated with the 1688 settlement was, of course, conservatism. This held that there is a 'natural history' to British development – an organic way of belonging within its traditions, institutions and laws. These in turn granted society the means to assess, reject and absorb modification, ensuring continuity based on the wisdom of its founding moment and its constant desire for its own progress in a changing world. In the twentieth century the left absorbed variants of this Burkean approach in both Fabianism and Labourism. Both shared a belief in gradualism and the virtuous administrator. They located the power necessary to effect reform in the honest State, not the vulgar impulses of the demos, arguing for reform, not revolution; but, like insurrectionary socialists, they focused on State power to initiate a social and economic transformation from poverty to plenty. Its uninspired incrementalism and innate dislike of vulgar commerce made Fabian-Labourism irredeemably statist – meaning that it looked to State authority to provide solutions – as it too renewed the prophylactic paternalism of the old regime.

Thatcher's market liberalism became the effective alternative to paternalism in both its traditional and Labour forms.

It sees individual initiative as the creator of wealth. The State may be necessary, but only because strong government is needed to clear the way for the free market and ensure competition. The Treasury values cited above are a good expression of market liberalism. Clearly they are not going to satisfy those with such modest principles as responsibility, justice and patriotism – or, perhaps, any principles at all. But when applied, they can unlock the colossal energy of free competition whose forces are, indeed, transforming societies across the world.

Marxism, as the insurrectionary form of socialism, saw the working class as the agent of change – which, stripped of its dignity, will rise up to overthrow capital and its handmaiden, the State. It held that knowledge of the future – of how best to make use of the productive potential of industry – is inscribed in its victims. One of the most powerful critiques of this view is that, for all its voluntarism and emphasis on action, Marxism is a doctrine of fate. It claims that there is a pre-ordained agent-in-waiting, in this case, below the stage rather than in the wings. There is, however, no such pre-inscribed class force. Yet those who scorn the notion often perpetrate their own forms of predestination. High Fabians believe that a select network of technocrats know the best path of amelioration. Labourism is even more attached to belief in its own people as an exclusive bulwark and battering-ram. Market liberalism's insistence on the individual as the only source of wealth and freedom proposes a more dynamic kind of fatalism, that of the hidden hand. Finally, Conservatism claims that the values we need already exist, in the past, which is the given guide to whatever might be best for the future. In this way all the familiar varieties of handling change, which fought each other so fiercely, share a belief that there already exists a social-historical gyroscope to point us in the right direction.

There is no such gyroscope. There is no source of certainty – not the underdog (Marxism), the cultivated (Fabianism), the organised (Labourism), the market (Liberalism) or the given (Conservatism). As the people cease to be mindless, the dialogue of control and change has altered in ways we still do not fully understand. Nonetheless, *purposive change* – including reforming our own behaviour, from diet and intimate relations to global pollution – is growing in confidence, even while blind market forces appear to have triumphed everywhere.

Strategy-making in these circumstances needs an approach that Tony Giddens of the London School of Economics has called 'utopian realism'. It offers no intrinsic solutions, nor does it propose any social force as the inherent bearer of a better society. In Giddens' definition it puts together 'realism . . . because radical politics has to grasp actual social processes to suggest ideas and strategies which have some purchase' alongside the utopian 'because . . . models of what could be the case can directly affect what comes to be the case'.[26] In more familiar language, utopian realism seeks to handle change by working backwards from the goal. The goal is a disclosure of hopes and objectives, not a blueprint, a plan, a god or a final solution. Thus utopian realism, like democracy itself, is procedural rather than substantive. It proposes a way of directing change, whatever the specific direction might be.

In some respects it is akin to the approach taken by Karl Popper in *The Open Society and its Enemies*. Popper argued that history bares no intrinsic meaning and has no special carrier, that 'instead of posing as prophets we must become the makers of our fate'. He argued for piecemeal social engineering. In our era of ecological risk and potentially catastrophic *laissez-faire* capitalism we need transforming change. As one of his more successful pupils put it, 'An open society is not merely the absence of government intervention and oppression. It is a complicated, sophisticated structure, and deliberate effort is needed to bring it into existence.'[27] We can see here the combination of possibility and practicality. As Popper put it in a moving passage on the need for humility in politics:

We can *learn*, we can *grow* in knowledge, even if we can never

> *know* – that is, know for certain. Since we can learn, there is no reason to despair of reason; and since we can never know, there are no grounds for smugness, or for conceit over the growth of our knowledge.[28]

'This is very idealistic but not practical,' I can hear it being said, and today the voices are more likely to be Labour ones than Tory. 'The next thing he'll be calling for is *imagination.*' Precisely. There is an outstanding example of utopian realism that, unfortunately, proved incomprehensible to the British political class at the time as its leading members, locked in tradition, lacked imagination. This was the creation of the European Union, or the Common Market as it was known when it began in 1958. Europe's founders deliberately laid down short-term measures justified by distant and ambitious goals. A glance at what happened shows utopian realism at work. Perry Anderson provides a penetrating description:

> It was an entirely novel combination: a style of political construction that was highly voluntaristic, yet pragmatically piecemeal – and yet vaultingly long-range . . . Monnet's strategy was an incremental totalisation . . . The implication of his undertaking did not escape him. 'We are starting a process of continuous reform', he wrote, 'which can shape tomorrow's world more lastingly than the principles of revolution so widespread outside the West.'[29]

Incremental totalisation: two words that sum up a careful, step-by-step approach guided by a transforming overview. Exactly the kind of approach needed for any large-scale constitutional project. Henri Spaak was the Belgium statesman who oversaw the 1956 report that set out the case. The British had told the core six Western European countries what Her Majesty's Government thought of the idea:

> The future treaty which you are discussing has no chance of being agreed; if it was agreed, it would have no chance of being ratified; and if it were ratified, it would have no chance of being applied. And if it was applied, it would be totally unacceptable to Britain.[30]

It was in these circumstances that Spaak made one last

appeal to try and convince the British to join. He went to see Rab Butler, the then Chancellor of the Exchequer and intellectually the most influential British Minister at the time. It was of critical importance to persuade Butler, for there to be any chance of turning the Cabinet around. Spaak's assistant describes what happened:

> It was obvious Spaak was not convincing Butler. I can still see him, very immobile, looking at Spaak without saying a word, and the colder he became, the warmer Spaak became, and the warmer Spaak became, the colder and colder Butler obviously became. After a while we realised that it was no use going on. We said goodbye and went off . . . As we walked back, Spaak turned round to us and said . . . I appealed to his imagination. I don't think I could have shocked him more if I had taken my trousers off.[31]

The *practical* cost of this lack of imagination was considerable. Britain staggered from balance of payments crisis to crisis over the next fifteen years, while community trade rose from $7,530 million to $49,830 million.

Utopian realism is the approach needed for constitutional reform. It means articulating clear, principled goals and then setting about them with practical measures that are given the space necessary to be assessed in a context of consent. New Labour has begun to implement its programme of constitutional reform – it is taking the first steps. But it decided against a statement of principles or a general paving motion that would have allowed MPs, press and public to debate the principles governing reform. So Britain is entering a period that will see the greatest constitutional change for a century (as Jack Straw, the Home Secretary, put it, and, if anything, this undersells the programme), yet the country has no clear idea what this means and where it is supposed to lead.

When Labour first spelt out the entire package of reforms that it intended to legislate if it won the election, it did promise just such a statement of purpose. On 5 March 1997, before the election campaign was officially announced, Labour and the Liberal Democrats published the 'Report of the Joint Consultative Committee on Constitutional Reform'.

This ponderous-sounding document set out a series of recommendations and agreements on how to reform the British political system. It was presented to the media by Robin Cook, MP and Robert Maclennan, MP, the joint Chairs of the committee, for Labour and for the Liberal Democrats respectively.

The report gave a succinct overview of the future government's ambitions. The joint announcement also demonstrated an understanding that reform of this kind requires a different sort of politics from either traditional party tribalism or confidential, unwritten understandings. The concluding paragraph of the report stated:

> The proposals set out in our Report are presented as distinct measures yet they are closely related. Through them runs the common thread of empowering the people. To make this clear the new Government should make an early declaration setting out the principles behind its programme of constitutional reform and outlining the more open and modern democracy it seeks to create.

The document's opening paragraphs give an idea of what these principles might be: 'A society that is open and free . . . power accountable to the collective wishes and interests of the people . . . equal rights and responsibilities . . . guaranteed civil liberty, social cohesion and economic opportunity'.

No such statement has been forthcoming. Derry Irvine resists producing more 'unnecessary paper'. Yet, as reform begins to bite, the need for an overall sense of purpose will become more pressing, not less. Reflecting on the votes in Scotland and Wales and on the state of local government in Britain, the *New Statesman* declared that Britain 'urgently needs . . . a worked-through strategic outline of what the government thinks its constitutional programme is intended to lead towards'.[32] It does not need to be *that* worked-through, provided it is clear and politically inspiring. For what is missing, for the English especially, is any sense of the real purpose of Labour's ambitious programme – just what is it ambitious for? The Scots do not have this problem – reform north of the border has not fragmented it into separate zones. Whatever view the Scots took in the referendum about the coming Parliament in Edinburgh, it unified the idea of constitutional change for them. It would have legislative power within a clear remit; it would be restrained by a Bill of Rights; there would be proportional representation likely to ensure cross-party co-operation, if not coalition. Without an equivalent image the English can hardly be blamed for not being able to see what reform means – how the different proposals will *add up*. The public cannot make sense of Labour's commitments; it cannot, literally, understand 'what they are all about'. Finally, a statement of intent would make it easier for the government to pace the changes, and even take them more slowly, without charges of betrayal or sell-out.

The joint report was cleared by Tony Blair, as Robin Cook made plain at its launch. It says that the government 'should' make an early declaration of principles, not that it must or that it will. In the narrow sense, the government falls within the report's guidelines if it does not do so. Constitutional reform is not a narrow matter, however. It is a broad ocean, as Rees-Mogg put it, and Labour has launched its boat upon it. On what new continent does it intend to land, for its purpose can hardly be a pleasure cruise that returns to home port?

The government is capable of articulating its aims.[33] For example in its defence of the first New Labour policy decision: Gordon Brown's announcement that he would give the Bank of England operational independence in deciding the base rate. This was a constitutional move of a high order, one that had been advocated by Nigel Lawson and rejected by Thatcher. In his memoirs, Lawson described it as 'a far more useful constitutional reform than any advocated by Charter 88 and other constitution-mongers'.[34] Brown himself has since explained and defended the decision in terms that connect it to the project of providing Britain with a new overall constitutional settlement. Here, one can see a small example of 'utopian realism', of taking a practical, realisable measure towards a highly ambitious general goal.

For this reason the decision deserves more attention. Utopian realism is not a matter of drawing up pinkprints, of trying to go from here to there in one mighty great leap. But nor is it piecemeal, determined only by what is practical at any given moment, in terms of the balance of demand and resistance. It is not motivated by the desire to preserve the existing system as a whole or to pre-empt challenges to it. Nor does it seek to replace it overnight. It means a form of change driven and justified by larger goals – in the case of the constitution, the goals of fairness, accountability, democracy and national dynamism, which call for an institutional restructuring – steered by the achievable. The decision to give partial independence to the Bank of England can be assessed within this framework.

When the decision was announced, it was widely attacked as a surrender of democratic control to unelected bankers – by Diane Abbot, MP, by Larry Elliot in the *Guardian*, by Melanie Phillips in the *Observer*, to name just a few. They saw the move, which shifts the power to decide interest rates from the Chancellor to a committee of the Bank of England, as a surrender to the demands of financial respectability, one that surbordinated government to the City and undermined the power of the people to influence policy through their elected representatives. Brown's critics argue that in the past, when the Chancellor decided interest rates, he had to answer to Parliament; and that by abolishing this line of accountability, Brown has diminished Britain's democracy.

This description of the role of the House of Commons is so threadbare that it could hardly be uttered outside a polemic. Far from holding the Chancellor to account, the Commons is a playground for a strong Executive. Over the medium term a Chancellor will be answerable (in terms of his political standing) for the general success or failure of the economy. This will still hold true. A strange thing is that the myth that the Commons is the site of real accountability exists alongside a contrary myth: that Ministers of the Crown are all-powerful and 'run the country', with virtually no let or restraint.

Ralph Dahrendorf, who is familiar with both the British and German political élites, once observed that even the wisest of British ex-Chancellors whom he had met could refer to the time they 'ran' the British economy, although they had been helpless as it swung from boom to recession. Yet their German equivalents did not assign themselves such sovereign influence, even when their economy had functioned smoothly, thanks in part to their policies.[35] In Germany they understood that it is a fantasy to think that a national economy can be 'run' by individuals. The Westminster system flatters its Ministers by feeding them this fantasy, surrounding it with the trappings of historic titles and great offices of State. Those who swallow the myth are consumed by it. Chancellors spend hours, if not days, calibrating the consequences of a quarter per cent rise or cut in the base rate. All the pressures of the market, the Bank of England, other central banks, the financial press, the popular media and their own Cabinet colleagues, focus upon them. They are forced into a concern with the short term, tempted by self-importance that makes them think they are 'running' things. Far from allowing them to be masters of history, the exercise of such power obliges them to become the servant, even the victim, of the immediate situation. By refusing to allow himself to be lured into this fantasy, Brown has enhanced his capacity to influence events. His real influence was always limited. But by bringing appearances into line with reality, his powers become more effective, not less.

Thanks to his decision, interest rates are now set by a Monetary Policy Committee comprising nine members, four appointed by the Chancellor himself, who will meet monthly. They will decide the base rate through majority votes, which allows the Governor of the Bank of England to be overruled. Their monthly discussions are published. This process is much more transparent and accountable than it was – including being more accountable to Members of Parliament through the Committee system.

There is an economic criticism of Brown's decision which argues that, by assigning the Bank of England the task of keeping inflation at 2.5 per cent, he implies that inflation is mechanically determined by the interest rate, and also that this should override other economic considerations, especially those of manufacturing. This criticism may be justified as a critique of the terms that have been laid down – the factors that the committee must take into account should, perhaps, be wider – but it does not touch the independence of the process.

The reform is democratic because it liberates policy from the portcullis of Parliament and is a step towards shared sovereignty. Instead of all decisions being monopolised by the Executive, which is supposedly accountable to the Commons but in fact controls the House almost completely, a specific decision will be taken by the relevant institution in an open way, and can then be challenged publicly, not least by MPs. Welcoming the move and linking it to Brown's other reforms of the City, Will Hutton claims:

> The Bank of England will never again play its old role. In transferring its regulatory functions . . . stripping it of debt management . . . and requiring it to set interest rates in the context of a nationally determined economic policy, Gordon Brown has turned the Bank from being the champion of the City to the servant of the British public.[36]

The shift was symbolised for me by an interview on *Newsnight* with Eddie George, the present Governor of the Bank of England. He defended the bank's new role, and claimed that countries with independent central banks experienced *lower* interest rates over the medium term. He was then obliged to answer questions about the impact on manufacturing and exports of the higher interest rates that he desires in the immediate future. Thus his traditional role was reversed. Instead of the Governor pressing for higher rates in the short term to defend the economy from inflation, he was having to justify his stance as not being deflationary. He was forced to accept, verbally at least (but this is a start), responsibility for the consequence of his views, now that he is charged with the power to implement them. And he committed himself to lower interest rates in the long run.

In his *Guardian* column Paul Foot attacked 'the bloodless triumph of the unelected Governor of the Bank of England in seizing control of interest rates' and commented acidly, 'The first act of Labour Ministers who had struggled for so long to get power was to give it away.' He went back thirty years to compare the decision to Harold Wilson's conflict with Lord Cromer, the Governor of the Bank of England in 1964. Then, too, Labour had just come to power after a long period of Tory rule. Cromer told Wilson that he had to raise interest rates. Wilson accused Cromer of undermining democracy, as he had been elected with the promise to keep them low. As Foot describes it, 'It took about eighteen days of entirely coincidental flights of sterling to bring Wilson to heel. Times have changed. Old Labour has become New Labour, and all those silly arguments between democracy and bankers' power are now irrelevant.'

This interpretation could not be more wrong. It was Wilson who capitulated to the established order from the start, as Foot himself once described in a masterly account written in 1967. The Labour government of 1964 inherited a massive balance of payments deficit. But Wilson ruled out the obvious step of devaluation, which many of his colleagues pressed on him. The proposals became known as 'the unmentionable'. He sacrificed the economy to the value of sterling and did so in defiance of the best political advice, both private and public, not least from the left.[37] He decided instead to protect Britain's world role. All Governor Cromer did was tell Wilson that if he wanted to retain an overvalued pound, he had to raise interest rates or foreigners would not hold sterling. Such advice was hardly a banker's conspiracy. On the contrary, Wilson's quarrel with Cromer followed entirely from his disastrous decision to fly in the face of realism. As a result he condemned Britain to years of unnecessary failure. The contrast with Brown's approach has been explained by the present Chancellor himself:

> A few weeks ago interest rate decisions were made by the Chancellor when he chose, announced when he and the Governor and the Bank chose, without any constitutional requirement for information or for explanation. The result was bad government: decisions serving the short-term party political interest rather than the long-term national interest, and as a result, suppressing debate about tough decisions that have to be made in the public interest.
>
> Our reforms move from the *ad hoc* and personalised to the formal and constitutional. They are based on clear rules; the government answerable to Parliament sets the objective, the Bank fulfils it and must report and inform on a regular basis.
>
> The Monetary Policy Committee will publish minutes of its deliberations and voting. What I call the open letter system means that that the Governor of the Bank explains to the public if inflation goes more than one percent above or below the target. And accountability to Parliament is strengthened so that full explanations can be questioned.
>
> So there is now openness and public accountability where once there was secrecy and personalised decision making.[38]

The Chancellor then developed a general overview of the principles that he believes will lead Britain towards reform, and what in his view lay behind Charter 88 from its beginning: 'neither a return to old-fashioned paternalism and state power, nor a belief in a dogmatic free-market liberalism'. To break out of these discredited alternatives, Brown argued, 'Britain needs a modern constitution and a modern view of the rule of government . . . The challenge of the 1990s is to create a new settlement that recognises both our rights and aspirations as individuals and our needs and shared values as a community.' It would be hard to find a better example of an imaginative statement of purpose linked to a limited, technical reform. Utopian realism in practice.

The example is also useful as an illustration of the *limits* of constitutional reform. Mistakes can still be made in the way the rate is set. The international market can still overturn the best-laid plans. The City will still put its priorities above manufacturing. Democracy is more procedural than substantive; it provides a method, not an outcome. But the exclusion summed up by the 'them' and 'us' syndrome has been diminished, and this in itself is good. It is now possible to watch the way that interest rates are decided and even to influence this, through MPs who will be questioning the Monetary Policy Committee before their own Select Committee. Previously the voices of those outside a small secretive circle were excluded from any intervention in decisions on interest rates. Now, such voices can be heard. It is a small reform, but a significant one.

In the conclusion of his classic *Introduction to the Study of the Law of the Constitution*, A. V. Dicey says that, thanks to his explanations, the British constitution no longer appears as a 'sort of maze'.[39] It still feels like a maze when you seek to leave it. There is no straightforward way out. Escaping can demand labyrinthine manoeuvres that feel more like an ambush than an exit. Most of us, in different ways, have suffered the painful experience of confidently striding into a British dead-end. The after-effect for many is an attitude best described as 'suspicion of the intellect combined with reluctance of the will'. This encourages the traditional, subordinate, resentful, grudging, incorporated attitude of the British underdog. Every possible device has been used to keep the natives in this state of mind. The events of 1997 show that this mentality can be cast aside. It is now time to ensure a lasting emancipation from deference. For this to happen Britain needs a democratic revival. One that joins a sense of larger purpose to practical measures based on consent. In terms of the constitution, this calls for a clear statement of principles and purpose. The sooner the better.

9
The English Question

> English, in the great tradition of music hall and penny dreadful, seaside pierrot show and pantomime, of radical dissent and continuous questioning, the other side of imperialism, if you like.
>
> Angela Carter[1]

AT THE OUTSET of this book I argued that all constitutions are lived, and how they are lived is more important than the way in which they are written – or, in the British case, unwritten. In Chapter 6 I developed this theme. A country's 'aspirations' are the most lived part of its constitution; they can find expression in words outside the formal, legal document of the constitution itself. They can also be lodged in symbols connected to the way society is organised. Since the 1975 referendum, the symbol of Europe – is it a glorious horizon or an ominous stormcloud? – has become a constitutional aspiration, namely the country's future, one that runs counter to the aspirations inherited from 1688. Today, the most important question about British identity is: does the country wish to be European? Nor is this a matter of a static state of mind. The Treaty of Rome of 1958 calls for 'ever closer union' of member states – is this Britain's aspiration?

Those who say 'No' and cite the EU's lack of democracy may not be democrats themselves. To date Britain has never aspired to be a full democracy, even while the country has prided itself, sometimes with good reason, on the degree of domestic consent. Instead, until recently the monarchy was 'the interpreter' of who the British are. When the monarchy did embody the country's aspirations, it was the figurehead of an embracing system of hierarchy and success. The respect and awe this induced was a product of the Victorian zenith – it was imperial, rather than merely royal. After 1945 these attitudes were reproduced out of loyalty and gratitude, rather than power, for a whole generation.

In 1997 it became clear that the monarch no longer personifies British aspirations. Not because she is at fault – she is what she was – but because her system has come to an end. Sensing that this was likely to be its fate, British royalty had re-projected itself at the end of the 1960s with considerable success, as an ideal *family*. A family worthy of emulation; to whom wealth came as naturally as the green grass on the fields where it picnicked in its television special. This ploy was reinforced by the royal wedding just over ten years later. Diana has shattered it.

I want to return briefly to what she did and what it led to. Not to the tunnel by the Seine, but to the September days that followed. They told us that the British constitution is now being lived differently. What mattered was the public's rejection of the royal family's attempt to bury Diana with as little fuss as possible. Through their massive applause for a dead princess, millions rejected the attitude of the living royals. Tony Blair was the immediate beneficiary; he became, at least temporarily, both Parliament *and* Crown. The uniqueness is in the conjunction, for no one else has ever been in this position before. The triumph that he enjoys is also negative. For it is a sign of the collapse of the old system: monarchy, Parliament (in terms of resistance to the Executive), the Conservative Party, the Lords (with no replacement in sight) – are broken. The record-breaking approval rating for Blair is a sign of the unparalleled decomposition of the rest of Britain's constitutional arrangements. The success and longevity of the 1688 settlement was due to the way it fused an alliance of élite forces that drew upon their own resources. It meant there was always an alternative. There was *even* an alternative when Margaret Thatcher claimed there was no alternative. The black side of 1997 is that there really is no alternative. All hopes rest on Blair and his team. A constitution that rejected personal rule and pioneered institutional flexibility has come down to one throw of the dice.

Except in this respect: the people (lower-case) are ahead of their leaders. They are not going to go back to the past. The stereotyped forms of appeal, whether to class struggle or to racism, raise little more than a disinterested eyebrow – 'Been there, done that'. The creation of Britain after 1688 rested heavily on overseas conflict, which mobilised what David Marquand has called 'pre-, even anti-enlightenment, nationalism: the nationalism of the anti-Jacobin mobs of the 1790s or the Powellite dockers of the 1960s: the nationalism of subjects defiantly asserting their subjecthood.'[2] This too has gone, and its loss is a significant gain.

The monarchy has been described as an enchanted glass, on which the public gazed to see a magical reflection of itself. This led to an extraordinary cult of the royal family as being just 'like-us'. In the popular mind, royals were contrasted to 'them' – the politicians, the system, the Establishment. It is difficult to recall this now, but it was only recently the mind-set of millions. Most nationalisms are based upon an idea of 'we-the-people'. The British State, pre-democratic to its fingertips, got there first. As democracy dawned, the royals became the regime's 'we-the-people'.[3]

For Diana, the image required of her became unbearable. She still believed in the glamour of royalty, but she wanted it to be the glamour of modernity, not of backwardness. She needed to recognise her own reflection in order to shine and found that, instead of walking through a Versailles-style Hall of Mirrors, she was being impersonated by a distortion. The charade threatened to become her asylum, as it seems actually to have become for other royals. She threw a brick at the mirror. The determination with which she did so is confirmed by the revelations of her persistent, covert guidance of Andrew Morton's original book, *Diana: Her True Story*, and the care she took to correct it, while denying any actual involvement. When the separation that followed was insufficient to give her the independence she needed, she threw another brick at the mirror in the form of her *Panorama* interview, in which she spoke at length, directly to the public. She authoritatively exposed the royal family as not being what it represented itself to be. She unveiled its dishonesty, its adultery and its callousness, as she had experienced it, and then declared that Charles was not suited to be King.

It is important to be dry-eyed both about what she did and the popular response after her death. In the absence of any political movement that really encourages their self-expression, people have to work with the materials that come to hand. Being more 'royal than the royals', Diana had the popularity to do the damage. Her constitutional coup was to turn the tables on the monarchy by stealing its clothes. She declared *herself* 'ordinary' – meaning vulnerable, unhappy, 'just like us' – and condemned the royals as being '*them*' the representatives of 'the Establishment' – explicitly and politically so in the *Panorama* interview. The full scale of the blow she delivered only became apparent when she died. For while she lived, the old element of identification lived on through her. Now, the lower-cases have made clear their disapproval of the monarch and her successor. *They* are no longer part of 'we-the-people'.

Of course, there has often been criticism of the royals before. There is a long tradition of 'stroppy', cynical noise directed at the monarchy and its Court. Indeed, one of the ways in which the royal order is made bearable is through mockery and complaint. This should give republicans pause to reflect. As the historian of the eighteenth century, Linda Colley, has observed, 'The shift in criticism of the monarchy which first became apparent in the 1780s, a shift away from anger at the institution to mockery of the individual royals and their foibles, helped – as it still helps – to preserve it'.[4]

But outspoken views on Elizabeth II in 1997 were not naughtiness of the kind that depends on the authority it provokes. There was anger, not mockery, in the first days of September, and there is a widespread sentiment now that the monarchy as a whole is past it; that the royal family now resembles the *Mir* space station, tumbling in its orbit, its systems constantly breaking down, its parts colliding, its wiser inhabitants keen to leave. It is no longer the star that guides.

With it, British identity also tumbles. Will its replacement be British or English, European or global, singular or plural or federal? I have argued that the government's constitutional reforms need a declaration of principles, of the kind half-promised when the programme was announced before the election. One reason why politicians instinctively resist such a proposal is that it is bound to raise questions of an awkward kind that relate directly to the old identity-mirror, the royal space station now under guidance from the control room of No. 10. Suppose, for example, the almost banal aim of non-discrimination is stated as an objective of constitutional renewal. Uncontentious in itself, once it is endorsed as a *principle*, it should follow that the Church of England should be disestablished, for the way that it currently enjoys a special status is clearly discriminatory, as, historically, it was meant to be. Technically, the professionals see only headaches if they have to try and disentangle the weightless occupants of the orbiting palaces from defending the faith.

This allows us to see a root cause of constitutional conservatism. Not so much 'leave well alone', as the conservatives would have it, but 'leave the unwell alone' for fear of contamination. An issue like disestablishment is important. It raises questions about what happens at the Coronation – how, and to whom, the Head of State swears allegiance; another example of how, with an unwritten constitution, touching a part touches the whole. Furthermore, there is a shadow of theocracy about Britain – ruled by God's representative on Earth. Establishment of the Church sanctifies the unwritten arrangements. Hitherto politicians had better things to do than raise such an issue. The monarch could say 'No' and the people loved her. This no longer describes the forces at work. The future monarch says he wants to defend 'all faiths', which is a nonsense on a personal basis and utterly secular intellectually. If the establishment of the Church of England ends, will not the pre-modern order also do so? When Charles was interviewed by Jonathan Dimbleby, he was asked – perhaps with the Church in mind – about the way he looked forward to being King of England. Charles replied in sombre tones (I am quoting from memory), 'King of Britain, Mr Dimbleby, King of Britain'. Disestablishment will free the Church from Britishness to be true to its name: the Church of *England*.

The different national questions of a multinational entity are posed by every constitutional reform, as the spirit flickers and the framework of the old *British* order folds. At present, the government declines to make the connections directly, perhaps fearing a fate similar to the royal *Mir*. Instead, it is taking a similar approach to the one adopted on Europe twenty years ago. It is doing the business, while insisting that this will preserve the form of Britain we have always been proud of. This is unlikely to prove satisfactory, not least because of pressure from the EU itself, probably in the shape of a common currency. The Prime Minister and his colleagues respond with talk about 'leading in Europe', as if this mantra will make the problem go away. 'We may not like *it*,' is the implication, 'but at least we can be ourselves by *leading* whatever it is.' Although his overall analysis is stuffed with cant, Enoch Powell saw through other people's cant on relations to Europe:

> We were great, we want to remain great, we must therefore belong to something big; and talking in the insufferable way that the English sometimes will talk they proceed to say: 'And we must therefore lead in Europe.' Now the notion of those who inhabit an offshore island 'leading' those who inhabit the continent is so ridiculous that the absurdity of it hardly needs to be mentioned.[5]

Yet it is not completely absurd. A fully engaged United Kingdom would create a triumvirate with France and Germany. This would place Britain, in one of John Major's few good phrases, 'at the heart of Europe'.

His formula begs the question, 'Do we want Europe to be in *our* heart?' For there has to be reciprocity in such matters. Talk of 'leading' avoids such a riposte – one can lead others without wanting to be like them. This option, however, is not on offer. It is, indeed, absurd to think that the European countries would be led by Britain, as if the UK were better than them. You cannot sell them your water, your remaining car industry and your famous merchant bank, and then claim that they need you to lead them. The term is used at conferences and on television for psychological reasons to handle the emotional problem that the EU poses for the UK. The heart of the issue is national. Do the British wish to be Europeans? Formally, I have argued that membership of the EU brought the 1688 settlement to an end. But the self-view of the complex country that emerged over 300 years, with all its stubborn individualism, has not ended. In the vital, lived sense, Britain has yet to join Europe.

In *Nationalism* Liah Greenfeld argues that the nation is 'the constitutive element of modernity . . . Rather than define nationalism by its modernity, I see modernity as defined by nationalism.' She attempts to prove her thesis with a panoramic survey of England (which she call's God's First-born), France, Russia, Germany and America. Tracing the rise of the first born nation in its parliamentary form, Greenfeld concludes that, 'English national consciousness was first and foremost the consciousness of one's dignity as an individual.'[6] One of the telling aspects of relations with Europe for many Britons, which shows they have not yet joined, is that the EU seems undignified to them, both individually and institutionally. This feeling is exploited by newspaper proprietors, especially Rupert Murdoch, who fears Brussels' regulation of the media. Thus a feeling that has deep roots is superficially manipulated by a global force, seeking to prevent the nation from co-operating with the continent. And if, during the election, all you did was read the British press you would have thought that Europe was *the* question.

In one way Europe is definitely 'the question'. Over the

next quarter-century the continent may need to react to immense, angry eruptions of people and regimes in North Africa or the Middle East; Russia or the Ukraine; the Balkans or Turkey. An expanded and strengthened EU may be more likely to respond constructively and peacefully, while a divided and competitive one is more likely to amplify divisions and import them. *This* question of Europe was not of the slightest moment in the British election – few people, if any, during the six-week election campaign, spoke about, or demanded to know about, how Europe should respond to such possible threats. Instead, as the quotations that I culled for Chapter 1 show (and it is a small gathering from among the acres), when the *Sun-Mail-Telegraph-Times* said that 'Europe is the issue', it did not mean that the future of Europe – the continent of which we are a part – is the issue. It meant the issue of 'Europe and us'. Equally, when the Euro was debated, Major was one of the few who mentioned that it might be a great success and asked, 'Then what would we do?' No one discussed whether they *wanted* it to succeed if it went ahead; let alone considered whether Germany's Chancellor Helmut Kohl was right to claim that peace depended on its success.

In most of this book I have taken a constitutional viewpoint. Modern sovereignty is no longer a singular, quasi-religious substance. In a democratic constitutional framework, sovereignty is shared and empowers citizens, cities, regions as well as nations; and it does so by adopting a different paradigm from absolutism, including parliamentary absolutism. But this is a conceptual way of putting something that touches us with feeling. And it is the feeling that decides the thinking. During the election the media was full of feeling – or, in some cases, the feeling of their proprietors. The obsession with the European Question was not with the constitutional arrangements of the continent, but with ourselves.

According to an opinion poll reported in the *Daily Telegraph* on 10 January 1997, only 34 per cent of Britons regard membership of the EU as a good thing. This compared to an average of twice that figure across the rest of the continent. The *Telegraph* was appalled by the support for the Union shown by the *other* countries. Why, it asked, do the 'supposedly more nationalistic' French think so positively about the EU, even when half of them also believe that Germany will emerge as its dominant power? Where are the Napoleonic virtues in the land of Nicolas Chauvin? The paper could not hide its disappointment. It is an important question. Why do the French, or the Germans, traditionally regarded as *more* nationalistic than the phlegmatic Brits, feel differently about the EU's threat to their national identity, which could be just as great as it is to ours? Have they lost their essence? Or – a possibility the *Telegraph* did not suggest – does the fault lie within us?

One explanation is that the entire EU escapade is really a vile plan to crush us. The *Telegraph* preceded its poll with a diatribe by Alan Clark, who was about to be re-selected as a parliamentary candidate by the Conservatives of Kensington and Chelsea. He saw the publication of the Euro-banknote designs at the Dublin summit as a warning. 'I make this prediction,' he wrote. 'Our own Munich crisis is not so far off.' Brussels is not the same as Hitler, he generously conceded, thus making the comparison by denying it. But the continent is ganging up to subjugate Britain. It will 'first isolate, then erode . . . British national identity and self-confidence'.

Clark virtually proposed himself as the new Winston Churchill. He called on those of us who live north of the Channel to stand our ground, as we did in 1939, and to overthrow EU regulations now being 'enforced by an army of quisling officials'. Doubtless members of his new constituency association thrilled to his language and it helped him win their votes, although his analysis is deeply flawed; the use to which he puts the Munich Agreement of 1938, for example, is perverse. Anyway, his was not really an argument about Germany; a country in which the British take far too little interest. When those like Clark attack the EU as a German plot to dominate Europe and fulfil Nazi dreams, they are struggling with developments in Britain, not abroad. Their language expresses their anger and grief at their own pain. 'Hitler' here means something equivalent to 'Smersh' in the James Bond films: 007's nemesis is out to dominate the world and eliminate virile Englishmen on the way. It is the English who want to re-fight the war. Ideally, they would like to win it single-handed this time (as Bond would have done), so that 'we can lead in Europe'.

Another, perhaps more telling way to identify the fundamental difference in British, compared to continental, attitudes is to examine the nature of *pro*-European support in the UK. Most advocates of British membership radiate a sense of loss. In other European countries, membership of the EU can reinforce feelings of nationhood, especially in the middle classes. Europhile French feel *more* French in the transcontinental spaces of the EU and in its negotiations with the rest of the world, even when these are led by an Englishman. They are willing to share their borders, if the alternative is to be confined within them. Many Germans feel *more* German in the EU, not because they want to be top dogs (there are some of those), but because theirs is a European culture, their history is federal and they dislike a strong German capital. Many Italians want to entrench their claim as an historic European nation, and exclusion from the Euro would be felt as a national loss, whatever the economic costs. Spaniards want to prove their modernity, and for them this means becoming a full partner of the EU.

In all these countries, sharing their sovereignty in Europe is experienced as an *identity gain*. Hence the much higher levels of support. A Catholic experience lies behind this, as it validates trans-European identity. But secular nationalism is the dominant mobilising force – and for the large nations of Europe (except Britain) the Union has enhanced, not subjugated, feelings of 'national identity and self-confidence', to echo Clark's words. It also did the nations of Europe a lot of good, economically and politically, when the Union was first formed.[7]

Similar feelings of enhancement can be even more intense

among the smaller states. Denmark, which looks to Britain, may be an exception. Ireland, which was attached to Britain, proves the point. In an elegant essay in *Prospect*, the former Premier of Ireland, Garrett Fitzgerald, and Paul Gilespie, foreign editor of the *Irish Times*, describe how 'EU membership has completed the project of Irish independence'.[8] Most politicians in Westminster, whether for or against the EU, would find this statement incomprehensible. They would regard the claim that a country completes its independence in Europe as contradictory. Yet the authors make a convincing case that Irish identity has been affirmed and consolidated through its European membership, which has released it from decades of inward-looking nationalism. Ireland has become more itself in the world, thanks to its participation in the EU. This is what the central European countries also hope for, as they demand the right to complete their journey to independence by becoming full members of the Union.

What Fitzgerald and Gilespie describe for Ireland is starting to happen in Scotland. Support for a Scottish Parliament is a product of the European process – this is as true for the Scottish National Party's hopes for an independent Parliament as it is for the White Paper's plan for a Scottish Parliament within Britain. Which brings us to the heart of British opposition to Europe. It is not British at all. It is English. Other Britons tend to share the continent-wide experience of membership of the Union as something that encourages them to feel more, not less, themselves: more Scottish, more Welsh. The English are different. They are already top dogs in a multinational union. They already enjoy an inter-national status larger than the sum of its parts, in the United Kingdom of Great Britain and Northern Ireland. The EU cannot be anything like as united an entity. But it does threaten to dissolve the leader-centric sovereignty of Westminster. Indeed, it is doing so already, as the *Prospect* authors point out, in Northern Ireland.

What is the difference between being English and being British? If you ask a Scot or a Welsh person about their Britishness, the question makes sense to them. They might say that they feel Scots first and British second. Or that they enjoy a dual-identity as Welsh-British, with both parts being equal. Or they might say, 'I'm definitely British first.' What they have in common is an understanding that there is a space between their nation and Britain, and they can assess the relationship between the two. The English, however, are more often baffled when asked how they relate their Englishness and Britishness to each other. They often fail to understand how the two can be contrasted at all. It seems like one of those puzzles that others can undo but you can't; Englishness and Britishness seem inseparable. They might prefer to be called one rather than the other – and today young people increasingly prefer English to British – but, like two sides of a coin, neither term has an independent existence from the other. This is how the relationship should be seen. It is an international coin, once called sterling, that has a home and an abroad as different sides of the same experience. At home we are English: it is the English countryside, one does not speak of a British cottage or a British village. Abroad, we are British: it is the British Embassy, we do not have English passports. It is not a border that is easily recognised when crossed; it is a simultaneous experience, uniting one's being at home and one's being in the world, while giving each a separate name. It is also protean, and the overlap has waxed and waned, but the two sides of the identity are that Englishness looks inward towards the countryside and Britishness looks outwards across the sea.

The history of the relationship between being English and being British is . . . well, it is the commanding history of the archipelago over the last 400 years. Linda Colley has shown how Protestantism was the force that made Great Britain after 1688, and how the 'Protestant construction of British identity' went hand-in-hand with remorseless imperial expansion. Britishness was created on the battlefield and the ocean waves. At home the struggle against Catholicism was led by a Protestant people elected by God and represented by Parliament. And Parliament was your representative, even if you did not choose its members yourself – an important point.[9]

The internal mobilisation of the population against the threat from Napoleonic France, the conscious creation of British-wide holdings by the landed class, the riotous penetration of press and voice, the new cult of the monarchy, coalesced into a single national-international experience: the English-British.

It lasted until the 1950s. In 'So There'll Always Be An England', Angela Carter describes the celebration of 'Empire Day' at her south London primary school and reflects:

> The idea of Britain was an English invention, like the spinning jenny and the steam engine. Why else did we celebrate the British Empire by singing: 'There'll always be an England'? Great Britain = Greater England. The greedy flag swallowed up its constituent parts and became a sign, not of a nation but of a state of mind.[10]

Slowly the state of mind has edged away. When the English politician looks at the world, especially if he is Tory, he still likes to think he represents more than a 'mere island'. He still hankers for Empire, the *British* Empire, or at least for its special relationship with America and the Far East. Hence the tears when Hong Kong was handed back. Then *Britannia* returned to England on its last voyage – another of those perfect moments in Britain's 1997.

But what country was she sailing to: was *Britannia* returning to Britannia, or had both taken their bow? For Britain in Europe cannot be imperial. When the UK joined the European partnership in the early 1970s, this is not how it was presented. Edward Heath and his supporters did exercise political arguments that foresaw intimate collaboration. But they did not argue how much Britain would need to change. Rather, the political argument used by the advocates of entry was that Britain's role and world influence could be *preserved* only if we joined the Union. They claimed membership was the only route left to the 'top table', and they thus presented themselves as the true protectors of Britain's greatness. They supported Europe negatively. Membership was in the country's overriding interest, because without it Britain would become even more vulnerable and weak.

Today many supporters of the UK's position in Europe – even Douglas Hurd while he was Conservative Foreign Secretary, for example – sigh with regret when they advocate its necessity. The past was nicer, they admit, but today our national interests mean that we cannot afford to be left out.

This is not a pro-European argument. It is a pro-British argument that takes a European form. It contains an enormous degree of suppressed resentment against Europe – for having developed such a dynamic project that to *preserve* its standing Britain must participate. But in order to prevent 'the loss' of a world role, the leaders of the UK abandoned their other preservative asset, the 1688 constitution. The two – the EU and the UK – are incompatible, international projects. Britain (the multinational 1688 experiment and the 1707 Treaty of Union, which took away a Parliament but not a nation in Scotland) was the first modern State in the world. One of the advantages this gave it was that it did not need to write down its constitution. It was under no pressure to do so. Internally, it had been formed not by a popular covenant but by an élite compromise in the aftermath of an early, hence 'incomplete', civil war. Externally, it constantly expanded and was under no pressure to redefine itself. Indeed, at first, it had the world almost to itself. The machinery of improvement and consent that resulted was more than just a matter of adaptation and prevention, but it never failed in these two vital respects. Now, as its days draw to a close, it faces a final, unprecedented challenge. Does it have the adaptive capacity to change itself into something else? The campaigns for this, from middle-class reformers, Scots, minorities and legal experts could all be frustrated. The irresistible pressure for an answer comes from the EU. The Powellite response, embedded yet suppressed in Thatcherism, was to pull out of Europe completely. This option is not on the agenda. The City and international companies would prevent it, as too many have invested in the UK in order to be inside the EU. Thatcher herself was thwarted in her efforts to integrate markets while seeking to avoid the regulation that accompanies this. In *On Living in an Old Country*, Patrick

Wright describes how the Falklands War allowed Thatcher to construct a national-popular project for her economic strategy:

> this small war enabled Thatcher to draw up the legitimising traditions of the 'nation' around a completely unameliorated 'modernising' monetarist programme. [Her] charismatic style of legitimation fused a valorisation of national tradition and identity with a policy and programme which is fundamentally destructive of the customary ways and values to which it appeals . . . In this respect it is a firmly contemporary project – able to mobilise feelings about past and nationhood which nevertheless remain at least partially distinct and which might, under different circumstances . . . find their way into very different forms of cultural and political expression.[11]

This was one of Thatcher's strengths, in terms of defining her image, and also a fatal weakness, seeding her approach with a divisiveness that meant she could never appeal successfully to one nation. The aftermath was the extraordinary fact that in the 1997 General Election, the Conservatives were completely wiped out in both Scotland and Wales, and became literally just an English party. I have called Thatcher's nationalism 'Great Englishness'. David Marquand put it bluntly: 'The State was Britain. The identity was English.'[12] The mix created was inherently unstable, it plucked at chauvinism in the inner isle and repelled its outer marches.

Now it is Blair's turn to mobilise feelings about past and nationhood in a different direction. He uses some of Thatcher's themes – enterprise, initiative – but combines them with compassion and inclusion. His is a 'giving' rather than a competing society, imagewise. He also attempts to draw on standard *Daily Mail* rhetoric of national greatness – being best in the world, *leading* in Europe, calling this 'enlightened patriotism' to distinguish it from Thatcher's surging romantic nationalism. It is Britain, quite clearly, that Blair and his disproportionately Scottish Cabinet wish to represent. They want a *modern* Britain.

The core arguments about how to achieve this are institutional. To be a modern beacon you must have a lighthouse that includes the machinery of modern democracy. Steps towards its construction are being taken. But the full constitutional consequences, including the limitations that this would impose on central power and the freedom of initiative it would decentralise to others, have not been formulated. Instead, Parliament has been identified as an old-fashioned, imperial-type institution, whose adversarial style is useless at providing accountability or representing what the public really feels. This contempt for Parliament should not be read as straightforward anti-democratic lust for neo-totalitarian power – although it could end up that way. Desperate to be a constructive opposition, Labour was scorned and ignored across nineteen years, even when its MPs were clearly right in the committee stage of Bills, such as the way pensions were being privatised. Current contempt reproduces Labour's real experience. They *know* that the House of Commons is not a modern, democratic institution.

But in trying to forge a modern Britain over the head of Parliament, they are entering a constitutionless zone, which beckons them on to reproduce on a grand scale the 'Mussolini' approach of William Waldegrave: turning government into marketing. Far from there being anything wrong with adopting marketing techniques, they are a welcome *addition* to democracy. But when it comes to power itself, such methods cannot be a substitute for actual decentralisation, freedom of information and independence, with all the energy and errors they acquit. The government, aware that any overall approach expresses a national direction, has decided to 're-brand' Britain. It may do so in a way that avoids the core issue of Englishness and seeks to separate its constitutional reforms from its redefinition of the nation. The most sustained advocacy of re-branding to appear so far is the Demos pamphlet *Britain™*. It is not government policy, but it has been read by government. Its core argument is that the country's definition of itself must break from imperial values and do so in terms of its international projection. It sees Thatcher as a moderniser who sought a strong British image. And sees that she failed:

> Her image of Britain was too nostalgic, too bound up with empire, too exclusive and, little more than five years after posters proclaimed that the great had been put back into Britain, a survey showed that half the population wanted to emigrate.[13]

The pamphlet is clear about the precipitous decline in identification with Britain. One extraordinary statistic is that 68 per cent of over 55-year-olds are proud of the way British democracy works, compared to only 7.5 per cent of 18- to 44-year-olds. Only 13 per cent of the population 'respect' the British monarchy. Only half the population think that Britishness is 'an important feature in their identity'. In order to turn round this allegiance, the pamphlet's author, Mark Leonard, argues for a co-operative, open identity that can be more lightly worn, rather than an exclusive, aggressive nationalism. This attractive idea would create a renewed Britishness out of positive elements of the past and present situation. The argument sees Britain as 'a world island'. The term comes from the analysis that political economists used to describe the UK's nineteenth-century role as the pioneering imperial centre of a global capitalism – an island that had a presence throughout the world. In Demos-speak the terms are neatly reversed: subject becomes object in the twenty-first century and the whole world has a presence in the island. This island is not, however, a world museum. It willingly draws the planet, its trade and cultures into its hub, and its mongrel population responds with value added, in a creative, hybrid and innovative site of fair play, highly interconnected and trading brilliantly.

The proposal to re-brand the country on these lines has come in for considerable sneering. But Britain must reform its identity to get away from its theme-park image. It should plan this in a businesslike fashion, based on polling evidence and through known and accountable processes, rather than the intuition of chaps. Furthermore, as Leonard states, 'Successful national re-branding exercises [such as Spain and Ireland] worked only because the new identity fitted with changed reality.' The case is that good branding can qualitatively improve what it projects. And the case is also convincing: branding that succeeds presents evidence in an attractive way; you can't re-brand *against* reality. In other words, if British manufacturing continues to make poor-quality products, 'Made in Britain' cannot succeed as a quality label.

A bold and original presentation, the weakness of *Britain*™ is what it leaves out, more than what it says. It assumes throughout that Britain is simply 'a nation'. It ignores its own evidence that identification with Scotland and Wales is growing, and with England too. Nor does it mention Europe. The latter might seem just part of the competitive, yet friendly identity environment. But the re-imagining of Britain which the pamphlet advocates is linked to the celebration of the millennium. It proposes the moment as a meridian for Britain – the cross-over into international recognition of the country as modern. Suppose that when the celebrations of 2000 begin, the core European countries are heading for the great adventure of a new, shared currency with the world markets behind them, while the UK has a dome that *proclaims* Britain is outward-looking and interconnected yet the government nervously bites its nails about the Euro. As the pamphlet says, you can only market what has been achieved. So branding Britain as 'a nation', when it isn't one, simply won't work. Similarly, branding Britain as forward-looking, interconnected and diverse won't work if its neighbours are interconnecting themselves in an even more forward-looking way that incorporates an entire continent of diversity, while Britain declares that everyone else is out of step. Since 1945, the decline in allegiance to Britishness that *Britain*™ documents was due not so much to the country failing to change internally, for both inhabitants and foreigners know that it has altered a great deal. What everyone also knows is that, despite this, Britain has always lagged behind other European countries. In marketing terms, the perception of a 'product' is comparative.

Put it this way. If Britain is to be a clever world island, as

Demos argues, why does it have a stupid Upper House and all those silly titles? What kind of country is it where pop stars take knighthoods, or are given them? This *is* the modernisation of the theme park. Britain has still to deal with its imperial legacy if it is to project a new one. The old image about which *Britain*™ complains is not completely unjustified. If the UK abolishes titles, handles and lordships – that is, not just the voting rights of hereditaries, but its daily use of the old snobbish rubbish – then the world will say, 'Ah, Britain has changed.' Corporate image-makers advise that if you have a re-design, it must be driven through the organisation. Even at the symbolic level, much of the ancient symbolism has to be cleared away, for in an exercise of the kind that *Britain*™ advocates, such symbolism matters. The Demos pamphlet leaves these awkward measures to one side. Britain is a modern, multi-national country. But its system of sovereignty is now a strait-jacket. It *has* to discard this, if it is to enjoy the future.

Before Blair, there was an argument between modernisers in the Labour Party as to whether Clause 4 of its constitution (which committed it to nationalisation) should be rewritten. Those against its removal argued that it was a dead letter, a sentimental formula, a piece of heritage, best left undisturbed – an argument once summed up by Harold Wilson, who, in the short period between becoming party leader and winning the 1964 election, said that Clause 4 was like the first chapters of Genesis on how God created the world: one didn't believe it, but one would not want it removed from the Bible. In fact, Clause 4 was a classic case of the past weighing on the minds of the living. Its dead letters were manacles. Their replacement was an emancipation, and Blair's success would not have been so stunning had he clung to the chains. Similarly, because Britain was an imperial construct, its reconstruction must replace not preserve the dead internal imperial attributes (Lords, ermine-style titles, Crown prerogative, etc.), even though the spirit has left them.

In an earlier Demos pamphlet, *The Battle over Britain*,

Philip Dodd argued for a pluralist English-British 'mongrelism'. This would contrast and oppose Thatcher's process of 'purification and exclusion'. Instead, 'What is needed now, then, not only in relationship to England but also with the whole of Britain, is a way of thinking about national identity that recognises the extraordinary diversity, past and present, within the islands.' And he warns that new constitutional arrangements will not be a sufficient response because the crisis of national identity, 'stretches far beyond the ceremonies of State into the very idioms of the language, and even the way we hold our bodies . . . to be resolved, it will have to be done across all aspects of our lives, and not merely in the formal political part.'[14]

This is surely right. But the new national identity for which Dodd calls cannot move *beyond* the ceremonies of State until it has dealt *with* them – they lie across its path. The danger of grand arguments about reconstructing identity is that already, before they have really begun, they threaten to reproduce what was one of the great failings of left and right in the Labour movement: both scorned liberals for their threat to 'distract' from their grand schemes with merely formal matters of constitutional procedure. In this way the over-ambition of socialism contributed to conservatism.

Nonetheless, the main point in dealing with institutional blockages is to help free the expression of complex contemporary sentiments. Hence the importance of the arguments in both of the Demos pamphlets for pluralism and diversity and for the new forms of nationalism to draw on vulgar and demotic British traditions. Dodd especially starts to take Thatcher's nationalism of 'purification and exclusion' by the throat. He sees the need to fight – to break her definition of English-Britishness. Perhaps fight is too macho a term, for Dodd spotted perceptively that the damage done to the monarchy by the treatment of Diana suggests that 're-imagining Britain and transforming masculinity may not be a million miles apart'. The mongrel, as against the bulldog, Britain that he argues for began to mobilise on the Mall.

At the same time, Dodd is less certain about where England

fits in, except that he sees it as an issue. So too do a clutch of conservative columnists who warned against a Scottish Parliament on the grounds that it would awaken the crude English nationalism of the kind with which Andrew Hargreaves enjoyed scaring Parliament on 20 February (quoted in Chapter 1). As the legislation for a Scottish Parliament passes through Westminster and the elections for it are held, its opponents will scratch at every anomaly to raise the crabby voice of old England. The English question is bound to arise when all around others are finding and renewing their identities. Furthermore, Englishness will be exploited to secure a bulwark in the referendum on the Europe currency. Fires are ready to burn, ignition could be provided by economic downturn, negligence is not advisable in exposing constitutional symbols to destruction. As the right seeks to raise a monster of Englishness from the depths of Britishness, who will oppose them and speak for another England, apart from Billy Bragg? Two voices, neither of them born in England, have been raised: that of Yasmin Alibhai-Brown, who called for the English to be English and reconstruct themselves in the process, and of David Hayes, who endorsed the aim of a democratic and dissenting Englishness but also warned of the consequences: 'Encouraging the English to be English (in Yasmin's words) will have costs and rewards. Losing the famed "taken-for-grantedness" of English identity would raise a mountain of dust. Peeling back the covers will expose a termites' feast'.[15]

Wariness, then. All the more reason to insist on the need for an Englishness that is not Thatcher's. A renovated, enlightened Britishness will not be sufficient; it will have to draw directly on the historic energy of the English – the majority nation by far in the UK – or its new Britishness could become a hollow dome.

One way to describe this contest is to see it as an attempt to replace the ethnic nationalism of Englishness (which Powell drew upon) with a civic nationalism that can trace its lineage back to the first modern fight for liberty in the seventeenth century. This will not be a purely civilising mission. In *Blood and Belonging*, a dignified study that combines witness and meditation, Michael Ignatieff reports on visits to six regions of conflict. He observes the tenacity of ethnic conflict. He had thought cosmopolitanism like his own was the wave of the future, but now he sees that it cannot escape from nationalism. He takes comfort in the distinction between civic and ethnic nationalism. The first defines nationalism in terms of belonging to a set of institutions, of having citizenship and rights embedded in the State, to which all are admitted; the second 'claims that an individual's deepest attachments are inherited, not chosen: it is the national community that defines the individual, not the individuals who define the national community'.[16] This distinction, which Ignatieff draws from Greenfeld, is part of a long line of attempts to differentiate between civilised patriotism on the one hand and barbaric chauvinism on the other, such as the Marxist effort to distinguish between progressive and reactionary nationalisms. The effort to separate the good from the bad forms of belonging.

Such an enlightened approach is not sufficient. Nationalism is one of the great passions and motive forces of our epoch – some would say *the* force. It has to be approached from below, not viewed from above like a surgeon wearing gloves. And the starting point for approaching nationalism, to quote from the work of Benedict Anderson, is that it is a force of such 'moral grandeur' that uncountable millions *died* for it. It is not the killing that it permitted, but rather the sacrifice that it inspired, that should make us pause.[17] All the historic civil nationalisms called forth their own victims with such appeals and also participated in their own ethnic cleansing, which the sacrifice seemed to justify. Like an umbilical cord through which they gained their first blood, there is no nationalism that does not carry the navel scar of its independence. Tom Nairn once argued that all nationalism is Janus-faced, looking back into the past in order to draw upon the forces that will confront the future. There is no nationalism, worthy of the name, that does not include elements of fate, scorn, anger, bloody-mindedness and historic enmity. Nationalisms can be contrasted in terms of the degree to which they embrace civic, constitutional democracy. None can be elevated to it alone.

But nation states now find themselves alongside other nations, in a world that is thick with them. The late twentieth-century wave of nationalism is less belligerent than its predecessors, whatever the publicity focused on the atrocities of the exceptions. Whereas previously each nation's nationalism represented itself (falsely) as organic and natural – a matter of instinct, not thought – nationalism today has become conscious of itself, aided by the immense literature on the nature of nationalism produced in the last twenty years. So we are seeing the emergence of a self-reflexive nationalism that is aware of itself as willed, rather than denying its created nature. There is a widespread consciousness that traditions have been invented and communities, a better phrase, imagined into existence. It does not follow that they are 'false' or unreal as a result of being imagined, any more than a constitution is false because it is the conscious work of humans.

So to counter Great Englishness, a democratic Englishness is needed. From the Magna Carta of 1215 to the Agreement of the People of 1647, and the Suffragettes and May 1940 it has plenty of indigenous resources and can make a fair claim on a lot of international ones as well. What could a democratic Englishness be like?

Among its qualities there could be literacy, a return to the exceptionally high levels of education that marked England in the sixteenth and seventeenth centuries. 'Education, education, education,' Blair said in the best passage in his pre-election party conference speech. The government had better mean it: from ensuring that poorer children are fed sufficiently to concentrate on lessons, to ending the strange arrangements whereby you can leave school early if you *fail* to gain qualifications. Old Britishness thrived on élite disdain for the great unwashed – and it kept them that way. An educated public, how can there be democracy without it?

Second, pluralism. Dodd stresses the historically mixed character and origins of Englishness. Now, after Empire, the English have become a world people, connected at every level with others abroad, while at home the mixed populations of the cities will soon be moving into the villages and countryside: a global nation, rather than a world island, capable of enjoying a modest but fortunate place.

Most countries fear the violence in their souls, for it has gone out of control: the Gulag, the concentration camp, slavery, segregation, the Mafia. England has done bad things. But, *relatively* speaking, not as bad, or as persistent, as most other empires, some of its behaviour in Ireland excepted. The usual way in which this is built into positive descriptions of Englishness is through emphasis on the peaceful, fair-minded, tolerant consequences. Such pastoralism is a myth. Rather, what is positive is that the English are more at ease with violence than most other national cultures. I don't mean hooliganism. Bill Buford has described in close-up the vacuousness of thugs – who have few hidden virtues.[18] But risk is essential to life, and a nationalism of difference and diversity which draws only on the virtues described by England's great historian A. J. P. Taylor as 'patience, toleration and generosity',[19] will wither. So, thirdly, while democracy means justice, it also means force, vulgarity and money-making. The English have these qualities in abundance, and a self-confidence in the expression of these undisguised, uncivilised attributes is a national virtue.

Fourth, gender. The most profound revolution of modern times, initiated in the sixties (in response to the sixties), has been feminism and the beginnings of equality for women. Nationalism, in its competitive, mobilising form, is exceptionally male in its leadership and in its internal organisation; it relied upon women, provided they were kept in their place. The fact that it took a woman Prime Minister to resuscitate this tradition as the men became 'wet' may show how deep that maleness went.[20] Aggression between nations and differentiation between the sexes thrived together. The dissolution of gender discrimination may relax the way in which nations define themselves against each other.

Fifth, ubanity. The English live in one of the most urbanised societies on earth. Empire Britishness, however, compressed the great industrial cities of the North and Midlands and the diverse, polyglot 'great wen' of London, out of their rightful role as the country's defining sites. The city was negated between the ocean swell and the rolling countryside. As the *New Departures* working papers have begun to argue, cities continue to be seen as problems rather than powerhouses. From commerce to parks, from streets to estates, England will defined by the richness and creativity of its town life – its citizenship.

Finally, England is historically older than Great Britain and its tradition of memory can be re-appropriated with popular support, as the History Workshop experience demonstrates. The historic nature of England is a resource and a source of departure. It is not an old country for England does not yet speak. It can hardly claim to be a new country. It is a historic country and the depth and range of its past is a contemporary value.

In exploring a positive English nationalism, I am not arguing for the break-up of the UK. I do not believe that Englishness will find a better, more free voice if the Scots and Welsh are told to go walk-about on their own – an argument with which some English nationalists are experimenting. At a time when nationalism is becoming less defining, both internally and in relationship to the rest of the world, and as other kinds of identification and relationship are created that cross traditional frontiers, the separation of the countries of the UK is likely to diminish range and harden each culture, even within the EU. And there are a large number of minority citizens living in England who regard themselves as British, and not English at all. This historically inherited multinational experience is also part of our country. Britishness was external but now contributes to the pluralism of all the UK's nations. Englishness is a European voice – its new, external field, where its traditional love of liberty, re-animated by constitutional democracy, is certainly needed. The price of this need not be the break-up of Britain.

10
THIS TIME

IN ECONOMICS IT is well known that to make a trend look good or bad you shift its starting point. Similarly, how you begin an argument is prompted by where you intend to end it. So I do not think that the constitutional debate should be decided in terms of its historical origins; it should be judged on its merits. Sovereignty and the constitution, however, raise issues of identity and nation. All four are steeped in history. And arguments against reform are always pitched in historical terms, though usually these are more sophisticated than Lord Hailsham's observation about 'time immemorial'. So it is fair to ask, 'What is your starting point?' And there are two possible starting points for the consideration of late twentieth-century British history. The usual one is May 1940, when Britain 'stood alone' in military resistance to Hitler after the defeat of France; the other is September 1938, the month of the Munich Agreement, when British appeasement opened the way to Hitler's aggression. Britain's history can be appreciated in different ways, depending on which date is adopted.

Certainly 1688 is not the starting point for contemporary argument over the meaning of Britain's constitution. Even though the 'Glorious Revolution' of that year (not so glorious for Ireland) initiated Britain's existing State machine, the legacy of that time has been re-worked across the centuries. Today we inhabit something that is fundamentally broken yet still immensely impressive: the Empire State created by the Victorians, restructured by universal franchise and then renewed by the wartime coalition led by Churchill. The Labour Government of 1945 should be seen as an extension of that coalition, which had placed Labour Ministers in high office since 1940. The arrangement incorporated the entire population. It did so militarily, by turning imperialism into defensive populism; economically, by the creation of full employment and the Welfare State; and politically, through consensus politics. The outcome was an upper-class polity that lasted into the 1960s and which relied upon lower-class acquiescence in a joint exercise of self-conscious defiance and sentimentality. It created that particular cross-class culture found in the aptly named *Carry On* movies. The wartime coalition was the origin of this way of life – political, social and economic. And its starting point was Britain's finest hour (the one made necessary by the almighty cock-up of appeasement).

The starting point that is still built into the mentality and attitudes of the contemporary body politic of Britain is May 1940. Within six weeks France would fall to Hitler's blitzkrieg; Poland was already partitioned between Germany and the Soviet Union, thanks to the Nazi-Soviet pact; the United States was neutral. Churchill declared, 'I have nothing to offer but blood, toil, tears and sweat.' An overwhelming and peculiarly British ideology emerged – Churchillism. It was a mixture distinct from the man himself: consensus politics, the Welfare State, the special (subordinate) relationship with America, the contrary notion of Britain defiant and going it alone, faith in a charismatic leader, belief in Britain's world standing (first Empire, then Commonwealth) while actually abandoning it – these became the tracks along which post-war politics took its course. Politicians debate modernisation, Europe and the nature of British sovereignty within these terms still. The need now is to leave them behind, but to do so with respect.

Margaret Thatcher used them for party purposes. The Falklands War allowed her to seize the banner of Churchillism from the hands of Labour, who had been its co-creators. This then enabled her to turn Churchillist rhetoric against consensus politics, all the while trumpeting its rhythms of 'one-nation'. I have described how her premiership wrecked the preserving formula of the British constitution – its conservatism, in a word. Thatcher was able to mobilise support materially, thanks to the revenues from North Sea oil, and ideologically because she reproduced the familiar tropes of Churchillism: Britain is different; our national destiny is special; we can lead but do not follow. This was to provide the template for the hostility towards Europe and its clichés, such as the *Daily Mail*'s 'Battle for Britain'.

Five months after the May 1997 landslide, Tony Blair had gone further than Thatcher. By the time of his speech to the Labour party conference in September he had reproduced an alliance akin to the wartime coalition itself: a Labour administration, Conservative policies, Liberal intellectuals, a united country, charismatic leadership, even a patriotic rhetoric that echoes the fusion between royalty and populace that Churchill managed,[1] also a personal alliance with the President of the United States and, finally, a declaration of belief in Britain's special international role, and the claim that it should lead in Europe. All this was joined by a consensus politics that seeks to end social exclusion and an economic underclass. Little wonder it produced wartime levels of public support.

But the sub-text of Blair's appeal is not Churchillist in one crucial respect – his pitch is progressive, not regressive, in international and historical terms. 'I have not become the King's First Minister in order to preside over the liquidation of the British Empire,' Churchill declared in 1942. In reality this was his role. But in terms of mentality, and the spirit of Britain, he presided over denial. British Prime Ministerial rhetoric ever since has wrestled with the consequences. How can Britain become modern and non-imperial? How, in other words, can it end the denial, and at the same time be true to – and not deny – ourselves? Churchill *was* an imperialist. He had fought with the cavalry at the Battle of Omdurman in 1898. Blair, by contrast, is not an old imperialist. Far from charging down the dervish army in the Sudan, he was the lead singer in the Ugly Rumours. And his New Labour project of re-branding Britain is a conscious attempt to wean the UK off its imperial and theme-park heritage – and end the denial. Blair's declared route is to 'lead' in Europe.

The last time that Britain led Europe was at the 1938 Munich conference. It was also the last time that London was to play a decisive role as a world power in an international conference without being under the wing of the United States. Instead of deciding to face Hitler down, Britain chose to appease him. If you take Munich as the starting point, rather than the fall of France to Hitler, then Britain is not as absolutely different from other European countries as it appears to be from the vantage point of May 1940. For a start, it is not free of any culpability in the rise of Nazism. More important, it becomes clear that Britain's domestic fate was determined by its European policy and not by its autonomous, global interests. Proclamations of British exceptionalism – that Britain is great, it has not changed, it is different from other European countries – tend to be seen as an expression of imperialism. But there were half a dozen other empires up to 1914 that were recognisably similar. It was the defensive experience of the Second World War that engrained this view of Britain. There was a better reason for it, too: Britain, although aided by Empire, *did* stand alone in Europe.

Return to 1938 and consider it from the view of contemporary Germany, France or Italy – not to speak of the Czechs. At Munich, Britain gave Hitler control of the strategic Czech Sudetenland (under the excuse of 'self-determination' for the Germans living there). It hugely strengthened the Nazi leader's domestic position and hold over the Army, ensured him the supplies of the large Czech arms factories, demoralised France and opened the way for Germany to neutralise Russia with a non-aggression treaty. In 1989, when the Cold War ended and Germany could reunite, Chancellor Kohl and President Mitterrand wanted to ensure *their* 'never again'; a shared concern to ensure their countries were never again divided or would go to war. Far from being an attempt to replay the war, as the Alan Clark tendency believes, their decision to impose a common currency was motivated by a wish to prevent another. They looked upon the catastrophe of what has been called Europe's thirty-year civil war, of 1914–1945, concluded that the system of competing sovereignties was at fault and decided to secure co-operation in the future through currency union.

Having arrived at the promised land of total popularity that his post-war predecessors wished was theirs, Blair must now leave it. (If he is tempted to stay, he might well meet the fate of Napoleon III – a thought from the editor of *New Left Review*).[2] This does not mean that Britain must go back to 1938 or 'redeem' itself for appeasement by entering monetary union. But it must abandon the Churchillist mind-set that grips politicians and popular press alike, even though much of the population has moved on. If Labour is to lead the country forward into modernity, or even normality, it needs to exchange the parameters of 1940 Churchillism for those of 1938, in the sense of recognising that decisions taken in Continental conferences prove that Europe was, and is, Britain's determining context, and not just a nearby trading zone. Begin the graph in 1940 with the heroic defiance of Churchill and it is us against the continent. Start it in 1938 and we are all in it together. We *are* all in it together, and Labour's decision to work for the success of the Euro and join if a majority agrees shows a welcome recognition.

Enough of starting points. They may haunt us, the only way to confine them to the turrets is by living differently. The new European process is based on shared sovereignty. This is the contemporary way to coexist and co-operate and Britain should join in fully. It does not mean that the European Union is all niceness and altruism. It is not a touchy-feely sharing, or a giving feeling. Absolutely not. The French and Germans exploit the EU for their own national advantage as much as they can. Indeed, they view the EU as a means of enhancing and enlarging their national interests. British governments need to handle it in a similar manner. But to do so, reform at home is needed. As Ferdinand Mount puts it, striving for calm recognition of the facts, 'The European Community has, in effect, endowed us with a written constitution and a Bill of Human Rights. The question is not whether we wish to have such newfangled things – we already have them – but whether we wish to *patriate* them'.[3] The emphasis is his. By 'patriate' he means that we should make British the way Europe has already changed us.

In her support for William Hague, however, in the final round of the Tory leadership contest, Margaret Thatcher declared, 'He stands for the things I believe in – above all he offers a clear vision of Britain as a free, sovereign nation with control over its own affairs.' According to reports, when she said this she was in the tea room of the House of Commons, holding Hague by the hand. She believes that she holds Blair by her other hand and that he too clutches at the same ideals. Thatcher's well-focused language provides a concise description of the issue. Those who belong to her Great English Party believe that Britain should be a free, sovereign nation with control over its own affairs. The realities of the existing EU are incompatible with this description. Its members are not completely free; their sovereignty is now shared; their control over their own affairs is limited. They are not single, they, like Britain, are partners for the indefinite future – it is a marriage meant to last.

Great Englanders deny this. They hold to the belief that no Parliament can bind its successor. Therefore, they argue, the new-fangled things can be undone. Hence they have not *really* happened. Any vows that were made were not genuinely meant, because the people were misled. They see the Europhiles, from Edward Heath onwards, as pimps who have sold our body politic to continental bureaucrats. In their view, no legitimate relationship has been consummated. They have an ongoing fear that any further 'concession' might make Britain lose its inner self-control and begin to 'mean' it. This fear is heightened by the knowledge that the system of centralised, secretive sovereignty which they advocate and defend is necessarily serviced by an élite cadre of civil servants in Whitehall, who are therefore all too capable of collaboration with their fellow mandarins in Brussels. Those who are most vociferous in warning the country against the threat to its democracy from Brussels are, paradoxically, the ones who most resist the extension of democracy in Britain, from a Freedom of Information Act to a Bill of Rights and decentralisation; that is, all the measures that would protect the UK from being subverted by Brussels.

The terms should be reversed. The EU is clearly unaccountable. To demand and obtain reform in Europe, and secure democracy at home, the UK needs to codify and entrench – to write down – its own constitution. This will help protect British democracy from the EU and create a better base for insisting on more democracy in the EU itself. When the Treaty of Maastricht was signed in 1992, a German opponent took his government to the German Constitutional Court, claiming that it violated the Basic Law of the Federal Republic, which states that 'all public authority emanates from the people'. In a long judgement, the court found that the Maastricht Treaty was constitutional, but that further extensions of the EU's powers might not be, and could not override the German Basic Law. It argued that:

> At present, the national populations impart democratic legitimacy through the national parliaments, limits are therefore set, from the point of view of the principle of democracy, to the extension of tasks and powers of the European Communities ... The European Union must respect the national identities of its Member States, whose systems of government are founded on democratic principles. In that respect, the Union preserves and builds on the democratic foundation existing in the Member States. Any further development of the European Union cannot take place outside that context.[4]

Of course, a judgement like this, being constitutional, cannot be relied upon. Its force depends upon how it is supported by the public. Nonetheless, it can both educate and transform the organisation of opinion. Here was a German court, using its national constitution, in part originally insisted upon by the British, holding the Maastricht Treaty to solemn scrutiny and assessing the priority of German democracy over it. As European co-operation deepens, Britain needs an equivalent codification of its own democracy and basic values in order to protect itself. Indeed, should joining a European common currency be put to a referendum, a second question could accompany the economic one, asking whether the electorate also wants to have a written constitution drawn up for its approval, to safeguard British democracy.

The inescapable, international framework of the EU presses reform on the British State. But there are overwhelming internal reasons for proceeding with reform anyway. The argument for constitutional decentralisation stands on its own merits. Contemporary society requires it. Quality in life calls for creativity not compliance, *self*-discipline grounded in autonomy rather than obedience. This is pretty obvious and would not bear repeating, were not pluralism still thought to be a disease of the lungs by many in Britain. Business experts, from Charles Handy to George Soros (who was once sceptical of the need for written constitutions, thanks to the influence of Harold Laski, his teacher at the LSE), suggest that the arguments for an institutionalised structure of democracy are overwhelming. Some communitarian thinkers also concur, Geoff Mulgan, for example:

> Any convincing vision of a future society must recognise the need for multiple structures of control: the coexistence of representative and direct democracy, rights of removal or veto, market-type controls and the control that is exercised through ethos and moral suasion. A convincing view of change also needs to reflect such pluralism of structures.[5]

Pluralism of structures is incompatible with the absolute sovereignty of Parliament, or anything else. There cannot be sustained economic development that includes all sections of society in the UK unless power is decentralised and sovereignty is vested in the people. Gordon Brown set out a form of this argument in his Crosland Lecture a month before the election was called. The basic principle: 'Everyone should have the chance to bridge the gap between what they are and what they have it in themselves to become.' The practical justification: 'What is right on ethical grounds is, in the 1990s, good for the economy too.' And the means:

> Political reform is central to this: it must enable people to have the chance to participate in decisions that affect them. This is about more than the concept of a classless society, it is about power and therefore about a truly democratic society. So we should see our constitutional proposals – which range from abolishing the hereditary principle in the Lords to devolution of power and free information – as part of a programme that makes sense of people's aspirations by redistributing power from the state, or any other vested interest, to the people themselves.[6]

In a memorable phrase Neal Ascherson once argued that you are anyway as likely to get equitable democracy from the existing British State as 'milk from a vulture'. This was when the system seemed to work. Now the case is even more overwhelming. Anthropologically, the final transition from status to contract has arrived.

Well, I say that. But the whistle has been heard for so long that the capacity for the British State to continue playing by its own rules cannot be underestimated. It has a legendary ability to pretend that each failure is an exception, each blast of the whistle a signal to someone else. Yet evidence that it is spiritually broken was provided by the Scott Report, which revealed the core relationship between officials, Ministers and Parliament to be an ethics-free zone. What *is* the system now? It has no formal existence. One reason why the constitution has remained unwritten was because it relies on gentlemen's agreements. These turn out to be in the interests of the gentlemen involved. They allow procedure, convention, funny names and 'self-regulation' to be a substitute for accountability. All the Executive has to do is smile and disappear up its Royal Prerogative – or is it or the supremacy of Parliament? – proclaiming the unwritten, invisible sanctity of sovereignty.

In *The Strange Death of Liberal England*, his tremendous historical account of the years before the outbreak of the First

World War, George Dangerfield recounts the passing of the 1911 Parliament Act – that set a limit the powers of the House of Lords. He describes the constitution as 'an unseen traveller, a mighty ghost' that left its footprints in the ribbed sands of English history, as with the Magna Carta or the Act of Union, while never taking visible form in flesh or words. And when, finally, the 1911 Parliament Act was passed, 'the Constitution, still unmaterialised in its mighty progress, had planted one more large footstep in the sands of history'.[7] Today, a patter of footprints bears down: referendums, Parliaments, assemblies, mayors, a Bill of Rights – can they really be the imprints of the same unseen traveller? One feels that we have been reduced to the age of Tolkien. That, instead of materialising as Dangerfield imagined, the mighty ghost will turn out to be a dwarf from the Cabinet Office riding a large plastic foot, like a pogo stick, hurling it onwards in a desperate effort to convince us that each imprint is the work of a monster as great as Dangerfield's spectre.

The constitution has become ridiculous. Yet the government remains reluctant to confront this fact, perhaps because the weakness has delivered enormous advantages to Labour. But also perhaps because while Labour politicians are often much better at seeing the merit of particular reforms than Tories, the Tories are generally superior in seeing the overall argument: they feel at home with ideas of sovereignty. They even, quite undemocratically, tend to regard them as their own. Conservative 2000 was founded as a small think-tank in 1995, when John Redwood stood for the leadership. Within eighteen months it had published a 200-page survey, *Conservatives and the Constitution* by Richard Wilson and Andrew Lansley, now MP for Cambridge South. When IPPR, a pro-Labour think-tank, published a full draft constitution in 1991 as a model for the United Kingdom, its main author, James Cornford, brought in a team of experts including Liberal Democrats and the exercise was educational, rather than being associated with any contending wing of the Labour Party. By contrast, Lansley and Wilson's document is a highly charged political synthesis. Far from having to educate the party about the importance of the issue, as the IPPR attempted for Labour, the Conservative 2000 booklet states confidently, 'The Constitution is a Conservative issue.' Grudgingly, the authors admit that others have now entered the terrain. They then set out to defend the status quo against New Labour's proposed reforms and the influence of the EU. But, they claim, 'It is for Conservatives to lead the debate on the constitution, not to follow it or, lamely, to respond to it.'[8]

This is a warning: Labour should not deceive itself about the viability of its disconnected reforms or presume that the Conservatives will settle for futile opposition. The Tories already see that the coherence of the old settlement, whose benefits they have enjoyed so fully, is at risk. They can grasp that a new constitutional framework will be needed after Labour's changes, and they are likely to realise that those who draft it can dominate the decades that follow. In which case they will use every means at their disposal to persuade Labour that this cannot be done – while calculating privately how they might best do it themselves.

This process started while this book was being written. In Chapter 8 I suggest that one of the reasons for the government's reluctance to provide an overview of its plans is uncertainty about where they will lead, a fear reinforced by warnings such as that of William Rees-Mogg, who told Labour that its incoherence meant that it was 'putting to sea in a sieve'. That was before the election. Within a week of the Labour government publishing its confident – and coherent – White Paper on a Scottish Parliament, Rees-Mogg reassessed the situation – as a good Conservative would. He congratulated William Hague for saying that the Tories would not abolish the Edinburgh Parliament, once endorsed by the referendum, and advised him to learn from Disraeli and steer for the destination:

> 1997 is the modern equivalent of 1832 . . . After 1832 the ship of the constitution had gone to sea, but had not arrived at its ultimate destination. Now Tony Blair's Government has put the ship out to sea again, but the first drafts are . . . inadequate . . . It is an historic decision but it does not remotely resemble

> an historic settlement. Disraeli's genius let him see that the Conservative Party should steer for the eventual port of settlement rather than hanker for a return to the port of departure.

The destination Rees-Mogg proposes is a 'fully federal system . . . the final constitutional settlement'.[9] This is agile seamanship.

So Conservatives are thinking about the constitution, and when they do so their approach is strikingly different from that of the governing party. Labour figures are interested in plausible steps that can be contained: those who want proportional representation are noticeably less interested in human rights; those concerned with human rights see little need for decentralisation. Whereas Conservatives tend absolutely to resist even small changes, sensing the consequences, but are interested in the impact of the system as a whole. Finally, when they turn to reform they want bold changes to the entire political environment. One (small 'c') conservative has produced precisely such an overview, timed for the first party conferences after the Labour victory. Robert Alexander, QC is a life peer, barrister and Chairman of the NatWest Group. His book, *The Voice of the People, A Constitution for Tomorrow*, presents a programme of overall reform covering everything from Rights, Lords reform and the Commons to regional decentralisation and local government. In the preface he advises the Conservative Party, in particular, to recall Talleyrand's maxim: 'The art of politics is to anticipate the inevitable and facilitate its occurrence.' He flatly opposes a written constitution as impractical and non-popular. Nonetheless, he is convinced that:

> Our Constitution is a living whole. We must not think we can tinker with or even amputate one part without considering how this will affect the whole. So we must not think of devolution without at the same time considering its impact on local government or upon the composition and functioning of the House of Commons.

And so on, every aspect being linked to another. But *how* will 'we' think about it? Alexander's answer is a Constitutional Commission, 'probably consisting largely of senior members of both Houses of Parliament'. As if this was highly practical and would be popular! The commission would carry out biannual reviews, oversee referendums, consider what legislation is constitutional from a strictly non-party standpoint (of course) and marshal the arguments for reform.[10] In short his commission, although Alexander might not put it like this, would embody the unwritten presumptions of the traditional 1688 approach. The historic settlement would be reduced to a board of advisors! The proposal resonates with Lord Armstrong's idea that the modernisation of the monarchy should be undertaken by a discrete committee small enough to fit around a dinner table, to keep the Head of State in touch with the spirit of the age.

Preposterous maybe, but not stupid. The proposal that a group of reliable senior chaps can safeguard the constitution or the monarchy, needs to be considered as a symptom. 'They' still have no intention of letting go. They still believe in themselves and their right to 'look after things', even if Alexander shows an energetic concern for participation. The resilience of such proposals should, incidentally, make republicans consider their position. Faced with another personal crisis in the monarchy, Alexander's Constitutional Commission would be quite capable of recommending Betty Boothroyd as temporary President, appointed by the non-party life peers of the House of Lords, while retaining all the traditional procedures, from privy council and prerogative power to the honours' system. Compared to the scenario of a written constitution, in which the public endorses the Windsors as Head of State by referendum, the latter emerges as a genuine constitutional democracy – infinitely preferable to a monarchist presidency. This allows us to see that the core issue is not republic versus monarchy, but democracy versus the old regime.

All the strange notions – commissions, dining committees, opinion polls on whether a fifteen-year-old should become the next King – are signs of the time and they are being read keenly by the Conservatives. Charles Powell wrote an editorial essay on Alexander's book for *The Times*. Private Secretary to the Prime Minister from 1984 to 1991 – that is, to two Premiers who set themselves against reform – Powell states bluntly, 'the idea that the constitution is sacrosanct and reform a no-go area can no longer be accepted.' He concludes, 'the Blair government should throw these issues open to the widest possible debate . . . A strong government should be able to galvanise the nation into the bold steps needed to complete the modernisation of Britain.'[11] The strength of this language contrasts to the throttled projection of Lord Chancellor Derry Irvine's 'measured and sensible' approach. For who will do the measuring? Already, before any of Labour's partial but significant reforms are on the statute book, experienced Tories are openly calling for no-holds-barred public debate on the constitution as a whole. They hope that *they* will do the measuring. And they will, if the government uses its strength to shut down democratic debate. It will then find itself outflanked, as the Conservatives move fast to claim the high ground with their own overall view.

Blair has declared that he wants Labour to win two full terms. Looking back, it does seem that one of the functions of Labour governments has been to allow the Conservatives to renew themselves. Twice, in the 1940s and 1960s, Labour administrations have been in a position to reshape and then dominate British politics. Both times Labour failed. To break this pattern would dwarf Blair's achievement in making Labour electable again. To spell it out: in 1924 the first Labour administration lasted nine months. It was followed by five years of Baldwin's Conservative manipulation. The second Labour government lasted thirty months, through 1929 to 1931. It opened the way to a decade of Conservative rule that culminated in the appeasement of Hitler. Labour's third moment of office began in triumph in 1945, with a huge majority and exceptionally able Ministers. Yet it lasted only six years and ended in rancorous splits, whereupon the Tories took over for nearly a decade and a half. Then, in 1964, the moment most comparable to 1997, Harold Wilson led Labour to a narrow victory, which he turned into a handsome majority two years later. Four years after that he was out. When the Tories faltered he returned briefly, and was succeeded as Labour Premier by the even less capable James Callaghan, who oversaw the débâcle of 1979 that banished Labour from Downing Street for what seemed an eternity of eighteen years.

The main reason why it has been a Conservative century in Britain is that when Labour has had a chance to govern, it has done so in the manner established beforehand by the Tories. I am not saying that Labour Ministers were 'traitors'. Accusations of betrayal are usually specious, as they serve their own myths and falsehoods. Certainly the leaders of the 1945 Labour administration genuinely regarded themselves as socialists. They governed, however, in the way they had learnt to during the years of their coalition under Churchill. In 1964 Harold Wilson likewise believed that he was modernising Britain. Yet he had been captivated by Harold Macmillan, the 'one-nation' Premier, author of *The Middle Way*, who had pulled off a great election victory for the Conservatives in 1959. Wilson saw Macmillan as a model for the successful management of Britain's peculiar inheritance. Today, an attempt is being made to ensure that Blair embraces Thatcher's approach to wielding political power. If, however, New Labour adopts the political methods of what, in 1980, Nigel Lawson called New Conservatism, then once again Labour will soon find itself replaced.

The simple reason why Labour should not copy the Tories is that, while Conservatives have rarely failed to be in office during modern times, they have been consistently disappointing in their exercise of it. They have virtually monopolised the State, but they have not exercised its power to the long-term benefit of Britain. Chamberlain's appeasement, Churchill's rejection of Europe after 1951, Eden's disastrous Suez mentality, Macmillan's complacency, Heath's domestic vacillations, Thatcher's monetarism and Europhobia, Major's feeble balancing act . . . this is a sorry record. In the last quarter of the nineteenth century the Conservatives created Britain's Empire State, extended the franchise and forged the modern party machine. Across most of the twentieth century they have overseen the collapse of the Empire State abroad and sharp, if relative, economic decline and loss of opportunity at home. Major neatly symbolised his party's failure in office and its success in keeping it. When they realised the strategic and electoral consequences of Thatcher's anti-European tirades and attachment to the Poll Tax, Tory MPs got rid of her. Their reward for having saved the nation from their own leadership was a further six and a half years of their own leadership. They drove the ship of State onto the rocks, then presented themselves as the best salvage company around. Then, once again, onto the rocks they sailed.

A Labour government has never benefited from this perverse logic. Nor should it. Labour could not have got away with the Scott Report, or the BSE scandal, for example. A prejudiced media imposes higher standards on it than on the Conservatives. This may be unfair. Nonetheless, should Blair and company try to rule like the Tories, they will be justly convicted and pilloried for letting Britain down. New Labour has understood that it would be fatal to govern like Old Labour. It will not take Britain back to consensus politics. Nonetheless, there is evidence that Blair looks on Thatcher in the same way that Wilson looked on Macmillan and Attlee on Churchill. But Thatcher's method of government was as flawed as her opposition to the previous 'consensus politics' was justified. If New Labour embraces the centralising, supremacy-fixated, bulldog definition of sovereignty that she established, it will reproduce the underlying pattern of the century – the deep structure, as it were, whereby Labour duplicates the approach of the immediately preceding Tory years. (Meanwhile, the Conservative Party will reassess and locate the best route for its return to power.)

This time, Labour needs to develop its own approach. It is right to reject any return to Labourism and post-war consensus politics. It also needs to discard what was dubbed 'conviction politics'. This was a false radicalism that preserved rule from above and retained the old-fashioned Churchillist premise that Britain is fundamentally different from everywhere else. Instead, Labour needs to embrace constitutional democracy.

To return back through *This Time*, Britain has to move on from the wartime constitution, in both its consensus and its conviction forms. It needs to recognise the multinational character of the United Kingdom, to create a modern form of Britishness compatible with being a European power. At the heart of this there has to be democratic Englishness, which draws on native radical traditions and a capacity to compromise. To achieve such a constitutional revolution an imaginative approach is needed, which can be called utopian realism, unless someone finds a better name. This involves clear statements of general goals and a practical approach to achieving them, testing and reflecting – moving fast where possible and cautiously where necessary, sharing the principles with the public and grounding progress on consent, so that means and ends cohere. This will break from the preservative methods of the 1688 settlement and the Victorian assumptions of administered, top-down government.

If the old order were not broken, it could preserve itself. Spiritually and administratively, however, its core values have withered or rotted. To replace the old settlement with a new written one, a broad understanding of a modern constitution needs to be established. Three requirements are clear: effective voice, realistic representation, clear accountability. Such overall reform, while fundamental, is neither abstract nor unreal. People – lower-case people – reflect and care and are confident that they can learn what is best. They – we – must become constitutionally sovereign. The swing voter (call her Worcester Woman) is interested in such an overview, even if the spin doctors do not wish her to be. We should do everything possible to ensure her participation, as this will affect the kind of modernisation that Britain will achieve. On offer is a centralising, demagogic and divisive but modern

American model. This was the way the Tories were taking Britain. The Labour Party implicitly, and the electorate explicitly and decisively, rejected this model. With it, the new corruption and its associated Great English ideologies of Powellism and Thatcherism went down, on the celebrated night of May 1st.

A measure of the shift that was registered across 1997 can be found in the editorials of the *Daily Telegraph* which prefigured Portillo's discovery of tolerance. As we have seen, before the election the newspaper defended David Evans MP against his critics, after he had called for the castration of 'black bastard' rapists and described the Labour candidate as 'a single girl with three bastard children'. The 'prissy ideologues who express deep shock at his words', the *Telegraph* proclaimed, 'are out of touch'. Six months later, on 11 September, as flowers still filled the Mall, another editorial appealed to the Scots to vote against a national Parliament in case they put at risk 'Britain's glory as the most tolerant and decent multinational state the world has ever seen'. No thanks to you, one felt like saying. But why be grudging? Everyone in Britain with life in them has been altered by the year. Nonetheless, the use of the word 'glory' is a small, warning alarm. To keep the multinational state 'tolerant and decent', a tolerant democratic constitution is essential: to consolidate the gains and enshrine the principles boosted by 1997; to protect them from the comeback of David Evans and his supporters; to ensure that the lure of a modern, centralist populism does not seduce New Labour; and to open the way for better arguments to come.

And good arguments are on their way. For the most decisive shift that ocurred in 1997 did not take place in *Daily Telegraph* editorials but in government policy towards Europe. In the passage on sovereignty at the start of Chapter 7, I described the way John Major balanced up the pros and cons of the European single currency when he was still Prime Minister, and then asked what would be best for Britain should the Euro become a success. One had to leave one's options open in case it was, was the gist of his argument. His stress on uncertainty was not based on the fallibility principle, which states that we need an open society in order to be able to respond to the unforseen. Britain under Major had made few moves to open up the European process. Rather, the Tories traded on the Brussel's regime of bureaucratic regulation to preserve public ill-will towards the EU. Open government is not soft government. At the very least a leader in Major's position should have told the public whether or not he and his government *wanted* the European currency union to succeed. On this defining question, I point out, John Major was silent. So too, however, was the Labour Party. On numerous occasions during the election campaign, Tony Blair emphasised that there was absolutely *'no difference'* between Labour Party and government policy on Europe, except in one respect: 'Labour is united and the Tories are divided'. In other words, Labour was even more silent on this defining question than were the Tories.

On Monday 27 October, 1997, on the first day of the new Parliamentary session, Gordon Brown spelt out a new government policy towards European monetary union: Britain wants it to succeed and will join if it does succeed, if circumstances are right and public assent is forthcoming in a referendum. Pro-Europeans were disappointed that there would be a delay. Given the hash they have made of British membership so far one might have hoped for greater modesty. For the government put behind it both of the hitherto dominant attitudes towards Europe. The Edward Heath one – the 'opposition is nonsense' approach which thinks the natives should belt up, respect their betters and stop their blather about democracy. Naturally, this damaged the cause. And the anti-European approach that seeks to halt integration with a referendum that trades on public fear and chauvinism, while it allows Great Englanders to fly the flag of democracy. New Labour's October decision was a breakthrough. For the first time clear support for continental integration was combined with a commitment to democratic assent. Furthermore, the government recognised that sovereignty will be shared and the consitutional situation altered by monetary union. A small and belated start is how some critics saw it. But a policy towards Europe that is both positive and honest is, truly, a significant shift. Labour would not have dared to undertake it without the historic alteration in attitudes that became public on and after 1 May.

In a statement in the *Sun* on 28 October, Blair emphasised the referendum: 'You, the people of Britain are the people who will make the final decision. It is too big to be any other way. For, in all honesty, it does mean pooling economic sovereignty'. Writing in the same day in the *Mirror*, which is pro-Europe, he was more forthright: 'We . . . committed ourselves to the principle of joining a single currency if it is successful and brings clear benefits . . . I am and always have been a believer that it is in our British national interests to be in Europe and that we should be a strong and leading player in Europe . . . The statement setting out our strategy was drafted by myself and Gordon Brown, in close consultation with our colleagues . . . A decision of this momentousness will require the explicit consent of the people in a referendum'. In politics especially, direction and momentum matter. Should this direction be maintained, then, by declaring their support for EMU, Tony Blair, Gordon Brown and Robin Cook will have rejected Thatcher's 'sacred mantle'.

Is all well, then? Not yet. Just the week before, Blair gave an interview to the 27 October edition of *Time* magazine to coincide with the Edinburgh gathering of the Commonwealth Heads of State, who were treated to a wincing, pop-video 'rebranding' of Britain. This was, from all accounts, the kind of stunt likely to persuade the world that Britain was still run by Terry Thomas style car salesmen. On cue, as it were, Rolls Royce was put out to tender.

Asked by *Time* about the meaning of the election, Blair told its editors that, 'the victory is an expression of the fact that a new generation has come on that doesn't have the outdated attitudes of the past'. It was 'a cultural change' that had 'found expression in politics'. Asked about Diana he saw this also as a cultural rather than political event:

> It said little about politics, but it said a lot about our character. For many people Princess Diana encapsulated the idea of somebody who could be immensely successful, glamorous, but basically a compassionate, decent person who was prepared to give her time and energy to other people. For many young people she was a symbol of what they would like to be.

One has to laugh. What Blair describes is obviously his own image. I write this self-critically. For I saw the response to Diana's death as an expression of inclusion that accepted difference, valued authenticity and supported criticism of the Establishment, a moment that separated the country's definition of success from monarchical values, even though Diana was a monarchist. Everyone seems able to project what they want to see onto the crowds that came out for Diana, as if they were a vast Rorschach test. New Labour does not see the Diana who walked out of her marriage, fought for her voice, lauded naturalness. And if most young people want to be as immensly successful and glamorous as her, there will be disappointment in store. It was not difference or pluralism that Blair idealised in his interview, but the culture of media glamour moderated by compassion for losers. A high-fashion form of paternalism without democracy.

In other words, the consequences of 1997 are still being contested. The May 1st election pulled down the curtain on Powellite bigotry and its associated definitions of Englishness, a fact the Diana events confirmed. This was the achievement of the year. What follows next is still an open question. The Labour government is probing to find its way. When it is tacky, it is very tacky. But when it is good, it is already better than anything since 1950. It has decided that it wants a new Britain. The events of the year have made this possible. There will, therefore, be a new Britain. What kind of new Britain is still undecided, and should not be decided by the government alone. A crucial part of the answer, however, lies in whether Labour creates a clear overall vision of its reform programme which can be appropriated by people across the UK, in the way that Scotland's parliament will belong to the Scots.

To argue in this fashion makes me return to the difficulty of what I have attempted in these pages. It is less a matter of content than what I feel to be a strangeness of voice. There are two familiar languages in British public life. The first, to which we are over-accustomed, reassures even when it raises some alarm or other, saying, basically, we British are OK, if not the best in the world, then nearly so. Sharp insights and creative meditations are possible within its parameters. Orwell's famous complaint, for example, that England is a family with the wrong members in control, reveals his Etonian perspective; as if all that was needed was to get the right people to run the show. The other language, which Orwell was also capable of, is the polemic that rests upon the imperative to revile and rail against the class system, its innate, irretrievable and insufferable brutality and stupidity, while really regarding one's criticism as futile. From sarcasm to rant to satire, England would be unbearable without its scurrilous, dissenting traditions. They are essential to our mental health. But in different ways, both the complacent and the radical attitudes assume the acquiescence of 'ordinary' people, that I discussed in the introduction.

I am not writing in either of these tones of voice. The consitutional system is rotten and broken. It is quite beyond the repair of better members of the family. The old constitution has to be replaced – period – for the country's structures of government to be opened up, made accountable and democratised. So stand by for the Freedom of Information Act, based on the principle that public papers belong to the people and not to the Crown. Such legislation is possible, and people like genuinely democratic policies. Radical change is now practical change. Its idiom is exceptional only within the confines of the twentieth-century British political discourse. One of its sources is the debate over the environment, which manages to combine a radical overview of the planet as a whole with practical, modern arguments about saving it. And those involved in the environment do not suffer from the still widespread sense in Britain that to speak and act politically one needs permission. We know how to scorn and laugh at government but we do not yet believe that it is our right to change the rules.

But it is. To do so constructively, and to overcome the remaining fear and reluctance, action is needed both at the centre and in society at large. A clear statement of the principles and aims of the government's reform agenda is essential. People like to act when there can be an outcome and abhor fruitless meetings. An overall statement of purpose and direction can help to tie in, and make sense of, the modest efforts that individuals can combine to make in their communities. For these also need (not mainly, but partially) to be constitutional. We are used to the idea that we have entitlements to education, to a health service and to equality before the law. We are not used to the idea of constitutional entitlement: that the way we are governed belongs to us-the-people.

The reform programme the government has embarked upon has not yet been presented in this – or any other – way. Certainly it has yet to endorse the ecological approach I have taken that would replace the mechanical 'absolute sovereignty' of parliament. Nonetheless, New Labour has already aroused expectations and broken inhibitions, for all its attempts to control events. Public energy will mount as the culture of effective citizenship develops. There will be an increase in calls for local and community action, essential to a society renewing its civic order. People will become more involved in what have been termed 'communities of purpose'. Not necessarily based on locality, these are free associations rather than communitarian-style communities of fate. They need funds, often very modest, relative to the volunteer resources they release. They enhance the networks essential to a flourishing contemporary society. They encourage and reinforce dissent. And they are needed to help prepare for a successful, written constitution. The media will assist officials in pouring scorn on the notion that such a historic transformation is possible or that it is wanted 'from below'. Until they wake up to the fact that, without any help, a sizeable majority of the public already believe that to make sense of the reforms taking place we should write down our constitution. Then, the cause will be jumped upon as if every articulate journalist and politician across the land has always known all along that Britain needs a new democratic settlement.

NOTES

Introduction: Voice, Class and a Nightmare:

1 G. H. L. Le May, *The Victorian Constitution*, London, 1979, p. 93.
2 *Daily Telegraph*, 11 September 1997, reported by Anthony King.
3 *Sunday Times*, 15 June 1997.
4 Speech delivered in Cardiff, 15 July 1994.
5 See my introduction to Anthony Barnett (ed.), *Power and the Throne*, London, 1992.
6 *Evening Standard*, 10 September 1997.
7 *Spectator*, 13 September 1997.
8 *The Times*, 13 September 1997.
9 Iain MacWhirter, *Scotsman*, 18 June 1997.
10 Lord Hailsham, *On the Constitution*, London, 1992, p. 7.
11 Robert Alexander (Lord Alexander of Weedon), *The Voice of the People*, London, 1997, pp. 199, 26.
12 Edmund Burke, *Reflections on the Revolution in France*, Penguin edition, p. 181.
13 For an important discussion of the relationships between individual autonomy and democracy see David Held, *Models of Democracy*, Cambridge, 1996, Chapter 9.
14 See Logie Barrow and Ian Bullock, *Democratic Ideas and the British Labour Movement 1880–1914*, Cambridge, 1996.
15 Mapped by Christopher Harvie in *The Centre of Things*, London, 1989. I discuss briefly how the British constitution has been 'intensely imagined' in the *Times Literary Supplementary*, 6 December 1991.

16 Tom Nairn, 'Sovereignty After the Election', paper for the Birkbeck Sovereignty Seminar, 25 June 1997.
17 H. N. Brailsford, *The Levellers and the English Revolution*, London, 1961, p. 255.
18 A. S. P. Woodhouse, *Puritanism and Liberty, Being the Army Debates (1647–9) from the Clarke Manuscripts*, London, 1951, pp. 52–3.
19 Eric Barendt, as reported by Alan Rusbridger in the *Guardian*, 24 May 1997.
20 A point made by Anthony Lester, QC, quoted by Alan Rusbridger in the *Guardian*, 26 June 1997.
21 John Smith, *A Citizen's Democracy*, p. 14, published by Charter 88, London, 1993. This includes his response to questions, from which I have quoted.

1. The Defeat of Fear

1 Peter Stothard, *The Times*, 25 April 1997.
2 Collected in *The Battle for the Constitution*, published by the Conservative Political Centre, September 1996.
3 Anthony Bevins, *Independent*, 6 June 1997.
4 Andrew Roberts, *The Sunday Times*, 27 April 1997.
5 *Independent*, 23 April 1997.
6 The quotations on these two episodes are taken from 'Three Bigots Bite the Dust', a post-election article by Nick Cohen, *Observer*, 4 May 1997. The third bigot was John Lines, who sought to exploit the German childhood of his Labour opponent Gisela Stuart by telling the electorate in Birmingham Edgbaston 'not to vote for a Kraut'. She took the seat with a swing of 10 per cent.
7 *Daily Mail*, 15 March 1997.
8 David Butler and Dennis Kavanagh, *The British General Election of February 1974*, London, 1974, p. 103.
9 R. W. Johnson presents a trenchant and compelling summary of 'the sheer size of the Powellite phenomenon' in the *London Review of Books*, 23 January 1997, which draws on the study of Douglas E. Schoen, *Enoch Powell and the Powellites*, London, 1977.
10 John Campbell, *Edward Heath*, London, 1993, p. 607.

11 Robert Shepherd, *Enoch Powell*, London, 1996, p. 449. Shepherd discusses the impact of the 'Wolverhampton epicentre' on the two elections, pp. 399–403 and 448–51.
12 For a helpful, recent debate see 'Dollar Democracy', *The Nation*, 5 May 1997. Martin Walker reported on the first billion-dollar election in the *Guardian*, 9 December 1995; see Anthony Barnett, 'The Creation of Democracy' in Paul Hirst and Sunil Khilnani (eds), *Reinventing Democracy*, Oxford, 1996.
13 *City of London and Westminster, Referendum Party News*, Issue No. 2.

2. A Velvet Revolution against Corruption

1 Ian Buruma, 'Smugness at Dawn', *Prospect*, May 1997.
2 *Guardian*, 15 May 1997.
3 *The Times*, 2 June 1997.
4 Peter Jenkins, *Mrs Thatcher's Revolution*, London, 1987, p. 30.
5 Richard Norton-Taylor, Mark Lloyd and Stephen Cook, *Knee Deep in Dishonour*, London, 1996, p. 187.
6 David Leigh and Ed Vulliamy, *Sleaze*, London, 1997, pp. 241–2.
7 See the *Guardian*, 21 March and 8 April 1997.
8 Leigh and Vulliamy, as above, p. 83.
9 As above, p. 149.
10 Trevor Smith, inaugural lecture, *British Politics in the Post-Keynesian Era*, London, 1985, and his contribution in the helpful Hansard Society reader, edited by F. F. Ridley and Alan Doig, *Sleaze: Politicians, Private Interests and Public Reaction*, Oxford, 1997.
11 Matthew Parris predicts that media 'vengeance will be terrible' on Labour when the press decides to expose its sexual behaviour ('No Labour Sleaze – Yet', *The Times*, 4 April 1997). Parris encourages the notion that the press was merely biased against the Conservatives. In this way he too diminishes the importance of the discrimination that needs to be made over financial corruption. If (perhaps one should say 'when') Labour MPs are uncovered abusing their new role for *financial* gain, the retribution will be tremendous. Not least because it will be motivated by Tory revenge for losing the honey pots.

12 Patrick Dunleavy and Stuart Weir, *Media, Opinion, and the Constitution*, in Ridley and Doig, as above, pp. 54–68.
13 All quotes and figures from the two documents produced by The Democratic Audit under the direction of Stuart Weir: a classic example of how determined research into public affairs can influence perception. In effect, Weir uncovered a secret State that had been referred to rhetorically – its existence was known – but had never been mapped; *Ego Trip, Extra-governmental Organisations in the UK and their accountability*, Stuart Weir and Wendy Hall (eds), London, 1995, and *The Untouchables, Power and Accountability in the Quango State*, by Wendy Hall and Stuart Weir, London, 1996.
14 Quoted in Roy Denman, *Missed Chances*, London, 1996, p. 290.
15 Shirley Williams asked for this information in the House of Lords. She declared that if a state of affairs were to last where the public was not informed about who was given public office and wielded official power, it would be 'the end of democracy'. Personal comment.
16 Kevin Morgan and Ellis Roberts, *The Democratic Deficit*, University of Wales Planning Paper No. 144, Cardiff, 1993.
17 Julian Barnes captures the moment well in his *Letters from London*, London, 1995, p. 172.
18 Francis Wheen's column, *Guardian*, 30 July 1997.
19 *Sunday Telegraph*, 27 June 1993.
20 Emma Nicholson, *Secret Society: Inside – and Outside – the Conservative Party*, London, 1996, pp. 12–13, 21–2.
21 Dunleavy and Weir, as above.
22 Roger Mortimore, 'Politics and Public Perceptions', in Ridley and Doig, as above, pp. 32–3.
23 *Daily Telegraph*, 4 July 1997.
24 See David Leigh, *Observer*, 22 June 1997. Leigh produced the *World in Action* film that led to Granada being sued by Aitken, along with the *Guardian*.
25 *The Times*, 8 July 1997.
26 In a leader on the Downey Report, 4 July 1997.
27 The letters from Edwina Currie, Kenneth Clarke and David Mellor are reproduced on pp 500–2 of Vol. II of the Downey Report. The quote from Hamilton is in Vol. III, p. 185.
28 The case for Mark Thatcher's exploitation of his mother's position to make himself, in his sister's words, 'swags of cash' is

set out at length in Paul Halloran and Mark Hollingsworth, *Thatcher's Gold*, London, 1995.

29 Vidal was hired by the BBC to cover the start of the election. His remarks were widely reported, and Labour protested vigorously. He described his experience in *The Nation*, 26 May 1997.

30 Richard Norton-Taylor and David Pallister, *Guardian*, 23 June 1997.

31 One can also draw a parallel with respect to the public-order acts that deprived the British of the right to silence, the right to assembly and even, had the government lasted, to the right not to have one's home bugged by the police at will and without a warrant. The public response in the UK to all this was at best lethargic. Despite the protests of liberal intellectuals in the Soviet-bloc countries, and outrage expressed in the West, communist authoritarian intrusion was likewise accepted passively by most of the public, with a shrug by those reduced to dependency and concerned for their jobs, saying, 'What can you expect?'

3. A Normal Country

1 William Hazlitt, *The Spirit of the Age*, London, World Classics edition, 1904, pp. 17–18.

2 James Laver, 'The mention of central heating coincides with the decay of the home', Ernest Barker, *The Character of England*, Oxford, 1947, p. 463.

3 Speech reported in full in the *Independent on Sunday*, 16 January 1994.

4 Report of the Child Poverty Action Group, suggesting the Conservatives had pursued a 'deliberate strategy of inequality', the *Guardian*, 28 April 1997, and reporting a Eurostat report that 12.8 million Britons lived below the poverty line of whom 3.9 million were children giving the UK the highest proportion of child poverty in the EU.

5 Nigel Lawson, *The View from No. 11*, London, 1993, p. 994.

6 Speech at the Nexus Conference, LSE, 1 March 1997 – the italics are mine.

7 *Daily Telegraph* and *Guardian*, 19 April 1997.

8 *The Times*, 24 January 1997.

9 *Daily Mail*, front page, 1 June 1997.

10 Tom Nairn, *The Enchanted Glass*, London, 1988, p. 27.
11 The *Guardian*, 16 June 1997.
12 Speech to the Institute of Socio-Economic Studies, 15 September 1975, in Margaret Thatcher, *The Revival of Britain, Speeches 1975–1988*, Alistair B. Cooke (ed.), London, 1989, p. 3.
13 The trend was first plotted by Ivor Crew and B. Sarlvik, 'Partisan Dealignment in Britain, 1946–74', *British Journal of Political Science*, 1977.
14 Paul Hirst and Grahame Thompson have helpfully insisted on the capacity of nations to resist globalisation in *Globalisation in Question*, Cambridge, 1966.
15 *Sunday Times*, 4 May 1997.
16 For this and extracts from the Derby and Southwark speeches that follow see Tony Blair, *New Britain, my vision of a young country*, London, pp. 291–309.
17 Martin Taylor, Chief Executive of Barclays' Bank and appointed by the government to chair an inter-departmental committee considering how to end the poverty trap, wrote an unfair review of Will Hutton's advocacy of stakeholding in the *Financial Times*, see Anthony Barnett *The Defining Moment*, London, 1995, for a discussion of the exchange, but Taylor did not reject the concept outright.

4. Worcester Woman

1 'Election turn-off for viewers', *Guardian*, 10 July 1997.
2 John Rentoul, *Tony Blair*, London, 1996 edition, pp. 456, 462.
3 *Observer*, 13 April 1997.
4 'The Anthony Crosland Memorial Lecture', 13 February 1997.
5 The Economist/MORI new government poll, *Economist*, 3 May 1997, p. 22.
6 Robert Harris, *The Sunday Times*, 4 May 1997. Harris travelled with Blair 'as a member of his private staff'.
7 Andrew Lansley, 'Accentuate the negative to win again', *Observer*, 3 September 1995.
8 *Evening Standard*, 29 April 1997.
9 Anatole Kaletsky, *The Times*, 22 April 1997.
10 *Daily Mail*, 16 April 1997.
11 Robert Harris, as above.
12 Marina Warner, *Monuments and Maidens, the Allegory of the*

Female Form, London, 1985, Chap. 3, which also contains a discussion of one of Worcester Woman's ancestors: Britannia.

13 Richard Norton-Taylor, *Guardian*, 9 May 1997.

14 Jerome Burne on vitamin supplements, *Independent*, 23 July 1997.

15 John Major, speech to the Centre for Policy Studies, 26 June 1996.

5. Diana: 'You was a Rose in a Garden of Weeds'

1 I want to thank David Hayes for an unsolicited letter about the Diana event which makes him co-author of some passages in this chapter.

2 *Independent*, 19 September 1997.

3 With great insight, Julie Burchill saw what had happened in 1992: 'One thing is sure; whatever she does, for the first time ever the love and loyalty of the people has shifted irretrievably from the ruling house – until death, beyond divorce and dishonour – to one individual. To the one and only People's – and Pop's – Princess.' *The Modern Review*, 1992, reprinted in the *Observer*, 7 September 1997.

4 Tina Brown makes the same point in her shrewd report on having lunch with Diana in New York in June 1997. Only Brown writes that since Churchill there has never been an occupant of Downing Street 'more charismatic' in the public's mind than the occupants of the Palace until Blair. This underestimates Thatcher's charisma rating. After the Falkland's War she certainly overtook the royals in this respect. But while Thatcher was more charismatic than the Queen she never scored as highly in her popularity ratings, for she was divisive and she needed the more low-charisma but comforting appeal of Elizabeth II. Blair, by contrast, is seeking to fashion a young One-Nation politics and for the first time the Queen is a *more divisive* figure than her Prime Minister. This is an astonishing turnabout. In one respect, however, Blair may need the throne as much as it needs him. Should Labour decide to enter Europe's single currency, the Queen could be an asset in neutralising patriotic fears. *New Yorker*, 15 September 1997.

5 *The Times*, 5 September 1997.

6 Shirley Williams, 'A Citizens' Monarchy', in Anthony Barnett (ed.) *Power and the Throne*, as cited.
7 Tina Brown, as above.
8 I am very grateful to Tim Miller for the comparison.
9 *Guardian*, 22 September 1997; for George VI, Margaret Driscoll, *The Sunday Times*, 7 September 1997.
10 Argument made when presenting her paper, *Sovereignty and the Media* to Birkbeck College Sovereignty Seminar 21 May 1997.
11 *Daily Express*, 10 March 1966.
12 Letter from Ms. Chris Charlesworth, *Independent*, 9 September 1997.
13 *Prospect*, October 1997.
14 *Daily Express*, 9 September 1997.
15 Robert Shepherd, *Enoch Powell*, London, 1996, p. 487.
16 Margaret Thatcher, 'Speech at Cheltenham', 3 July 1982. The speech is reproduced in full in Anthony Barnett, *Iron Britannia*, London, 1982, pp. 149–53.
17 Speech given on 9 April 1976, quoted in Paul Gilroy, *There Ain't No Black in the Union Jack*, London, 1987, p. 43.
18 Shepherd, as above, pp. 276, 366.
19 As above, p. 45.
20 *Sunday Telegraph*, 7 September 1997.
21 Andrew Morton, *Diana: Her True Story – In Her Own Words*, Revised Edition, London, 1997, p. 28.
22 *Sunday Times*, 17 March 1997.
23 Anthony Barnett, 'The Divorce', *Soundings*, July 1996, p. 17.
24 Walter Bagehot, *The English Constitution*, London, 1963, p. 262.
25 As above, pp. 105, 65.
26 Tom Nairn, *The Enchanted Glass* and Ferdinand Mount in *The British Constitution Now* have both argued that Bagehot's analysis is wrong. Robert Rhodes James has also, from a royalist point of view: he claims that the Queen, far from being decorative, exercises an important, continuing power whose beneficial effects depend on it remaining secret, *Journal of the Royal Society of Arts*, April 1994. I discuss these arguments in *Power and the Throne*, as above, pp. 28–30. A longer, detailed critique by a master of Britain's constitutional niceties, Peter Hennessy, can be found in his *The Hidden Wiring*, London, 1995, pp. 49–55. He shows Bagehot was 'plain wrong' to assert

that 'a republic has insinuated itself beneath the folds of a monarchy'.

27 The group's existence was publicised in 1996. It consisted of senior royals and at least four male advisors, see *Daily Telegraph*, 20 August 1996.

28 Christian Tyler, 'Plainclothes Royals', *Financial Times*, 20 April 1997.

6. What a Constitution Is

1 Thus Paine was wrong, when, in his response to Burke's attack on the French Revolution, he wrote in *The Rights of Man*, 'Can then Mr Burke produce the English Constitution? If he cannot, we may fairly conclude, that though it has been so much talked about, no such thing as a constitution exists, or ever did exist, and consequently that the people have yet a constitution to form'. Thomas Paine, *Collected Writings*, New York, 1995, p. 468.

2 For a succinct account that links the incident to its wider significance, see Hugo Young, *One of Us*, London, 1991, pp. 285–8, and Clive Ponting, *The Right to Know*, London, 1985.

3 Peter Hennessy, *The Hidden Wiring*, London, 1995, p. 76, reported by Malcolm Rifkind.

4 I have discussed this (drawing on Garry Wills, *Lincoln at Gettysburg*, New York, 1992) in 'Creating Democracy', in *Reinventing Democracy*, Paul Hirst and Sunil Khilnani (eds), Oxford, 1996.

5 Walter Bagehot, *The English Constitution*, London, 1963, p. 266.

6 David Held, *Models of Democracy*, 2nd edition, Oxford, 1996, p. 197.

7 See Chapter 2, 'Oliver Franks: a man for all treasons', in Trevor Smith and Alison Young, *The Fixers*, London, 1996, p. 12.

8 Quoted by James Cornford, in 'Official Secrecy and Freedom of Information', in *1688–1988, Time for a New Constitution*, Richard Holmes and Michael Elliot (eds), London, 1988, p. 143.

9 Keynote speech by Gordon Brown, MP to the Economist/Charter 88 Conference, 12 July 1997.

10 William Waldegrave, *Recruiting to the Little Platoons*, Social Market Foundation pamphlet, London, 1994, p. 6. Justifying

the modernisation of government, Waldegrave noted that the first model of British government was 'the model of an army. Disciplined, hierarchical; responsive to commands, an organisation with an explicit ethos of its own set consciously against the ethos of the "civilian" world. It is not long since diplomats actually went in for uniforms.'

11 Apparently over 100 legal articles have now appeared on this case, known as *Pepper v. Hart*. I am grateful to Anthony Lester for encouraging me to witness the small constitutional earthquake. He has published an accessible overview, 'Pepper v. Hart Revisited', in *Statute Law Review*, Vol. 15, No. 1, 1994.

12 Vernon Bogdanor, *The Monarchy and the Constitution*, Oxford, 1995, p. 215.

13 With the *Brown v. Board of Education* decision that ended legal segregation; Stanley Katz, 'The Strange Birth and Unlikely History of Constitutional Equality', *Journal of American History*, December 1988, pp. 747–8.

14 Francesca Klug, *Reinventing Community, the Rights and Responsibilities Debate*, Charter 88, 1996, p. 15, outlines vividly the emergence of the UN and European human rights declarations after 1945, 'to make a reality of the phrase "never again"'.

15 Speaking in an interview I did with him for *Red Pepper*, June 1997.

16 Its lineage continued to the publication in 1991 by the IPPR of a full draft for *A British Bill of Rights*, edited by James Cornford with Anthony Lester chairing the working party. It was reissued in a second edition in 1996.

17 Letter to the *Independent*, 10 October 1991, the newspaper that sponsored the convention and hosted a pioneering debate in its pages on the call for a new constitution.

18 David Selbourne, *The Principle of Duty*, pp. 36, 234, 276–7.

19 Murray Hunt, *Using Human Rights Law in English Courts*, Oxford, 1997, p. 324.

20 Jeffrey Jowell, 'Politics, Principle and Judicial Review,' in *Current Legal Problems*, Oxford, 1997

21 This happened in the United States, where the Supreme Court decided that abortion was a constitutional right. In fact, it was an issue that the constitution did not address. If the US judges had not been so interventionist, different state legislatures would have made their own rulings and public opinion would have

worked through the issue, there being – for obvious reasons – a quiet, natural majority against abortion being illegal. Instead, by substituting itself for the democratic process, the US Supreme Court distorted the debate, helped to evacuate politics of relevance and provided opponents of abortion with a focus for populist rhetoric.

22 Lord Hailsham, *On the Constitution*, London, 1992, p. 105.

23 Earl of Carnarvon and others, *Second Chamber, Some Remarks on Reforming the House of Lords*, London, 1995, p. 1.

24 David Butler, Andrew Adonis and Tony Travers, *Failure in Britain's Government: The Politics of the Poll Tax*, Oxford, 1994, pp. 78–9.

25 *Sunday Telegraph*, 12 April 1992. The full account of how it did *not* work is to be found in Butler, Adonis and Travers, as above, who conclude that whatever personal mistakes and misjudgements may have been made, 'it appears to us incontrovertible that system failure was also to blame', p. 302.

26 See Godfrey Hodgson, *A Squinting Eye to Democracy*, Charter 88, 'Violations' No. 8, London, 1993.

27 James Fishkin has pioneered both studies and practical examples, including for Channel 4, see *The Voice of the People*, New Haven and London, 1995. I am grateful to him for a helpful conversation on applying deliberative polling to a second chamber.

28 Among the proposals there is one by me, *A House of Peers: the Athenian Solution*, discussion paper for Charter 88 Council, Spring 1996. Another is by Peter Carty. We are planning to collaborate on a joint publication.

29 House of Lords debate, 4 July 1996.

30 A. J. P. Taylor, *English History 1914–45*, Oxford, 1965, p. 569.

31 *Taking Charge: The Rebirth of Local Democracy*. The final report of the Commission for Local Democracy, London, 1995.

32 Speech to CPC seminar at Conservative Central Office, 1 July 1996.

33 I am using the famous distinction of Albert O. Hirschman, *Exit, Voice and Loyalty*, Cambridge, Mass., 1970.

34 Trevor Smith, private conversation.

35 I discuss this issue at length in *In Support of Consent*, Charter 88's response to the Labour Party's consultation paper (circulated but not published).

36 In 'Constitutional Possibilities', *Political Quarterly*, October–December 1997.
37 The Constitution Unit, *Scotland's Parliament: Fundamentals for a New Scotland Act*, London, 1996.
38 John Osmond (ed.), *The Nation Question Again*, Llandysul, 1985.
39 Walter Bagehot, as above, pp. 65–6.
40 Stanley de Smith and Rodney Brazier, *Constitutional and Administrative Law*, 7th edition, London, 1994, p. 575.
41 D. Osborne and T. Gaebler, *Reinventing Government*, Reading, Mass., 1992, pp. 166–7.
42 Peter Miller, 'The Limits of Accounting', in Hirst and Khilnani (eds), as above) pp. 57–69.
43 Speech of 5 July 1993, quoted in Weir and Hall, *Ego Trip*, as above, p. 12.
44 Historical debate as we know it over proportional voting starting in the early nineteenth century, Jennifer Hart, *Proportional Representation, Critics of the British Electoral System 1820–1945*, Oxford, 1992.
45 In his review of Vernon Bogdanor's *Power and the People*, in the *Guardian*, 12 June 1997.
46 Figures based on Table 1–1 in David Butler and Austin Ranney, *Referendums Around the World*, London, 1994. These include Switzerland's, which held over half the world's referendums up to 1993 – which skew the figures, but the general picture is clear: referendums are still infrequent but their numbers have exploded since the 1960s. The volume also contains a collection of helpful essays, including an admirable comparative survey of referendums across Europe by Vernon Bogdanor.
47 Frank Vibert's *Europe: A Constitution for the Millennium*, London, 1995, pp. 53–5.
48 Paper number 51, *The Federalist Papers*, edited by Isaac Kramnick, London, 1987, p. 320.
49 *Sunday Telegraph*, 12 December 1993.
50 *Daily Telegraph*, 25 September 1997.
51 Vernon Bogdanor, *Power and the People*, London, 1997, p. 11.
52 de Smith and Brazier, as above, pp. 6, 73, 83–4.
53 A. W. Bradley, 'Sovereignty in Parliament – in Perpetuity?', in Jeffrey Jowell and Dawn Oliver, *The Changing Constitution*, 3rd edition, Oxford, 1996, p. 89.
54 In other words, if a despairing government were to suddenly try

and surrender sovereignty over Ulster without a referendum, it would be taken to court for breaching the 1973 Act. How the courts would then decide between different arguments over the nature of Parliament's sovereignty would depend, if it ever came about, on the judges at the time. A generation ago they might have endorsed the view that Parliament can always stand on its head. This is less likely to be the view today.

7. Ours is Broke, a story of Nerve Gas and Eton

1 *The Economist*, 11 November 1995.
2 Enoch Powell, 'Parliamentary Sovereignty in the 1990s', in Philip Norton (ed.), *New Directions in British Politics?*, Aldershot, 1991, p. 134.
3 Quoted by Trevor Smith, 'Causes, Concerns and Cures', Ridley and Doig, (eds), *Sleaze*, as cited, p. 9.
4 *Committee on Standards and Privileges*, First Report, Vol. III, July 1997, p. 79.
5 *Guardian*, 22 March 1997.
6 *Daily Telegraph*, 4 June 1997.
7 This short account is drawn from the full story in Leigh and Vulliamy, *Sleaze*, as cited, pp. 190–99.
8 Francesca Klug, Keir Starmer, Stuart Weir, *The Three Pillars of Liberty*, London, 1996, pp. 83–9.
9 *The Times*, 24 January 1997.
10 As above. (Note 8) p. 304.
11 A. S. P. Woodhouse, *Puritanism and Liberty, being the Army Debates (1647–9) from the Clarke Manuscripts*, London, 1951, p. 54.
12 Simon Jenkins, *Accountable to None*, London, 1995, pp. 64, 255, 258.
13 Andrew Marr, *Ruling Britannia*, London, 1995, pp. 143–53.
14 John Sweeney, *Trading with the Enemy*, London, 1993, pp. 80–83.
15 Richard Norton-Taylor, *Truth is a Difficult Concept, Inside the Scott Inquiry*, London, 1995, p. 6.
16 The pipes episode provides an illuminating cameo of trustworthiness of the culture of integrity in British government. At the time of the dockland seizure of the pipes in 1990, Nicholas

Ridley, Minister for Trade and Industry, said that the Government had 'only recently' become aware of the supergun project. In fact the Conservative MP, Sir Hal Miller, had passed on the manufacturer's alarm about the military specifications in *June 1988*. Ridley's statement went through eight drafts, the third of which went to Thatcher in Downing Street. Early versions had 'last year' instead of 'recently'. Ridley's private secretary argued that 'recently' is a word whose 'interpretation depends very much upon its context' and helpfully explained what he meant with two examples: 'recent history suggest a different timescale to recent weather.' Then he added that as the Minister's own personal awareness was 'only days old', 'Ridley will have felt that Government awareness was genuinely recent, if only because of his own recent exposure to the facts'. Unwittingly, this use of the word 'genuinely' concedes that Parliament was presented with a counterfeit.

17 Paul Johnson, *Wake Up Britain!* London, 1994, pp. 44–5.
18 House of Commons, Public Service Committee Report on *Ministerial Accountability and Responsibility*, Vol. III, July 1996, pp. 67, 138–9.
19 Alan Clark, *Diaries*, London, 1993, p. 30.
20 Hennessy recounts this episode in the opening chapter of *The Hidden Wiring*, London, 1995.
21 The word 'knowingly' made its first appearance in a draft proposal for a Civil Service Code drawn up by the Treasury and Civil Service committee in 1994. It was seized upon by the government. I am grateful to Amy Baker for her help in clarifying the episode.
22 Public Service Committee, Vol. III, 1996, as cited, p. 138.
23 As above, p. 121.
24 David Gladstone, *Must We Keep the Crown Prerogative?*, unpublished draft, 1997.

8. Mending it – a Theory of Change

1 *The Times*, 27 September 1997.
2 The Lord Chancellor was interviewed by Andrew Adonis and Patrick Wintour, *Observer*, 27 July 1997.
3 *The Times*, 12 July 1998.
4 As above.

5 Lord Irvine of Lairg, the Lord Chancellor, 'Keynote Address to the Conference on a Bill of Rights for the United Kingdom', London, 4 July 1997. The subsequent quotes are from this speech.
6 Alan Watkins has pointed out that Hansard does not provide a record of 'exactly what the man or woman said at the time' in the preface to his *A Conservative Coup*, London 1991, p. viii.
7 *The Times*, 10 March 1997 – it was the week after Labour and the Liberal Democrats came to their joint agreement on constitutional reform.
8 See Anthony Lester in 'Can we achieve a new Constitutional Settlement?' in Colin Crouch and David Marquand (eds.) *Reinventing Collective Action*, Oxford 1995.
9 See the quotation in the Introduction pp. 21–22.
10 Ernest Gellner, *Thought and Change*, London, 1964, p. 136.
11 Will Hutton, *The State We're In*, London, 1995, p. 319.
12 'The Empire State', in *Power and the Throne*, London 1995.
13 See Gregory Elliot, *Labourism and the English Genius*, London, 1993, pp. 183–96, from which this discussion is drawn. Like him I am indebted to the Nairn/Anderson theses which situated the question of British modernisation in terms of its comparative history, see especially Perry Anderson's brilliant 'Origins of the Present Crisis', reprinted in *English Questions*, London, 1992.
14 Graham Allen MP, *Reinventing Democracy*, London, 1995, p. 3.
15 In his 1980 Lecture, 'The New Conservatism' reproduced in Lawson, *The View from No. 11*, as cited, p. 1045.
16 Hugo Young, *One of Us*, as cited, p. 223.
17 Simon Jenkins, *Accountable to None*, as cited, p. 1.
18 F. A. Hayek *The Constitution of Liberty*, London, 1960, p. 182. He also defends the need for bills of rights 'in spite of their inevitable incompleteness' and even advocates them as an important measure for advancing the awareness of 'the public mind', pp. 216–17. Hayek's argument here is circumscribed by his overall effort to laud the British, empirical tradition at the expense of the French, rationalist one which, notoriously, declaimed the rights of man. But by the mid-twentieth century the advantages of bills of rights could be justified in an organic, almost Burkian fashion.
19 Stuart Hall, 'The Great Moving Right Show', in Stuart Hall and Martin Jacques, *The Politics of Thatcherism*, London, 1983,

p. 34. The book is a collection of the pioneering articles published in *Marxism Today*.

20 The key moment that allowed her to do this was the Falklands War. I give an account of what happened in *Iron Britannia*, London, 1982, where I describe the important influence of 'Churchillism', also discussed in Chapter 10 below.

21 *Financial Times*, 23 October 1993.

22 The document was leaked to *The Times*, 17 July 1996. These quotes are from an article about it the following day by the paper's Economics Editor Anatole Kaletsky, who concludes that the entire Treasury team should be locked up, 'throwing the key in the Thames'.

23 Simon Jenkins, who argues that local government must be able to spend and answer for it at the polls, if democracy is to revive, identifies the Treasury as the driving force behind the destruction of local finance. Commenting on its baleful influence on the plans for the capital, he wrote after the Green Paper on London was published: 'The next crucial battle is . . . with the Treasury . . . now the biggest block on constitutional reform in Britain. Its apparatchiks on Whitehall committees rant in defence of their beloved "control". They so neutered the Green Paper's few paragraphs on financing the new London authority as to render it totally incoherent. This one-time intellectual powerhouse is now a jaded freemasonry.' *The Times*, 30 July 1997.

24 Paul Johnson, *Daily Telegraph*, 16 March 1997.

25 Chantal Mouffe, 'Democracy Citizenship and the Political Community', in Chantal Mouffe (ed.), *Dimensions of Radical Democracy*, London, 1992. Paul Hirst, *Associational Democracy*, Cambridge, 1994.

26 Tony Giddens, *Beyond Left and Right, the future of radical politics*, Cambridge, 1994, p. 251.

27 George Soros, 'The Capitalist Threat', *The Atlantic Monthly*, January, 1997, p. 53.

28 Karl Popper, *The Open Society and its Enemies*, London, 1995, pp. 510, 525; and see his brief and pointed discussion of democracy, 390–92.

29 Perry Anderson, 'Under the Sign of the Interim', *London Review of Books*, 4 January 1996.

30 Quoted in Roy Denman, *Missed Chances*, London, 1996, p. 198.

31 As above, p. 199.

32 *New Statesman*, 26 September 1997.
33 This has been my view, since Blair and Brown gained the leadership; see *The Defining Moment*, Charter 88, 1994, in which I argued in 1994: 'A new Labour government *can* introduce successful constitutional reform. Its leaders are young enough not to be awed by the past. They are alert enough to the country's interests to want to proceed democratically.'
34 Nigel Lawson, as cited, p. 868.
35 Private conversation.
36 *Observer*, 25 May 1997.
37 Paul Foot, *The Politics of Harold Wilson*, Harmondsworth, 1968, pp. 153–65.
38 Speech by Gordon Brown MP to the Economist/Charter 88 Conference, 12 July 1997.
39 A. V. Dicey, *The Law Of The Constitution*, 8th edition, London, 1920, p. 465.

9. The English Question

1 Angela Carter, *Shaking a Leg*, London, 1997, p. 603.
2 David Marquand, *The New Reckoning*, Cambridge, 1997, p. 154.
3 See Tom Nairn, *The Enchanted Glass*, London, 1988, for a full description, the quote is p. 188.
4 Linda Colley, *Britons: Forging the Nation 1707–1837*, London, 1992, p. 210.
5 Enoch Powell, 'Parliamentary Sovereignty in the 1990s', in Philip Norton (ed.), *New Directions in British Politics*, Aldershot, 1991, p. 137.
6 Liah Greenfeld, *Nationalism*, Cambridge, Mass., 1992, pp. 18, 86.
7 See Alan Millward's *The European Rescue of the Nation State*, London, 1992.
8 *Prospect*, January 1997.
9 Linda Colley, *Britons*, as cited, pp. 51–4. Royalty is representative but not voted for. Parliament too could be experienced as their representative body by those who could not vote, especially women. Colley shows how from the early eighteenth century, Parliament, though chosen by relatively few men was celebrated as representing all Protestant Britain. Of course, it had cut down

a King, still a live memory. If the development of Britishness was fundamentally linked to Protestantism, as Colley argues, then Parliament can be seen less as a medieval court than a synod of the British nation. Church councils are also experienced as representative by people who can never vote for them.

10 Angela Carter, as cited, p. 186.

11 Patrick Wright, *On Living in an Old Country*, London, 1985, p. 186. His assessment is a partial corrective to my own analysis in *Iron Britannia*.

12 David Marquand, as cited, p. 175.

13 Mark Leonard, *Britain™*, Demos, London, 1997, p. 71.

14 Philip Dodd, *The Battle for Britain*, London, 1995, pp. 9, 26, 41. 'Mongrel' is a reference to Daniel Defoe's poem, *The True Born Englishman*, 'From whence a Mongrel-half-bred Race there came/With neither Name nor Nation, Speech or Fame.' See also Marina Warner's Reith lecture, Chap. 6, *Managing Monsters*, London, 1994.

15 *New Stateman*, 11 July and 27 August 1997.

16 Michael Ignatieff, *Blood and Belonging*, London, 1993, pp. 3–14.

17 Benedict Anderson, *Imagined Communities*, London, 1991, p. 144.

18 Bill Buford, *Among the Thugs*, London, 1991, see pp. 192–3.

19 The three virtues identified by A. J. P. Taylor at the conclusion to his *English History 1914–1945*, Oxford, 1965, p. 600.

20 Judith Herrin has studied the way Empresses drew on 'their experience of orthodoxy' to revive traditional Byzantine icon worship across a century that saw exceptional periods of direct rule by women, while the Empire was threatened by the rise of Islam, *Women in Purple*, forthcoming.

10. This Time

1 In his Humble Address to the Sovereign on winning the war in Europe, Churchill stated, 'the prerogatives of the Crown have become the privileges of the people', a wonderful formula that sums up British democracy – an intense and genuine consent fused to monarchical presumptions, which leaves people without any formal rights or constitutional distribution of power. The

speech is quoted in David Marquand, *The New Reckoning*, Cambridge, 1997, p. 167.

2 Robin Blackburn, 'Reflections on Blair's Velvet Revolution', *New Left Review,* 223, May–June 1997.

3 Ferdinand Mount, *The British Constitution Now*, London, 1992, p. 223.

4 Judgement of the German Federal Constitutional Court, 12 October 1993, English translation pp. 46, 85.

5 Geoff Mulgan, *Politics in an Anti-political Age*, Oxford, 1994, p. 129.

6 Gordon Brown, 'The Anthony Crosland Memorial Lecture', London, 13 February 1997, pp. 5, 7.

7 George Dangerfield, *The Strange Death of Liberal England*, London, 1936, pp. 34, 63.

8 Andrew Lansley and Richard Wilson, *Conservatives and the Constitution*, London, 1997, p. 7.

9 William Rees-Mogg, *The Times*, 31 July 1997.

10 Robert Alexander, *The Voice of the People, A Constitution for Tomorrow*, London, 1997, pp. vii, 206–9. A curt focus on his main idea inevitably does Alexander an injustice, for his discussion of Conservative abuse of basic rights between 1979 and 1997 is passionate and compelling, and he stresses the need to encourage participation. But people participate in organisations which belong to them. His reluctance to risk democracy is a basic flaw, which is reflected in the Commission proposal.

11 *The Times*, 4 September 1997.

Index

Abbot, Diane 276
accountability 152–3, 193–9
Accountable to None, the Tory Nationalisation of Britain 227–9
Adam Smith Institute 63
Additional Member System (AMS) 203
Administration of Justice 255
Agreement of the People (1647) 17–18, 304
Aitken, Jonathan 19–21, 34, 71–2, 74, 222
al-Fayed, Dodi 121, 132
al-Fayed, Mohammed 52, 54–6, 71–2
Al-Yamamah deal 74
Albania 76
Alexander, Lord (Robert), QC 12–13
  Constitutional Commission 319
  The Voice of the People, A Constitution for Tomorrow 318–20
Alibhai-Brown, Yasmin 302
American
  Bill of Rights 165
  Constitution (1787) 84–5, 164–5, 204–5
  Declaration of Independence 165, 205, 267
  Revolution 93
Americanisation 94–6, 99
Anatomy of Britain (1962) 87
Anderson, Benedict 303
  Imagined Communities 134
Anderson, Bruce 9–10
Anderson, Perry 272
Anne, Princess 137
Arab dealers 52
Arabs 132
aristocracy 8, 206
arms to Iraq 42, 230–50
Armstrong, Lord 319
  Daily Telegraph 208
Army 8, 17, 206, 210
Ascherson, Neal 315
Ashdown, Paddy 31, 59, 92, 104
Athenian Solution 180
Attlee, Clement 33, 245–6, 322
Austinian view of sovereignty 216

Australia, compulsory voting 202

Bagehot, Walter 154, 194, 254
  The Economist 213
  The English Constitution 141–2
Baghdad, Embassy 233
Baldwin, Stanley 320
Balmoral 129
Bank of England 27, 102, 275–80
Barings Bank 76
Barker, Sir Ernest 81–2
Basic Rights 255
Battle of Omdurman (1898) 309
The Battle over Britain 300–1, 304–5
BBC
  constitutional institution 210, 262
  News at 9 pm. 101
  Newsnight, George, Eddie 278
  Panorama interview 116, 138–9, 285
  Radio, *World at One* 65
  Today programme 123
Beck, Ulrich, *The Risk Society* 190
Beeston, Nicholas, *The Times* 231–2
Belgrano, sinking 150
Bell, Martin 56–7
Beloff, Max 166–7
Benn, Tony 41, 178
Berlin 83
  Wall 50, 78, 130
Big Bang 75, 86, 93
Bill of Human Rights 312
Bill of Rights 22, 24, 164, 167, 169–70, 193, 255, 275, 313, 316
  (1689) 34, 149, 160–1, 222–4
  (1968) pamphlet 166
  Thatcher, Margaret 166
Birmingham 40–1
  Hall Green 39
Black, Conrad 35
Blair, Tony 4, 28, 32, 40
  battle-bus 108
  biography 102
  British voting system 104
  Clause 4; 22, 300
  Clinton, Bill 90
  constitution 6, 256
  Derby 98
  Diana, Princess of Wales 118–19, 135, 283, 327
  education 304
  election campaign (1997) 32, 50
  Elizabeth II, Queen 91
  Far East tour 97–8
  government 35, 46, 94, 284, 317, 320
  image 102, 309
  Iron Lady mantle 268
  Labour Manifesto preface 254
  Labour Party modernisation 92
  Mirror 326
  Oxford 92
  political advisors 221–2
  Prime Minister 143
  Report on Constitutional Reform 275
  single currency 38, 311, 325–6
  Southwark Cathedral 98

stakeholder capitalism 98
Sun 38, 326
Thatcher, Margaret 79, 266–7, 321–2
Time magazine 326
Trade Union Congress (September 1997) 79, 118
Blenheim 126
Blitz 66, 126, 128
Blood and Belonging 302–3
BMW 76
BNFL 250
Bogdanor, Vernon 116, 211–12
The Monarchy and the Constitution 163
Bohr, Niels 211
Bollocks Constitution 249
Boothroyd, Betty 319
Bradberry, Grace, *The Times* 126
Bradshaw, Ben 39, 59
Branson, Richard 72
Brazil 122
Britain 297–300
Britain
civilisation 82
communitarians 168
Constitution 205, 217–18, 251, 253
constitutional court 161–2
courts 20
domestic administration 185
Empire State 83, 309
ex-Chancellors 277
Glorious Revolution 194
Law
European Convention on Human Rights 253
European Human Rights 214
libel 20
meaning of 293
modernisation 94–5
parliamentary history 83
Parliaments, Scotland 93
unwritten constitution 23, 84, 113, 228, 262
voting system 104–5
Britannia 294
British
State 6, 123, 171, 185, 284, 315
European Union reforms 314
The British Constitution Now 263, 311–12
Brooke, Peter 66
Brooks-Baker, Sir Harold 88
Brown, Gordon 92, 102–3, 113, 157
Bank of England 275–9
Crosland Lecture 103, 314
election campaign (1997) 32
European monetary union 325–6
political advisors 221–2
Brown, Tina, *The New Yorker* 121
Brussels 36, 288, 313, 325
BSE disaster 42, 53, 70, 157, 250, 322
Buckingham Palace 115, 118, 123, 128, 138
Budgen, Nicholas 42, 45
Buford, Bill 305
Bulpitt, Jim, *Territory and Power in the United Kingdom* 181
Burchill, Julie 118
Burke, Edmund 13, 15, 19, 165–6

Burke's Peerage 88
Buruma, Ian 50, 130
Butler Doctrine 247–8
Butler, Rab 273
Butler, Sir Robin 5–6, 89, 222, 231, 236, 242–5, 247–8

Cabinet
  government 141
  Office 160, 316
  Overseas and Defence Committee 232–3
Callaghan, James 321
Campbell, Alastair 54, 108, 110–1, 118, 163
Campbell, Colin and Graham Wilson, *The End of Whitehall* 227
capitalism 153
Carlton TV monarchy programme 140
Carnarvon, Lord 175–6, 178
Caroline, Princess 93
Carry On movies 308
Carter, Angela 16–17, 282
  So There'll Always Be An England 294
Catholicism 293
centralised form of rule 77
Chamberlain, Neville 321
change, theory of 251–81
Channel Tunnel 36
Channon, Paul 244
The Character of England 81–2
Charles, Prince 83, 136, 139, 207–9, 285
  Church of England 163
  Diana, Princess of Wales 137, 206–7
  wedding (1981) 117, 128, 132, 136, 283
  Parker–Bowles, Camilla 121, 129
Charter 88; 15–17, 21, 111, 230, 280
  Constitutional Convention (1991) 166–7
Chartists 15
Chauvin, Nicholas 290
chemical warfare (CW) 234–5, 240
China, Gang of Four 131
A Choice for England 184
Church, document on poverty and unemployment 102
Church of England 8, 82, 163, 206, 224, 286–7
Churchill, Winston 126–7, 290, 311, 321–23
  coalition government 308–09, 321
  'finest hour' declaration 83
  Iron Curtain speech 77
Churchillism 308–9, 311
Citizens 269
  Charters 195, 197
  Juries 195, 201
  Monarchy 120
City of London 8, 75, 206, 276, 278, 280, 295
  'Big Bang' 75, 86, 93
  institutions 258
  jobs 60
Civil Service 8, 27, 87, 151, 156, 210, 222, 230, 243, 248, 262 civil society courts 168
Civil War 208
Clark, Alan 58, 244–5, 290–1, 311

Diary 59
Clark, Kenneth 34–5, 64, 66, 68, 73
Clark, Nick 65
Clausewitz, Carl von 159
Cleese, John 16
Clinton, Bill 90, 95
Club, loyalty 224
Cold War 51, 77–8, 83, 310
Coleridge, Samuel Taylor 15
Colley, Linda 285, 293
Commission for Local Democracy 182
communism 154
consensual order 262
consensus politics 99, 262
Conservatism 269–70
Conservative
  Central Office 55
  Party 41, 51–5, 321
    conference (1996) 54–5
    constitution 88, 318
    donations 60, 67
    General Elections
      (1987) poster 107
      (1997) 31–4, 41, 48, 55
    Manifesto (1983) 263
    Research 105
    swing voters 51–3, 105
  200, *Conservatives and the Constitution* 316–17
Conservatives and the Constitution 316–17
constitution
  (1688) 16, 249, 259–60, 265–6, 269, 283–4, 288, 295, 307
  arrangements 82
  aspirations 203–12
  court 177
  development 245
  devolution 228
  institutions 210
  law 7
  normalisation 85
  reforms 1, 21, 29–30, 81, 99–100, 108, 110, 149–212
The Constitution of Liberty 263
Constitutional Convention (1991), Charter 88; 166–7
constitutions 84, 149–212
Cook, Robin 54, 326
  Foreign Secretary 248–9
  Joint Consultative Committee, Report on Constitutional Reform 274–5
  Scott Report 241–2, 244
Cornford, James 189, 316–17
Coronation (1953), Elizabeth II, Queen 128, 286
corruption 1, 50–76, 78
Cranborne, Lord 176, 180
Criminal Justice and Public Order Act (1994) 225
Cromer, Lord 279
Cromwell, Oliver 17, 19
Crosland Lectures 103, 314
Crown 88–9, 118, 123, 131, 142, 144, 206, 257, 328
  Ministers 276–7
  Parliament 2, 161
Currie, Edwina 73
Customs and Excise 238

Daily Mail 10, 29–30, 35, 41–2, 53, 107
  Battle for Britain 36–7, 215, 309

Europe 289
national greatness 296
Daily Telegraph 2, 39, 41, 45, 50, 70–1, 73, 324
Armstrong, Lord 208
Establishment figures 207
European Union poll 289–90
Evans, David outburst 39, 324
Hill, Jonathan 222
Johnson, Paul 267–8
Portillo, Michael 324
single currency 37
Tatton constituency 56–7
Dalyell, Tam 150
d'Ancona, Matthew 134–5
Dangerfield, George, *The Strange Death of Liberal England* 315–16
Darendorf, Ralph 277
De Smith, Stanley and Rodney Brazier 211
debate, full and free 179
decentralisation 99, 175, 185, 318
defence business 237
defence equipment market 234
Delhi, India 137
democracy 1–2, 24, 95, 144, 149, 153–4, 176, 280, 314
democratic
constitution 120
decentralisation 99
englishness 304–6
exchange (1647) 199
reform 154
Democratic Audit
election (1997) 202–3
The Three Pillars of Liberty 225–6, 228–9
Demos pamphlets
The Battle over Britain 300–1, 304–5
Britain 297–300
Denmark 106, 202, 228, 292
Denton, Baroness 62
Derby, Blair, Tony 98
devolution 45
Dewar, Donald 54–5, 189
Diana: Her True Story 284–5
Diana, Princess of Wales 1–3, 9–10, 21, 93, 115–45, 284–5, 301
Angola, minefields 121
death 10, 21, 48, 90, 110, 117, 121–3, 145
The Times 208
funeral 2, 80, 125, 127, 130
Panorama interview 116, 138–9, 285
wedding (1981) 117, 128, 132, 136, 283
Dicey, A.V. 15, 254
Introduction to the Study of the Law of the Constitution 281
Dimbleby, Jonathan 287
Disraeli, Benjamin 15, 317–18
Dodd, Philip, *The Battle over Britain* pamphlet 300–1, 304–5
Dorrell, Stephen 29, 123, 182–3
Downey, Sir Gordon 55–6, 71–2, 74–5, 220–1
Commission 219–20
investigations 56
Report 101
Downing Street 5, 118, 123, 223
constitutional amendment

223–4
Dublin summit 290
Dykes, Hugh 41

Eastern Europe 51, 75–6, 84, 93–4, 131
revolutions 130
economic democracy 99
The Economist, 62
Bagehot, Walter 213
Eden, Anthony 321
Edinburgh
Commonwealth Heads of State 326
Parliament 1, 3, 6, 27–8, 173–4, 188, 255, 275, 292, 301–2, 317, 328
Egyptians 134
electoral systems 200, 251
Elizabeth I, Queen 187
Elizabeth II, Queen 3, 90–1, 94, 110, 118, 123–4, 128–9, 145, 209
(1997) 110, 285
advisors 208
Blair, Tony 91
Coronation (1953) 128, 286
Diana, Princess of Wales's death 208
live television broadcast 127
loyalty to 224
Major, John 140
monarchy 143
seventieth birthday 116
speech 10, 50
Spencer, Charles 137
Spencer, Earl 138
taxation 123
Windsor Castle fire 66–7
Elizabeth, Queen Mother 128, 138
Elliot, Larry, *Guardian* 276
Empire 7, 82–3, 160, 206, 294
Day 294
State 8, 17, 152, 258, 307, 322
The End of Whitehall 227
Engel, Matthew 50
English
Constitution 194
courts, human rights law 170
question 255, 282–306
The English Constitution, Bagehot, Walter 141–2
Enlightenment 155
ERM fiasco (1992) 53–4, 66
essential services 65
Essex University, Democratic Audit 202–3, 225–6
Establishment 3, 81, 87, 93, 204, 208, 285
consensus 89
culture 99
figures, *Daily Telegraph* 207
politics 143
routines 92
ethnic question 42
Eton 87, 244–49, 328
Euro–banknote designs 290
Europe: a Constitution for the Millenniium 204
European
Convention on Human Rights 84
British Law 214, 253, 260
Courts 173, 212
Exchange Rate 106
Parliament
elections (1999) 199
Prescott, John 183
proportional

representation 217
single currency 35–7, 215, 325
referendum 199
Union 209, 251, 272, 289
accession 8, 260
British State reforms 314
constitution 167, 203–4
law 212–13
membership 212
national identities 290
public expenditure 216
sovereignty 213–14, 291
VAT 216
Europeanisation 94
Europhiles 291, 312
Europhobia 131, 321
Eurosceptics 34–5, 37–8, 41, 45, 89
Evans, David 39, 41, 324
Evening Standard 9, 106
Evita 122
Executive 73, 101, 151–2, 159–60, 172–3, 210, 214, 237, 250, 254, 266, 276, 278, 315

Fabian Society, Twigg, Stephen 89
Fabian-Labourism 12, 269–70
Falklands War 44, 82, 93, 133, 296, 308
victory parade 133
Far East tour, Blair, Tony 97
fascism 154
fear, defeat of 27–49
Felixstowe 127
Ferguson, Adam 190
Ferguson, Sarah 128
Fermoy, Lady 138
First World War 156, 315–16
first-past-the-post system 200
Fitzgerald, Garret, *Prospect* 292
Foot, Paul, *Guardian* 279
Ford, Henry 100
Foreign Office
chemical warfare 240
foreign policy 78, 248–9, 251
paper on defence equipment market 234
Forsyth, Michael 29
Forth Estate 14
Foster, Christopher and Francis Plowden, *The State underStress* 227
France 228, 294, 307–8
European Union 311
revolution (1789) 13, 93, 256
Franco, Fransisco 141
Franks, Lord 156–8
Free-market populism 258, 261–8
Freedom of Information 163–4, 215, 250
Act 27, 55, 91, 110, 156–7, 313, 328
freedom and rights, individual 164
Fulton, Missouri, iron curtain speech (1946) 77
fundamental rights 251

Gallup polls 30, 33, 70
Gellner, Ernest, *Thought and Change* 256–8
General Elections
(1970) 43–4
(1974 February) 43–4
(1979) 44, 264

(1987) 107
(1997) 3–4, 6, 32, 64, 77, 80, 88, 93, 109, 202–3, 296
European Questions 289
Scottish and Welsh votes 40
(next) 199
George, Eddie 278
George IV, King 93
George V, King 137
Spencer family 138
George VI, King 124, 128, 138
German Constitutional Court 313
Germany 314
European Union 311
Republic 77, 177, 277, 313
Gettysberg 153
Giddens, Tony 271
Giddy, Pam, *Violations of Rights in Britain* 160–1
Gilespie, Paul, *Irish Times* 292
Gilroy, Paul, *There Ain't No Black in the Union Jack* 134
Gladstone, David 250
Glasgow, Paisley 75
globalisation 95, 298
Glorious Revolution (1688) 16, 259–60, 265–6, 269, 283–4, 288, 295, 307
Glover, Stephen 71–4
Godsmark, Chris 61
Godwin, William, *Enquiry Concerning Political Justice* 79
Goldsmith, Sir James 30, 46–8
Gorbachev, Mikhail 78
Granada Television 19–20
Gray, John, Nexus rally 87–8
Great English
ideologies 7, 14, 75, 115, 324–5
Party 35–6, 312
Great Reform Act (1832) 259
Greater London Council (GLC) 15, 186
Greece, compulsory voting 202
Green Paper, London 186
Greenfeld, Liah, *Nationalism* 288, 303
Greenpeace 250
Greer, Ian 56
Greer–Hamilton case 221
Grey, Lord 259
Guardian 19–20, 34, 41, 50, 54–6, 71, 220
Elliot, Larry 276
Foot, Paul 279
Greer-Hamilton case 221
Hamilton, Neil 223
Hirst, David 233
MacAskill, Ewen 159
Nevin, Charles 138
Norton–Taylor, Richard 237
White, Michael 90–1
Guiness, John 250
Gulag 305
Gulf War 82

Hague, William 29, 48, 118, 123, 251, 312, 317
Hailsham, Lord 173, 252, 307
On the Constitution 12
Hall, Stuart 103, 264
Hallabjeh, Iraq, bombing 231–3
Hamilton, Neil 34, 56–8, 71, 73, 106, 219–20
Guardian 223

Major, John 223
Thatcher, Lady 223
Hand, Justice Learned 8
Handy, Charles 98, 314
Hansard 160–1
Hargreaves, Andrew 39–41, 302
Harris, Robert 108
Harrison, Tony 23
Harrods 10
Hattersley, Roy 3, 91, 200
Havel, Vaclav 50
Hayek, Frederick 166
The Constitution of Liberty 263
Hayes, David 302
Hazell, Robert 189
Hazlitt, William
Godwin, William 79
Spirit of the Age (1825) 79
Heads of State 21, 319
hereditary 141
Health Service 268
Heath, Edward 43–4, 91, 184, 294, 312, 321, 325
Heffer, Simon 35, 42
heirs to the throne 129, 136
Held, David 153–4
Helping the Exporter, Morris, Michael 244
Hennessy, Peter 245
hereditary peers 176, 180–1, 252
Heseltine, Michael 35, 56, 65–6, 150
Scott Report 230–1
Hill, Jonathan 221–2
Hirst, David, *Guardian* 233
history 100
History of England from the Accession of James the Second 259–60
Hitler, Adolf 207, 290–1, 307–8, 310, 320
Hobbesian view 15, 172
Hoffman, Lord 223
Hogg, Douglas 107
Holden, Anthony 131
Holland 2
Hong Kong 11, 83, 294
honours for donations 60
House of Commons 160–1, 178, 262, 266, 273, 276, 297
adversarial culture 160
All-Party Public Accounts Committee 61
Committee system 277
Constitution debate 39–40, 254
elections 180
power 173–4
Select Committees (1979–) 198
Strangers' Gallery 161
House of Lords 92, 95, 160, 175–81, 193, 215, 255, 283, 319
Constitution debate 218–19
Criminal Justice and Public Order Act (1994) 225
powers 173–4, 316
reform 22, 251, 318
virtue of 180
House of Peers 180
Houses of Parliament 163, 251
Howard, Michael 35, 53
Howe, Sir Geoffrey 230–2
arms to Iraq 237, 240
Scott Inquiry 234–5
Thatcher memoirs 264–5
'The Economic

Consequences of Peace in the Gulf' 232–4
Hume, David 15, 190
Hunt, Murray 170
Hurd, Douglas 68, 244, 295
Hussein, Saddam 235, 238
Hutton, Will 278
The State We're In 227, 257–8

Ignatieff, Michael, *Blood and Belonging* 302–3
immigration controls 42
improper privilege 63
Incorporation of the European Convention on Human Rights (1997), White Paper 171–2
incremental totalisation 272–3
Independent 38, 41, 61, 115, 130
Independent on Sunday 62
industrialisation 153
Information Technology 23
The Inquiry into the Export of Defence Related Equipment to Iraq and the Related Prosecutions *see* Scott Report
international sovereignty 251
Introduction to the Study of the Law of the Constitution 281 IPPR (think-tank) 189
full draft constitution (1991) 316–17
IRA 4
Iran 232, 242
Iran-Contra scandal 8
Iraq
arms to 42, 230–50
chemical warfare (CW) 234–5
exports to 232–3, 238, 242
Iran ceasefire 232
Kuwait invasion 237–38
Ireland 4, 292
Ireton, General 18, 226
Irish Sea 74
Irish Times, Gilespie, Paul 292
Irvine, Derry 161–2, 214, 255–6, 320
European Convention on Human Rights 253, 260
Labour Manifesto 252
Observer 253
Scotland and Wales referendums 274
The Times 252–3
Italy, referendums 201
Ivy League colleges 244

Jack, Iain 108
Jacobin mobs (1790) 284
Jacques, Martin 103, 264
James I, King of England 187
James VI, King of Scotland 187
Jay, Sir Anthony 207
Jenkins, Peter 53
Jenkins, Roy 108, 166
Jenkins, Simon 72, 74–5
Accountable to None, the Tory Nationalisation of Britain 227–9
Johnson, Melanie 39
Johnson, Paul 241
Daily Telegraph 267–8
Joint Consultative Committee, Report on Constitutional Reform 273–4
Joseph Rowntree Reform Trust

70
State of the Nation MORI survey 112–13
Jowell, Jeffrey 170

Kaletsky, Anatole, *The Times* 106
Kane, Pat 10
Kay, John 98
Kennedy, President 122
Kensington Palace 9, 122, 134
Keynes, John Maynard 85
Keynesian full-employment policies 261
King, Lord of Wartnaby 72
King, Tom 244
Kings, divine rights 81
Kinnock, Neil 91–2
Knights of the Realm 143
Kohl, Chancellor Helmut 289, 310
Korea, inward investment 76
Kurds 213, 233–7

Labour Party 14, 55, 75
  Campaign for Electoral Reform 33
  Clause 4; 22, 300
  constitutional programme 4–5, 28, 252–3, 256
  decentralisation 175
  European Union 78
  General Election (1997) 31–2, 40–1, 96, 102
  Governments 50
    (1945) 33, 308, 321
    (1964) 279
  Key Seats Unit 103–5
  Manifesto 113, 252–4
  Millbank centre 50, 55, 103
  October (1996) conference 98, 102
  Prime Ministers 89–90
  reforms 92, 215, 328–9
  War Book 55
  see also New Labour; Old Labour
Lamont, Norman 45, 106
Lansley, Andrew 105, 316–17
Laski, Harold 314
Law Lords 161, 177
Lawson, Nigel 86–7, 261, 268, 275, 321
leadership, Major, John 45
Lenin, Vladimir, tradition 166
Leonard, Mark 298
Lester, Anthony QC 160–1
  Bill of Rights pamphlet (1968) 166
Levellers 15, 18
Liberal Democrats 14, 31, 178, 257
  General Election (1997) 30–1
  Report on Constitutional Reform 273–4
  researchers 55
  Scottish Constitutional Convention 189
Liberalism 12, 270
liberty 202, 224–30
Liberty (pressure group) 225
Lincoln, Abraham 153–4
Linklater, Magnus 10
Littlejohn, Richard 39
Livingstone, Ken 15
Lloyd, John 119
lobbying 60
lobbyists 68, 73–4
local government 182, 274, 318
Locke 15

Lombroso, Cesare 41
London 64, 83, 133, 215
  Mayor 27, 173–4, 185, 187–8, 192, 199
  palaces 117, 127
  School of Economics 271

Maastrich paving debate 106
MacAskill, Ewen, *Guardian* 159
Macaulay, Lord 15, 260, 262–3
  History of England from the Accession of James the Second 259–60
McEwan, Ian 16
Mackay, Lord 218–22, 224, 229, 245
Maclennan, Robert, Joint Consultative Committee, Report on
  Constitutional Reform 274
Macmillan, Harold 322
  The Middle Way 321
Madison, James 204
MAFF 110
Mafia 305
Magna Carta (1215) 18, 304, 316
Mail on Sunday 38, 43, 90
Major, John 32, 42, 66, 76, 91–3, 96–7, 110–11, 118
  balancing act 321–2
  constitution 29, 111–12, 224
  corruption 56, 58
  economy 64–5
  election campaign 55, 101, 215
  Elizabeth II, Queen 140
  European Exchange Rate policy 106
  European Union 287–9
  government 106, 324
    Bill of Rights (1689) 149
  Great English Party 35
  Hamilton, Neil 58, 223
  leadership 45, 106–7, 268
  party line on Europe 101
  Political Secretary 221–2
  proportional representation (PR) 203
  Scotland referendum 28–9
  Scott Report 230–1, 243
  SERPS 229–30
  single currency 37–8, 215–16, 289, 324
  Thatcher, Margaret 267
Mandela, Nelson 50
Mandelson, Peter 6, 54, 107
manifesto politics 200
Mao 76
Margaret, Princess 137
Marquand, David 227, 284, 296
Marr, Andrew 38, 249
  Ruling Britannia, the failure and future of British Democracy 229
Marshall, Sir Michael 244
Marx, Karl 257
Marxism 256, 270, 303
Mather, Graham 248
Matrix–Churchill 238, 242–3
Mawhinney, Brian 217
Maxwell, Robert gagging writs 20
May (1940) 304
May Day (1997) 27–50, 94, 100, 124, 131, 155, 202–3
mechanical politics 100

Mellor, David 106, 244
Merchant, Piers 59
Methley, Pamela 110
MI6; 239
Middle East, Western forces 238
Middle England 29–30, 38, 80
The Middle Way 321
Mill 15
Miller, Peter 196
Milton, John 15
miners' strike 93
Ministers conduct 245
Mir space station 286–7
Mirror, Blair, Tony 326
Mitterand, President 310
modernisers 197, 267
modernity 79, 99, 288, 311
monarchy 2, 81, 87, 89, 91, 109, 115–16, 123, 129, 141, 143, 207, 209, 251, 262, 284–5
  Elizabeth II, Queen 143
  modernisation 319
Monarchy Conference (1993) 119–20
The Monarchy and the Constitution 163
monetarism 12, 321
Monetary Policy Committee 277, 280–1
Monroe, Marilyn 122
Montesquieu, Charles-Louis, *The Spirit of the Laws* (1748) 193–5
Moore, Suzanne, *Independent* 115
MORI
  polls 38, 70
  survey, *State of the Nation* 112–13
Morris, Michael, *Helping the Exporter* 244
Morton, Andrew 138
  Diana: Her True Story 284–5
Moscow 77
Mouffe, Chantal 269
Mount, Ferdinand
  The British Constitution Now 263, 311–12
  Conservative Manifesto (1983) 263
MPs, extra-parliamentary incomes 68
Mulgan, Geoff 314
Munich
  Agreement (1938) 83, 290, 307, 310
  conference (1938) 310
  crisis 290
municipal government 151
Murdoch, Rupert 78, 117–18, 288
Muslims 132
Mussolini, Benito 197, 297

Nadir, Asil 67
Nairn, Tom 186, 188–9, 193, 303
Napoleon III 311
national
  anthem 205
  curriculum 63
National Audit Office (NAO) 61, 195
National Health Service 23, 96, 268
National Westminster Bank 67
Nationalism 288
nationalism 296, 301, 303–4
nations 186–92

Nazi-Soviet pact 308
Nazism 290–1, 310
Needham, Richard 244
nerve gas 231–37
Nevin, Charles, *Guardian* 138
New Conservatism 321
New Labour 33, 80, 95–7, 99–101, 106–7, 109, 135, 254–5, 263, 266, 279, 322, 329
New Left Review 311
New Statesman 274
The New Yorker 121
Nexus rally 87–8
Nicholson, Emma 71
  Secret Society 67–8
Nixon, Richard 76
Nolan Commission 54, 68
Nolan, Lord 57–8
  Standards in Public Life report (1995) 246
nomenklatura 63
NOP 33, 193
normal country 77–100
North Sea oil 309
Northern Ireland
  Constitution Act (1973) 212
  terrorism 226
Norton-Taylor, Richard, *Guardian* 237
Norway, constitutional devolution 228
nuclear deterrence 77

Observer 41, 103, 105
  Irvine, Derry 253
  Phillips, Melanie 276
Official
  secrecy 158
  Secrets Act 150–1, 267
Old Bailey 238
Old Labour 14–15, 279, 322
Old School 224
On the Constitution 12
On Living in an Old Country 295–6
One-Nation Tories 37
Onslow, Sir Cranley 254
open government 239, 274
The Open Society and Its Enemies, Popper, Karl 271
Orwell, George 328
Oxbridge 244
  Cabinet (1966) 87
Oxford, Blair, Tony 92
Oxford University Press, *The Character of England* 81–2

Paine, Tom 165–6, 178
Panorama interview, Diana 116, 138–9, 285
Paris, Ritz Hotel 52, 56, 72
Parker-Bowles, Camilla 121, 129
Parliament 161–2, 211, 246, 250, 255, 297
  Members 151, 277
  sovereignty 75, 155, 159, 174, 213–18, 314
Parliament Act (1911) 316
party system 87
People with the Necessary Qualities (PNQs) 219–22, 224, 237,240, 243
Pepper v. Hart 162–3
perestroika 78
Pergau Dam, Malaysia 70, 74, 250
Phillips, Melanie, *Observer*

276
Phipps, Simon 141
Pinter, Harold 16
Plaid Cymru, General Election (1997) 30
Pleming, Mr QC 220–1
Poland 140, 308
Police Act 225
political
  advertising 47–8
  institutions 99
  parties 81
  rights and freedoms 225–6
Poll Tax 179, 230, 250, 262, 268, 322
Polly Peck 67
Ponting, Clive 150, 152, 243
Pope, Alexander 230
Popper, Karl, *The Open Society and Its Enemies* 271
Portillo, Michael 33–5, 45, 85–6, 88–9
  Daily Telegraph 324
  Observer 41
Portugal, constitutional devolution 228
post-Establishment General Election 91
Potter, Denis 16
Powell, Charles
  Kurds 233
  The Times 320
Powell, Enoch 7, 43–6, 48, 75, 133–4, 184, 213–14, 287
  Falklands victory parade 133
  'rivers of blood' speech (1968) 45
Powellism 1, 80, 92–3, 216, 263, 268, 324
Powellite dockers (1960s) 284
power stations 76
powers, distribution of 172–5
Presbyterian fundamentalism 191
Prescott, John 183
presidential power 91
Press Secretary, Prime Minister 159
pressure groups 198, 225
Prideaux, John 61
Prime Ministers, Press Secretaries 159
prison ship 48
private medicine 64
privatisations 60
proportional representation (PR) 104, 203, 217
Prospect 50, 292
protestantism 293
public
  accountability 197–8
  Accounts Committee 56
  Interest Immunity Certificates 238–9
  schools 64
  Service Committee 248
  services 52, 60, 63
Putney, democratic exchange (1647) 17–19, 199

Quangocrats 61–2
quangos 60–3, 210
Questions of Procedure for Ministers (QPM) 245–6

rail
  depots 61
  windfall 61
Rainsborough, Colonel 18–19
Redwood, John 35, 43, 89, 316

Rees-Mogg, William 53, 255–6, 275, 317–18
Referendum Party 30, 33, 43, 46–8
referendums 200–1, 251
  (1975) 260, 282
  Europe's single currency 199, 325
regions 22, 181–6
Reinventing Government 196
Rentoul, John, Blair, Tony, biography 102
Republicans 117, 142, 319
revolutions 93, 130, 194, 256–7
  see also Glorious Revolution (1688); velvet revolution
Riddell, Peter 253
rights and liberty 227 and *see* Bill of Rights
The Risk Society, Beck, Ulrich 190
Roberts, Andrew 31
Robertson, Geoffrey, QC 221, 239
Rogers, Adrian 39
Rolls Royce 326
Romania 76
Rover 76
Royal
  Automobile Club 88
  family 90–1, 120, 136, 209, 284–86
    Blitz 66, 128
    Diana, Princess of Wales's death 207, 283
    television film (1969) 128
  Household 128, 138
  Prerogative 120, 250, 315
  Yacht episode 89–90, 141
Ruling Britannia, the failure and future of British Democracy 229
ruling system 81
Rumbold, Dame Angela 36, 38, 45
Rushdie, Salman 16
Ruskin College, Prescott, John 183
Russia, peasants 208

Sachs, Albie 166
Sainsbury, Timothy 244
St John Stevas, Norman 123
St Pancras Station 142
Sampson, Anthony, *Anatomy of Britain* (1962) 87
Sandringham estate 137
Santerre, Jacques 106
Scargillism 268
Scarman, Lord (Leslie) 16, 166–7
science 153
Scotland 191, 292–3, 295
  British Parliaments 93
  constitutional reform 186, 215
  General Election (1997) 296
  Home Rule 1, 3–4, 10–11
  opinion poll 193
  Parliament 1, 3, 6, 27–8, 173–4, 188, 255, 275, 292, 301–2, 317, 328
  referendum 3, 9, 27–8, 131, 274–5
  voice 187–8
Scotland's Parliament, White Paper 188–90, 253, 292, 317
Scotsman 11
Scott, Sir Richard 230–1, 236,

239–40, 242
Inquiry 213, 234–5, 239–40
Report 53, 106, 198, 218, 230–2, 234–7, 239–45, 247, 315, 322
Cook, Robin 241–2, 244
Scottish
Cabinet 296
Constitutional Convention 189
National Party (SNP) 30, 186, 292
Seaton, Jean 125
second chamber 173, 178–9
Second World War 81–2, 156, 160, 260, 262, 310
Secret Society 67–8
Sedgefield 32
Selbourne, David 168
Senna, Ayrton 122
SERPS (State earnings–related pension scheme) 229, 250, 297
Sheerman, Barry 244
Shelley, Percy Bysshe 15
Shepherd, Richard 158
Simon, Lord 223–4
Single Transferable Votes 203
Skinner, Quentin 269
Skoal Bandits 73–4
Smith, Adam 190
Smith, John 21–2, 92, 256
Smith, Tim 56, 219–21
Smith, Trevor 58
So There'll Always Be An England 294
Soames, Nicholas 138
Soros, George 271, 314
South Africa
Apartheid 166, 205
constitution 166, 170–1, 205
Southwark Cathedral 98
sovereignty 3, 24, 28, 85, 141, 174, 199, 213–18, 307
Soviet-bloc 63, 94
Spaak, Henri 272–3
Spain
constitution 141, 228
referendum 141
Special People with the Necessary Qualities (SPNQs) 244
Spectator 9, 35
Spencer, Earl (Charles) 137
funeral address 127
Spencer, Earl (John) 138
Spencer family 137–8
spin doctors 54, 110, 118
Spirit of the Age (1825) 79
The Spirit of the Laws (1748) 193–5
St James's Palace 9
stakeholding 97–8
Standards in Public Life report (1995) 246
Star Chamber 20
State of the Nation 112–13
State services, reorganisation 196
The State under Stress 227
The State We're In 227, 257–8
Stewart, John 63
Stonehenge 225
The Strange Death of Liberal England 315–16
Straw, Jack 273
Suez 82, 321
Suffragettes 304
Sun 10, 37–8, 45, 58, 67, 89, 117, 141
Blair, Tony 326
Europe 289

Sunday Express 128
Sunday Telegraph 42, 67
  Poll Tax 179
Sunday Times 31, 38, 97
Supreme Court 15
Sweden 144, 228
Switzerland, referendums 201
Sykes, Paul 35

Talleyrand 318
taxation 184
Taylor, A.J.P. 181–2, 305
Tebbit, Lord (Norman) 35, 107, 132, 168
television 198
Territory and Power in the United Kingdom 181
Thatcher, Margaret 24, 44, 46, 51, 83, 86, 151, 166, 283–4,297–8
  American/Soviet antagonism 77
  anti-European stance 78, 295, 322
  Bill of Rights 166
  Blair, Tony 79, 266–7, 321–2
  Cabinet members 265
  constitution 6, 262, 275
  Falklands War 93, 133, 296, 308
  free-market ideas 263
  Hague, William 312
  Hamilton, Neil 223
  Kurds 233
  Major, John 267
  market liberalism 269–70
  memoirs 264–5
  monetarism 321
  outsider thinking 263
  Poll Tax 179
  premiership 7, 35, 52, 91, 117, 132, 259, 266
  Press Secretary 159
  quangos 63
  radicalism 264
  Scott Report 213, 230–1
  single currency 37
  society 5, 131
Thatcher, Mark 74
Thatcher-Major years 53, 228
Thatcher-Murdoch modernity 100
Thatcherism 86–7, 93, 131, 261, 264–5, 295, 324
  Powellite core 35, 134
There Ain't No Black in the Union Jack 134
Thomas, Terry 326
Thompson, Emma 16
THORP (nuclear processing plant) 250
Thought and Change 256–8
The Three Pillars of Liberty 225–6, 228–9
Tiananmen Square (1976) 130
Time magazine, Blair, Tony 326
The Times 28, 41, 72, 110, 116
  Beeston, Nicholas 231–2
  Bradberry, Grace 126
  Diana, Princess of Wales's death 208
  Europe 289
  Irvine, Derry 252–3
  Kaletsky, Anatole 106
  Linklater, Magnus 10
  Lloyd, John 119
  Powell, Charles 320
titles 60, 207
Tolkein, J.R.R. 316

Tolstoy, Leo 81–2
Touche Ross 67
Trade Unions 14, 264
  Congress (September 1997) 79, 118
traditional reform 258-60
Transport, Department of 61
Treasury 5
  'Key Assumptions' 266–7, 270
  Declaration of Independence 267
  reviews 228
Treaties of
  Maastricht (1992) 313–14
  Rome (1958) 209, 282
  Union (1707) 17, 29, 295, 316
Trotsky, Leon 10
truth, the quiet voice 221–2
Tudor law 20
Twigg, Stephen, Fabian Society 89

Union Jack 115
United Kingdom
  European Union 288
  institutions 253, 254
United States 46–7, 59, 73
Utopian realism 258, 268–81

velvet revolution 50–76, 78, 135
Vibert, Frank, *Europe: a Constitution for the Millennium* 204
Victoria, Queen 2, 93, 115
Vidal, Gore 74
Vietnam War 234
Violations of Rights in Britain, Giddy, Pam 160–1
The Voice of the People, A Constitution for Tomorrow 318–20
voting 199–203
  compulsory 202
Voting Reform Group 9

Waldegrave, William 53, 70–1, 197, 205–6, 244–5, 297
  constitution 29
  Scott Inquiry 239–40
Wales 62–3, 192–3
  Assembly 27, 193
  General Election (1997) 296
  referendum 27, 274
Warsaw Pact 76
Washington, special relationship 77
water utilities 76
'Way Ahead' group 142–3
Weir, Stuart and Patrick Dunleavy 60
Welfare State 97, 99, 260, 308
Welsh Development Agency 62
West Lothian question 255
Westminster 17, 19
  Abbey 125–6
  mythical power 183
  Scottish MPs 253
  sovereignty 292
  system 277
White, Michael, *Guardian* 90–1
White Papers
  Freedom of Information 110
  Incorporation of the European Convention on Human Rights (1997) 171–2
  Scotland's Parliament 188–90, 253, 292, 317

White Wednesday 106
Whitehall secrecy 77
Widdecombe, Anne 53
William and Harry, Princes 3
Williams, Raymond 115
Williams, Shirley 62, 119–20
Wilson, A.N. 9
Wilson, Harold 43–4, 279, 300, 321–2
  Oxbridge Cabinet (1966) 87
Wilson, Richard and Andrew Lansley, *Conservatives and the Constitution* 316–17
Wilson–Callaghan government (1974–9) 91
windfall bonuses 60
Windsor
  Castle fire 66–7
  family 2–3, 137, 319
Wolmar, Christian 61
Woolf, Virginia, *Orlando* 187
Worcester Woman 101–14, 208, 223, 323
working order 206
working-class expectations 15
Worsthorne, Peregrin 214–15
Wright, Patrick, *On Living in an Old Country* 295–6
Wright, Tony 242, 247
written constitutions 2, 5, 7–8, 24, 112, 255, 329

Zhou Enlai, Tiananmen Square (1976) 130